Kawasaki EX & ER500
Service and Repair Manual

by Alan Ahlstrand and
John H Haynes Member of the Guild of Motoring Writers

(2052-240-4AH4)

Models covered
EX500A (GPZ500S). 498 cc. UK 1987 to 1993
EX500D (GPZ500S). 498 cc. UK 1994 to 2001
EX500E (GPZ500S). 498 cc. UK 2002 to 2004
ER500A (ER-5). 498 cc. UK 1997 to 1999
ER500C (ER-5). 498 cc. UK 2000 to 2007
EX500A. 498 cc. US 1987 to 1993
EX500D (Ninja). 498 cc. US 1994 to 2008

ABCDE

© Haynes Publishing 2008

A book in the **Haynes Service and Repair Manual Series**

All rights reserved. No part of this book may be reproduced or transmitted in any form or by any means, electronic or mechanical, including photocopying, recording or by any information storage or retrieval system, without permission in writing from the copyright holder.

ISBN **978 1 78521 293 2**

British Library Cataloguing in Publication Data
A catalogue record for this book is available from the British Library.

Library of Congress Control Number 2008934244

Printed in the USA

Haynes Publishing
Sparkford, Yeovil, Somerset BA22 7JJ, England

Haynes North America, Inc
861 Lawrence Drive, Newbury Park, California 91320, USA

Haynes Publishing Nordiska AB
Box 1504, 751 45 UPPSALA, Sverige

Printed using 33-lb Resolute Book 65 4.0 from Resolute Forest Products Calhoun, TN mill. Resolute is a member of World Wildlife Fund's Climate Savers programme committed to significantly reducing GHG emissions. This paper uses 50% less wood fibre than traditional offset. The Calhoun Mill is certified to the following sustainable forest management and chain of custody standards: SFI, PEFC and FSC Controlled Wood.

Contents

Contents

REPAIRS AND OVERHAUL

REFERENCE

Kawasaki
The Green Meanies

by Julian Ryder

Kawasaki Heavy Industries

Kawasaki is a company of contradictions. It is the smallest of the big four Japanese manufacturers but the biggest company, it was the last of the four to make and market motorcycles yet it owns the oldest name in the Japanese industry, and it was the first to set up a factory in the USA. Kawasaki Heavy Industries, of which the motorcycle operation is but a small component, is a massive company with its heritage firmly in the old heavy industries like shipbuilding and railways; nowadays it is as much involved in aerospace as in motorcycles.

In fact it may be because of this that Kawasaki's motorcycles have always been quirky, you get the impression that they are designed by a small group of enthusiasts who are given an admirably free hand. More realistically, it may be that Kawasaki's designers have experience with techniques and materials from other engineering disciplines. Either way, Kawasaki have managed to be the factory who surprise us more than the rest. Quite often, they do this by totally ignoring a market segment the others are scrabbling over, but more often they hit us with pure, undiluted performance.

The origins of the company, and its name, go back to 1878 when Shozo Kawasaki set up a dockyard in Tokyo. By the late 1930s, the company was making its own steel in massive steelworks and manufacturing railway locos and rolling stock. In the run up to war, the Kawasaki Aircraft Company was set up in 1937 and it was this arm of the now giant operation that would look to motorcycle engine manufacture in post-war Japan.

They bought their high-technology experience to bear first on engines which were sold on to a number of manufacturers as original equipment. Both two- and four-stroke units were made, a 58 cc and 148 cc OHC unit. One of the customer companies was Meihatsu Heavy Industries, another company within the Kawasaki group, which in 1961 was shaken up and renamed Kawasaki Auto Sales. At the same time, the Akashi factory which was to be Kawasaki's main production facility until the Kobe earthquake of 1995, was opened. Shortly afterwards, Kawasaki took over the ailing Meguro company, Japan's oldest motorcycle maker, thus instantly obtaining a range of bigger bikes which were marketed as Kawasaki-Meguros. The following year, the first bike to be made and sold as a Kawasaki was produced, a 125 cc single called the B8 and in 1963 a motocross version, the B8M appeared.

The three cylinder two-stroke 750

Model development

Kawasaki's first appearance on a road-race circuit came in 1965 with a batch of disc-valve 125 twins. They were no match for the opposition from Japan in the shape of Suzuki and Yamaha or for the fading force of the factory MZs from East Germany. Only after the other Japanese factories had pulled out of the class did Kawasaki win, with British rider Dave Simmonds becoming World 125 GP Champion in 1969 on a bike that looked astonishingly similar to the original racer. That same year Kawasaki reorganised once again, this time merging three companies to form Kawasaki Heavy Industries. One of the new organisation's objectives was to take motorcycle production forward and exploit markets outside Japan.

KHI achieved that target immediately and set out their stall for the future with the astonishing and frightening H1. This three-cylinder air-cooled 500 cc two-stroke was arguably the first modern pure performance bike to hit the market. It hypnotised a whole generation of motorcyclists who'd never before encountered such a ferocious, wheelie inducing power band or such shattering straight-line speed allied to questionable handling. And as for the 750 cc version ...

The triples perfectly suited the late '60s, fitting in well with the student demonstrations of 1968 and the anti-establishment ethos of the Summer of Love. Unfortunately, the oil crisis would put an end to the thirsty strokers but Kawasaki had another high-performance ace up their corporate sleeve. Or rather they thought they did.

The 1968 Tokyo Show saw probably the single most significant new motorcycle ever made unveiled: the Honda CB750. At Kawasaki it caused a major shock, for they also had a 750 cc four, code-named New York Steak, almost ready to roll and it was a double, rather than single, overhead cam motor. Bravely, they took the decision to go ahead - but with the motor taken out to 900 cc. The result was the Z1, unveiled at the 1972 Cologne Show. It was a bike straight out of the same mould as the H1, scare stories spread about unmanageable power, dubious straight-line stability and frightening handling, none of which stopped the sales graph rocketing upwards and led to the coining of the term 'superbike'. While rising fuel prices cut short development of the big two-strokes, the Z1 went on to found a dynasty, indeed its genes can still be detected in Kawasaki's latest products like the ZZ-R1100 (Ninja ZX-11).

This is another characteristic of the way Kawasaki operates. Models quite often have very long lives, or gradually evolve. There is no major difference between that first Z1 and the air-cooled GPz range. Add water-cooling and you have the GPZ900, which in turn metamorphosed into the GPZ1000RX and then the ZX-10 and the ZZ-R1100. Indeed, the

The first Superbike, Kawasaki's 900 cc Z1

One of the two-stroke engined KH and KE range - the KE100B

The GT750 - a favourite hack for despatch riders

last three models share the same 58 mm stroke. The bikes are obviously very different but it's difficult to put your finger on exactly why.

Other models have remained effectively untouched for over a decade: the KH and KE single-cylinder air-cooled two-stroke learner bikes, the GT550 and 750 shaft-drive hacks favoured by big city despatch riders and the GPz305 being prime examples. It's only when they step outside the performance field that Kawasakis seems less sure. Their first factory

The high-performance ZXR750

customs were dire, you simply got the impression that the team that designed them didn't have their heart in the job. Only when the Classic range appeared in 1995 did they get it right.

Racing success

Kawasaki also have a more focused approach to racing than the other factories. The policy has always been to race the road bikes and with just a couple of exceptions that's what they've done. Even Simmonds' championship winner bore a strong resemblance to the twins they were selling in the late '60s and racing versions of the 500 and 750 cc triples were also sold as over-the-counter racers, the H1R and H2R. The 500 was in the forefront of the two-stroke assault on MV Agusta but wasn't a Grand Prix winner. It was the 750 that made the impact and carried the factory's image in F750 racing against the Suzuki triples and Yamaha fours.

The factory's decision to use green, usually regarded as an unlucky colour in sport, meant its bikes and personnel stood out and the phrase 'Green Meanies' fitted them perfectly. The Z1 motor soon became a full 1000 cc and powered Kawasaki's assault in F1 racing, notably in endurance which Kawasaki saw as being most closely related to its road bikes.

That didn't stop them dominating 250 and 350 cc GPs with a tandem twin two-stroke in the late '70s and early '80s, but their path-breaking monocoque 500 while a race winner never won a world title. When Superbike arrived, Kawasaki's road 750s weren't as track-friendly as the opposition's out-and-out race replicas. This makes Scott Russell's World title on the ZXR750 in 1993 even more praiseworthy, for the homologation bike, the ZXR750RR, was much heavier and much more of a road bike than the Italian and Japanese competition.

The company's Supersport 600 contenders have similarly been more sports-tourers than race-replicas, yet they too have been competitive on the track. Indeed, the flagship bike, the ZZ-R1100, is most definitely a sports tourer capable of carrying two people and their luggage at high speed in comfort all day and then doing it again the next day. Try that on one of the race replicas and you'll be in need of a course of treatment from a chiropractor.

Through doing it their way Kawasaki developed a brand loyalty for their performance bikes that kept the Z1's derivatives in production until the mid-'80s and turned the bike into a classic in its model life. You could even argue that the Z1 lives on in the shape of the 1100 Zephyr's GPz1100-derived motor. And that's another Kawasaki invention, the retro bike. But when you look at what many commentators refer to as the retro boom, especially in Japan, you find that it is no such thing. It is the Zephyr boom. Just another example of Japan's most surprising motorcycle manufacturer getting it right again.

Cheap but definitely not nasty

Kawasaki's tendency not to do the obvious was never better demonstrated than when they launched the GPZ500S (EX500 in the US) in 1987. Four-stroke parallel twins were a nearly extinct breed and examples with sporting pretensions were definitely defunct. So what to make of the EX500? Was it a warmed-over version of the underwhelming old 450LTD factory custom? Thankfully, no. It shared the 74 x 58 mm dimensions of that big bruiser the GPZ1000RX (Ninja 1000R in the US) and turned out to behave much more like half a 1000 than an LTD.

Which was a good job because the faired and unfaired versions of the Yamaha RD350 Power Valve were the sporting middleweight benchmarks and the Kawasaki was seen as a four-stroke LC. Not that the EX500 was ever an out-and-out performer, it was much more of an all-rounder. It was just as at home in town on the commuter run as it was scratching on country lanes, in other words a typical four-stroke. It could lug along at low revs but when the tacho got above 7000 rpm it fair howled along. Kawasaki had obviously built it down to a price as far as possible to keep it competitive with the LC.

There was no adjustment on the forks, the belly pan was an option in certain markets, there was only one front disc and the rear brake was a drum. It was, however, capable of squealing the front tyre with just two-finger pressure on the lever. Where the Yen-pinching showed was in the slightly squidgy rear suspension. And pre-load adjustment was by double lock-nuts on the shock body so changing things was not an easy job. The Kawasaki's cleverest trick was to be as small and manageable as its two-stroke rival despite those cams and valves on top of the motor, something which endeared it to women and newly qualified riders of both genders.

The EX500A model

But while the LC was a creature of the 1980s, the GPZ500S soldiered on, as Kawasakis tend to, into the '90s with hardly a change. Except to its image. The only real change in specification came in 1994 when the EX500D superseded the long-running EX500A. The main changes on the D model were its rear disc brake which replaced the drum brake fitted to previous models, the repositioned front disc (now mounted to the right-hand side), its new bodywork and instruments. Mechanical changes were minor apart from modifications to the ignition system. The EX500D continued unchanged in the US market, but in the UK it was renamed the EX500E in 2002 and its braking was uprated to a twin front disc brake system.

The EX500 has filled the gap between 125 cc learner bikes and the increasingly racy 600 sport bikes. There weren't many bikes which a newly qualified rider could feel both safe and excited on but this was one of them.

This concept was taken further in 1997 with the ER-5, a bike unashamedly built down to a price. Where the GPZ had a square-section frame and café-racer style accoutrements the ER-5 had a utilitarian tubular frame, round headlight, twin rear shocks and no bodywork. The styling wasn't self-consciously retro like the Zephyr range but neat and up-to-date. In the UK, it was launched with a flurry of incentives and heavy emphasis on its price tag.

Changes to the original ER500A were few apart from the fitment of a fuel gauge and adjustable handlebar levers. The most significant change came in 2001 with the launch of the ER500C, which had restyled bodywork.

Acknowledgements

Our thanks are due to Kawasaki Motors (UK) Ltd for permission to reproduce certain illustrations used in this manual and for supplying colour transparencies. We would also like to thank NGK Spark Plugs (UK) Ltd for supplying the colour spark plug condition photos, the Avon Rubber Company for supplying information on tyre fitting, and Kevin Wood who did the mechanical work and provided numerous technical tips.

Thanks are also due to GT Motorcycles of Yeovil, Riders of Bridgwater and Taylors of Crewkerne who supplied some of the motorcycles featured in the photographs. The introduction 'Kawasaki – The Green Meanies' was written by Julian Ryder.

About this Manual

The aim of this manual is to help you get the best value from your motorcycle. It can do so in several ways. It can help you decide what work must be done, even if you choose to have it done by a dealer; it provides information and procedures for routine maintenance and servicing; and it offers diagnostic and repair procedures to follow when trouble occurs.

We hope you use the manual to tackle the work yourself. For many simpler jobs, doing it yourself may be quicker than arranging an appointment to get the motorcycle into a dealer and making the trips to leave it and pick it up. More importantly, a lot of money can be saved by avoiding the expense the shop must pass on to you to cover its labour and overhead costs. An added benefit is the sense of satisfaction and accomplishment that you feel after doing the job yourself.

References to the left or right side of the motorcycle assume you are sitting on the seat, facing forward.

We take great pride in the accuracy of information given in this manual, but motorcycle manufacturers make **alterations and design changes during the production run of a particular motorcycle of which they do not inform us. No liability can be accepted by the authors or publishers for loss, damage or injury caused by any errors in, or omissions from, the information given.**

Model development

GPZ500S

The GPZ500S was introduced in 1987.

The engine was a liquid cooled, two-cylinder four-stroke with double overhead camshafts driven by chain from the centre of the crankshaft. Four valves per cylinder were operated by forked rocker arms located on the underside of each camshaft. The crankcases were two-piece, split horizontally, with a separate cylinder block. A balancer shaft, gear-driven off the crankshaft, was located in the front of the crankcase.

Drive was transmitted to the six-speed gearbox by chain through a cable-operated, five-spring multi-plate clutch, and to the rear wheel by chain and sprockets.

Fuel was drawn into the engine via two 34 mm constant vacuum Keihin carburettors, and Kawasaki's Clean Air System, initially only fitted to US market models, reduced the level of unburned hydrocarbons in the exhaust gasses. The exhaust system was a two-into-two design.

The chassis comprised a square-section, steel duplex cradle frame with a box-section swingarm. Front suspension was by conventional, non-adjustable telescopic forks and rear suspension was by Kawasaki Uni-Trak rising rate mono-shock with spring pre-load adjustment only.

Braking was by a single, two-piston caliper disc brake at the front and a drum brake at the rear.

The GPZ500S was equipped with three-spoke, cast aluminium wheels and a two-section fairing, split in the middle to allow unimpeded air-flow to the radiator. A rectangular headlight was fitted in the upper fairing section and the handlebars were two separate units clamped to the tops of the front fork tubes.

Technically the GPZ500S series remained unchanged until 1994 when a rear disc brake was added and the front disc brake was moved from the left-hand to right-hand fork. A caliper with differential piston bores was used on the front brake. Wheel diameters were increased from sixteen to seventeen inches and a wider rear tyre was fitted. Minor changes were made to the fairing and switchgear and a new instrument cluster was fitted.

The Kawasaki Clean Air System was fitted to all market models in 2001.

ER5

The ER5 was introduced in 1997.

The engine and transmission unit was the same liquid cooled, two-cylinder four-stroke as was fitted to the GPZ500S, in a slightly milder state of tune. A two-into-one exhaust system was fitted.

The chassis, although similar in design, was constructed from round-section tubular steel, and rear suspension was by twin shock absorbers with pre-load adjustment only.

Braking was by a single, two-piston caliper disc brake at the front and a drum brake at the rear.

Styled as a touring/commuter machine, the ER5 was fitted with a single, round headlight, one-piece handlebars and individual designed speedometer and tachometer units.

Technically the ER5 series remained unchanged until 2001 when the Kawasaki Clean Air System was fitted to all market models. Minor changes were made to the design of the front brake caliper, bodywork side covers and tail piece.

Bike spec

Engine

Type	Liquid cooled, in-line 2-cylinder
Capacity	98 cc
Bore	74.0 mm
Stroke	58.0 mm
Compression ratio	
EX models	10.8:1
ER models	9.8:1
Camshafts	DOHC, chain driven
Valves	4 valves per cylinder
Fuel system	2 x Keihin CVK34 carburettors
Clutch	Wet multi-plate, cable operated
Transmission	6 speed constant mesh
Final drive	
Chain	
EX models	EK 520SX-O (104 links)
ER models	EK 520SX-O (106 links)
Sprockets	
EX500A1 to A3 models	17 tooth front/42 tooth rear
EX500A4 to A7 models	16 tooth front/42 tooth rear
EX500D and E models	16 tooth front/41 tooth rear
ER models	17 tooth front/42 tooth rear

Weights and dimensions

Wheelbase
EX500A . . . . .1440 mm
EX500D and E . . . . .1435 mm
ER500A and C . . . . .1430 mm
Overall length
EX500A1
UK model . . . . .2050 mm
US model . . . . .2125 mm
EX500A2 to A7 . . . . .2110 mm
EX500D and E . . . . .2095 mm
ER500A . . . . .2040 mm
ER500C . . . . .2070 mm
Overall height
EX500A . . . . .1165 mm
EX500D and E . . . . .1160 mm
ER500A and C . . . . .1070 mm

Overall width
EX500A . . . . .675 mm
EX500D and E . . . . .700 mm
ER500A and C . . . . .730 mm
Seat height
EX500A . . . . .770 mm
EX500D and E . . . . .775 mm
ER500A . . . . .780 mm
ER500C . . . . .800 mm
Ground clearance
EX500A, D and E . . . . .120 mm
ER500A and C . . . . .125 mm
Dry weight
EX500A . . . . .171 kg
EX500D . . . . .177 kg
EX500E . . . . .179 kg
ER500A . . . . .174 kg
ER500C . . . . .179 kg

Chassis

Type . . . . .Tubular steel double cradle
Rake . . . . 27.0°
Trail
EX models . . . . 91 mm
ER models . . . . 102 mm
Front suspension
Type . . . . Oil-damped telescopic forks
Travel
EX models . . . . .130 mm
ER models . . . . 125 mm
Adjustments . . . . .None
Rear suspension
Type
EX models .Rising rate with monoshock
ER models . . . . .Twin shock
Travel
EX models . . . . 100 mm
ER500A models . . . . 105 mm
ER500C models . . . . 114 mm
Adjustment (all models) . . . . .Spring pre-load

Tyre sizes
Front
EX500A models 100/90 16 54H
EX500D and E models .110/70 17 54H
ER models 110/70 17 54H
Rear
EX500A models 120/90 16 63H
EX500D and E models .130/70 17 62H
ER models 130/70 17 62H
Brakes
Front
EX500A and D models . . . . .1 x disc with two-piston caliper
EX500E models . . . . .2 x disc with two-piston calipers
ER models . . . . .1 x disc with two-piston caliper
Rear
EX500A models . . . . 160 mm drum brake
EX500D and E models . . . . .1 x disc with single-piston caliper
ER models . . . . 160 mm drum brake

Professional mechanics are trained in safe working procedures. However enthusiastic you may be about getting on with the job at hand, take the time to ensure that your safety is not put at risk. A moment's lack of attention can result in an accident, as can failure to observe simple precautions.

There will always be new ways of having accidents, and the following is not a comprehensive list of all dangers; it is intended rather to make you aware of the risks and to encourage a safe approach to all work you carry out on your bike.

Asbestos

● Certain friction, insulating, sealing and other products - such as brake pads, clutch linings, gaskets, etc. - contain asbestos. Extreme care must be taken to avoid inhalation of dust from such products since it is hazardous to health. If in doubt, assume that they do contain asbestos.

Fire

● Remember at all times that petrol is highly flammable. Never smoke or have any kind of naked flame around, when working on the vehicle. But the risk does not end there - a spark caused by an electrical short-circuit, by two metal surfaces contacting each other, by careless use of tools, or even by static electricity built up in your body under certain conditions, can ignite petrol vapour, which in a confined space is highly explosive. Never use petrol as a cleaning solvent. Use an approved safety solvent.

● Always disconnect the battery earth terminal before working on any part of the fuel or electrical system, and never risk spilling fuel on to a hot engine or exhaust.

● It is recommended that a fire extinguisher of a type suitable for fuel and electrical fires is kept handy in the garage or workplace at all times. Never try to extinguish a fuel or electrical fire with water.

Fumes

● Certain fumes are highly toxic and can quickly cause unconsciousness and even death if inhaled to any extent. Petrol vapour comes into this category, as do the vapours from certain solvents such as trichloro-ethylene. Any draining or pouring of such volatile fluids should be done in a well ventilated area.

● When using cleaning fluids and solvents, read the instructions carefully. Never use materials from unmarked containers - they may give off poisonous vapours.

● Never run the engine of a motor vehicle in an enclosed space such as a garage. Exhaust fumes contain carbon monoxide which is extremely poisonous; if you need to run the engine, always do so in the open air or at least have the rear of the vehicle outside the workplace.

The battery

● Never cause a spark, or allow a naked light near the vehicle's battery. It will normally be giving off a certain amount of hydrogen gas, which is highly explosive.

● Always disconnect the battery ground (earth) terminal before working on the fuel or electrical systems (except where noted).

● If possible, loosen the filler plugs or cover when charging the battery from an external source. Do not charge at an excessive rate or the battery may burst.

● Take care when topping up, cleaning or carrying the battery. The acid electrolyte, evenwhen diluted, is very corrosive and should not be allowed to contact the eyes or skin. Always wear rubber gloves and goggles or a face shield. If you ever need to prepare electrolyte yourself, always add the acid slowly to the water; never add the water to the acid.

Electricity

● When using an electric power tool, inspection light etc., always ensure that the appliance is correctly connected to its plug and that, where necessary, it is properly grounded (earthed). Do not use such appliances in damp conditions and, again, beware of creating a spark or applying excessive heat in the vicinity of fuel or fuel vapour. Also ensure that the appliances meet national safety standards.

● A severe electric shock can result from touching certain parts of the electrical system, such as the spark plug wires (HT leads), when the engine is running or being cranked, particularly if components are damp or the insulation is defective. Where an electronic ignition system is used, the secondary (HT) voltage is much higher and could prove fatal.

Remember...

✗ **Don't** start the engine without first ascertaining that the transmission is in neutral.

✗ **Don't** suddenly remove the pressure cap from a hot cooling system - cover it with a cloth and release the pressure gradually first, or you may get scalded by escaping coolant.

✗ **Don't** attempt to drain oil until you are sure it has cooled sufficiently to avoid scalding you.

✗ **Don't** grasp any part of the engine or exhaust system without first ascertaining that it is cool enough not to burn you.

✗ **Don't** allow brake fluid or antifreeze to contact the machine's paintwork or plastic components.

✗ **Don't** siphon toxic liquids such as fuel, hydraulic fluid or antifreeze by mouth, or allow them to remain on your skin.

✗ **Don't** inhale dust - it may be injurious to health (see Asbestos heading).

✗ **Don't** allow any spilled oil or grease to remain on the floor - wipe it up right away, before someone slips on it.

✗ **Don't** use ill-fitting spanners or other tools which may slip and cause injury.

✗ **Don't** lift a heavy component which may be beyond your capability - get assistance.

✗ **Don't** rush to finish a job or take unverified short cuts.

✗ **Don't** allow children or animals in or around an unattended vehicle.

✗ **Don't** inflate a tyre above the recommended pressure. Apart from overstressing the carcass, in extreme cases the tyre may blow off forcibly.

✔ **Do** ensure that the machine is supported securely at all times. This is especially important when the machine is blocked up to aid wheel or fork removal.

✔ **Do** take care when attempting to loosen a stubborn nut or bolt. It is generally better to pull on a spanner, rather than push, so that if you slip, you fall away from the machine rather than onto it.

✔ **Do** wear eye protection when using power tools such as drill, sander, bench grinder etc.

✔ **Do** use a barrier cream on your hands prior to undertaking dirty jobs - it will protect your skin from infection as well as making the dirt easier to remove afterwards; but make sure your hands aren't left slippery. Note that long-term contact with used engine oil can be a health hazard.

✔ **Do** keep loose clothing (cuffs, ties etc. and long hair) well out of the way of moving mechanical parts.

✔ **Do** remove rings, wristwatch etc., before working on the vehicle - especially the electrical system.

✔ **Do** keep your work area tidy - it is only too easy to fall over articles left lying around.

✔ **Do** exercise caution when compressing springs for removal or installation. Ensure that the tension is applied and released in a controlled manner, using suitable tools which preclude the possibility of the spring escaping violently.

✔ **Do** ensure that any lifting tackle used has a safe working load rating adequate for the job.

✔ **Do** get someone to check periodically that all is well, when working alone on the vehicle.

✔ **Do** carry out work in a logical sequence and check that everything is correctly assembled and tightened afterwards.

✔ **Do** remember that your vehicle's safety affects that of yourself and others. If in doubt on any point, get professional advice.

● If in spite of following these precautions, you are unfortunate enough to injure yourself, seek medical attention as soon as possible.

Frame and engine numbers

The frame serial number or VIN (Vehicle Identification Number) is stamped into the right-hand side of the steering head. The engine number is stamped into the top of the crankcase on the right-hand side of the engine. Both of these numbers should be recorded and kept in a safe place so they can be furnished to law enforcement officials in the event of a theft. There is also an identification number on each carburettor body.

The frame serial number, engine serial number and carburettor identification number should also be kept in a handy place (such as with your driver's licence) so they are always available when purchasing or ordering parts for your machine.

The procedures in this manual identify the bikes by model prefix (EX or ER model) and if necessary also by the model suffix (eg EX500A6). Note that this model code corresponds with the production year as shown in the table below, although the production year will not necessarily be the same as the year of registration; if in doubt use the frame and engine number details to identify your bike. The following identification data relates to UK and US market models.

Buying spare parts

Once you have found all the identification numbers, record them for reference when buying parts. Since the manufacturers change specifications, parts and vendors (companies that manufacture various components on the machine), providing the ID numbers is the only way to be reasonably sure that you are buying the correct parts.

Whenever possible, take the worn part to the dealer so direct comparison with the new component can be made. Along the trail from the manufacturer to the parts shelf, there are numerous places that the part can end up with the wrong number or be listed incorrectly.

The two places to purchase new parts for your motorcycle – the accessory store and the franchised dealer – differ in the type of parts they carry. While dealers can obtain virtually every part for your motorcycle, the accessory dealer is usually limited to normal high wear items such as shock absorbers, tune-up parts, various engine gaskets, cables, chains, brake parts, etc. Rarely will an accessory outlet have major suspension components, cylinders, transmission gears, or cases.

Used parts can be obtained for roughly half the price of new ones, but you can't always be sure of what you're getting. Once again, take your worn part to the breaker's yard for direct comparison.

Whether buying new, used or rebuilt parts, the best course is to deal directly with someone who specialises in parts for your particular make.

UK models	Prod Yr	Initial Frame no.	Initial Engine no.
EX500A1 (GPZ500S)	1987	EX500A 000001	EX500AE 000001
EX500A2 (GPZ500S)	1988	EX500A 010501	EX500AE 008001
EX500A3 (GPZ500S)	1989	EX500A 020501	EX500AE 018001
EX500A4 (GPZ500S)	1990	EX500A 033001	EX500AE 018001
EX500A5 (GPZ500S)	1991	EX500A 048001	EX500AE 018001
EX500A6 (GPZ500S)	1992/3	EX500A 060001	EX500AE 018001
EX500D1 (GPZ500S)	1994	EX500D 000001	EX500AE 018001
EX500D2 (GPZ500S)	1995	EX500D 009001	EX500AE 018001
EX500D3 (GPZ500S)	1996/7	EX500D 025001	EX500AE 018001
EX500D5 (GPZ500S)	1998	EX500D 040001	EX500AE 018001
EX500D6 (GPZ500S)	1999	JKAEX500DDA 048001	EX500AE 018001
EX500D7 (GPZ500S)	2000/1	JKAEX500DDA 056001	EX500AE 018001
EX500E9 (GPZ500S)	2002	JKAEX500DDEA 070001	EX500AE 018001
EX500E10 (GPZ500S)	2003/4	JKAEX500DDEA 070001	EX500AE 018001
ER500A1 (ER-5)	1997	JKAER500AAA 000001	EX500AE 018001
ER500A2 (ER-5)	1998	JKAER500AAA 015001	EX500AE 018001
ER500A3 (ER-5)	1999	JKAER500AAA 028001	EX500AE 018001
ER500A4 (ER-5)	2000	JKAER500AAA 041001	EX500AE 018001
ER500C1 (ER-5)	2001/2	JKAER500ACA 051001to 067000	EX500AE 018001
ER500C3 (ER-5)	2003	JKAER500ACA 067001	EX500AE 018001
ER500C4P (ER-5)	2004	JKAER500ACA 072001	EX500AE 018001
ER500C5P (ER-5)	2005 to 07	JKAER500ACA 082001	EX500AE 018001
US models	**Prod Yr.**	**Frame no.**	**Engine no.**
EX500A1	1987	JKAEXA1 HA000001	EX500AE 000001
EX500A2	1988	JKAEXA1 JA010501	EX500AE 008001
EX500A3	1989	JKAEXVA1 KA020501	EX500AE 018001
EX500A4	1990	JKAEXVA1 LA033001	EX500AE 018001
EX500A5	1991	JKAEXVA1 MA048001	EX500AE 018001
EX500A6	1992	JKAEXVA1 NA060001	EX500AE 018001
EX500A7	1993	JKAEXVA1 PA075001	EX500AE 018001
EX500D1 (Ninja)	1994	JKAEXVA1 RA000001	EX500AE 018001
EX500D2 (Ninja)	1995	JKAEXVA1 SA009001	EX500AE 018001
EX500D3 (Ninja)	1996	JKAEXVA1 TA025001	EX500AE 018001
EX500D4 (Ninja)	1997	JKAEXVA1 VA035001	EX500AE 018001
EX500D5 (Ninja)	1998	JKAEXVA1 WA040001	EX500AE 018001
EX500D6 (Ninja)	1999	JKAEXVA1 XA048001	EX500AE 018001
EX500D7 (Ninja)	2000	JKAEXVD1 YA056001	EX500AE 018001
EX500D8 (Ninja)	2001	JKAEXVD1 1A064001	EX500AE 018001
EX500D9 (Ninja)	2002	JKAEXVD1 2A070001	EX500AE 018001
EX500D10 (Ninja)	2003	JKAEXVD1 3A079001	EX500AE 018001
EX500D11 (Ninja)	2004	JKAEXVD1 4A085001	EX500AE 018001
EX500D12 (Ninja)	2005	JKAEXVD1 5A090001	EX500AE 018001
EX500D6F (Ninja)	2006	Not available	Not available
EX500D7F (Ninja)	2007	Not available	Not available
EX500D8F (Ninja)	2008	Not available	Not available

The engine number is stamped into the top of the crankcase on the right-hand side of the engine.

The frame number is stamped on the right-hand side of the steering head

Note: *The daily (pre-ride) checks are also outlined in the bike's owner's manual and on a sticker stuck to the underside of the seat (EX models) or inside the right-hand side cover (ER models).*

Coolant level check

⚠️ **Warning: DO NOT remove the radiator pressure cap to add coolant. Topping up is done at the coolant reservoir tank. DO NOT leave open containers of coolant about, as it is poisonous.**

Before you start:

✔ The engine must be cold for the results to be accurate, so always perform this check before starting the engine for the first time each day.

✔ Make sure the motorcycle is on level ground and on its centrestand.
✔ Make sure you have a supply of coolant available – a mixture of 50% distilled water and 50% corrosion inhibited ethylene glycol anti-freeze is needed.

Bike care:

● Use only the specified coolant mixture. It is important that anti-freeze is used in the system all year round, and not just in the winter. Do not top the system up using only water, as the system will become too diluted.

● Do not overfill the reservoir tank. If the coolant is significantly above the FULL level line at any time, the surplus should be siphoned or drained off to prevent the possibility of it being expelled out of the breather hose.

● If the coolant level falls steadily, check the system for leaks (see Chapter 1). If no leaks are found and the level continues to fall, it is recommended that the machine is taken to a Kawasaki dealer for a pressure test.

EX500A models

1 The coolant level marks are visible through the slot in the inner side of the upper fairing. The coolant level should lie between the LOW and FULL lines marked on the reservoir.

2 To top up, remove the inspection cover – it is retained by a single screw . . .

3 . . . unscrew the reservoir cap and add the recommended coolant mixture until the FULL level is reached.

EX500D and E models

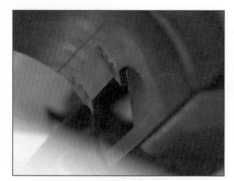

4 View the coolant reservoir from the lower right-hand side of the upper fairing. The coolant level should lie between the LOW and FULL lines marked on the reservoir.

5 To top up, unscrew the reservoir cap from the top of the upper fairing right-hand side . . .

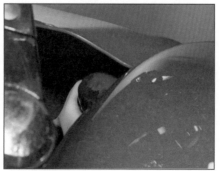

6 . . . and add the recommended coolant mixture until the FULL level is reached.

ER models

7 Remove the seat to access the coolant reservoir (see Chapter 8).

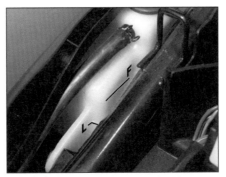

8 The coolant level should lie between the LOW and FULL lines marked on the reservoir.

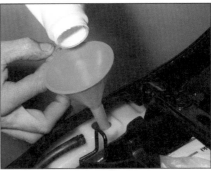

9 To top up, pry off the filler cap and add the recommended coolant mixture until the FULL level is reached.

Engine/transmission oil level check

Before you start:
✔ Start the engine and allow it to reach normal operating temperature.

Caution: Do not run the engine in an enclosed space such as a garage or workshop.

✔ Stop the engine. Place the bike on its centrestand and allow it to sit undisturbed in a level position for about five minutes.

Bike care:
● If you have to add oil frequently, you should check whether you have any oil leaks. If there is no sign of oil leakage from the joints and gaskets, the engine could be burning oil (see *Fault Finding*).

1 With the engine stopped, check the oil level in the window located at the lower part of the right-hand crankcase cover. The oil level should be between the Maximum and Minimum level marks next to the window.

2 If the level is below the Minimum mark, remove the oil filler cap from the right-hand crankcase cover.

3 Add enough oil of the recommended grade and type to bring the level up to the Maximum mark. Do not overfill.

The correct oil
● Modern, high-revving engines place great demands on their oil. It is very important that the correct oil for your bike is used.
● Always top up with a good quality oil of the specified type and viscosity and do not overfill the engine.

Oil type	API grade SE, SF or SG
Oil viscosity Up to 15°C (60°F) Above 5°C (40°F)	 SAE 10W40 or 10W50 SAE 20W40 or 20W50

Brake fluid level checks

Note: *This text relates to hydraulic disc brakes only. The drum rear brake checks for EX500A and ER models appear in 'Legal and safety checks'*

⚠ ***Warning: Brake hydraulic fluid can harm your eyes and damage painted surfaces, so use extreme caution when handling and pouring it and cover surrounding surfaces with rag. Do not use fluid that has been standing open for some time, as it absorbs moisture from the air which can cause a dangerous loss of braking effectiveness.***

Before you start:

✔ Position the bike on its centrestand.
✔ When checking the front brake fluid level turn the handlebars until the top of the master cylinder is as level as possible.
✔ Make sure you have the correct hydraulic fluid. DOT 4 is recommended. The brake fluid type is also marked on the fluid reservoir cap. Do not mix different brands of brake fluid in the reservoir, as they may not be compatible.

Bike care:

● The fluid in the front and rear brake master cylinder reservoirs will drop slightly as the brake pads wear down.
● If any fluid reservoir requires repeated topping-up this is an indication of an hydraulic leak somewhere in the system, which should be investigated immediately.
● Check for signs of fluid leakage from the hydraulic hoses and components – if found, rectify immediately.
● Check brake operation before taking the machine on the road; if there is evidence of air in the system - spongy feel to lever (front) or pedal (rear) – it must be bled as described in Chapter 7.

1 The front brake fluid level is checked via the inspection window in the master cylinder reservoir. Make sure that the fluid level is above the LOWER mark on the reservoir.

2 If the level is below the LOWER level mark, remove the screws and lift off the cover and rubber diaphragm. **Note:** *Do not operate the brake with the cover removed.*

3 Add new, clean brake fluid of the recommended type until the level is above the inspection window in the reservoir.

4 Install the rubber diaphragm and the plate. Install the cover and tighten the screws evenly, but do not overtighten them. Wipe any spilled fluid off the reservoir body.

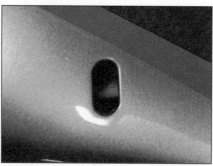

5 The rear brake fluid level can be checked through the slot provided in the right-hand rear side cover. The level must be between the UPPER and LOWER lines.

6 To top up, remove the side cover (see Chapter 8), unscrew the reservoir cap and withdraw the plate and diaphragm.

7 Add new clean brake fluid of the recommended type until the level is between the UPPER and LOWER lines.

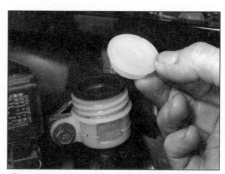

8 Install the rubber diaphragm and plate, then screw the reservoir cap into place.

Tyre checks

Tyre care:

● Check the tyres carefully for cuts, tears, embedded nails or other sharp objects and excessive wear. Operation of the motorcycle with excessively worn tyres is extremely hazardous, as traction and handling are directly affected.
● Check the condition of the tyre valve and ensure the dust cap is in place.
● Pick out any stones or nails which may have become embedded in the tyre tread. If left, they will eventually penetrate through the casing and cause a puncture.
● If tyre damage is apparent, or unexplained loss of pressure is experienced, seek the advice of a tyre fitting specialist without delay.

The correct pressures:

● The tyres must be checked when **cold**, not immediately after riding. Note that low tyre pressures may cause the tyre to slip on the rim or come off. High tyre pressures will cause abnormal tread wear and unsafe handling.
● Use an accurate pressure gauge.
● Proper air pressure will increase tyre life and provide maximum stability and ride comfort.

Tyre tread depth:

● At the time of writing UK law requires that tread depth must be at least 1 mm over 3/4 of the tread breadth all the way around the tyre, with no bald patches. Many riders, however, consider a minimum of 2 mm tread depth to be a safer limit. Kawasaki recommend a minimum of 1 mm on the front and 2 mm on the rear (3 mm on the rear if machine is used at speeds above 70 mph (110 kmh).
● Many tyres now incorporate wear indicators in the tread. Identify the triangular pointer on the tyre sidewall to locate the indicator bar and replace the tyre if the tread has worn down to the bar.

Tyre pressures		
EX500A models:	**Front**	**Rear**
Up to 97.5 kg (215 lbs)	1.9 bars (28 psi)	2.25 bars (32 psi)
97.5 to 184 kg (215 to 406 lbs)	2.25 bars (32 psi)	2.5 bars (36 psi)
EX500D and E models	2.25 bars (32 psi)	2.5 bars (36 psi)
ER models:		
Up to 97.5 kg (215 lbs)	2.25 bars (32 psi)	2.5 bars (36 psi)
97.5 to 181 kg (215 to 400 lbs)	2.25 bars (32 psi)	2.8 bars (41 psi)

1 Check the tyre pressures when the tyres are **cold** and keep them properly inflated.

2 Measure tread depth at the centre of the tyre using a tread depth gauge.

3 Tyre tread wear indicator bar and its location marking (usually either an arrow, a triangle or the letters TWI) on the sidewall (arrowed).

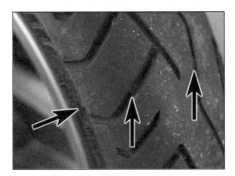

4 Look for the tyre information label on the chainguard.

Suspension, steering and drive chain checks

Suspension and Steering:
● Check that the front and rear suspension operates smoothly without binding.
● Check that the suspension is adjusted as required (see Chapter 6 for adjustment).
● Check that the steering moves smoothly from lock-to-lock.

Final drive:
● Check that the drive chain slack isn't excessive, and adjust if necessary (see Chapter 1).
● If the chain looks dry, lubricate it (see Chapter 1).

Legal and safety checks

Lighting and signalling:
● Take a minute to check that the headlight, sidelight, tail light, brake light, instrument lights and turn signals all work correctly.
● Check that the horn sounds when the buttom is pressed.
● A working speedometer graduated in mph is a statutory requirement in the UK.

Safety:
● Check that the throttle grip rotates smoothly and snaps shut when released, in all steering positions. Also check for the correct amount of freeplay (see Chapter 1).
● Check that the engine shuts off when the kill switch is operated.
● Check that the sidestand return spring holds the stand securely up when retracted. The same applies to the centerstand.

● Check that the clutch lever operates smoothly and with the correct amount of freeplay (see Chapter 1).
● On EX500A and ER models check the operation of the rear drum brake. If brake stopping power is poor or the brake does not free off when the pedal is released investigate the problem immediately.

Fuel:
● This may seem obvious, but check that you have enough fuel to complete your journey. If you notice signs of fuel leakage – rectify the cause immediately.
● Ensure you use the correct grade fuel – unleaded or low-lead (subject to local regulations), minimum 91 RON (Research Octane Number).

Chapter 1
Routine maintenance and servicing

Contents

Degrees of difficulty

Easy, suitable for novice with little experience		**Fairly easy,** suitable for beginner with some experience		**Fairly difficult,** suitable for competent DIY mechanic		**Difficult,** suitable for experienced DIY mechanic		**Very difficult,** suitable for expert DIY or professional	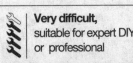

Specifications

Note: *A certain amount of maintenance data is included on a sticker stuck to the underside of the seat (EX models) or on the inside of the right-hand side cover (ER models)*

Engine

Spark plug type
  EX500A models (UK and Canada) .... NGK DR8ES or ND X27ESR-U
  EX500D, E and ER models (UK and Canada) .... NGK DR9EA or ND X27ESR-U
  All EX models (US) .... NGK D9EA or ND X27ES-U
Spark plug gap gap .... 0.6 to 0.7 mm (0.024 to 0.028 in)
Engine idle speed
  EX500A models – UK and US except California) .... 1200 ± 50 rpm
  EX500A California models .... 1300 ± 50 rpm
  EX500D, E and ER models .... 1200 ± 50 rpm
Valve clearances (COLD engine)
  Inlet .... 0.13 to 0.18 mm (0.005 to 0.007 in)
  Exhaust .... 0.18 to 0.23 mm (0.007 to 0.009 in)
Cylinder compression pressure – acceptable range
  EX models .... 128 to 196 psi (8.8 to 13.5 bars)
  ER models .... 139 to 213 psi (9.8 to 15.0 bars)
Carburettor synchronisation (vacuum difference
  between cylinders) .... Less than 2 cm (0.391 in) Hg
Cylinder numbering (from left side to right side of bike) .... 1 – 2

Cycle parts

Brake pad minimum thickness .... 1.0 mm (0.04 in)
Brake shoe lining minimum thickness .... 2.0 mm (0.08 in)
Brake pedal position below the top of the footrest
  EX500A models .... 0 to 20 mm (0 to 0.8 in)
  ER models .... approx. 50 mm (1.97 in)
  For EX500D and E models refer to Chapter 7

Cycle parts (continued)

Freeplay adjustments
    Throttle grip . . . . 2 to 3 mm (0.08 to 0.12 in)
    Clutch lever (gap between lever and lever bracket
        when freeplay is taken up) . . . . 2 to 3 mm (0.08 to 0.12 in)
    Rear brake pedal (EX500A and ER models) . . . . 20 to 30 mm (0.8 to 1.2 in)
    Choke lever . . . . 2 to 3 mm (0.08 to 0.12 in)
Drive chain
    Slack
        Standard . . . . 35 to 40 mm (1.38 to 1.57 in)
        Service limit . . . . 45 mm (1.77 in)
    20-link length . . . . 323 mm (12.73 in) maximum
Battery electrolyte specific gravity . . . . 1.280 at 20°C (68°F)
Tyre pressures and tread depth . . . . see Daily (pre-ride) checks

Torque specifications

Oil drain plug . . . . 29 Nm (22 ft-lbs)
Oil filter . . . . 17 Nm (12.5 ft-lbs)
Coolant drain bolt
    EX500A models . . . . 12 Nm (104 in-lbs)
    EX500D, E and ER models . . . . 11 Nm (95 in-lbs)
Spark plugs . . . . 14 Nm (120 in-lbs)
Valve cover bolts . . . . 9.8 Nm (87 in-lbs)

Recommended lubricants and fluids

Engine/transmission oil type . . . . API grade SE, SF or SG
Engine/transmission oil viscosity
    In cold climates – up to 15°C (60°F) . . . . SAE 10W40 or 10W50
    In warm climates – above 5°C (40°F) . . . . SAE 20W40 or 20W50
Engine/transmission oil capacity
    Oil change only . . . . 2.8 litres (3.0 US qt, 4.9 Imp pt)
    Oil and filter change . . . . 3.0 litres (3.2 US qt, 5.3 Imp pt)
    Engine dry (after overhaul) . . . . 3.4 litres (3.6 US qt, 6.0 Imp pt)
Coolant type . . . . 50/50 mixture of ethylene glycol based antifreeze and soft water
Capacity – total
    EX models . . . . 1.8 litres (2.0 US qt, 3.1 Imp pt)
    ER models . . . . 1.7 litres (3.0 Imp pt)
Brake fluid . . . . DOT 4
Fork oil type . . . . SAE 10W20
Fork oil capacity – EX500A models
    At oil change . . . . Approx. 245 cc
    Dry fill (after overhaul) . . . . 287 ± 2.5 cc
Fork oil capacity – EX500D and E models
    At oil change . . . . Approx. 300 cc
    Dry fill (after overhaul) . . . . 352 ± 4 cc
Fork oil capacity – ER500A models
    At oil change . . . . Approx. 315 cc
    Dry fill (after overhaul) . . . . 370 ± 4 cc
Fork oil capacity – ER500C1 and C3 models
    At oil change . . . . Approx 295 cc
    Dry fill (after overhaul) . . . . 346 ± 2 cc
Fork oil capacity – ER500C4 and C5 models
    At oil change . . . . Approx 298 cc
    Dry fill (after overhaul) . . . . 351 ± 2 cc
Fork oil level*
    EX500A models . . . . 131 ± 2 mm (5.15 ± 0.08 in)
    EX500D and E models . . . . 117 ± 2 mm (4.61 ± 0.08 in)
    ER500A models . . . . 118 ± 2 mm (4.65 ± 0.08 in)
    ER500C1 and C3 models . . . . 127 ± 2 mm
    ER500C4 and C5 models . . . . 120 ± 2 mm
Drive chain . . . . SAE 90 oil or aerosol chain lubricant suitable for O-ring chains
Wheel bearings . . . . Medium weight, lithium-based multi-purpose grease
Swingarm and Uni-Trak pivot bearings . . . . Medium weight, lithium-based multi-purpose grease
Cables and lever pivots . . . . Chain and cable lubricant or 10W30 motor oil
Sidestand/centerstand pivots . . . . Medium-weight, lithium-based multi-purpose grease
Brake pedal/gearchange lever pivots . . . . Chain and cable lubricant or 10W30 motor oil
Throttle grip . . . . Multi-purpose grease or dry film lubricant

Measured from the top of the fork tube with the fork compressed and the spring removed

EX500A (all markets), EX500D (US and Canada)

Note: *The daily (pre-ride) checks at the beginning of the manual cover those items which should be inspected on a daily basis. Always perform the pre-ride inspection at every maintenance interval (in addition to the procedures listed). The intervals listed below are the intervals recommended by the manufacturer for the models covered in this manual. If in doubt, check with a Kawasaki dealer.*

Daily or before riding
See *'Daily (pre-ride) checks'* at the beginning of this manual.

Every 300 km (200 m)
☐ Lubricate the drive chain (Section 1)

After the initial 800 km (500 m)
Note: *This check is usually performed by a Kawasaki dealer after the first 800 km (500 m) from new. Thereafter, maintenance is carried out according to the following intervals of the schedule.*

Every 800 km (500 m)
☐ Check/adjust the drive chain slack (Section 2)

Every 5000 km (3100 m)
☐ Clean and gap the spark plugs (Section 3)
☐ Check the operation of the air suction valves (if equipped) (Section 4)
☐ Check/adjust the idle speed (Section 5)
☐ Check/adjust the carburettor synchronisation (Section 6)
☐ Check the evaporative emission control system (California models) (Section 7)
☐ Check/adjust the clutch freeplay (Section 8)
☐ Check the drive chain and sprockets for wear (Section 9)
☐ Check the brake system (Section 10)
☐ Check the brake pads and shoe linings (Section 11)
☐ Check/adjust the brake pedal position – drum brake (Section 12)
☐ Lubricate all cables (Section 13)
☐ Lubricate the clutch and brake lever pivots (Section 13)
☐ Lubricate the gearchange/brake lever pivots and the sidestand/centerstand pivots (Section 13)
☐ Check the tyres and wheels (Section 14)
☐ Check the battery electrolyte level (Section 15)
☐ Check the steering head bearings for freeplay (Section 16)
☐ Check the suspension (Section 17)
☐ Check the fuel hoses (Section 22)

Every 10,000 km (6200 m)
Carry out all the items under the 5000 km (3100 mile) check, plus the following:
☐ Check the throttle for smooth operation and correct freeplay (Section 18)
☐ Check the choke cable freeplay (Section 18)
☐ Adjust the valve clearances (Section 19)
☐ Change the engine oil and oil filter (Section 20)
☐ Clean the air filter element (Section 21)
☐ Clean the fuel filter and check the fuel and vacuum hoses (Section 22)
☐ Lubricate the swingarm needle bearings and Uni-trak linkage (Section 23)
☐ Check the cooling system for leaks and the hose condition (Section 24)
☐ Check the exhaust system for leaks and check the tightness of the fasteners (Section 25)
☐ Check the tightness of the fasteners (Section 26)
☐ Clean the carburettor warmer filter (Chapter 3)

Every 20,000 km (12,420 m) or two years
Carry out all the items under the 10,000 km (6200 mile) check, plus the following:
☐ Change the brake fluid (Section 27)
☐ Lubricate the steering head bearings (Section 28)
☐ Renew the air filter element (Section 21)
☐ Lubricate the rear brake cam – drum brakes (Section 29)

Every 30,000 km (18,630 m) or two years
Carry out all the items under the 10,000 km (6200 mile) check, plus the following:
☐ Change the coolant (Section 30)
☐ Change the fork oil (Section 31)

Every two years
☐ Overhaul the brake caliper(s) and master cylinder(s) (Section 32)

Every four years
☐ Renew the fuel hoses (Section 33)
☐ Renew the hydraulic brake hose(s) (Section 34)

Non-scheduled maintenance
☐ Cylinder compression check (Section 35)

ER500D and E (UK), ER500 (all markets)

Note: *The daily (pre-ride) checks at the beginning of the manual cover those items which should be inspected on a daily basis. Always perform the pre-ride inspection at every maintenance interval (in addition to the procedures listed). The intervals listed below are the intervals recommended by the manufacturer for the models covered in this manual. If in doubt, check with a Kawasaki dealer.*

Daily or before riding

See *'Daily (pre-ride) checks'* at the beginning of this manual.

Every 600 km (400 m)

☐ Lubricate the drive chain (Section 1)

After the initial 1000 km (600 m)

Note: *This check is usually performed by a Kawasaki dealer after the first 1000 km (600 m) from new. Thereafter, maintenance is carried out according to the following intervals of the schedule.*

Every 1000 km (600 m)

☐ Check/adjust the drive chain slack (Section 2)

Every 6000 km (3700 m)

☐ Clean and gap the spark plugs (Section 3)
☐ Check the operation of the air suction valves (if equipped) (Section 4)
☐ Change the engine oil (Section 20)
☐ Check/adjust the clutch freeplay (Section 8)
☐ Check the drive chain and sprockets for wear (Section 9)
☐ Check the brake system (Section 10)
☐ Check the brake pads and shoe linings (Section 11)
☐ Check/adjust the brake pedal position – drum brake (Section 12)
☐ Check the steering head bearings for freeplay (Section 16)
☐ Check the tyres and wheels (Section 14)
☐ Check the battery electrolyte level – EX models (Section 15)
☐ Check the fuel hoses (Section 22)

Every 12,000 km (7400 m)

Carry out all the items under the 6000 km (3700 m) check, plus the following:
☐ Adjust the valve clearances (Section 19)
☐ Clean/inspect the air filter element (Section 21)

Every 12,000 km (7400 m) (continued)

☐ Check the throttle for smooth operation and correct freeplay (Section 18)
☐ Check the choke cable freeplay (Section 18)
☐ Check/adjust the idle speed (Section 5)
☐ Check/adjust the carburettor synchronisation (Section 6)
☐ Change the engine oil and oil filter (Section 20)
☐ Check the suspension (Section 17)
☐ Lubricate the swingarm needle bearings and Uni-trak linkage (Section 23)
☐ Lubricate all cables (Section 13)
☐ Lubricate the clutch and brake lever pivots (Section 13)
☐ Lubricate the gearchange/brake lever pivots and the sidestand/centerstand pivots (Section 13)
☐ Check the exhaust system for leaks and check the tightness of the fasteners (Section 25)
☐ Check the tightness of the fasteners (Section 26)
☐ Check the evaporative emission control system (California models) (Section 7)
☐ Clean the fuel filter and check the fuel and vacuum hoses (Section 22)
☐ Check the cooling system for leaks and the hose condition (Section 24)
☐ Clean the carburettor warmer filter (Chapter 3)

Every 24,000 km (14,900 m) – or every two years

Carry out all the items under the 12,000 km (7400 m) check, plus the following:
☐ Change the coolant (Section 30)
☐ Change the brake fluid (Section 27)
☐ Lubricate the steering head bearings (Section 28)
☐ Change the fork oil (Section 31)

Every four years

☐ Overhaul the brake caliper(s) and master cylinder(s) (Section 32)

Non-scheduled maintenance

☐ Lubricate the rear brake cam – ER drum brake (Section 29)
☐ Renew the fuel hoses (Section 33)
☐ Renew the hydraulic brake hose(s) (Section 34)
☐ Cylinder compression check (Section 35)

EX models

1   Rear brake fluid reservoir (EX500D and E)
2   Clutch cable adjuster
3   Coolant reservoir
4   Front brake fluid reservoir

5   Engine/transmission oil filter
6   Coolant drain plug
7   Engine/transmission oil drain bolt
8   Engine/transmission oil filler

9   Engine/transmission oil level sightglass
Note: For rear brake freeplay adjuster and rear brake cam locations on the EX500A refer to the ER-5 model component location illustration

EX models

1   Clutch cable adjuster
2   Steering head bearings
3   Air suction valves (also fitted to ER500C models)

4   Air filter
5   Battery
6   Drive chain adjusters
7   Idle speed adjuster (throttle stop screw)

8   Fuel filter
9   Front fork drain plug (EX500A)
10 Fork oil seals

ER models

1	Coolant reservoir	5	Coolant drain plug	8	Engine/transmission oil level sightglass
2	Clutch cable adjuster	6	Engine/transmission oil drain bolt	9	Rear brake freeplay adjuster
3	Front brake fluid reservoir	7	Engine/transmission oil filler	10	Rear brake cam
4	Engine/transmission oil filter				

ER models

1	Clutch cable adjuster	4	Battery	6	Idle speed adjuster (throttle stop screw)
2	Steering head bearings	5	Drive chain adjusters	7	Fork oil seals
3	Air filter				

Deciding where to start or plug into the routine maintenance schedule depends on several factors. If you have a motorcycle whose warranty has recently expired, and if it has been maintained according to the warranty standards, you may want to pick up routine maintenance as it coincides with the next mileage or calendar interval. If you have owned the machine for some time but have never performed any maintenance on it, then you may want to start at the nearest interval and include some additional procedures to ensure that nothing important is overlooked. If you have just had a major engine overhaul, then you may want to start the maintenance routine from the beginning. If you have a used machine and have no knowledge of its history or maintenance record, you may desire to combine all the checks into one large service initially and then settle into the maintenance schedule prescribed.

The Sections which outline the inspection and maintenance procedures are written as step-by-step comprehensive guides to the performance of the work. They explain in detail each of the routine inspections and

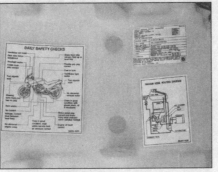

Decals provide information on safety, emission control, servicing and vacuum hose routing . . .

. . . and drive chain care

maintenance procedures on the check list. References to additional information in applicable Chapters is also included and should not be overlooked.

Before beginning any maintenance or repair, the machine should be cleaned thoroughly, especially around the oil filter, spark plugs, cylinder head covers, side covers, carburettors, etc. Cleaning will help ensure that dirt does not contaminate the

engine and will allow you to detect wear and damage that could otherwise easily go unnoticed.

Maintenance information is printed on decals under the seat (EX models) or under the right-hand side cover (ER models) and on the chain guard (see illustrations). If the information on the decals differs from that included here, use the information on the decal.

Maintenance procedures

1 Drive chain – lubrication

Note: *If the chain is extremely dirty, it should be removed and cleaned before it's lubricated* (see Chapter 6).

1 The best time to lubricate the chain is after the motorcycle has been ridden. When the chain is warm, the lubricant will penetrate the joints between the side plates, pins, bushings and rollers to provide lubrication of the internal load bearing areas.

2 Use a good quality chain aerosol chain lubricant (marked as being suitable for O-ring chains) and apply it to the area where the side

plates overlap – not the middle of the rollers (see illustration). With the bike on its centerstand, hold the plastic nozzle near the edge of the chain and turn the wheel by hand as the lubricant sprays out - repeat the procedure on the inside edge of the chain.

3 After applying the lubricant, let it soak in a few minutes before wiping off any excess.

2 Drive chain –
check and adjustment

Check – all models

1 A neglected drive chain won't last long and

can quickly damage the sprockets. Routine chain adjustment isn't difficult and will ensure maximum chain and sprocket life.

2 To check the chain, place the bike on its centerstand and shift the transmission into Neutral. Make sure the ignition switch is OFF.

3 Push up on the bottom run of the chain and measure the slack midway between the two sprockets (see illustration), then compare your measurements to the value listed in this Chapter's Specifications. As wear occurs, the chain will actually stretch, which means adjustment by removing some slack from the chain. In some cases where lubrication has been neglected, corrosion and galling may cause the links to bind and kink, which effectively shortens the chain's length. If the chain is tight between the sprockets, rusty or kinked, it's time to renew it. **Note:** *Repeat the chain slack measurement along the length of the chain – ideally, every inch or so. If you find a tight area, mark it with felt pen or paint and repeat the measurement after the bike has been ridden. If the chain's still tight in the same area, it may be damaged or worn. Because a tight or kinked chain can damage the transmission output shaft bearing, it's a good idea to renew it.*

Adjustment – EX500A models

4 Rotate the rear wheel until the chain is positioned with the least amount of slack present.

5 Remove the R-pin from the torque link nut and loosen the nut, then remove the split pin

1.2 Apply chain lubricant to the joints between the side plates and the rollers - not in the centre of the rollers

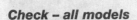

2.3 Push up on the bottom run of the chain and measure how far it deflects

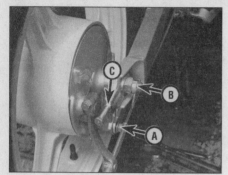

2.5 Loosen the torque link nut (A) and the axle nut (B), then back-off the chain adjuster locknut (C)

2.6 When the adjuster bolts (A) are set evenly, the adjuster marks (C) on both sides should line up with the same marks in the swingarm. Secure the locknuts (B)

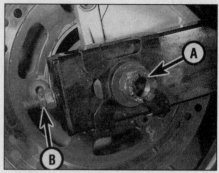

2.10 Slacken the axle nut (A) and back off the adjuster locknut (B) on each side

and loosen the axle nut (see illustration). Loosen and back-off the locknuts on the adjuster bolts.

6 Turn the adjuster bolts on both sides of the swingarm until the proper chain tension is obtained (get the adjuster on the chain side close, then set the adjuster on the opposite side) (see illustration). If the adjusting bolts reach the end of their travel, the chain is excessively worn and should be renewed (see Chapter 6).

7 When the chain has the correct amount of slack, make sure the marks on the adjusters correspond to the same relative marks on each side of the swingarm. Tighten the axle nut to the torque listed in Chapter 7 Specifications, then install a new split pin. If necessary, turn the nut an additional amount to line up the

cotter pin hole with the castellations in the nut – don't loosen the nut to do this.

8 Tighten the adjuster bolt nuts against the chain adjusters. Tighten the torque link nut to the torque listed in Chapter 7 and fit the R-pin.

Adjustment – EX500D and E models

9 Rotate the rear wheel until the chain is positioned with the least amount of slack present.

10 Remove the split pin from the axle nut and loosen the nut. Back off the chain adjuster locknut on each side (see illustration).

11 Turn the adjuster nuts on both sides of the swingarm until the proper chain tension is obtained (get the adjuster on the chain side

close, then set the adjuster on the opposite side) (see illustration). Turn the nuts in (clockwise) to tighten the chain. In the event that the chain is too tight, back off the adjuster nuts and kick the rear wheel forwards to reposition the chain adjuster in the swingarm slots. Make sure that the single mark on the top of each chain adjuster aligns with the same mark on each side of the swingarm (see illustration), if necessary turn the adjuster nuts as required to achieve this.

12 Tighten the axle nut to the torque listed in Chapter 7 Specifications, then install a new split pin. If necessary, turn the nut an additional amount to line up the cotter pin hole with the castellations in the nut – don't loosen the nut to do this.

13 Tighten the locknuts against the adjuster nuts.

Adjustment – ER models

14 Rotate the rear wheel until the chain is positioned with the least amount of slack present.

15 Remove the R-pin from the torque link nut and loosen the nut, then remove the split pin and loosen the axle nut (see illustration). Loosen and back-off the locknuts on the adjusters.

16 Turn the adjuster nuts on both sides of the swingarm until the proper chain tension is obtained (get the adjuster on the chain side close, then set the adjuster on the opposite side) (see illustration). Turn the nuts in

2.11a Adjusting the chain tension

2.11b Chain adjuster plate notch and wheel alignment marks

2.15 Remove the split pin and slacken the axle nut

2.16a Back off the locknuts before making adjustment

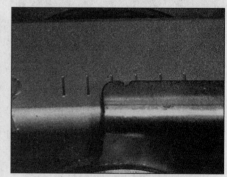

2.16b Chain adjuster plate notch and wheel alignment marks

3.2a Rotate the spark plug caps back and forth to loosen them . . .

3.2b . . . then pull them off the plugs and check them for brittleness and cracking

3.2c Use an extension and a deep socket (preferably one with a rubber insert to prevent damage to the plug) to remove the spark plugs

(clockwise) to tighten the chain. In the event that the chain is too tight, back off the adjuster nuts and kick the rear wheel forwards to reposition the chain adjuster in the swingarm slots. Make sure that the notch on the top of each chain adjuster aligns with the same mark on each side of the swingarm **(see illustration)**, if necessary turn the adjuster nuts as required to achieve this.

17 Tighten the axle nut to the torque listed in Chapter 7 Specifications, then install a new split pin. If necessary, turn the nut an additional amount to line up the cotter pin hole with the castellations in the nut – don't loosen the nut to do this.

18 Tighten the locknuts against the adjuster nuts. Tighten the torque link nut to the torque listed in Chapter 7 and fit the R-pin.

> **HAYNES HiNT** *The marks on the swingarm and chain adjusters are a guide to correct wheel in alignment. To check wheel alignment refer to Chapter 7.*

3 Spark plugs – clean and regap

Note: *This motorcycle is equipped with spark plugs that have 12 mm threads and an 18 mm wrench hex. Make sure your spark plug socket is the correct size before attempting to remove the plugs. A suitable tool should be included in the bike's toolkit.*

1 Remove the fuel tank to access the spark plugs (see Chapter 4).

2 Disconnect the spark plug caps from the spark plugs **(see illustrations)**. If available, use compressed air to blow any accumulated debris from around the spark plugs. Remove the plugs **(see illustration)**.

3 Inspect the electrodes for wear. Both the centre and side electrodes should have square edges and the side electrode should be of uniform thickness. Look for excessive deposits and evidence of a cracked or chipped insulator around the centre electrode. Compare your spark plugs to the colour spark plug reading chart on the inside rear cover. Check the threads, the washer and the ceramic insulator body for cracks and other damage.

4 If the electrodes are not excessively worn, and if the deposits can be easily removed with a wire brush, the plugs can be regapped and reused (if no cracks or chips are visible in the insulator). If in doubt concerning the condition of the plugs, renew them, as the expense is minimal.

5 Cleaning spark plugs by sandblasting is permitted, provided you clean the plugs with a high flash-point solvent afterwards.

6 Before installing new plugs, make sure they are the correct type and heat range. Check the gap between the electrodes, as they are not preset. For best results, use a wire-type gauge rather than a flat gauge to check the gap **(see illustration)**. If the gap must be adjusted, bend the side electrode only and be very careful not to chip or crack the insulator nose **(see illustration)**. Make sure the washer is in place before installing each plug.

7 Since the cylinder head is made of aluminium, which is soft and easily damaged, thread the plugs into the heads by hand. Slip a short length of hose over the end of the plug to use as a tool to thread it into place **(see illustration)**. The hose will grip the plug well enough to turn it, but will start to slip if the plug begins to cross-thread in the hole – this will prevent damaged threads and the accompanying repair costs

8 Once the plugs are finger tight, the job can be finished with a socket. If a torque wrench is available, tighten the spark plugs to the torque listed in this Chapter's Specifications. If you do not have a torque wrench, tighten the plugs finger tight (until the washers bottom on the cylinder head) then use a wrench to tighten them an additional 1/4 turn. Regardless of the method used, do not over-tighten them.

9 Reconnect the spark plug caps.

10 Install the fuel tank (see Chapter 4).

> **HAYNES HiNT** *Stripped plug threads in the cylinder head can be repaired with a thread insert – see 'Tools and workshop tips' in the Reference section.*

3.6a Spark plug manufacturers recommend using a wire type gauge when checking the gap

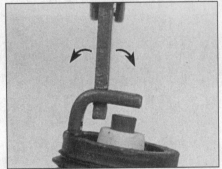

3.6b To change the gap, bend the side electrode only, as indicated by the arrows

3.7 A length of rubber hose will save time and prevent damaged threads when installing the spark plugs

4.3a Squeeze the spring clip, slide it back along the hose and detach the hose from the air suction valve

4.3b There's an air suction valve mounted on the valve cover above each cylinder

5.3a Throttle stop screw – EX models (carburettors removed from engine for clarity)

4 Air suction valves – check

1 The air suction valves, installed on US and ER500C models, are one-way check valves that allow fresh air to flow into the exhaust ports. The suction developed by the exhaust pulses pulls the air from the air cleaner, through a hose to the air switching valve, through a pair of hoses and a pair of reed valves, and finally into the exhaust ports. The introduction of fresh air helps ignite any fuel that may not have been burned by the normal combustion process.
2 Remove the fuel tank (see Chapter 4).
3 Disconnect the hoses from the air suction valves (see illustration). Remove the bolts (see illustration) and lift off the covers.
4 Check the valves for cracks, warping, burning or other damage. Check the area where the reeds contact the valve holder for scratches, separation and grooves. If any of these conditions are found, renew the valve.
5 Wash the valves with solvent if carbon has accumulated between the reed and the valve holder.
6 Installation of the valves is the reverse of removal. Be sure to use a new gasket.

5 Idle speed – check and adjustment

1 The idle speed should be checked and adjusted after the carburettors are synchronised and when it is obviously too high or too low. Before adjusting the idle speed, make sure the valve clearances and spark plug gaps are correct.

HAYNES HiNT *Turn the handlebars back-and-forth and see if the idle speed changes as this is done. If it does, the accelerator cable may not be adjusted correctly, or it may be worn out. Be sure to correct this problem before proceeding.*

2 The engine should be at normal operating temperature, which is usually reached after 10 to 15 minutes of stop and go riding. Place the motorcycle on the centerstand with the transmission in neutral and engine idling.
3 Turn the throttle stop screw until the idle speed listed in this Chapter's Specifications is obtained. The throttle stop screw is located on the left-hand side of the bike, just to the rear of the carburettor for cylinder no. 1 on EX models (see illustration), and just below the fuel tap on the left-hand side on ER models (see illustration).
4 Snap the throttle open and shut a few times, then recheck the idle speed. If necessary, repeat the adjustment procedure.
5 If a smooth, steady idle can't be achieved, the fuel/air mixture may be incorrect. Refer to Chapter 4 for additional carburettor information.

6 Carburettor synchronisation – check and adjustment

> **Warning: Gasoline (petrol) is extremely flammable, so take extra precautions when you work on any part of the fuel system. Don't smoke or allow open flames or bare light bulbs near the work area, and don't work in a garage where a natural gas-type appliance (such as a water heater or clothes dryer) is present. If you spill any fuel on your skin, rinse it off**

5.3b Throttle stop screw (arrowed) – ER models

immediately with soap and water. When you perform any kind of work on the fuel system, wear safety glasses and have a fire extinguisher suitable for a class B type fire (flammable liquids) on hand.

> **Warning: Take great care not to burn your hand on the hot engine unit when accessing the gauge take-off points on the inlet manifolds. Do not allow exhaust gases to build up in the work area; either perform the check outside or use an exhaust gas extraction system.**

1 Carburettor synchronisation is simply the process of adjusting the carburettors so they pass the same amount of fuel/air mixture to each cylinder. This is done by measuring the vacuum produced in each cylinder. Carburettors that are out of synchronisation will result in decreased fuel mileage, increased engine temperature, less than ideal throttle response and higher vibration levels.
2 To properly synchronise the carburettors, you will need a set of two vacuum gauges or calibrated tubes (manometer) to indicate engine vacuum. **Note:** *Because of the nature of the synchronisation procedure and the need for special instruments, most owners leave the task to a Kawasaki dealer.*
3 Start the engine and let it run until it reaches normal operating temperature, then shut it off.
4 Remove the fuel tank (see Chapter 4).
5 Detach the vacuum hoses or caps from the fitting on the front of each carburettor body (see illustrations), then hook up the vacuum

6.5a Disconnect the carburettor vacuum hoses

6.5b Front view of the carburettors

A *Vacuum hose (disconnect to expose fitting)*
B *Fitting*
C *Synchronisation screw*

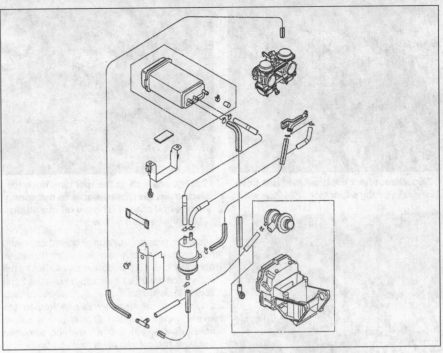

7.2 Emission control system details

gauge set or the manometer according to the manufacturer's instructions. Make sure there are no leaks in the set-up, as false readings will result.

6 Disconnect the fuel delivery pipe to the carburettors and in its place, connect a longer length of pipe to a remote fuel tank. Have an assistant hold the remote fuel tank out of the way, but in such a position that fuel can still be delivered and access to the carburettors is unobstructed.

7 Start the engine and make sure the idle speed is correct.

8 The vacuum readings for both of the cylinders should be the same, or at least within the tolerance listed in this Chapter's Specifications. If the vacuum readings vary, adjust as necessary.

9 To perform the adjustment, synchronise the carburettors by turning the butterfly valve adjusting screw, as needed, until the vacuum is identical or nearly identical for both cylinders **(see illustration 6.5b)**. Note: *Do not press down on the screw whilst adjusting it, otherwise a false reading will be obtained.*

10 When the adjustment is complete, recheck the vacuum readings and idle speed, then stop the engine. Remove the vacuum gauge or manometer and attach the hoses or

caps to the fittings on the carburettors. Reinstall the fuel tank and seat.

7 Evaporative emission control system (California models only) – check

1 This system, installed on California models to conform to stringent emission control standards, routes fuel vapours from the fuel system into the engine to be burned, instead of letting them evaporate into the atmosphere. When the engine isn't running, vapours are stored in a carbon canister.

Hoses

2 To begin the inspection of the system, remove the seat and fuel tank (see Chapters 4 and 8 if necessary). Inspect the hoses from the fuel tank, carburettors and liquid/vapour

separator to the canister for cracking, kinks or other signs of deterioration **(see illustration)**.

Liquid/vapour separator test

3 Disconnect the breather hose from the separator and inject about 20 cc of gasoline into the fitting with a syringe.

4 Disconnect the fuel return hose from the tank and place the end of the hose in a container level with the top of the tank.

5 Start the engine and let it idle. If the fuel comes out of the hose, the separator is good; if not, renew it.

Component inspection

6 Label and disconnect the hoses, then remove the separator and canister from the machine. Note: *For system inspection, it's easiest to remove the separator, canister, fuel tank bracket and air suction switching valve as a unit (see illustrations).*

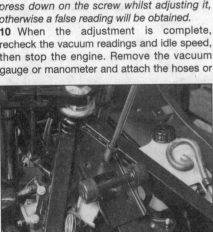

7.6a To remove the components, unbolt the tank bracket from the frame . . .

7.6b . . . disconnect the purge hose from the canister fitting (arrowed) (the other canister hose can be left connected and the canister-to-tank bracket bolts can be left in place) . . .

7.6c . . . follow the vacuum hose from the T-fitting (A) and disconnect its other end; disconnect the air suction hose from each cylinder (B) and from the air box (C)

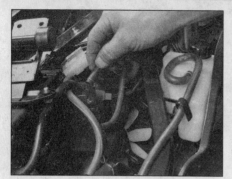
7.6d Disconnect the breather hose from the separator . . .

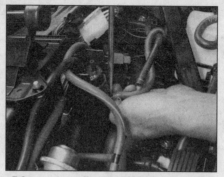
7.6e . . . as well as the fuel tank hose (to disconnect the hoses, squeeze the spring clamps and push the hoses off the fittings with a screwdriver)

7.6f Remove the air switching valve, separator, canister and fuel tank bracket

7.7 To renew the separator, disconnect its hoses and remove it from the bracket

7 Check the separator closely for cracks or other signs of damage. If these are found, renew it **(see illustration)**.

8 Inspect the canister for cracks or other signs of damage. Tip the canister so the nozzles point down. If fuel runs out of the canister, the liquid/vapour separator is probably bad – check it as described above. The fuel inside the canister has probably caused damage, so it would be a good idea to renew it also.

8 Clutch - check and adjustment

1 Correct clutch freeplay is necessary to ensure proper clutch operation and reasonable clutch service life. Freeplay normally changes because of cable stretch and clutch wear, so it should be checked and adjusted periodically.

2 Clutch cable freeplay is checked at the lever on the handlebar. Slowly pull in on the lever until resistance is felt, then note how far the lever has moved away from its bracket at the pivot end **(see illustration)**. Compare this distance with the value listed in this Chapter's Specifications. Too little freeplay may result in the clutch not engaging completely. If there is too much freeplay, the clutch might not release fully.

3 Freeplay adjustments can be made at the clutch lever by loosening the lockwheel and turning the adjuster until the desired freeplay is obtained. Always retighten the lockwheel once the adjustment is complete. If the lever adjuster reaches the end of its travel, try adjusting the cable at its bracket on the engine.

4 Loosen the adjusting nuts at the lower end of the cable completely **(see illustration)**.

5 Loosen the knurled lockwheel at the clutch lever and turn the adjuster in or out to expose approximately 5 or 6 mm of threads between the adjuster and the lockwheel.

6 Pull the clutch cable tight to remove all slack, then tighten the adjusting nuts against the bracket at the lower end of the cable.

7 Turn the adjuster at the clutch lever until the correct freeplay is obtained, then tighten the lockwheel.

8 If the proper amount of freeplay still can't be obtained, the cable must be renewed (see Chapter 2).

9 Once the cable is adjusted properly, turn the numbered adjusting wheel (span adjuster) to position the clutch lever a comfortable distance from the handlebar.

9 Drive chain and sprockets – wear check

1 Remove the chain guard (it's held on by two bolts). Check the entire length of the chain for damaged rollers, loose links and pins. Hang a 20 lb (9 kg) weight on the bottom run of the chain and measure the length of 20 links (21 pins) along the top run **(see illustration)**. Rotate the wheel and repeat this check at several places on the chain, since it may wear unevenly. Compare your measurements with the maximum 20-link length listed in this

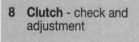

8.2 Check clutch freeplay measurement point (A), adjuster lockwheel (B) and adjuster (C)

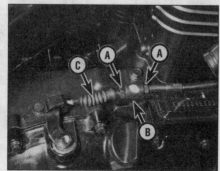
8.4 Lower adjuster nuts (A), bracket (B) and dust cover (C)

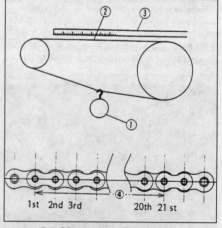
9.1 Measuring chain stretch

1   20 lb (9 kg) weight
2   Top run of chain
3   Rule
4   20 link length

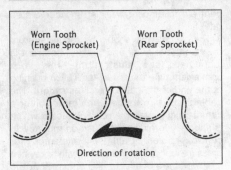

9.2 Check the sprockets in the areas indicated to see if they are worn excessively

10.6 To adjust the rear brake light switch, hold the switch body and turn the adjusting nut (arrowed)

11.2a Checking the front brake pads for wear

Chapter's Specifications. If any of your measurements exceed the maximum, renew the chain.

 Never install a new chain on old sprockets, and never use the old chain if you install new sprockets – renew the chain and sprockets as a set.

2 Remove the engine sprocket cover (see Chapter 6). Check the teeth on the engine sprocket and the rear sprocket for wear **(see illustration).**

10 Brake system – general check

1 A routine general check of the brakes will ensure that any problems are discovered and remedied before the rider's safety is jeopardised.
2 Check the brake lever and pedal for loose connections, excessive play, bends, and other damage. Renew any damaged parts (see Chapter 7).
3 Make sure all brake fasteners are tight. Check the brake pads and shoe linings for wear (see Section 11) and make sure the fluid level in the reservoir(s) is correct (see *Daily (pre-ride) checks*). Look for leaks at the hose connections and check for cracks in the

hoses. If the lever is spongy, bleed the brakes as described in Chapter 7.
4 Make sure the brake light operates when the brake lever is depressed. The front brake light switch is not adjustable. If it fails to operate properly, renew it (see Chapter 9).
5 Make sure the brake light is activated when the rear brake pedal is depressed approximately 15 mm (0.6 inch) on EX500A models and ER models, and 10 mm (0.4 inch) on EX500D and E models.
6 If adjustment is necessary, hold the switch and turn the adjusting nut on the switch body **(see illustration)** until the brake light is activated when required. Turning the switch out will cause the brake light to come on sooner, while turning it in will cause it to come on later. If the switch doesn't operate the brake lights, check it as described in Chapter 9.

11 Brake pads and shoe linings – wear check

1 The brake pads (disc brakes) and shoe linings (drum brakes) should be checked at the recommended intervals and renewed when worn beyond the limit listed in this Chapter's Specifications.

Brake pads

2 Brake pad wear can be checked without removing the brake caliper **(see illustrations).**

The brake pads should have at least the specified minimum amount of lining material remaining on the metal backing plate **(see illustration).** If the pads are dirty or if you are in doubt as to the amount of friction material remaining, remove them for inspection (see Chapter 7) and measure the thickness of the friction material.
3 If the pads are worn excessively, they must be renewed (see Chapter 7).

Brake shoe linings

4 To check the rear brake linings, press the brake pedal firmly and look at the indicator on the brake drum **(see illustration).** If the pointer is beyond the Usable Range scale, renew the brake shoes (see Chapter 7).

12 Brake pedal position and play – check and adjustment (drum brakes)

1 Rear brake pedal position is largely a matter of personal preference. Locate the pedal so that the rear brake can be engaged quickly and easily without excessive foot movement. The recommended factory setting is listed in this Chapter's Specifications and is expressed as the difference in height bewteen the brake pedal tip (when at rest) and the top of the footrest rubber.
2 To adjust the position of the pedal, loosen the locknut on the adjusting bolt, turn the bolt

11.2b Checking the rear brake pads for wear

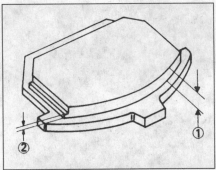

11.2c Brake pad friction material thickness when new (1) and worn down to wear limit step (2)

11.4 If the pointer goes past the Usable Range indicator toward the rear of the bike, the linings are worn and must be renewed

12.2a Brake pedal position bolt locknut (arrowed) – EX500A models

12.2b Brake pedal position bolt locknut (arrowed) – ER models

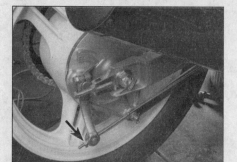

12.4 Turn the adjuster at the rear of the brake rod (arrowed) to adjust pedal freeplay

13.3a Disconnect the clutch cable from the lever after aligning the slots in the adjuster and lockwheel

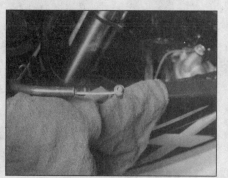

13.3b The bushing at the end of the cable should be checked for wear; lubricate it with high-temperature grease

13.3c Lubricating a cable with a cable oiler clamp (make sure the tool seats around the inner cable)

to set the pedal position and tighten the locknut **(see illustrations)**.

3 With the pedal position adjusted correctly, check freeplay. Apply the rear brake and compare the pedal travel with that listed in this Chapter's Specifications.

4 To adjust the freeplay, turn the adjuster at the rear end of the brake rod **(see illustration)**.

3 If necessary, adjust the brake light switch (see Section 10).

13 Lubrication – general

1 Since the controls, cables and various other components of a motorcycle are exposed to the elements, they should be lubricated periodically to ensure safe and trouble-free operation.

2 The footrests, clutch and brake lever, brake pedal, gearchange lever and side and centerstand pivots should be lubricated frequently. In order for the lubricant to be applied where it will do the most good, the component should be disassembled. However, if chain and cable lubricant is being used, it can be applied to the pivot joint gaps and will usually work its way into the areas where friction occurs. If motor oil or light grease is being used, apply it sparingly as it may attract dirt (which could cause the

controls to bind or wear at an accelerated rate).

3 The clutch cable should be separated from the handlebar lever and bracket before it is lubricated **(see illustration)**. This is a convenient time to inspect the Teflon bushing at the end of the cable **(see illustration)**. The cable should be treated with motor oil or a commercially available cable lubricant which is specially formulated for use on motorcycle control cables. Cable oiler clamps for pressure lubricating the cables with spray can lubricants are available and ensure that the cable is lubricated along its entire length **(see illustration)**. If motor oil is being used, tape a funnel-shaped piece of heavy paper or plastic to the end of the cable, then pour oil into the funnel and suspend the end of the cable upright **(see illustration)**. Leave it until the oil runs down into the cable and out the other end. When attaching the cable to the lever, be sure to lubricate the barrel-shaped fitting at the end with high-temperature grease.

4 To lubricate the throttle and choke cables, disconnect the cable(s) at the lower end, then lubricate the cable with a pressure lube adapter **(see illustration 13.3c)**. See Chapter 4 for the choke cable removal procedure.

5 Refer to Chapter 9 and remove the speedometer cable. Lubricate the inner cable, taking care not to lubricate the upper few inches of the cable as the lubricant may travel up into the instrument head.

14 Wheels and tyres – general check

1 Routine tyre and wheel checks should be made with the realisation that your safety depends to a great extent on their condition.

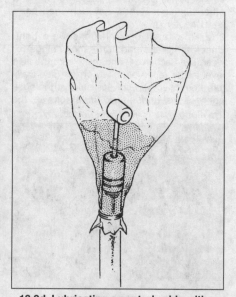

13.3d Lubricating a control cable with a makeshift funnel and motor oil

14.3 When checking the wheel bearings for play attempt to push and pull the wheel about the hub

15.2 Lift the junction box and bracket to gain access to the battery - note the position of the battery vent tube (lower arrow) and carburettor vent tube (upper arrow)

15.4 Detach the negative cable (left arrow) from the battery first, then detach the positive cable (right arrow)

Wheels

2 The cast wheels used on all models are virtually maintenance free, but they should be kept clean and checked periodically for cracks and other damage. Never attempt to repair damaged cast wheels; they must be renewed. Check the valve rubber for signs of damage or deterioration and have it renewed if necessary. Also, make sure the valve stem cap is in place and tight.

3 The wheel bearings will wear over a period of time and result in handling problems. Place the motorcycle on its centerstand and take the weight off the front wheel. Check for any play in the bearings by pushing and pulling the wheel against the hub **(see illustration)**. Also rotate the wheel and check that it rotates smoothly.

4 If any play is detected in the hub, or if the wheel does not rotate smoothly (and this is not due to brake drag), the wheel bearings must be renewed (see Chapter 7).

Tyres

5 Refer to *Daily (pre-ride) checks*.

15 Battery electrolyte level/specific gravity – check

Caution: Be extremely careful when handling or working around the battery. The electrolyte is very caustic and an explosive gas (hydrogen) is given off when the battery is charging.

EX models

Level check

1 Remove the seat (see Chapter 8).

2 Unbolt the junction box bracket and lift it off together with the junction box **(see illustration)**. Note the position of the carburettor vent tube and battery vent tube.

3 It may be possible to view the battery level marks without disconnecting its leads and lifting it out of its box. The electrolyte level is visible through the translucent battery case – it should be between the Upper and Lower level marks.

4 To remove the battery, remove the bolts securing the battery cables to the battery terminals (remove the negative cable first, positive cable last) **(see illustration)**. Pull the battery straight up to remove it, having first disconnected the vent tube from its side.

5 To top up the battery, remove the cell caps and fill each cell to the upper level mark with distilled water. Do not use tap water (except in an emergency), and do not overfill. If the level is within the marks on the case, additional water is not necessary. Refit the cell caps and mop up any water spills.

> **HAYNES HiNT** *The cell holes are quite small, so it may help to use a clean plastic squeeze bottle with a small spout to add the water.*

6 Slip the battery back into its holder and reconnect the vent tube making sure that it is not pinched at any point **(see illustration)**. Reconnect the cables to the battery, attaching the positive cable first and the negative cable last; install the plastic cap over the positive terminal. Install the junction box bracket. Ensure that the end of the carburettor tube is well away from the air intake before installing the seat.

Specific gravity check

7 A specific gravity check measures the state

of charge of the battery. If the specific gravity is low, the battery is not fully charged. This may be due to corroded battery terminals, a dirty battery case, a malfunctioning charging system, or loose or corroded wiring connections. On the other hand, it may be that the battery is worn out, especially if the machine is old, or that infrequent use of the motorcycle prevents normal charging from taking place.

8 You will need a battery hydrometer to measure specific gravity and the battery must be removed from the bike and cell caps removed as described above **(see illustration)**.

9 Refer to *Checking battery specific gravity* in the Fault Finding Equipment section of Reference at the end of this manual. Specific gravity should be 1.280 at 20°C (68°F) in a good condition charged battery.

ER models

10 A maintenance-free battery is fitted to ER models. Apart from making sure that the battery leads are well secured to the battery terminals and there is no trace of corrosion, there are no maintenance requirements for this type of battery.

11 If the battery is discharged or you suspect that it is worn out refer to Chapter 9 for futher information.

15.6 The clear plastic vent tube supplied with the battery fits inside the motorcycle's drain tube (arrowed) when the battery is installed

15.8 Check the specific gravity with a hydrometer

16.4 Check for freeplay in the steering head bearings

16.6 Loosen the lower pinch bolt on each fork (arrowed)

16.7 Loosen the steering stem bolt

16 Steering head bearings – check and adjustment

1 This motorcycle is equipped with ball-and-cone type steering head bearings. Steering head bearings can become dented, rough or loose during normal use of the machine and in extreme cases can cause steering wobble.

Check

2 To check the bearings, place the motorcycle on the centerstand and block the machine so the front wheel is in the air.
3 Point the wheel straight ahead and slowly move the handlebars from side-to-side. Dents or roughness in the bearing races will be felt and the bars will not move smoothly.
4 Next, grasp the fork legs and try to move the wheel forward and backward **(see illustration)**. Any looseness in the steering head bearings will be felt. If play is felt in the bearings, adjust the steering head as follows:

Adjustment

5 Remove the fuel tank to provide easier access (see Chapter 4).
6 Loosen the fork lower pinch bolts **(see illustration)**. This allows the necessary vertical movement of the steering stem in relation to the fork tubes.
7 Loosen (DO NOT remove) the steering stem

bolt **(see illustration)**. On ER models, displace the handlebars to access the stem bolt (see Chapter 6).
8 Use a C-spanner wrench to loosen the bearing adjuster nut **(see illustration)**.
9 Carefully tighten the bearing adjuster nut until the steering head is tight but does not bind when the forks are turned from side-to-side. The object is to set the adjuster nut so that the bearings are under a very light loading, just enough to remove any freeplay. *Caution: Take great care not to apply excessive pressure because this will cause premature failure of the bearings.*
10 Retighten the steering stem bolt and the fork pinch bolts, in that order, to the torque values listed in the Chapter 6 Specifications.
11 Recheck the steering head bearings for play as described above. If necessary, repeat the adjustment procedure. Reinstall all parts previously removed.
12 Refer to Chapter 6 for steering head bearing lubrication and replacement procedures.

17 Suspension – check

1 The suspension components must be maintained in top operating condition to ensure rider safety. Loose, worn or damaged

suspension parts decrease the bike's stability and control.
2 While standing alongside the motorcycle, lock the front brake and push on the handlebars to compress the forks several times. See if they move up-and-down smoothly without binding. If binding is felt, the forks should be disassembled and inspected as described in Chapter 6.
3 Carefully inspect the area around the fork seals for any signs of oil leakage **(see illustration)**. If leakage is evident, the seals must be renewed as described in Chapter 6.
4 Check the tightness of all suspension nuts and bolts to be sure none have worked loose.
5 Inspect the rear shock absorber(s) for fluid leakage and tightness of the mounting nuts. If leakage is found, the shock(s) should be renewed.
6 Set the bike on its centerstand. Grab the swingarm on each side, just ahead of the axle **(see illustration)**. Rock the swingarm from side to side – there should be no discernible movement at the rear. If there's a little movement or a slight clicking can be heard, make sure the pivot shaft nuts are tight. If the pivot nuts are tight but movement is still noticeable, the swingarm will have to be removed and the bearings renewed as described in Chapter 6.
7 Inspect the tightness of the rear suspension nuts and bolts.

16.8 Use a C-spanner to loosen or tighten the bearing adjuster nut (handlebars removed for clarity)

17.3 Check above and below the fork seals (arrowed) for signs of oil leakage

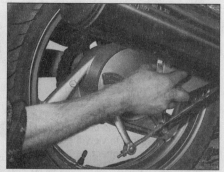

17.6 Check for freeplay in the swingarm

18.2 Measure throttle freeplay at the grip flange

18.3 Loosen the accelerator cable lockwheel (1) and turn the adjuster (2) in or out to obtain the correct throttle freeplay

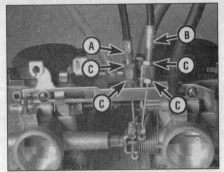

18.5 Throttle cable connections at carburettors – accelerator cable (A), decelerator cable (B), adjuster nuts (C)

18 Throttle and choke operation/grip freeplay – check and adjustment

Throttle freeplay check

1 With the engine stopped, make sure the throttle grip rotates easily from fully closed to fully open with the front wheel turned at various angles. The grip should return automatically from fully open to fully closed when released. If the throttle sticks, check the throttle cables for cracks or kinks in the housings. Also, make sure the inner cables are clean and well-lubricated.

2 Check for a small amount of freeplay at the grip and compare the freeplay to the value listed in this Chapter's Specifications (see illustration).

Throttle cable adjustment

Note: These motorcycles use two throttle cables – an accelerator cable and a decelerator cable.

3 Freeplay adjustments can be made at the throttle end of the cable. Loosen the lockwheel on the cable where it leaves the handlebar (see illustration). Turn the adjuster until the desired freeplay is obtained, then retighten the lockwheel.

4 If the cables can't be adjusted at the grip end, adjust them at the lower ends. To do this, first remove the fuel tank (see Chapter 4).

5 Fully back off the upper adjuster nut towards the cable ferrul on each cable, then screw the lower adjuster nut up the thread (see illustration). This will create a large amount of freeplay at the throttle grip.

6 Make sure the throttle grip is in the fully closed position.

7 Working on the decelerator cable first, back off the lower adjuster nut, then thread the upper nut down the thread until the inner cable just becomes tight; tighten both nuts against the bracket.

8 Back off the accelerator cable lower nut and thread the upper nut down the thread until the desired freeplay is obtained at the throttle grip, then tighten both nuts against the bracket.

9 Make sure the throttle linkage lever contacts the throttle stop screw when the throttle grip is in the closed throttle position.

⚠️ Warning: Turn the handlebars all the way through their travel with the engine idling. Idle speed should not change. If it does, the cables may be routed incorrectly. Correct this condition before riding the bike.

Choke cable check

10 There should be a small amount of freeplay at the choke lever. Observe the choke plunger end on the carburettors and very slowly operate the choke lever on the handlebar until the choke linkage shaft contacts the plunger (see illustration). Using a ruler measure the distance when the choke lever is in this position to its OFF position (see illustration). Compare with the value listed in this Chapter's Specifications.

11 If freeplay is incorrect, locate the cable adjuster inside the left-hand side of the fairing on EX models (see illustration) or under the fuel tank on ER models (see illustration). Loosen the locknut, turn the adjusting nut to set freeplay and tighten the locknut.

18.10a Operate the choke lever until the linkage shaft and plunger touch . . .

18.10b . . . then measure the amount of lever freeplay

18.11a Choke cable adjuster (arrowed) on EX models (fairing removed for clarity)

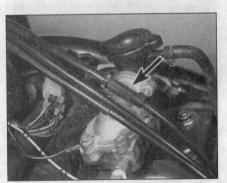

18.11b Choke cable adjuster (arrowed) on ER models

19.5 Unscrew the covers from the crankshaft rotation bolt and timing window

19.6a Turn the crankshaft clockwise with a socket . . .

19.6b . . . until the T mark on the rotor aligns with the timing notch . . .

19 Valve clearances – check and adjustment

1 The engine must be completely cool for this maintenance procedure, so let the machine sit overnight before beginning.
2 Disconnect the cable from the negative terminal of the battery (see Section 15).
3 Refer to Chapter 4 and remove the fuel tank.
4 Remove the valve cover (see Chapter 2).
5 Remove the covers from the crankshaft rotation bolt and timing inspection holes **(see illustration)**.

6 Position the no. 1 piston (on the left-hand side of the engine) at Top Dead Centre (TDC) on the compression stroke. Do this by turning the crankshaft clockwise, with a socket placed on the crankshaft bolt, until the T mark on the rotor is aligned with the timing mark on the crankcase **(see illustrations)**. Now, check the position of the no. 1 cylinder cam lobes – they should be pointing upward **(see illustration)**. Piston no. 1 is now at TDC compression.
7 With the engine in this position, all of the valves for cylinder no. 1 can be checked.
8 Start with the no. 1 inlet valve clearance. Insert a feeler gauge of the thickness listed in this Chapter's Specifications between each

valve stem and adjuster screw **(see illustration)**. Pull it out slowly – you should feel a slight drag. If there's no drag, the clearance is too loose. If there's a heavy drag, the clearance is too tight.
9 If the clearance is incorrect, loosen the adjuster screw locknut and turn the adjuster screw in or out, as needed. A small flat-bladed screwdriver and slim open-end spanner can be used to adjust the valves, although access is limited because of the oil lines. Alternatively, an aftermarket valve adjusting tool can be used **(see illustration)**.
10 Hold the adjuster screw with a screwdriver (or the special tool) to keep it from turning and tighten the locknut. Recheck the clearance to make sure it hasn't changed.
11 Now adjust the no. 1 exhaust valves, following the same procedure you used for the inlet valves. Make sure to use the correct size feeler gauge – the clearance differs for the exhaust valves.
12 Rotate the crankshaft clockwise to align the C mark on the rotor with the timing mark on the crankcase, which will position piston no. 2 at TDC compression **(see illustration)**. The cam lobes for no. 2 cylinder should now point upward **(see illustration)**.
13 Adjust all four valves on cylinder no. 2 as previously described.
14 Install the valve cover and all of the components that had to be removed to get it off.
15 Install the fuel tank and reconnect the cable to the negative terminal of the battery.

19.6c . . . and the no. 1 cam lobes point upward

19.8 For the most accurate measurement, use a pair of feeler gauges because each rocker arm operates two valves

19.9 Adjusting the valves with an aftermarket tool - the socket (A) loosens and tightens the locknut while the screwdriver (B) turns the adjusting screw

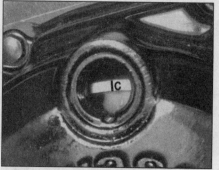

19.12a Turn the crankshaft until the C mark on the rotor aligns with the timing notch . . .

19.12b . . . and the no. 2 cam lobes point upward

20.4 Remove the oil pan drain plug (arrowed)

20.5a Remove the oil filter with a special adapter like this or a strap wrench

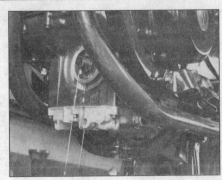

20.5b Let the oil drain completely from the drain plug and filter openings

20 Engine oil/filter – change

Note: *For some models the oil and filter renewal intervals are separate; for a straightforward oil change, ignore the filter information.*

1 Consistent routine oil and filter changes are the single most important maintenance procedure you can perform on a motorcycle. The oil not only lubricates the internal parts of the engine, transmission and clutch, but it also acts as a coolant, a cleaner, a sealant, and a protectant. Because of these demands, the oil takes a terrific amount of abuse and should be renewed often with new oil of the recommended grade and type.

> **HAYNES HINT**
> *Saving a little money on the difference in cost between a good oil and a cheap oil won't pay off if the engine is damaged.*

2 Before changing the oil and filter, warm up the engine so the oil will drain easily. Be careful when draining the oil, as the exhaust pipes, the engine, and the oil itself can cause severe burns. If the oil filter is being renewed on EX models you are advised to remove the lower fairing (see Chapter 8).
3 Put the motorcycle on the centerstand over a clean drain pan. Remove the oil filler cap to vent the crankcase and act as a reminder that there is no oil in the engine.
4 Next, remove the drain plug from the front of the sump **(see illustration)** and allow the oil to drain into the pan. Discard the sealing washer on the drain plug; it should be renewed whenever the plug is removed.
5 As the oil is draining, remove the oil filter **(see illustrations)**. If additional maintenance is planned for this time period, check or service another component while the oil is allowed to drain completely.
6 Wipe any remaining oil off the filter sealing area of the crankcase.
7 Check the condition of the drain plug threads.
8 Coat the gasket on a new filter with clean engine oil. Install the filter and tighten it to the

amount listed in this Chapter's Specifications.
9 Slip a new sealing washer over the drain plug, then install and tighten the plug. Tighten the drain plug to the torque listed in this Chapter's Specifications. Avoid overtightening, as damage to the engine case will result.

> **HAYNES HINT**
> *Before refilling the engine, check the old oil carefully. If the oil was drained into a clean pan, small pieces of metal or other material can be easily detected. If the oil is very metallic coloured, then the engine is experiencing wear from break-in (new engine) or from insufficient lubrication. If there are flakes or chips of metal in the oil, then something is drastically wrong internally and the engine will have to be disassembled for inspection and repair. If there are pieces of fibre-like material in the oil, the clutch is experiencing excessive wear and should be checked.*

10 Refill the crankcase to the proper level with the recommended oil and install the filler cap. Start the engine and let it run for two or three minutes. Shut it off, wait a few minutes, then check the oil level as described in Daily (pre-ride) checks, and top up if necessary. Check that there are no oil leaks around the drain plug and filter.
11 The old oil drained from the engine cannot

be reused in its present state and should be disposed of. Check with your local refuse disposal company, disposal facility or environmental agency to see whether they will accept the oil for recycling. Don't pour used oil into drains or onto the ground. After the oil has cooled, it can be drained into a suitable container (capped plastic jugs, topped bottles, etc.) for transport to a disposal site.

> **OIL CARE**
> FOLLOW THE CODE
> OIL BANK LINE
> **0800 66 33 66**

Note: It is antisocial and illegal to dump oil down the drain. To find the location of your local oil recycling bank, call this number free.

In the USA, note that any oil supplier must accept used oil for recycling.

21 Air filter element – servicing

EX models

1 Remove the seat (see Chapter 8).
2 Remove the fuel tank and its bracket (see Chapter 4).
3 Move the wiring harness and carburettor vent tube aside, then remove the housing cover screws **(see illustrations)**.

21.3a Note the location of the carburettor vent tube (arrowed) and the wiring harness; they must be positioned in the groove as shown

21.3b Remove the cover screws, set the harness and vent tube aside . . .

21.4 . . . and lift the cover to expose the element

21.10a Remove the three screws to free the cover . . .

21.10b . . . and withdraw the element

4 Lift off the housing cover and remove the air filter element (see illustration). Wipe out the housing with a clean rag.

5 Clean the element with solvent. If compressed air is available, use it to clean the element by blowing from the inside out (from the mesh side toward the foam side). If the foam is extremely dirty or torn, renew the element.

6 Soak a clean, lint-free cloth in SAE 30 engine oil. Tap the cloth on the foam to oil it.

7 Reinstall the filter by reversing the removal procedure. Make sure the element is seated properly in the filter housing before installing the cover. Make sure the carburettor vent hose is routed correctly so it won't be pinched and so it's not near the air inlet (see illustration 21.3a).

8 Reinstall the fuel tank bracket, fuel tank and seat.

ER models

9 Remove the seat and the left-hand side cover (see Chapter 8).

10 Remove the three screws to free the air filter cover and withdraw the element (see illustrations).

11 Tap the element down on a hard surface to dislodge any large particles of dirt. If compressed air is available, use it to clean the element by blowing from the inside out (from the paper side to the mesh side). If the paper is extremely dirty or torn, renew the element.

12 Reinstall the filter by reversing the removal procedure. Make sure the element is seated

properly in the filter housing before installing the cover.

13 Install the left-hand side cover and seat (see Chapter 8).

22 Fuel system –
check and filter cleaning

⚠️ **Warning: Gasoline (petrol) is extremely flammable, so take extra precautions when you work on any part of the fuel system. Don't smoke or allow open flames or bare light bulbs near the work area, and don't work in a garage where a natural gas-type appliance (such as a water heater or clothes dryer) is present. If you spill any fuel on your skin, rinse it off immediately with soap and water. When you perform any kind of work on the fuel system, wear safety glasses and have a fire extinguisher suitable for a class B type fire (flammable liquids) on hand.**

1 Check the fuel tank, the fuel tap, the fuel hoses and the carburettors for leaks and evidence of damage.

2 If carburettor gaskets are leaking, the carburettors should be disassembled and rebuilt by referring to Chapter 4.

3 If the fuel tap is leaking, tightening the screws may help. If leakage persists, the tap should be disassembled and repaired or renewed.

4 If the fuel hoses are cracked or otherwise deteriorated, renew them.

5 Check the vacuum hose connected to the fuel tap. If it is cracked or otherwise damaged, renew it.

6 The fuel filter may become clogged and should be removed and cleaned periodically. In order to clean the filter, the fuel tank must be drained. On EX models the fuel filter is integral with the fuel tap. On ER models, two fuel filters are fitted in the base of the tank with a hose leading from the union on each filter to the remote fuel tap.

7 Remove the fuel tank (see Chapter 4). Drain the fuel into an approved fuel container.

8 On EX models, loosen and remove the screws that attach the fuel tap to the tank (see illustration). Remove the tap and filter. On ER models pull the hose off each filter union and unscrew the union bodies from the tank (see illustration).

9 Clean the filter (see illustration) with solvent and blow it dry with compressed air. If the filter is torn or otherwise damaged, renew the entire fuel tap (EX models) or the individual filters (ER models).

10 On EX models use a new O-ring at the tap-to-tank joint and renew the two mounting bolt washers if they are damaged. On ER models renew the O-ring between the filter union and tank.

11 Install the tank. Refill the tank and check carefully that there are no leaks.

22.8a The fuel tap is secured to the tank by two screws on EX models

22.8b Fuel filter unions on ER models (arrowed)

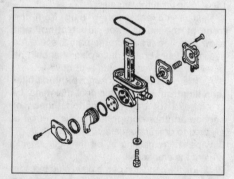

22.9 Fuel tap and filter details – EX models

24.7a The cooling system pressure cap is located on the thermostat housing – EX models . . .

24.7b . . . and ER models

23 Rear suspension – lubrication

1 Refer to Chapter 6 and dismantle the swingarm and Uni-trak linkage for lubrication of the needle roller bearings.

24 Cooling system – check

 Warning: The engine must be cool before beginning this procedure.

Note: Refer Daily (pre-ride) checks and check the coolant level before performing this check.
1 The entire cooling system should be checked carefully at the recommended intervals. Look for evidence of leaks, check the condition of the coolant, check the radiator for clogged fins and damage and make sure the fan operates when required.
2 Remove the fuel tank (Chapter 4).
3 Examine each of the rubber coolant hoses along its entire length. Look for cracks, abrasions and other damage. Squeeze each hose at various points. They should feel firm, yet pliable, and return to their original shape when released. If they are dried out or hard, renew them.
4 Check for evidence of leaks at each cooling system joint. Tighten the hose clamps carefully to prevent future leaks.
5 Check the radiator for evidence of leaks and other damage. If leaks are noted, remove the radiator (refer to Chapter 3) and have it professionally repaired.

HAYNES HiNT *Leaks in the radiator leave telltale scale deposits or coolant stains on the outside of the core below the leak*

Caution: Do not use a liquid leak stopping compound to try to repair leaks.
6 Check the radiator fins for mud, dirt and insects, which may impede the flow of air through the radiator. If the fins are dirty, force water or low pressure compressed air through the fins from the backside. If the fins are bent or distorted, straighten them carefully with a screwdriver.
7 Remove the pressure cap by turning it counterclockwise (anticlockwise) until it reaches a stop. If you hear a hissing sound (indicating there is still pressure in the system), wait until it stops. Now, press down on the cap with the palm of your hand and continue turning the cap counterclockwise until it can be removed **(see illustrations)**. Check the condition of the coolant in the system. If it is rust coloured or if accumulations of scale are visible, drain, flush and refill the system with new coolant. Check the cap gaskets for cracks and other damage. Have the cap tested by a dealer service department or renew it. Install the cap by turning it clockwise until it reaches the first stop, then push down on the cap and continue turning until it can turn no further.
8 Check the antifreeze content of the coolant with an antifreeze hydrometer **(see illustration)**. Sometimes coolant may look like it's in good condition, but might be too weak to offer adequate protection. If the hydrometer indicates a weak mixture, drain, flush and refill the cooling system (see Section 30).
9 Start the engine and let it reach normal operating temperature, then check for leaks again. As the coolant temperature increases, the fan should come on automatically and the temperature should begin to drop. If it does not, refer to Chapter 3 and check the fan and fan circuit carefully.
10 If the coolant level is consistently low, and no evidence of leaks can be found, have the entire system pressure checked by a Kawasaki dealer.
11 On models equipped with a carburettor warmer system, check that the filter is not blocked (see Chapter 3, Section 10).

25 Exhaust system – check

1 Periodically check all of the exhaust system joints for leaks and loose fasteners. The lower fairing (EX models) will have to be removed to do this properly (see Chapter 8). If tightening the clamp bolts fails to stop any leaks, renew the gaskets (a procedure which requires disassembly of the system).
2 The exhaust pipe flange nuts at the cylinder heads are especially prone to loosening, which could cause damage to the head. Check them frequently and keep them tight.

26 Fasteners – check

1 Since vibration of the machine tends to loosen fasteners, all nuts, bolts, screws, etc.

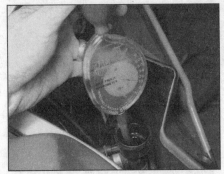

24.8 An antifreeze hydrometer is used for determining the condition of the coolant

should be periodically checked for proper tightness.

2 Pay particular attention to the following:
Spark plugs
Engine oil drain plug
Gearchange lever
Footrests, sidestand and centerstand
Engine mounting bolts
Front fork pinch bolts
Rear shock absorber mounting bolts
Uni-trak linkage bolts
Front axle and clamp bolt
Rear axle nut

3 If a torque wrench is available, use it along with the torque specifications at the beginning of this, or other, Chapters.

27 Brake fluid – renewal

1 The brake fluid should be renewed at the prescribed interval or whenever a master cylinder or caliper overhaul is carried out.
2 Refer to the brake bleeding section in Chapter 7, noting that all old fluid must be pumped from the fluid reservoir and hydraulic line before filling with new fluid.

HAYNES HiNT *Old brake fluid is invariably much darker in colour than new fluid, making it easier to see when old fluid has been expelled from the system.*

28 Steering head bearings – lubrication

1 Refer to Chapter 6, Section 8 and remove the steering stem/lower triple clamp from the frame headstock. There is no need to remove the lower bearing race from the stem or to remove the bearing outer races from the headstock; remove all old grease, check them for wear and apply new grease before reassembly.
2 If the bearings show signs of wear renew them; renew the top and bottom bearing sets at the same time.

29 Rear brake cam – lubrication (drum brakes)

1 Refer to Chapter 7, Section 9 and remove the brake cam from the brake panel. Remove all traces of old grease from the surface of the cam and its hole in the brake panel. Apply a smear of high melting-point grease to the two bearing surfaces of the cam and the operating flat on its end. Also apply a smear of high melting-point grease to the brake shoe pivot on the brake panel and the spring hooks

where they engage the holes in the brake shoes.
2 Assemble the brake cam and shoes in the brake panel as described in Chapter 7, Section 9.
Caution: Do not apply too much grease otherwise there is a risk of it contaminating the brake shoe linings.

30 Coolant – renewal

⚠ *Warning: Allow the engine to cool completely before performing this maintenance operation. Also, don't allow antifreeze to come into contact with your skin or painted surfaces of the motorcycle. Rinse off spills immediately with plenty of water. Antifreeze is highly toxic if ingested. Never leave antifreeze lying around in an open container or in puddles on the floor; children and pets are attracted by its sweet smell and may drink it. Check with local authorities (councils) about disposing of used antifreeze. Many communities have collection centres which will see that antifreeze is disposed of safely. Antifreeze is also combustible, so don't store or use it near open flames.*

Draining
1 Remove the fuel tank on all models (see Chapter 4). On EX models also remove the upper and lower fairings and on ER models remove the rear bodywork (see Chapter 8).
2 Loosen the pressure cap **(see illustration 24.7a or b)**.
3 Place a large, clean drain pan under the right-hand side of the engine. Remove the drain bolt from the bottom of the water pump cover **(see illustration)** and allow the coolant to drain into the pan. **Note:** *The coolant will rush out with considerable force, so position the drain pan accordingly. Remove the pressure cap completely to ensure that all of the coolant can drain.*
4 Drain the coolant reservoir. Refer to Chapter 3 for the reservoir removal procedure. Wash the reservoir out with water.

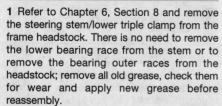
30.3 The coolant drain bolt is located in the bottom of the water pump cover

Flushing
5 Flush the system with clean tap water by inserting a garden hose in the radiator filler neck. Allow the water to run through the system until it is clear when it exits the drain bolt hole. If the radiator is extremely corroded, remove it by referring to Chapter 3 and have it cleaned by a professional.
6 Check the drain bolt gasket. Renew it if necessary.
7 Clean the hole, then install the drain bolt and tighten it to the torque listed in this Chapter's Specifications.
8 Fill the cooling system with clean water mixed with a flushing compound. Make sure the flushing compound is compatible with aluminium components, and follow the manufacturer's instructions carefully.
9 Start the engine and allow it to reach normal operating temperature. Let it run for about ten minutes.
10 Stop the engine. Let the machine cool for a while, then cover the pressure cap with a heavy rag and turn it counterclockwise (anticlockwise) to the first stop, releasing any pressure that may be present in the system. Once the hissing stops, push down on the cap and remove it completely.
11 Drain the system once again and refit the drain bolt.
12 Fill the system with clean water, then repeat Steps 9, 10 and 11.

Refilling
13 Fill the system with the proper coolant mixture (see this Chapter's Specifications); pour the coolant in slowly to avoid trapping air in the system. When the system is full (all the way up to the bottom of the reservoir tank hose union in the radiator cap filler neck), fully install the cap and start the engine **(see illustration)**. Allow the engine to reach normal operating temperature, then shut it off.
14 Let the engine cool down, cover the radiator cap with a heavy rag and loosen it to

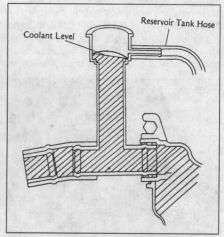
30.13 Fill the system up to the bottom of the reservoir tank hose union in the filler neck

Coolant Level
Reservoir Tank Hose

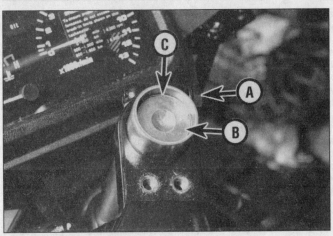

31.3a Loosen the upper pinch bolt (A), press down on the top plug (B) and remove the retaining ring (C)

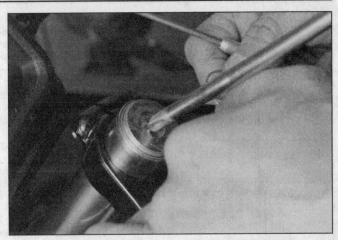

31.3b Release the spring tension on the top plug

the first stop to allow any pressure in the system to bleed off before the cap is removed completely. Recheck the coolant level in the radiator filler neck. If it's low, add more coolant until it reaches the bottom of the reservoir tank hose union.

15 Leave the pressure cap off and start the engine. Let it idle and observe the coolant in

the filler neck. When no more air bubbles can be seen in the coolant the system is bled of air. Stop the engine, top up the coolant if necessary and refit the pressure cap.

16 Fill the reservoir tank with coolant up to the correct level (see *Daily (pre-ride) checks*). Check that there are no coolant leaks and install the bodypanels and fuel tank.

17 Do not dispose of the old coolant by pouring it down a drain. Instead, pour it into a heavy plastic container, cap it tightly and take it to an authorised disposal site or a service station.

position a jack with a block of wood on the jack head under the engine.

2 Remove the handlebar from one side (see Chapter 6).

3 Loosen the upper pinch bolts **(see illustration)**. Push the top plug downward against spring pressure with a Phillips screwdriver or similar tool, remove the retaining ring and release the spring pressure **(see illustration)**.

4 Lift out the top plug and O-ring **(see illustration)**.

5 Lift out the fork spring **(see illustration)**.

6 Place a drain pan under the fork leg and remove the drain screw **(see illustration)**.

31.4 Lift out the top plug and inspect its O-ring

31 Fork oil – renewal

EX500A models

1 Place the motorcycle on the centerstand. Remove the lower fairing (if equipped) and

⚠️ *Warning: Do not allow the fork oil to contact the brake disc, pads or tyre. If it does, clean the disc with brake system cleaner, wipe off the tyre, and renew the pads before riding the motorcycle. Make up a cardboard chute to direct oil away from the disc and tyre.*

7 After most of the oil has drained, slowly

31.5 Lift out the fork spring

31.6 There's a fork drain screw (arrowed) at the bottom of each fork leg

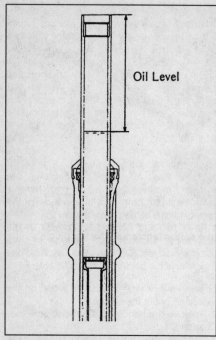

31.10 Measure oil level in the fork with a stiff tape measure; add or drain oil to correct the level

compress and release the forks to pump out the remaining oil. An assistant will most likely be required to do this procedure.

8 Check the drain screw gasket for damage and renew it if necessary. Clean the threads of the drain screw with solvent and let it dry, then install the screw and gasket, tightening it securely.

9 Pour the type and amount of fork oil, listed in this Chapter's Specifications, into the fork tube through the opening at the top.

> **HAYNES HiNT**
> *Remove the jack from under the engine and slowly pump the forks a few times to purge the air from the upper and lower chambers.*

10 Fully compress the front forks (you may need an assistant to do this). Insert a stiff tape measure into the fork tube and measure the

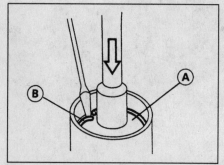

31.17 Depress the top plug (A) and remove the retaining ring (B) from its groove

distance from the oil to the top of the fork tube **(see illustration)**. Compare your measurement to the value listed in this Chapter's Specifications. Drain or add oil, as necessary, until the level is correct.

11 Check the O-ring on the top plug, then coat it with a thin layer of multi-purpose grease. Install the fork spring with its tapered end facing downwards. Install the top plug, push it down against the spring pressure, install the retaining ring and slowly release the top plug.

12 Tighten the fork tube pinch bolts to the torque listed in the Chapter 6 Specifications. Install the handlebar, tightening the bolts to the torque listed in the Chapter 6 Specifications.

13 Repeat the procedure to the other fork. Note that it is essential that the oil quantity and level is identical in each fork.

14 Install the lower fairing (if equipped).

EX500D, E and ER models

15 The forks on these models are not fitted with drain plugs. To change the fork oil, the forks must be removed from the bike as described in Chapter 6, Section 6.

16 On ER models prise out the rubber cap from the top of the fork.

17 Extend the fork leg fully, and with the aid of an assistant push the top plug downward against spring pressure with a Phillips screwdriver or similar tool, remove the retaining ring and release the spring pressure **(see illustration)**.

Caution: Beware of the tool slipping and causing injury when depressing the top plug. You may find it easier to clamp the fork back in the triple clamps to do this (although make sure that the bike is well supported) or to clamp the fork tube between the padded jaws of a vice.

18 Lift out the top plug and O-ring.

19 Lift out the spacer, spring seat and fork spring **(see illustration)**.

20 Tip the fork upside down to drain the oil. Pump the fork to aid draining.

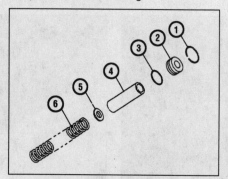

31.19 Fork top components

1 Retaining ring
2 Top plug
3 Top plug O-ring
4 Spacer
5 Spring seat
6 Spring

21 Pour the type and amount of fork oil, listed in this Chapter's Specifications, into the fork tube and slowly pump the forks a few times to purge the air from the upper and lower chambers.

22 Fully compress the front forks (you may need an assistant to do this). Insert a stiff tape measure into the fork tube and measure the distance from the oil to the top of the fork tube **(see illustration 31.10)**. Compare your measurement to the value listed in this Chapter's Specifications. Drain or add oil, as necessary, until the level is correct.

23 Check the O-ring on the top plug, then coat it with a thin layer of multi-purpose grease. Install the fork spring with its tapered end facing downwards, followed by the spring seat and spacer. Install the top plug, push it down against the spring pressure, install the retaining ring and slowly release the top plug. On ER models insert the rubber cap in the top of the fork.

24 Repeat the procedure to the other fork. Note that it is essential that the oil quantity and level is identical in each fork.

25 Install the forks in the triple clamps as described in Chapter 6, Section 6.

32 Brake caliper and master cylinder – overhaul

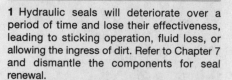

1 Hydraulic seals will deteriorate over a period of time and lose their effectiveness, leading to sticking operation, fluid loss, or allowing the ingress of dirt. Refer to Chapter 7 and dismantle the components for seal renewal.

33 Fuel hoses – renewal

> ⚠ *Warning: Petrol (gasoline) is extremely flammable, so take extra precautions when you work on any part of the fuel system. Don't smoke or allow open flames or bare light bulbs near the work area, and don't work in a garage where a natural gas-type appliance (such as a water heater or clothes dryer) is present. Since gasoline is carcinogenic, wear latex gloves when there's a possibility of being exposed to fuel, and, if you spill any fuel on your skin, rinse it off immediately with soap and water. When you perform any kind of work on the fuel system, wear safety glasses and have a fire extinguisher suitable for a Class B type fire (flammable liquids) on hand.*

1 Remove the fuel tank (see Chapter 4). Disconnect the fuel hoses from the fuel tank and/or tap and from the carburettors, noting the routing of each hose and where it connects (see Chapter 4 if required). It is

35.2 A compression gauge with a threaded fitting for the spark plug hole is recommended

advisable to make a sketch of the various hoses before removing them to ensure they are correctly installed.

2 Secure each new hose to its unions using new clamps. Run the engine and check that there are no leaks before taking the machine out on the road.

34 Brake hose(s) – renewal

1 The hydraulic hoses will in time deteriorate with age and should be renewed regardless of their apparent condition. Refer to Chapter 7.

35 Cylinder compression – check

1 Among other things, poor engine performance may be caused by leaking valves, incorrect valve clearances, a leaking head gasket, or worn pistons, rings and/or cylinder walls. A cylinder compression check will help pinpoint these conditions and can also indicate the presence of excessive carbon deposits in the cylinder heads.

2 The only tools required are a compression gauge and a spark plug wrench. A compression gauge with a threaded end for the spark plug hole **(see illustration)** is preferable to the type which requires hand pressure to maintain a tight seal. Depending on the outcome of the initial test, a squirt-type oil can may also be needed.

3 Make sure the valve clearances are correctly set (see Section 19) and that the cylinder head bolts are tightened to the correct torque setting (see Chapter 2).

4 Refer to *Fault Finding Equipment* in the Reference section for details of the compression test. Compression specifications are given at the beginning of this Chapter.

Notes

Chapter 2
Engine, clutch and transmission

Contents

Degrees of difficulty

Easy, suitable for novice with little experience		Fairly easy, suitable for beginner with some experience		Fairly difficult, suitable for competent DIY mechanic		Difficult, suitable for experienced DIY mechanic		Very difficult, suitable for expert DIY or professional	

Specifications

General
Bore .... 74.0 mm (2.913 in)
Stroke .... 58.0 mm (2.283 in)
Displacement .... 498 cc
Compression ratio
 EX models .... 10.8 : 1
 ER models .... 9.8 : 1

Camshaft and rocker arms

Lobe height (inlet and exhaust) – EX models
    Standard . . . . 35.635 to 35.761 mm (1.403 to 1.408 in)
    Minimum . . . . 35.55 mm (1.40 in)
Lobe height (inlet) – ER models
    Standard . . . . 35.474 to 35.590 mm (1.3966 to 1.4012 in)
    Minimum . . . . 35.37 mm (1.3925 in)
Lobe height (exhaust) – ER models
    Standard . . . . 35.475 to 35.591 mm (1.3967 to 1.4012 in)
    Minimum . . . . 35.38 mm (1.3929 in)
Bearing oil clearance
    Standard . . . . 0.030 to 0.071 mm (0.001 to 0.003 in)
    Maximum . . . . 0.16 mm (0.006 in)
Journal diameter
    Standard . . . . 24.950 to 24.970 mm (0.982 to 0.983 in)
    Minimum . . . . 24.92 mm (0.981 in)
Camshaft runout
    Standard – EX models . . . . 0.03 mm (0.0012 in) or less
    Standard – ER models . . . . 0.02 mm (0.0008 in) or less
    Maximum – all models . . . . 0.1 mm (0.003 in)
Camshaft chain 20-link length (maximum) . . . . 128.9 mm (5-5/64 in)
Rocker arm inside diameter
    Standard . . . . 12.50 to 12.518 mm (0.492 to 0.493 in)
    Maximum . . . . 12.55 mm (0.494 in)
Rocker shaft diameter
    Standard . . . . 12.466 to 12.484 mm (0.490 to 0.491 in)
    Minimum . . . . 12.44 mm (0.489 in)

Cylinder head, valves and valve springs

Cylinder head warpage limit . . . . 0.05 mm (0.002 in)
Valve stem bend limit . . . . 0.05 mm (0.002 in)
Valve stem diameter
    Standard
        Inlet . . . . 5.475 to 5.490 mm (0.2155 to 0.216 in)
        Exhaust . . . . 5.455 to 5.470 mm (0.2147 to 0.215 in)
    Minimum
        Inlet . . . . 5.46 mm (0.2149 in)
        Exhaust . . . . 5.44 mm (0.2141 in)
Valve head thickness
    Standard
        Inlet . . . . 0.5 mm (0.020 in)
        Exhaust . . . . 1.0 mm (0.039 in)
    Minimum
        Inlet . . . . 0.25 mm (0.010 in)
        Exhaust . . . . 0.7 mm (0.027 in)
Valve guide inside diameter (inlet and exhaust)
    Standard . . . . 5.50 to 5.512 mm (0.2165 to 0.2170 in)
    Maximum . . . . 5.58 mm (0.2196 in)
Valve seat width (inlet and exhaust) . . . . 0.5 to 1.0 mm (0.020 to 0.040 in)
Valve stem-to-guide clearance
    Standard
        Inlet . . . . 0.02 to 0.04 mm (0.0008 to 0.0016 in)
        Exhaust . . . . 0.07 to 0.14 mm (0.0028 to 0.0055 in)
    Maximum
        Inlet . . . . 0.22 mm (0.0087 in)
        Exhaust . . . . 0.27 mm (0.0106 in)
Valve spring free length
    Standard
        Inner . . . . 36.3 mm (1.429 in)
        Outer . . . . 40.4 mm (1.59 in)
    Minimum
        Inner . . . . 35 mm (1.378 in)
        Outer . . . . 39 mm (1.535 in)

Cylinder block

Bore diameter
    Standard . . . . 74.0 to 74.012 mm (2.9133 to 2.9138 in)
    Maximum . . . . 74.11 mm (2.9177 in)
Taper limit . . . . 0.05 mm (0.002 in)
Out-of-round limit . . . . 0.05 mm (0.002 in)

Pistons

Piston diameter
  Standard .... 73.942 to 73.957 mm (2.9111 to 2.9116 in)
  Minimum .... 73.79 mm (2.905 in)
Piston-to-cylinder clearance
  Standard .... 0.044 to 0.070 mm (0.0017 to 0.0027 in)
  Maximum .... 0.17 mm (0.0066 in)
Oversize pistons and rings .... + 0.5 mm (+0.020 in) (one oversize only)
Ring-to-groove clearance
  Standard
    Top .... 0.03 to 0.07 mm (0.0017 to 0.0027 in)
    Second .... 0.02 to 0.06 mm (0.0007 to 0.0023 in)
  Maximum
    Top .... 0.17 mm (0.0066 in)
    Second .... 0.16 mm (0.0062 in)
Ring groove width
  Standard
    Top .... 0.82 to 0.84 mm (0.032 to 0.033 in)
    Second .... 1.01 to 1.03 mm (0.039 to 0.040 in)
    Oil (EX500A only) .... 2.01 to 2.03 mm (0.079 to 0.080 in)
  Maximum
    Top .... 0.92 mm (0.036 in)
    Second .... 1.12 mm (0.044 in)
    Oil (EX500A only) .... 2.11 mm (0.083 in)
Ring thickness (top and second)
  Standard
    Top .... 0.77 to 0.79 mm (0.030 to 0.031 in)
    Second .... 0.97 to 0.99 mm (0.038 to 0.039 in)
  Minimum
    Top .... 0.7 mm (0.027 in)
    Second .... 0.9 mm (0.035 in)
Ring end gap
  Standard
    Top and second .... 0.2 to 0.35 mm (0.008 to 0.013 in)
    Oil .... 0.2 to 0.7 mm (0.008 to 0.027 in)
  Maximum
    Top and second .... 0.7 mm (0.027 in)
    Oil .... 1.0 mm (0.039 in)

Crankshaft and bearings

Main bearing oil clearance
  Standard .... 0.020 to 0.044 mm (0.0008 to 0.0017 in)
  Maximum .... 0.08 mm (0.003 in)
Main bearing journal diameter
  No mark on crank throw .... 35.984 to 35.992 mm (1.4166 to 1.4170 in)
  '1' mark on crank throw .... 35.993 to 36.000 mm (1.4170 to 1.4173 in)
Main bearing bore diameter
  No mark on case .... 39.009 to 30.016 mm (1.5357 to 1.5360 in)
  'O' mark on case .... 39.000 to 39.008 mm (1.5354 to 1.5357 in)
Crankshaft endplay
  Standard .... 0.05 to 0.25 mm (0.002 to 0.010 in)
  Maximum .... 0.4 mm (0.016 in)
Crankshaft runout limit .... 0.05 mm (0.002 in)
Connecting rod side clearance
  Standard .... 0.13 to 0.38 mm (0.005 to 0.015 in)
  Maximum .... 0.5 mm (0.019 in)
Connecting rod bearing oil clearance – EX500A models
  Standard .... 0.036 to 0.066 mm (0.0016 to 0.0025 in)
  Maximum .... 0.1 mm (0.004 in)
Connecting rod bearing oil clearance – EX500D, E and ER models
  Standard .... 0.043 to 0.073 mm (0.0017 to 0.0029 in)
  Maximum .... 0.1 mm (0.004 in)
Connecting rod big-end bore diameter
  No mark on side of rod .... 41.000 to 41.008 mm (1.6141 to 1.6144 in)
  'O' mark on side of rod .... 41.009 to 41.016 mm (1.6145 to 1.6148 in)
Connecting rod journal (crank pin) diameter
  No mark on crank throw .... 37.984 to 37.994 mm (1.4954 to 1.4958 in)
  'O' mark on crank throw .... 37.995 to 38.000 mm (1.4958 to 1.4960 in)
Connecting rod bend and twist, maximum .... 0.2 mm (0.008 in) per 100 mm (3.94 in)
Primary chain 20-link length (maximum) .... 193.4 mm (7.614 in)

Oil pump and relief valve

Oil pressure (warm) . . . .   40 to 48 psi (2.8 to 3.3 Bars) @ 4000 rpm
Relief valve opening pressure . . . .   63 to 85 psi (4.3 to 5.9 Bars)

Balancer shaft

Balancer shaft bearing oil clearance
  Standard . . . .   0.02 to 0.05 mm (0.0008 to 0.0019 in)
  Maximum . . . .   0.09 mm (0.0035 in)
Balancer shaft journal diameter
  No mark on balancer . . . .   27.987 to 27.993 mm (1.1018 to 1.1020 in)
  'O' mark on balancer . . . .   27.994 to 28.000 mm (1.1021 to 1.1023 in)
Balancer shaft bearing bore diameter – EX500A models
  No mark on case . . . .   30.014 to 31.025 mm (1.1817 to 1.2215 in)
  'O' mark on case . . . .   31.000 to 31.013 mm (1.2205 to 1.2210 in)
Balancer shaft bearing bore diameter – EX500D, E and ER models
  No mark on case . . . .   30.017 to 31.024 mm (1.1818 to 1.2214 in)
  'O' mark on case . . . .   31.008 to 31.016 mm (1.2208 to 1.2211 in)

Clutch

Spring free length
  Standard . . . .   34.2 mm (1.346 in)
  Minimum . . . .   33.1 mm (1.303 in)
Friction plate thickness
  Standard . . . .   2.9 to 3.1 mm (0.114 to 0.122 in)
  Minimum . . . .   2.75 mm (0.108 in)
Friction and steel plate warpage
  Standard . . . .   0.2 mm (0.008 in)
  Limit . . . .   0.3 mm (0.012 in)

Transmission

Gear ratios – EX models
  1st gear . . . .   2.571 to 1 (36/14T)
  2nd gear . . . .   1.777 to 1 (32/18T)
  3rd gear . . . .   1.380 to 1 (29/21T)
  4th gear . . . .   1.125 to 1 (27/24T)
  5th gear . . . .   0.961 to 1 (25/26T)
  6th gear . . . .   0.851 to 1 (23/27T)
Gear ratios – ER models
  1st gear . . . .   2.571 to 1 (36/14T)
  2nd gear . . . .   1.722 to 1 (31/18T)
  3rd gear . . . .   1.333 to 1 (28/21T)
  4th gear . . . .   1.125 to 1 (27/24T)
  5th gear . . . .   0.961 to 1 (25/26T)
  6th gear . . . .   0.851 to 1 (23/27T)
Gear backlash (EX models)
  Standard . . . .   0.02 to 0.19 mm (0.0008 to 0.0074 in)
  Maximum . . . .   0.23 mm (0.009 in)
Selector fork groove width in gears
  Standard . . . .   5.05 to 5.15 mm (0.199 to 0.202 in)
  Maximum . . . .   5.3 mm (0.208 in)
Selector fork ear thickness
  Standard . . . .   4.9 to 5.0 mm (0.193 to 0.197 in)
  Minimum . . . .   4.8 mm (0.189 in)
Selector fork guide pin diameter
  Standard . . . .   7.9 to 8.0 mm (0.311 to 0.315 in)
  Minimum . . . .   7.8 mm (0.307 in)
Selector drum groove width
  Standard . . . .   8.05 to 8.2 mm (0.317 to 0.323 in)
  Maximum . . . .   8.3 mm (0.326 in)

Torque specifications

Valve cover bolts . . . .   9.8 Nm (87 in-lbs)
Camshaft bearing cap bolts
  EX500A models . . . .   8.8 Nm (78 in-lbs)
  EX500D, E and ER models . . . .   12 Nm (104 in-lbs)
Camshaft sprocket bolts . . . .   15 Nm (11 ft-lbs)
Rocker arm shafts . . . .   39 Nm (29 ft-lbs)

Torque specifications (continued)

Oil pipe bolts (on camshaft bearing caps)
  EX500A models . . . . not specified
  EX500D, E and ER models . . . . 11 Nm (95 in-lbs)
Camshaft chain tensioner cap . . . . 4.9 Nm (43 in-lbs)
Camshaft chain tensioner mounting bolts
  EX500A models . . . . 8.8 Nm (78 in-lbs)
  EX500D, E and ER models . . . . 11 Nm (95 in-lbs)
Cylinder head bolts
  6 mm bolts . . . . 9.8 Nm (87 in-lbs)
  8 mm bolts . . . . 51 Nm (38 ft-lbs)
Crankcase bolts
  6 mm bolts . . . . 12 Nm (104 in-lbs)
  8 mm bolts . . . . 27 Nm (20 ft-lbs)
Connecting rod nuts . . . . 36 Nm (27 ft-lbs)
Primary chain guide bolts . . . . 12 Nm (104 in-lbs)
Clutch cover bolts
  EX500A models . . . . not specified
  EX500D, E and ER models . . . . 11 Nm (95 in-lbs)
Clutch spring bolts . . . . 9.3 Nm (82 in-lbs)
Clutch hub nut . . . . 130 Nm (98 ft-lbs)
Oil pan bolts . . . . 12 Nm (104 in-lbs)
Oil pipe-to-cylinder head union bolts
  EX500A models . . . . 20 Nm (174 in-lbs)
  EX500D, E and ER models . . . . 12 Nm (104 in-lbs)
Oil pipe-to-crankcase union bolts
  Left front corner of case . . . . 12 Nm (104 in-lbs)
  Left side of case (upper bolt) . . . . 7.8 Nm (69 in-lbs)
  Left side of case (lower bolt) . . . . 12 Nm (104 in-lbs)
  Bottom of case (inside oil pan) . . . . 12 Nm (104 in-lbs)
  Right rear corner of engine . . . . 7.8 Nm (69 in-lbs)
  Cylinder head 'Y' line to crankcase . . . . 20 Nm (174 in-lbs)
Relief valve-to-oil pan . . . . 15 Nm (11 ft-lbs)

1 General information

The engine/transmission unit is a water-cooled, in-line, parallel twin. The valves are operated by double overhead camshafts which are chain driven off the crankshaft. The engine/transmission assembly is constructed from aluminium alloy. The crankcase is divided horizontally.

The crankcase incorporates a wet sump, pressure-fed lubrication system which uses a gear-driven, dual-rotor oil pump, an oil filter and by-pass valve assembly, a relief valve and an oil pressure switch. Also contained in the crankcase is the balancer shaft and the starter motor clutch.

Power from the crankshaft is routed to the transmission via the clutch, which is of the wet, multi-plate type and is chain-driven off the crankshaft. The transmission is a six-speed, constant-mesh unit.

2 Operations possible with the engine in the frame

The components and assemblies listed below can be removed without having to remove the engine from the frame. If, however, a number of areas require attention at the same time, removal of the engine is recommended.

Gear selector mechanism external components
Water pump
Starter motor
Alternator
Clutch assembly (except housing)
Oil pan and relief valve
Valve cover, camshafts and rocker arms
Cam chain tensioner
Cylinder head
Cylinder block and pistons

3 Operations requiring engine removal

It is necessary to remove the engine/transmission assembly from the frame and separate the crankcase halves to gain access to the following components:

Clutch housing
Crankshaft, connecting rods and bearings
Transmission shafts
Selector drum and forks
Balancer shaft
Starter motor clutch
Cam chain
Primary chain
Oil pump

4 Major engine repair – general note

1 It is not always easy to determine when or if an engine should be completely overhauled, as a number of factors must be considered.

2 High mileage is not necessarily an indication that an overhaul is needed, while low mileage, on the other hand, does not preclude the need for an overhaul. Frequency of servicing is probably the single most important consideration. An engine that has regular and frequent oil and filter changes, as well as other required maintenance, will most likely give many miles of reliable service. Conversely, a neglected engine, or one which has not been broken in properly, may require an overhaul very early in its life.

3 Exhaust smoke and excessive oil consumption are both indications that piston rings and/or valve guides are in need of attention. Make sure oil leaks are not responsible before deciding that the rings and guides are bad. Refer to Chapter 1 and perform a cylinder compression check to determine for certain the nature and extent of the work required.

4 If the engine is making obvious knocking or rumbling noises, the connecting rod and/or main bearings are probably at fault.

5 Loss of power, rough running, excessive valve train noise and high fuel consumption rates may also point to the need for an overhaul, especially if they are all present at the same time. If a complete tune-up does not remedy the situation, major mechanical work is the only solution.

6 An engine overhaul generally involves restoring the internal parts to the specifications of a new engine. During an overhaul the piston rings are renewed and the cylinder walls are bored and/or honed. If a rebore is done, then new pistons are also required. The main and connecting rod bearings are generally renewed and, if necessary, the crankshaft is also renewed. Generally the valves are serviced as well, since they are usually in less than perfect condition at this point. While the engine is being overhauled, other components such as the carburettors and the starter motor can be rebuilt also. The end result should be a like-new engine that will give as many trouble free miles as the original.

7 Before beginning the engine overhaul, read through all of the related procedures to familiarise yourself with the scope and requirements of the job. Overhauling an engine is not all that difficult, but it is time consuming. Plan on the motorcycle being tied up for a minimum of two weeks. Check on the availability of parts and make sure that any necessary special tools, equipment and supplies are obtained in advance.

8 Most work can be done with typical shop hand tools, although a number of precision measuring tools are required for inspecting parts to determine if they must be renewed. Often a dealer service department or motorcycle repair shop will handle the inspection of parts and offer advice concerning reconditioning and renewal. As a general rule, time is the primary cost of an overhaul so it doesn't pay to install worn or substandard parts.

9 As a final note, to ensure maximum life and minimum trouble from a rebuilt engine, everything must be assembled with care in a spotlessly clean environment.

5 Engine – removal and installation

Note: *Engine removal and installation should be done with the aid of an assistant to avoid damage or injury that could occur if the engine is dropped. A hydraulic floor jack should be used to support and lower the engine if possible.*

Removal

1 Set the bike on its centerstand.
2 Remove the seat (see Chapter 8). Remove the battery (see Chapter 9). Remove the fuel tank (see Chapter 4).
3 Remove both side covers on EX500A and ER models. Remove the left-hand side cover on EX500D and E models. On all EX models, remove the upper fairing and lower fairing (see Chapter 8).
4 Drain the coolant and the engine oil (see Chapter 1).
5 Remove the air cleaner housing (see Chapter 5).
6 Remove the air suction valve and the vacuum switching valve, where fitted (see Chapter 1).
7 Remove the carburettors (see Chapter 4) and plug the inlet openings with rags.
8 Remove the radiator, radiator hoses and coolant tubes (see Chapter 3).
9 Remove the ignition coils and brackets (see Chapter 5).
10 Remove the exhaust system (see Chapter 4).
11 Remove the gearchange pedal (see Section 21).
12 Remove the engine sprocket cover, then remove the sprocket and chain from the engine (see Chapter 6).
13 Disconnect the lower end of the clutch cable from the lever and bracket (see Chapter 1).
14 Mark and disconnect the wires from the oil pressure switch, neutral switch and the starter motor. Unplug the alternator, sidestand and pick-up coil electrical connectors (see Chapters 5 and 9). Unbolt the battery negative lead from the top of the crankcase.
15 Support the engine under the crankcase with a floor jack and a wood block.
16 Remove the engine front mounting bolt, nut and spacer and the bolts holding the downtube to the frame **(see illustrations)**.
17 Remove the nuts from the rear mounting bolts **(see illustration)**.
18 With the engine supported, pull the rear mounting bolts out. Make sure no wires or hoses are still attached to the engine assembly.
19 Slowly and carefully lower the engine

5.16a Remove the nut from the front mounting bolt . . .

5.16b . . . then pull out the bolt and spacer (engine removed for clarity)

5.16c Remove two lower bolts . . .

5.16d . . . and two upper bolts that secure the frame downtube

5.17 Remove the nuts from the rear engine mounting bolts (arrowed)

5.19 With the engine supported by a floor jack, have an assistant help you lower it and guide it out of the frame

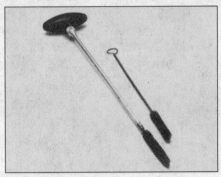

6.2a A selection of brushes is required for cleaning holes and passages in the engine components

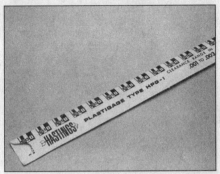

6.2b Type HPG-1 Plastigauge is needed to check the crankshaft, connecting rod and camshaft oil clearances

assembly to the floor, then guide it out from under the bike **(see illustration)**.

Installation

20 Installation is the reverse of removal. Note the following points:
  a) Don't tighten any of the engine mounting bolts until they all have been installed.
  b) Use new gaskets at all exhaust pipe connections.
  c) Tighten the engine mounting bolts and frame downtube bolts securely.
  d) Adjust the drive chain, throttle cables, choke cable and clutch cable following the procedures in Chapter 1.
  e) Refill the engine with oil and the cooling system with coolant (see Chapter 1).

6 Engine disassembly and reassembly – general information

1 Before disassembling the engine, clean the exterior with a degreaser and rinse it with water. A clean engine will make the job easier and prevent the possibility of getting dirt into the internal areas of the engine.
2 In addition to the precision measuring tools mentioned earlier, you will need a torque wrench, a valve spring compressor, oil gallery brushes and a clutch holder tool (which is described in Section 19). Some new, clean

engine oil of the correct grade and type, some engine assembly lube (or moly-based grease), a tube of Kawasaki Bond liquid gasket (part no. 92104-1003) or equivalent, and a tube of RTV (silicone) sealant will also be required. Although it may not be considered a tool, some Plastigauge (type HPG-1) should also be obtained to use for checking bearing oil clearances **(see illustrations)**.
3 An engine support stand made from short lengths of 2 x 4's bolted together will facilitate the disassembly and reassembly procedures **(see illustration)**. The perimeter of the mount should be just big enough to accommodate the engine oil pan. If you have an automotive-type engine stand, an adapter plate can be made from a piece of plate, some angle iron and some nuts and bolts.
4 When disassembling the engine, keep 'mated' parts together (including gears, cylinders, pistons, etc. that have been in contact with each other during engine operation). These 'mated' parts must be reused or renewed as an assembly.
5 Engine/transmission disassembly should be done in the following general order with reference to the appropriate Sections.
  Remove the cylinder head
  Remove the cylinder block
  Remove the pistons
  Remove the clutch (except the housing)
  Remove the oil pan
  Remove the external gearchange mechanism

  Remove the alternator rotor/stator coils and starter clutch (see Chapter 9)
  Separate the crankcase halves
  Remove the crankshaft and connecting rods
  Remove the balancer shaft and gears
  Remove the clutch housing, transmission shafts/gears
  Remove the selector drum/forks
6 Reassembly is accomplished by reversing the general disassembly sequence.

7 Valve cover – removal and installation

Note: The valve cover can be removed with the engine in the frame. If the engine has been removed, ignore the steps which don't apply.

Removal

1 Set the bike on its centerstand.
2 Drain the engine coolant (see Chapter 1).
3 Remove the fuel tank (see Chapter 4).
4 On EX models, prop the ends of the upper fairing out of the way (see Chapter 8).
5 Disconnect the coolant tubes and on ER models also remove the thermostat housing (see Chapter 3). Remove the air suction valve and the vacuum switching valve, where fitted (see Chapter 1). Disconnect the throttle and choke cables at their lower ends (see Chapter 4).
6 Pull the spark plug caps off the spark plugs. If necessary for removal access, remove the ignition coils and their brackets (see Chapter 5). Unbolt the fuel tank mounting bracket from the frame and disconnect the throttle cables from the bracket hook.
7 Remove the valve cover bolts **(see illustration)**.
8 Lift the cover off the cylinder head **(see illustration overleaf)**. If it's stuck, don't attempt to pry it off – tap around the sides with a plastic hammer to dislodge it. The cover is a close fit between the frame tubes on early ER models – lift up the right side of the cover slightly, then pull it rearwards and upwards. **Note:** Pay attention to the locating dowels as you remove

6.3 An engine stand can be made from short lengths of 2 x 4 wood

7.7 Remove the valve cover bolts (arrowed)

7.8 Lift the cover off the engine – if it's stuck, tap gently on the side with a soft-faced hammer

7.9 Be careful not to lose the locating dowels (arrowed) or let them fall into the engine

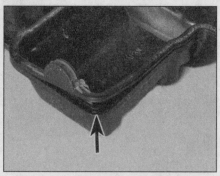

7.11a Be sure the gasket seats securely in the groove (arrowed)

the cover – if they fall into the engine, major disassembly may be required to get them out.

Installation

9 Remove the locating dowels from the valve cover **(see illustration)**. Peel the rubber gasket from the cover. If it's cracked, hardened, has soft spots or shows signs of general deterioration, renew it.

10 Clean the mating surfaces of the cylinder head and the valve cover with lacquer thinner, acetone or brake system cleaner. Apply a thin film of RTV sealant to the half-circle cutouts on each side of the head.

11 Install the gasket to the cover. Make sure it fits completely into the cover groove **(see illustration)**. Apply a small amount of silicone sealer to the corners of the half-circle portions of the gasket **(see illustration)**.

12 Position the cover on the cylinder head, making sure the gasket doesn't slip out of place.

13 Check the rubber seals on the valve cover bolts, renewing them if necessary. Install the bolts, tightening them evenly to the torque listed in this Chapter's Specifications.

14 The remainder of installation is the reverse of removal. Fill the cooling system with the recommended type and amount of coolant (see Chapter 1).

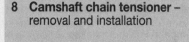

8 Camshaft chain tensioner – removal and installation

EX500A models

Removal

Caution: Once you start to remove the tensioner bolts, you must remove the tensioner all the way and reset it before tightening the bolts. The tensioner extends and locks in place, so if you loosen the bolts part way and then retighten them, the tensioner or cam chain will be damaged.

1 Loosen the tensioner cap bolt while the tensioner is still installed **(see illustration)**.

2 Remove the tensioner mounting bolts and take it off the engine.

3 Remove the tensioner cap bolt and O-ring.

Installation – original tensioner

4 Check the O-ring on the tensioner body for cracks or hardening. It's a good idea to renew this O-ring whenever the tensioner is removed.

5 Place the tensioner mounting bolts where you can reach them with one hand while the other hand holds the tensioner in position in Step 7.

6 Press the end of the rod that contacts the chain into the tensioner body. At the same time, turn the other end of the rod clockwise with a screwdriver until the rod protrudes about 10 mm (3/8-in) from the tensioner body **(see illustration)**.

Caution: Don't turn the rod counterclockwise (anticlockwise) or it may separate from the tensioner. If this happens it can't be reassembled.

7 Place the tensioner in position on the engine. Push it firmly against the engine, remove the screwdriver, and install the mounting bolts finger-tight.

Caution: If the tensioner moves away from the engine before you tighten the bolts, the rod will extend too far. If this happens (or you think it might have happened), remove the tensioner and repeat Step 6, then continue with Step 7.

8 Tighten the mounting bolts to the torque listed in this Chapter's Specifications.

9 Install the tensioner cap and O-ring. Tighten the cap to the torque listed in this Chapter's Specifications.

Installation – new tensioner

10 New tensioners come with a keeper that fits in the tensioner rod slot and holds the rod in the correct position for installation **(see**

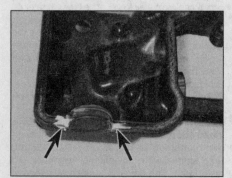

7.11b Apply a small amount of silicone sealant to the corners of the half-circle portions of the gasket (arrowed)

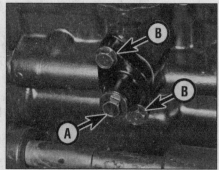

8.1 Loosen the tensioner cap bolt (A) while the tensioner is still on the engine, then remove the mounting bolts (B)

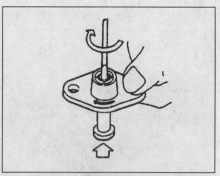

8.6 Turn the slotted end of the tensioner clockwise and press the plunger in until it extends 10 mm from the body of the tensioner

illustration). The new tensioner will also be supplied with new O-rings and a new cap bolt.

11 Place the tensioner on the engine. Install the mounting bolts and tighten them to the torque listed in this Chapter's Specifications.

12 Pull the keeper out with needle nosed pliers. **Note:** *Save the keeper and place it in your toolbox for future use. You can use it to hold the tensioner rod in position next time you install the tensioner, leaving both hands free.*

13 Install the tensioner cap and O-ring. Tighten the cap to the torque listed in this Chapter's Specifications.

EX500D, E and ER models

Caution: Once you start to remove the tensioner bolts, you must remove the tensioner all the way and reset it before tightening the bolts. The tensioner extends and locks in place, so if you loosen the bolts part way and then retighten them, the tensioner or cam chain will be damaged.

Removal

14 Loosen the tensioner cap bolt while the tensioner is still installed **(see illustration 8.1)**.

15 Remove the tensioner mounting bolts and take it off the engine.

16 Remove the tensioner cap bolt and washer.

17 Examine the tensioner components for signs of wear or damage.

18 Release the ratchet mechanism from the

8.10 New tensioners come with a keeper (arrowed) to hold the rod in position for installation

tensioner plunger and check that the plunger moves freely in and out of the tensioner body **(see illustration 8.20)**.

19 If the tensioner or any of its components are worn or damaged, or if the plunger is seized in the body, the tensioner must be replaced. Individual components are not available.

Installation

20 Release the ratchet mechanism and press the tensioner plunger all the way into the tensioner body **(see illustration)**.

21 Fit a new gasket onto the tensioner body, then install the tensioner in the engine. Tighten the mounting bolts to the torque setting

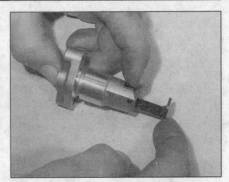

8.20 Release the ratchet and press the plunger into the body

specified at the beginning of the Chapter.

22 Check the condition of the sealing washer on the cap bolt and renew it if it is worn or damaged. Install the spring and cap bolt and tighten the bolt to the torque setting specified at the beginning of the Chapter.

---

9 Camshafts, rocker arm shafts and rocker arms – removal, inspection and installation

Note: *This procedure can be performed with the engine in the frame.*

Camshafts

Removal

1 Remove the valve cover (see Section 7).

2 Remove the camshaft chain tensioner (see Section 8).

3 Turn the engine to position no. 2 cylinder at TDC compression (see Chapter 1 – Valve clearances – check and adjustment). When the engine is positioned correctly, the EX mark on the exhaust camshaft and the IN mark on the inlet camshaft will align with the cylinder head top surface **(see illustrations)**. To ease reassembly, mark the sprockets and chain with felt pen **(see illustration)**.

4 Remove the upper chain guide **(see illustration)**.

5 Remove the bolts and lift the oil pipes and O-rings from the cylinder head **(see illustration)**.

9.3a Position the EX mark on the exhaust camshaft even with the cylinder head surface and the sprocket punch mark up (arrowed) . . .

9.3b . . . the IN mark on the inlet camshaft should also be even with the head surface and the sprocket punch mark should be up . . .

9.3c . . . once the camshafts are positioned correctly, mark across the chain and sprocket with felt pen to ease reassembly

9.4 The centre four camshaft bearing cap bolts also secure the chain guide; its arrow points toward the front of the engine

9.5 Remove the oil line bolts (arrowed) and lift the oil pipes and O-rings out of the engine

9.6 The camshaft bearing caps have letter marks to indicate position; the caps must be reinstalled in their original locations

9.7a Lift the camshafts out of the head and disengage them from the chain

9.7b The camshafts are identified by punch marks

6 Unscrew the bearing cap bolts for one of the camshafts, a little at a time, until they are all loose, then unscrew the bearing cap bolts for the other camshaft. Remove the bolts and lift off the bearing caps. Note the letters on the bearing caps which correspond to those on the cylinder head **(see illustration)**. When you reinstall the caps, be sure to install them in the correct positions.
Caution: If the bearing cap bolts aren't loosened evenly, the camshaft may bind.
7 Pull up on the camshaft chain and carefully guide the camshaft out **(see illustration)**. With the chain still held taut, remove the other

9.8 This protrusion in the bottom of the engine case is designed to prevent the cam chain from falling out of mesh with the crankshaft sprocket

camshaft. Look for marks on the camshafts **(see illustration)**. The inlet camshaft should have an IN mark and the exhaust camshaft should have an EX mark. If you can't find these marks, label the camshafts to ensure they are installed in their original locations. **Note:** *Don't remove the sprockets from the camshafts unless absolutely necessary.*
8 While the camshafts are out, don't allow the chain to go slack – there's a protrusion inside the crankcase that's designed to keep the chain from falling off the sprocket on the crankshaft **(see illustration)**, but if it's worn, the chain may fall off and bind between the crankshaft and case, which could damage these components. Wire the chain to another component to prevent it from dropping down. Also, cover the top of the cylinder head with a rag to prevent foreign objects from falling into the engine.

Inspection

Note: *Before renewing camshafts or the cylinder head and bearing caps because of damage, check with local machine shops specialising in motorcycle engine work. In the case of the camshafts, it may be possible for cam lobes to be welded, reground and hardened, at a cost far lower than that of a new camshaft. If the bearing surfaces in the cylinder head are damaged, it may be possible for them to be bored out to accept bearing inserts. Due to the cost of a new cylinder head*

it is recommended that all options be explored before condemning it as trash!
9 Inspect the cam bearing surfaces of the head and the bearing caps. Look for score marks, deep scratches and evidence of spalling (a pitted appearance).
10 Check the camshaft lobes for heat discoloration (blue appearance), score marks, chipped areas, flat spots and spalling **(see illustration)**. Measure the height of each lobe with a micrometer **(see illustration)** and compare the results to the minimum lobe height listed in this Chapter's Specifications. If damage is noted or wear is excessive, the camshaft must be renewed. Also, be sure to check the condition of the rocker arms, as described later in this Section.
11 Next, check the camshaft bearing oil clearances. Clean the camshafts, the bearing surfaces in the cylinder head and the bearing caps with a clean, lint-free cloth, then lay the cams in place in the cylinder head, with the IN and EX marks on the gears facing away from each other and level with the valve cover gasket surface of the cylinder head **(see illustrations 9.3a and 9.3b)**. Engage the cam chain with the cam gears, so the camshafts don't turn as the bearing caps are tightened.
12 Cut eight strips of Plastigauge (type HPG-1) and lay one piece on each bearing journal, parallel with the camshaft centreline **(see illustration)**.
13 Make sure the bearing cap dowels are

9.10a Check the lobes of the camshaft for wear – here's a good example of damage which will require renewal

9.10b Measure the height of the camshaft lobes with a micrometer

9.12 Position a strip of Plastigauge on each cam bearing journal, parallel with the centreline of the crankshaft

9.13a Make sure the bearing cap dowels (arrowed) are in position

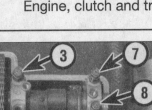

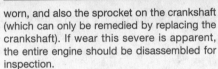

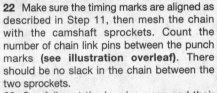

9.13b Camshaft bearing cap tightening sequence (the centre four bolts also secure the chain guide) – tighten the no. 1 and no. 2 bolts evenly to specifications first, then tighten the others in numerical order

installed (**see illustration**). Install the bearing caps in their original positions (the arrows on the caps must face toward the front of the engine and the letters on the caps must correspond with those on the cylinder head) and install the bolts. Tighten the bolts in three steps, following the recommended sequence (**see illustration**), to the torque listed in this Chapter's Specifications. While doing this, DO NOT let the camshafts rotate!

14 Now unscrew the bolts, a little at a time, and carefully lift off the bearing caps.

15 To determine the oil clearance, compare the crushed Plastigauge (at its widest point) on each journal to the scale printed on the Plastigauge container (**see illustration**). Compare the results to this Chapter's Specifications. If the oil clearance is greater than specified, measure the diameter of the cam bearing journal with a micrometer (**see illustration**). If the journal diameter is less than the specified limit, renew the camshaft and recheck the clearance. If the clearance is still too great, renew the cylinder head and bearing caps (see the Note that precedes Step 9).

16 Except in cases of oil starvation, the camshaft chain wears very little. If the chain has stretched excessively, which makes it difficult to maintain proper tension, renew it (see Section 28).

17 Check the sprockets for wear, cracks and other damage, renewing them if necessary. If the sprockets are worn, the chain is also

worn, and also the sprocket on the crankshaft (which can only be remedied by replacing the crankshaft). If wear this severe is apparent, the entire engine should be disassembled for inspection.

18 If you remove the sprockets, be sure to install them correctly; they're identical, with each sprocket having bolt holes for the inlet and exhaust camshafts. The inlet camshaft sprocket uses the bolt holes labelled IN; the exhaust camshaft sprocket uses the bolt holes labelled EX (**see illustration**).

19 Check the cam chain guide for wear or damage. If it is worn or damaged, the chain is worn out or improperly adjusted. Renewal of the guide requires removal of the cylinder head and cylinder block.

Installation

20 Make sure the bearing surfaces in the cylinder head and the bearing caps are clean, then apply a light coat of engine assembly lube or moly-based grease to each of them.

21 Apply a coat of moly-based grease to the camshaft lobes. Make sure the camshaft bearing journals are clean, then lay the camshafts in the cylinder head (do not mix them up), ensuring the marks on the cam sprockets are aligned properly (**see illustrations 9.3a, 9.3b and 9.3c**).

22 Make sure the timing marks are aligned as described in Step 11, then mesh the chain with the camshaft sprockets. Count the number of chain link pins between the punch marks (**see illustration overleaf**). There should be no slack in the chain between the two sprockets.

23 Carefully set the bearing caps and their dowels in place (arrows pointing toward the front of the engine and in their proper positions) (**see illustration 9.6**) and install the bolts. Tighten them in the recommended sequence (**see illustration 9.13b**), to the torque listed in this Chapter's Specifications.

24 Insert your finger or a wood dowel into the cam chain tensioner hole and apply pressure to the cam chain. Check the timing marks to make sure they are aligned (see Step 3) and there are still the correct number of link pins between the punch marks on the cam sprockets (**see illustration 9.22**). If necessary, change the position of the sprocket(s) on the chain to bring all of the marks into alignment.

Caution: If the marks are not aligned exactly as described, the valve timing will be incorrect and the valves may contact the pistons, causing extensive damage to the engine.

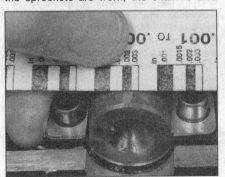

9.15a Compare the width of the crushed Plastigauge to the scale on the Plastigauge envelope to obtain the clearance

9.15b Measure the cam bearing journal with a micrometer

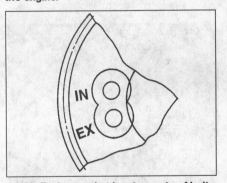

9.18 Each sprocket has two sets of bolt holes; those labelled EX are used for the exhaust camshaft, while those labelled IN are used for the inlet camshaft

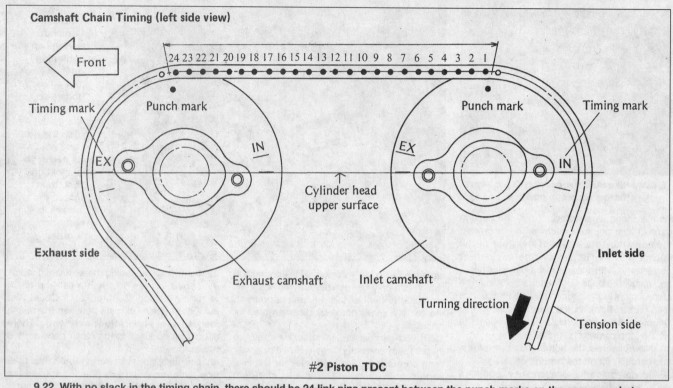

Camshaft Chain Timing (left side view)

Front

24 23 22 21 20 19 18 17 16 15 14 13 12 11 10 9 8 7 6 5 4 3 2 1

Timing mark   Punch mark   Punch mark   Timing mark

EX   IN   EX   IN

Cylinder head upper surface

Exhaust side   Inlet side

Exhaust camshaft   Inlet camshaft

Turning direction   Tension side

#2 Piston TDC

9.22 With no slack in the timing chain, there should be 24 link pins present between the punch marks on the cam sprockets

9.30a Insert an Allen wrench into the rocker shaft head (a bit like this one is necessary for tightening the plug to specifications) . . .

9.30b . . . unscrew the shaft and pull it out

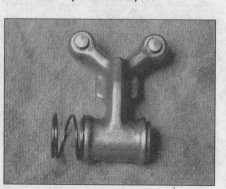

9.31 Remove the rocker arms and springs

9.33 Inspect the rocker arms, especially the faces that contact the cam lobes, for wear

25 Install the tensioner as described in Section 8.
26 Adjust the valve clearances (see Chapter 1).
27 Turn the engine with a socket on the crankshaft rotation bolt. If you feel a sudden increase in resistance, stop turning. The valves may be hitting the pistons due to incorrect assembly. Find the problem and fix it before turning the engine any further, or serious damage may occur.
28 The remainder of installation is the reverse of removal.

Rocker arm shafts and rocker arms

Removal

29 Remove the camshafts following the procedure given above. Be sure to keep tension on the camshaft chain.
30 Unscrew one rocker shaft from the cylinder head and pull it out **(see illustrations)**.
31 Remove the rocker arms and springs **(see illustration)**.
32 Repeat the above Steps to remove the other rocker arm shafts and rocker arms. Keep all of the parts in order so they can be reinstalled in their original locations.

Inspection

33 Clean all of the components with solvent and dry them off. Blow through the oil passages in the rocker arms with compressed air, if available. Inspect the rocker arm faces for pits, spalling, score marks and rough spots **(see illustration)**. Check the rocker arm-to-

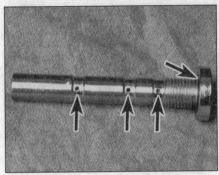

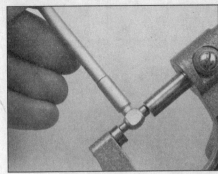

9.34a Check the rocker shaft for wear, make sure the oil holes (lower arrows) are clear and inspect the O-ring under the head (upper arrow)

9.34b Measure the inside diameter of the rocker arm using a telescoping gauge . . .

9.34c . . . then measure the gauge with a micrometer

shaft contact areas and the adjusting screws, as well. Look for cracks in each rocker arm. If the faces of the rocker arms are damaged, the rocker arms and the camshafts should be renewed as a set.

34 Measure the diameter of the rocker arm shafts, in the area where the rocker arms ride, and compare the results with this Chapter's Specifications. Also measure the inside diameter of the rocker arms **(see illustrations)** and compare the results with this Chapter's Specifications. If either the shaft or the rocker arms are worn beyond the specified limits, renew them as a set.

35 Check the O-ring under the head of the rocker arm shaft, renewing it if necessary.

Installation

36 Position a rocker arm and spring in the cylinder head, with the spring toward the centre of the cylinder head **(see illustration)**.

37 Lubricate the rocker arm shaft with engine oil and slide it into the cylinder head and through the rocker arm and spring. Tighten it to the torque listed in this Chapter's Specifications.

38 Repeat Steps 36 and 37 to install the remaining rocker arms and shafts.

39 Install the camshafts following the procedure described earlier in this Section.

10 Cylinder head – removal and installation

Caution: The engine must be completely cool before beginning this procedure, or the cylinder head may become warped.

Note: *This procedure can be performed with the engine in the frame. If the engine has been removed, ignore the steps which don't apply.*

Removal

1 Set the bike on its centerstand.

2 Remove the valve cover (see Section 7).

3 Remove the exhaust system and the carburettors (see Chapter 4).

4 Remove the cam chain tensioner (see Section 8).

5 Remove the camshafts (see Section 9).

6 Remove the oil pipe banjo bolts and washers from the rear of the cylinder head **(see illustration)**.

7 Remove the small cylinder block-to-cylinder head bolts and the main oil pipe mounting bolt **(see illustrations)**.

8 Loosen the cylinder head bolts, a little at a time, using the reverse order of the tightening sequence **(see illustrations)**.

9 Pull the cylinder head off the cylinder block

9.36 The rocker arm springs (arrowed) go between the rocker arm and the centre of the head

10.6 Remove the oil line banjo bolts

10.7a Remove one small head-to-block bolt (upper arrow), the oil line mounting bolt (lower arrow) . . .

10.7b . . . and one small head-to-block bolt located inside the head

10.8a Use a deep socket to remove the head bolts

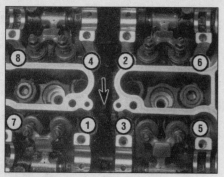

10.8b Head bolt TIGHTENING sequence – the arrow points to the front of the engine

10.9 Lift the head off the cylinder block

10.10 Remove the old gasket

(see illustration). If the head is stuck, tap upward against the rocker shaft heads with a rubber mallet to jar it loose, or use two wooden dowels inserted into the inlet or exhaust ports to lever the head off. Don't attempt to pry the head off by inserting a screwdriver between the head and the cylinder block – you'll damage the sealing surfaces.

10 Lift the head gasket off the cylinder block (see illustration).

11 Stuff a clean rag into the cam chain tunnel to prevent the entry of debris.

12 Locate the two dowel pins to make sure they haven't fallen into the engine. If they are in the head, put them in their holes in the cylinder block.

13 Check the cylinder head gasket and the mating surfaces on the cylinder head and block for leakage, which could indicate warpage. Refer to Section 12 and check the flatness of the cylinder head.

14 Clean all traces of old gasket material from the cylinder head and block. Be careful not to let any of the gasket material fall into the crankcase, the cylinder bores or the water passages.

Installation

15 Lay the new gasket in place on the cylinder block. Make sure the UP mark on the gasket is positioned on the right-hand side of the engine (see illustration). Never reuse the old gasket and don't use any type of gasket sealant.

16 Carefully lower the cylinder head over the studs. It is helpful to have an assistant support the camshaft chain with a piece of wire so it doesn't fall and become kinked or detached from the crankshaft. When the head is resting against the cylinder block, wire the cam chain to another component to keep tension on it.

17 Install the long 8 mm head bolts. Using the proper sequence (see illustration 10.8b), tighten the bolts to approximately half of the torque listed in this Chapter's Specifications.

18 Using the same sequence, tighten the bolts to the full torque listed in this Chapter's Specifications.

19 Install the small 6 mm cylinder block-to-cylinder head bolts, tightening them to the torque listed in this Chapter's Specifications.

20 Install the oil line mounting and banjo bolts. Use new washers on the banjo bolts (see illustration).

21 Install the camshafts and the valve cover (see Sections 9 and 7).

22 Change the engine oil (see Chapter 1)

11 Valves/valve seats/valve guides – servicing

1 Because of the complex nature of this job and the special tools and equipment required, most owners leave servicing of the valves, valve seats and valve guides to a professional.

2 The home mechanic can, however, remove

the valves from the cylinder head, clean and check the components for wear and assess the extent of the work needed, and, unless a valve service is required, grind in the valves (see Section 12).

3 The dealer will remove the valves and springs, replace the valves and guides, recut the valve seats, check and replace the valve springs, spring retainers and collets (as necessary), replace the valve seals with new ones and reassemble the valve components.

4 After the valve service has been performed, the head will be in like-new condition. When the head is returned, be sure to clean it again very thoroughly before installation on the engine to remove any metal particles or abrasive grit that may still be present from the valve service operations. Use compressed air, if available, to blow out all the holes and passages.

12 Cylinder head and valves – disassembly, inspection and reassembly

1 As mentioned in the previous Section, valve servicing and valve guide replacement should be left to a Kawasaki dealer. However, disassembly, cleaning and inspection of the valves and related components can be done (if the necessary special tools are available) by the home mechanic. This way no expense is incurred if the inspection reveals that service work is not required at this time.

2 To properly disassemble the valve components without the risk of damaging them, a valve spring compressor is absolutely necessary.

Disassembly

3 Remove the rocker arm shafts and rocker arms (see Section 9). Store the components in such a way that they can be returned to their original locations without getting mixed up (labelled plastic bags work well).

4 Before the valves are removed, scrape away any traces of gasket material from the head gasket sealing surface. Work slowly and do not nick or gouge the soft aluminium of the head. Gasket removing solvents, which work

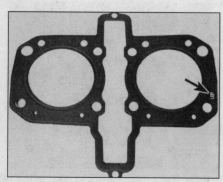

10.15 The UP mark on the head gasket goes toward the right side of the engine

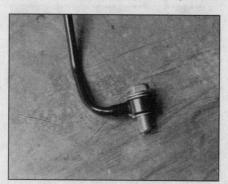

10.20 Use a new washer on each side of the oil line banjo bolt fittings

12.7a Compressing the valve springs with a valve spring compressor

12.7b Remove the valve keepers/collets with needle-nose pliers or tweezers

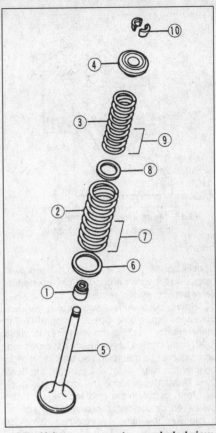

12.7c Valve components – exploded view

1	Oil seal	7	Tightly wound
2	Outer spring		coils
3	Inner spring	8	Inner spring seat
4	Valve spring	9	Tightly wound
	retainer		coils
5	Valve	10	Keepers/collets
6	Outer spring seat		

very well, are available at most motorcycle shops and auto parts stores.

5 Carefully scrape all carbon deposits out of the combustion chamber area. A hand held wire brush or a piece of fine emery cloth can be used once the majority of deposits have been scraped away. Do not use a wire brush mounted in a drill motor, or one with extremely stiff bristles, as the head material is soft and may be eroded away or scratched by the wire brush.

6 Before proceeding, arrange to label and store the valves along with their related components so they can be kept separate and reinstalled in the same valve guides they are removed from (again, plastic bags work well for this).

7 Compress the valve spring on the first valve with a spring compressor, then remove the keepers/collets **(see illustrations)** and the retainer from the valve assembly. Do not compress the springs any more than is absolutely necessary. Carefully release the valve spring compressor and remove the springs and the valve from the head **(see illustration)**. If the valve binds in the guide (won't pull through), push it back into the head and deburr the area around the keeper/collet groove with a very fine file or whetstone **(see illustration)**.

8 Repeat the procedure for the remaining valves. Remember to keep the parts for each valve together so they can be reinstalled in the same location.

9 Once the valves have been removed and

labelled, pull off the valve stem seals with pliers and discard them (the old seals should never be reused), then remove the spring seats.

10 Next, clean the cylinder head with solvent and dry it thoroughly. Compressed air will speed the drying process and ensure that all holes and recessed areas are clean.

11 Clean all of the valve springs, keepers/collets, retainers and spring seats with solvent and dry them thoroughly. Do the parts from one valve at a time so that no mixing of parts between valves occurs.

12 Scrape off any deposits that may have formed on the valve, then use a motorised wire brush to remove deposits from the valve heads and stems. Again, make sure the valves do not get mixed up.

Inspection

13 Inspect the head very carefully for cracks and other damage. If cracks are found, a new head will be required. Check the cam bearing surfaces for wear and evidence of seizure. Check the camshafts and rocker arms for wear as well (see Section 9).

14 Using a precision straight-edge and a feeler gauge, check the head gasket mating surface for warpage. Lay the straight-edge lengthways, across the head and diagonally (corner-to-corner), intersecting the head bolt holes, and try to slip a 0.05 mm (0.002 in) feeler gauge under it, on either side of each combustion chamber **(see illustration)**. If the feeler gauge can be inserted between the

head and the straight-edge, the head is warped and must either be machined or, if warpage is excessive, renewed.

15 Examine the valve seats in each of the combustion chambers. If they are pitted, cracked or burned, the head will require valve service that is beyond the scope of the home mechanic. Measure the valve seat width **(see illustration)** and compare it to this Chapter's

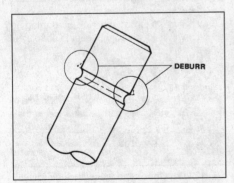

12.7d If the valve binds in the guide, deburr the area above the keeper/collet groove

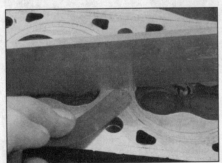

12.14 Lay a precision straight-edge across the cylinder head and try to slide a feeler gauge of the specified thickness under it

12.15 Measuring the valve seat width

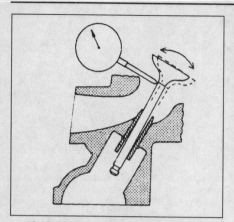

12.16 Measuring valve stem to guide clearance using the 'wobble' method

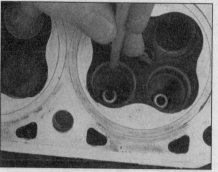

12.17a Insert a small hole gauge into the valve guide and expand it so there's a slight drag when it's pulled out

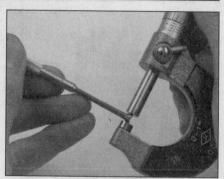

12.17b Measure the small hole gauge with a micrometer

Specifications. If it is not within the specified range, or if it varies around its circumference, valve service work is required.

16 Kawasaki specify a valve stem-to-guide clearance figure (see Specifications). This is measured by inserting the valve into its guide (both components have already been cleaned) and mounting a dial gauge so that its tip rests against the valve stem just beneath the head **(see illustration)**. Move the valve head back and forth to obtain the clearance figure. If the measured clearance exceeds the limit, go on to measure the valve stem diameter (Step 19)

and valve guide diameter (Step 17) to determine which component is worn.

17 Clean the valve guides to remove any carbon build-up, then measure the inside diameters of the guides (at both ends and the centre of the guide) with a small hole gauge and a micrometer **(see illustrations)**. The guides are measured at the ends and at the centre to determine if they are worn in a bell-mouth pattern (more wear at the ends). If they are, guide renewal is an absolute must. Compare your measurements with the minimum diameter given in the Specifications.

18 Carefully inspect each valve face for cracks, pits and burned spots. Check the valve stem and the keeper/collet groove area for cracks

(see illustration). Rotate the valve and check for any obvious indication that it is bent. Check the end of the stem for pitting and excessive wear. The presence of any of the above conditions indicates the need for valve servicing.

19 Measure the valve stem diameter **(see illustration)** and compare it to this Chapter's Specifications. Also check the valve stem for bending. Set the valve in a V-block with a dial gauge touching the middle of the stem **(see illustration)**. Rotate the valve and note the reading on the gauge. If the stem runout exceeds the value listed in this Chapter's Specifications, renew the valve.

20 Check the end of each valve spring for wear and pitting. Measure the free length **(see illustration)** and compare it to this Chapter's Specifications. Any springs that are shorter than specified have sagged and should not be reused. Stand the spring on a flat surface and check it for squareness **(see illustration)**.

21 Check the spring retainers and keepers/collets for obvious wear and cracks. Any questionable parts should not be reused, as extensive damage will occur in the event of failure during engine operation.

Reassembly

22 Before installing the valves in the head, they should be lapped to ensure a positive seal between the valves and seats. This procedure requires fine valve lapping compound (available from auto accessory stores) and a valve lapping

12.18 Check the valve face, stem and keeper groove for signs of wear and damage

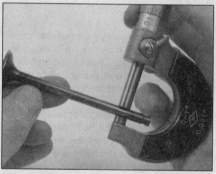

12.19a Measure the valve stem diameter with a micrometer

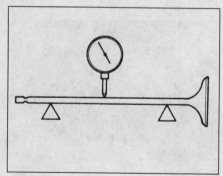

12.19b Check the valve stem for bends with a V-block (or blocks, as shown here) and a dial gauge

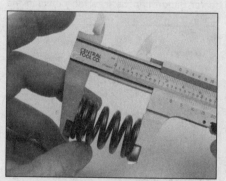

12.20a Measure the free length of the valve springs

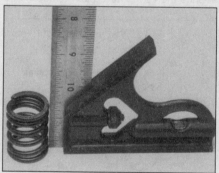

12.20b Check the valve springs for squareness

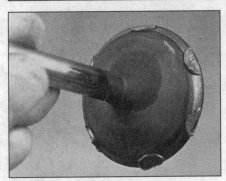

12.23 Apply the lapping compound very sparingly, in small dabs, to the valve face only

12.24a A hose, pushed over the end of the valve, can be used to turn the valve back and forth

12.24b After lapping, the valve face should exhibit a uniform, unbroken contact pattern (arrowed) . . .

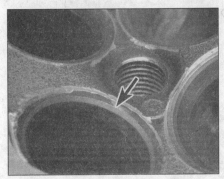

12.24c . . . and the seat should be the specified width (arrowed) with a smooth, unbroken appearance

tool. If a lapping tool is not available, a piece of rubber or plastic hose can be slipped over the valve stem (after the valve has been installed in the guide) and used to turn the valve.

23 Apply a small amount of fine lapping compound to the valve face **(see illustration)**, then slip the valve into the guide. **Note:** *Make sure the valve is installed in the correct guide and be careful not to get any lapping compound on the valve stem.*

24 Attach the lapping tool (or hose) to the valve and rotate the tool between the palms of your hands. Use a back-and-forth motion rather than a circular motion **(see illustration)**. Lift the valve off the seat and turn it at regular intervals to distribute the lapping compound properly. Continue the lapping procedure until the valve face and seat contact area is of uniform width and unbroken around the entire circumference of the valve face and seat **(see illustrations)**.

25 Carefully remove the valve from the guide and wipe off all traces of lapping compound. Use solvent to clean the valve and wipe the seat area thoroughly with a solvent soaked cloth. Repeat the procedure for the remaining valves.

26 Lay the spring seats in place in the cylinder head, then install new valve stem seals on each of the guides. Use an appropriate size deep socket to push the seals into place until they are properly seated. Don't twist or cock them, or they will not seal properly against the valve stems. Also, don't remove them again or they will be damaged.

27 Coat the valve stems with assembly lube or moly-based grease, then install one of them into its guide. Next, install the springs and retainers, compress the springs and install the collets. **Note:** *Install the springs with the tightly wound coils at the bottom (next to the spring seat). When compressing the springs with the valve spring compressor, depress them only as far as is absolutely necessary to slip the collets into place. Apply a small amount of grease to the keepers* **(see illustration)** *to help hold them in place as the pressure is released from the springs. Make certain that the collets are securely locked in their retaining grooves.*

28 Support the cylinder head on blocks so the valves can't contact the workbench top, then very gently tap each of the valve stems with a soft-faced hammer. This will help seat the collets in their grooves.

> **HAYNES HiNT** *Once all of the valves have been installed in the head, check for proper valve sealing by pouring a small amount of solvent into each of the valve ports. If the solvent leaks past the valve(s) into the combustion chamber area, disassemble the valve(s) and repeat the lapping procedure, then reinstall the valve(s) and repeat the check. Repeat the procedure until a satisfactory seal is obtained.*

13 Cylinder block – removal, inspection and installation

Removal

1 Following the procedure given in Section 10, remove the cylinder head. Make sure the crankshaft is positioned at Top Dead Centre (TDC) for cylinder no. 2.

2 Remove the water pump together with the water pipe (see Chapter 3).

3 Remove the oil pipe mounting bolt **(see illustration)**.

4 Lift out the camshaft chain rear guide **(see illustration)**.

12.27 A small dab of grease will help hold the keepers/collets in place on the valve spring while the valve is released

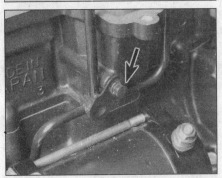

13.3 If you haven't already done so for cylinder head removal, remove the oil pipe mounting bolt

13.4 Lift the rear cam chain guide out of the engine (cylinder block removed for clarity)

13.5 Lift the cylinder block up and off the crankcase and pistons

13.6 Place rags under the pistons to protect them and keep debris out of the crankcase

13.8a Measure the cylinder bore with a telescoping gauge (then measure the gauge with a micrometer)

5 Lift the cylinder block straight up to remove it **(see illustration)**. If it's stuck, tap around its perimeter with a soft-faced hammer. Don't attempt to pry between the block and the crankcase, as you will ruin the sealing surfaces. As you lift, note the location of the dowel pins. Be careful not to let these drop into the engine.

6 Stuff clean shop towels around the pistons **(see illustration)** and remove the gasket and all traces of old gasket material from the surfaces of the cylinder block and the cylinder head.

Inspection

Caution: Don't attempt to separate the liners from the cylinder block.

7 Check the cylinder walls carefully for scratches and score marks.

8 Using the appropriate precision measuring tools, check each cylinder's diameter near the top, centre and bottom of the cylinder bore, parallel to the crankshaft axis **(see illustrations)**. Next, measure each cylinder's diameter at the same three locations across the crankshaft axis. Compare the results to this Chapter's Specifications. If the cylinder walls are tapered, out-of-round, worn beyond the specified limits, or badly scuffed or

scored, have them rebored and honed by a Kawasaki dealer or an engineer. If a rebore is done, oversize pistons and rings will be required as well. **Note:** *Kawasaki supplies pistons in one oversize only, +0.020 in (+0.5 mm).*

9 As an alternative, if the precision measuring tools are not available, the dealer or engineer will make the measurements and offer advice concerning servicing of the cylinders.

10 If they are in reasonably good condition and not worn to the outside of the limits, and if the piston-to-cylinder clearances can be maintained properly (see Section 14), then the cylinders do not have to be rebored; honing is all that is necessary.

11 To perform the honing operation you will need the proper size flexible hone with fine stones, or a 'bottle brush' type hone, plenty of light oil or honing oil, some shop towels and an electric drill motor. Hold the cylinder block in a vice (cushioned with soft jaws or wood blocks) when performing the honing operation. Mount the hone in the drill motor, compress the stones and slip the hone into the cylinder. Lubricate the cylinder thoroughly, turn on the drill and move the hone up and down in the cylinder at a pace which will produce a fine crosshatch pattern on the cylinder wall with the crosshatch lines intersecting at approximately a 60° angle. Be sure to use plenty of lubricant and do not take off any more material than is absolutely necessary to produce the desired effect. Do

not withdraw the hone from the cylinder while it is running. Instead, shut off the drill and continue moving the hone up and down in the cylinder until it comes to a complete stop, then compress the stones and withdraw the hone. Wipe the oil out of the cylinder and repeat the procedure on the remaining cylinder. Remember, do not remove too much material from the cylinder wall. If you do not have the tools, or do not desire to perform the honing operation, a dealer service department or motorcycle repair shop will generally do it for a reasonable fee.

12 Next, the cylinders must be thoroughly washed with warm soapy water to remove all traces of the abrasive grit produced during the honing operation. Be sure to run a brush through the bolt holes and flush them with running water. After rinsing, dry the cylinders thoroughly and apply a coat of light, rust-preventative oil to all machined surfaces.

Installation

13 Lubricate the cylinder bores with plenty of clean engine oil. Apply a thin film of moly-based grease to the piston skirts.

14 Install the dowel pins, then place a new cylinder base gasket on the crankcase with the sealant ripple in the gasket upward **(see illustration)**. Some gaskets also have an arrow, which must point to the front of the engine.

15 Slowly rotate the crankshaft until all of the pistons are at the same level. Slide lengths of welding rod or pieces of a straightened-out coat hanger under the pistons, on both sides of the connecting rods. This will help keep the pistons level as the cylinder block is lowered onto them.

16 Attach two piston ring compressors to the pistons and compress the piston rings. Large hose clamps can be used instead – just make sure they don't scratch the pistons, and don't tighten them too much. Note that ring compressors aren't essential – you can feed the rings into the bores by hand if care is taken.

17 Install the cylinder block over the pistons and carefully lower it down until the piston crowns fit into the cylinder liners. While doing this, pull the camshaft chain up, using a hooked

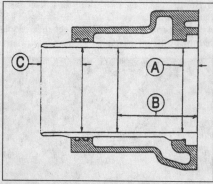

13.8b Specified measuring points in the bore

A	10 mm
B	60 mm
C	40 mm (EX models), 20 mm (ER models)

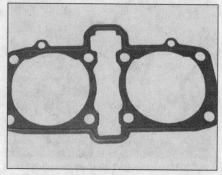

13.14 Install the base gasket with the ridge upward

tool or a piece of coat hanger. Push down on the cylinder block, making sure the pistons don't get cocked sideways, until the bottoms of the cylinder liners slide down past the piston rings. A wood or plastic hammer handle can be used to gently tap the block down, but don't use too much force or the pistons will be damaged.

18 Remove the piston ring compressors or hose clamps (if used), being careful not to scratch the pistons. Remove the rods from under the pistons.

19 Install the cam chain rear guide **(see illustration 13.4)**.

20 The remainder of installation is the reverse of removal.

14 Pistons – removal, inspection and installation

1 The pistons are attached to the connecting rods with piston pins that are a slip fit in the pistons and rods.

2 Before removing the pistons from the rods, stuff a clean shop towel into each crankcase hole, around the connecting rods **(see illustration 13.6)**. This will prevent the circlips from falling into the crankcase if they are inadvertently dropped.

Removal

3 Using a sharp scribe, scratch the number of each piston into its crown. Each piston should also have an arrow pointing toward the front of the engine **(see illustration)**. If not, scribe an arrow into the piston crown before removal. Support the first piston, grasp the circlip with needle-nose pliers and remove it from the groove. If the pin won't come out, fabricate a piston pin removal tool from threaded stock (stud), nuts, washers and a piece of pipe.

4 Push the piston pin out from the opposite end to free the piston from the rod. You may have to deburr the area around the groove to enable the pin to slide out (use a triangular file for this procedure). Repeat the procedure for the other piston.

Inspection

5 Before the inspection process can be

14.3 Using a sharp scribe, scratch the cylinder numbers into the piston crowns – also note the arrow, which must point to the front

carried out, the pistons must be cleaned and the old piston rings removed.

6 Using a piston ring installation tool or simply using your fingertips, carefully remove the rings from the pistons **(see illustration)**. Do not nick or gouge the pistons in the process.

7 Scrape all traces of carbon from the tops of the pistons. A hand-held wire brush or a piece of fine emery cloth can be used once most of the deposits have been scraped away. Do not, under any circumstances, use a wire brush mounted in a drill motor to remove deposits from the pistons; the piston material is soft and will be eroded away by the wire brush.

8 Use a piston ring groove cleaning tool to remove any carbon deposits from the ring grooves. If a tool is not available, a piece broken off the old ring will do the job. Be very careful to remove only the carbon deposits. Do not remove any metal and do not nick or gouge the sides of the ring grooves.

9 Once the deposits have been removed, clean the pistons with solvent and dry them thoroughly. Make sure the oil return holes below the oil ring grooves are clear.

10 If the pistons are not damaged or worn excessively and if the cylinders are not rebored, new pistons will not be necessary. Normal piston wear appears as even, vertical wear on the thrust surfaces of the piston and slight looseness of the top ring in its groove. New piston rings, on the other hand, should always be used when an engine is rebuilt.

14.6 Remove the piston rings with a ring removal and installation tool

11 Carefully inspect each piston for cracks around the skirt, at the pin bosses and at the ring lands **(see illustration)**.

12 Look for scoring and scuffing on the thrust faces of the skirt, holes in the piston crown and burned areas at the edge of the crown. If the skirt is scored or scuffed, the engine may have been suffering from overheating and/or abnormal combustion, which caused excessively high operating temperatures. The oil pump and cooling system should be checked thoroughly. A hole in the piston crown, an extreme to be sure, is an indication that abnormal combustion (pre-ignition) was occurring. Burned areas at the edge of the piston crown are usually evidence of spark knock (detonation). If any of the above problems exist, the causes must be corrected or the damage will occur again.

13 Measure the piston ring-to-groove clearance by laying a new piston ring in the ring groove and slipping a feeler gauge in beside it **(see illustration)**. Check the clearance at three or four locations around the groove. Be sure to use the correct ring for each groove; they are different. If the clearance is greater than specified, new pistons will have to be used when the engine is reassembled.

14 Check the piston-to-bore clearance by measuring the bore (see Section 13) and the piston diameter. Make sure that the pistons and cylinders are correctly matched. Measure the piston across the skirt on the thrust faces at a 90° angle to the piston pin, about 13 mm (1/2-in) up from the bottom of the skirt **(see illustration)**.

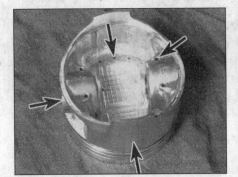

14.11 Check the piston pin bore and the piston skirt for wear, and make sure the internal holes are clear (arrowed)

14.13 Measure the piston ring-to-groove clearance with a feeler gauge

14.14a Measure the piston diameter with a micrometer

14.14b If you don't have a micrometer, piston clearance, out-of-round and cylinder taper can be measured with a piece of feeler gauge stock

14.15 Slip the pin into the piston and try to wiggle it back-and-forth; if it's loose, renew the piston and pin

15.3a Square the ring in the bore by turning the piston upside down and tapping on the ring . . .

Subtract the piston diameter from the bore diameter to obtain the clearance. If it is greater than specified, the cylinders will have to be rebored and new oversized pistons and rings installed. If the appropriate precision measuring tools are not available, the piston-to-cylinder clearances can be obtained, though not quite as accurately, using feeler gauge stock. Feeler gauge stock comes in 12-in lengths and various thicknesses and is generally available at auto parts stores. To check the clearance, select a 0.07 mm (0.002 in) feeler gauge and slip it into the cylinder along with the appropriate piston **(see illustration)**. The cylinder should be upside down and the piston must be positioned exactly as it normally would be. Place the feeler gauge between the piston and cylinder on one of the thrust faces (90° to the piston pin bore). The piston should slip through the cylinder (with the feeler gauge in place) with moderate pressure. If it falls through, or slides through easily, the clearance is excessive and a new piston will be required. If the piston binds at the lower end of the cylinder and is loose toward the top, the cylinder is tapered, and if tight spots are encountered as the feeler gauge is placed at different points around the cylinder, the cylinder is out-of-round. Repeat the procedure for the remaining piston and cylinder. Be sure to have the cylinders and pistons checked by a Kawasaki dealer or an engineer to confirm your findings before purchasing new parts.

15 Apply clean engine oil to the pin, insert it

into the piston and check for freeplay by rocking the pin back-and-forth **(see illustration)**. If the pin is loose, new pistons and pins must be installed.

16 Refer to Section 15 and install the rings on the pistons.

Installation

17 Install the pistons in their original locations with the arrows pointing to the front of the engine. Lubricate the pins and the rod bores with clean engine oil. Install new circlips in the piston grooves (don't reuse the old circlips). Push the pins into position from the opposite side and install new circlips. Compress the circlips only enough for them to fit in the piston. Make sure the clips are properly seated in their grooves.

15 Piston rings – installation

1 Before installing the new piston rings, the ring end gaps must be checked.

2 Lay out the pistons and the new ring sets so the rings will be matched with the same piston and cylinder during the end gap measurement procedure and engine assembly.

3 Insert the top (No. 1) ring into the bottom of the first cylinder and square it up with the cylinder walls by pushing it in with the top of

the piston **(see illustration)**. The ring should be about one inch above the bottom edge of the cylinder. To measure the end gap, slip a feeler gauge between the ends of the ring **(see illustration)** and compare the measurement to the Specifications.

4 If the gap is larger or smaller than specified, double check to make sure that you have the correct rings before proceeding.

5 If the gap is too small, it must be enlarged or the ring ends may come in contact with each other during engine operation, which can cause serious damage. The end gap can be increased by filing the ring ends very carefully with a fine file **(see illustration)**. When performing this operation, file only from the outside in.

6 Excess end gap is not critical unless it is greater than 1 mm (0.040 in). Again, double check to make sure you have the correct rings for your engine.

7 Repeat the procedure for each ring that will be installed in the first cylinder and for each ring in the remaining cylinder. Remember to keep the rings, pistons and cylinders matched up.

8 Once the ring end gaps have been checked/corrected, the rings can be installed on the pistons.

9 The oil control ring (lowest on the piston) is installed first. It is composed of three separate components. Slip the expander into the groove, then install the upper side rail **(see illustrations)**. Do not use a piston ring

15.3b . . . then check the piston ring end gap with a feeler gauge

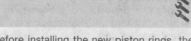
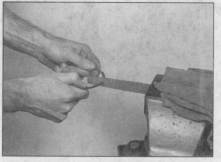

15.5 If the end gap is too small, clamp a file in a vice and file the ring ends (from the outside in only)

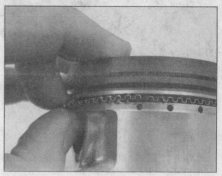

15.9a Installing the oil ring expander – make sure the ends don't overlap

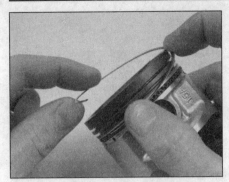

15.9b Installing an oil ring side rail – don't use a ring installation tool to do this

installation tool on the oil ring side rails as they may be damaged. Instead, place one end of the side rail into the groove between the spacer expander and the ring land. Hold it firmly in place and slide a finger around the piston while pushing the rail into the groove. Next, install the lower side rail in the same manner.

10 After the three oil ring components have

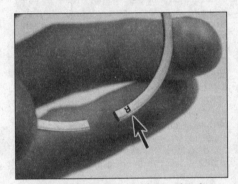

15.12 Make sure the marks on the rings (arrowed) face up when the rings are installed on the pistons

been installed, check to make sure that both the upper and lower side rails can be turned smoothly in the ring groove.

11 Install the no. 2 (middle) ring next. It can be readily distinguished from the top ring by its cross-section shape **(see illustration)**. Do not mix the top and middle rings.

12 To avoid breaking the ring, use a piston ring installation tool and make sure that the identification mark (N or R) is facing up **(see illustration)**. Fit the ring into the middle groove on the piston. Do not expand the ring any more than is necessary to slide it into place.

13 Finally, install the no. 1 (top) ring in the same manner. Make sure the identifying mark is facing up.

14 Repeat the procedure for the remaining

piston and rings. Be very careful not to confuse the no. 1 and no. 2 rings.

15 Once the rings have been properly installed, stagger the end gaps, including those of the oil ring side rails **(see illustrations)**.

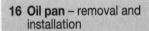

16 Oil pan – removal and installation

Note: *The oil pan can be removed with the engine in the frame.*

Removal

1 Set the bike on its centerstand.

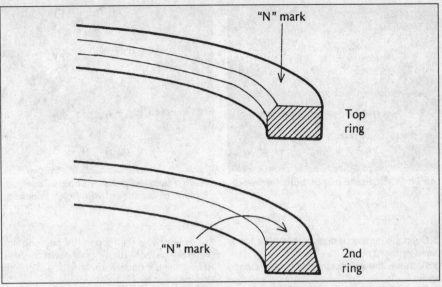

15.11 Don't confuse the top ring with the second (middle) compression ring

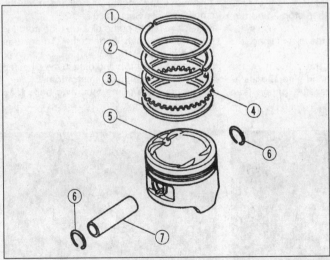

15.15a Piston and piston ring components

1 Top compression ring
2 Second compression ring
3 Oil ring side rails
4 Oil ring expander
5 Arrow mark
6 Circlip
7 Piston pin

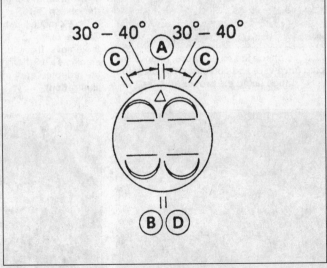

15.15b Piston ring end gap positions

A Top compression ring
B Second compression ring
C Oil ring side rails
D Oil ring expander

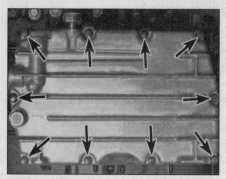

16.5a Remove the oil pan bolts (arrowed)

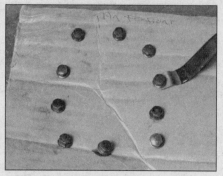

16.5b Place the bolts in a holder, such as a piece of cardboard with holes punched in it

16.7 Make sure the O-rings are in position (arrowed); the three O-rings to the left have a flat side, which goes upward (against the crankcase and away from the oil pan)

2 Drain the engine oil and remove the oil filter (see Chapter 1).
3 Remove the exhaust system (see Chapter 4).
4 Remove the small screw and disconnect the wire from the oil pressure switch (see Chapter 9).
5 Remove the oil pan bolts and detach the pan from the crankcase **(see illustrations)**.
6 Remove all traces of old gasket material from the mating surfaces of the oil pan and crankcase.

Installation

7 Check the small O-rings in the oil passages in the crankcase and the large O-ring around

17.3 To check the oil pressure, remove the plug (arrowed) and connect an oil pressure gauge using the proper adapter

the oil filter hole (in the pan) for cracking and general deterioration **(see illustration)**. Renew them if necessary. The flat side of the O-rings must face the crankcase.
8 Position a new gasket on the oil pan. A thin film of RTV sealant can be used to hold the gasket in place. Install the oil pan and bolts, tightening the bolts to the torque listed in this Chapter's Specifications, using a criss-cross pattern.
9 The remainder of installation is the reverse of removal. Install a new filter and fill the crankcase with oil (see Chapter 1), then run the engine and check that there are no leaks.

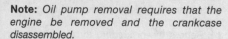

17 Oil pump – pressure check, removal, inspection and installation

Note: *Oil pump removal requires that the engine be removed and the crankcase disassembled.*

Oil pressure check

1 Warm up the engine, then stop it and turn the ignition OFF.
2 On EX models remove the lower fairing (see Chapter 8).
3 Remove the plug at the bottom of the crankcase on the right-hand side and install the adapter and oil pressure gauge **(see illustration)**.

 Warning: Be very careful to avoid scalding your hands on the hot oil or hot components.

4 Start the engine and watch the gauge while increasing engine speed to 4000 rpm. The pressure should stay within the relief valve opening pressure listed in this Chapter's Specifications. Only run the engine at this speed for sufficient time to read the gauge, then turn it OFF.
5 If the pressure is too high, the relief valve is stuck closed. To check it, see Section 18.
6 If the pressure is lower than the standard, either the relief valve is stuck open, the oil pump is faulty, or there is other engine damage. Begin diagnosis by checking the relief valve (see Section 18), then the oil pump. If those items check out okay, chances are the bearing oil clearances are excessive and the engine needs to be overhauled.

Removal

7 Remove the engine and disassemble the crankcase (see Sections 5 and 22).
8 Remove the oil pump pick-up tube from the pump so you can inspect the O-ring **(see illustration)**.
9 Remove the circlip and detach the oil pump gear from the shaft **(see illustration)**.
10 Remove the pump mounting bolts **(see illustration)**.

17.8 Unbolt the pickup from the pump so you can inspect the O-ring

17.9 Remove the circlip and the pump drive gear

17.10 Remove the pump mounting bolts

17.11 Lift out the pump and its oil pipe; if necessary, unbolt the pipe from the pump and remove them separately

11 Remove the pump and its oil pipe (**see illustration**).

Inspection

12 Remove the oil pump cover screws and lift off the cover (**see illustration**).

13 Remove the oil pump shaft, pin, inner rotor and outer rotor from the pump. Mark the rotors so they can be installed in the same relative positions.

14 Wash all the components in solvent, then dry them off. Check the pump body, the rotors and the cover for scoring and wear. Make sure the pick-up screen isn't clogged. Kawasaki doesn't publish clearance specifications, so the condition of the pump components can only be determined by visual examination. If the pump rotors are scored or chipped they should be renewed.

15 Reassemble the pump by reversing the disassembly steps, but before installing it, prime it by pouring oil into it while turning the shaft by hand – this will ensure that it begins to pump oil quickly.

Installation

16 Installation is the reverse of removal, with the following additions:

a) *Make sure the pick-up O-ring is in place.*

b) *Use non-permanent thread locking agent on the pick-up mounting screws and the oil pump mounting screws.*

c) *Install the drive gear with its recessed side away from the pump (**see illustration**).*

18 Oil pressure relief valve – removal, inspection and installation

Removal

1 Remove the oil pan (see Section 16).

2 Unscrew the relief valve from the oil pan (**see illustration**).

Inspection

3 Clean the valve with solvent and dry it, using compressed air if available.

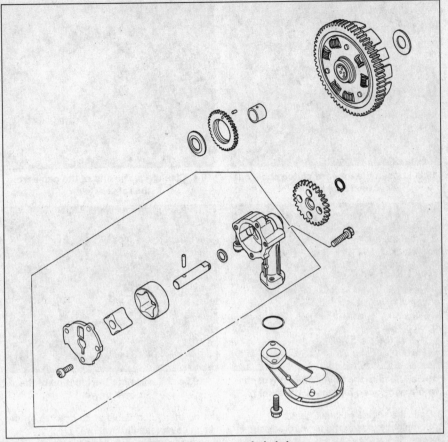

17.12 Oil pump – exploded view

4 Using a wood or plastic tool, depress the steel ball inside the valve and see if it moves smoothly. Make sure it returns to its seat completely. If it doesn't, renew it (don't attempt to disassemble and repair it).

Installation

5 Apply a non-permanent thread locking compound to the threads of the valve and install it into the oil pan, tightening it to the torque listed in this Chapter's Specifications.

6 The remainder of installation is the reverse of removal.

19 Clutch – removal, inspection and installation

Note: *The clutch (except the housing) can be removed with the engine in the frame. Removal of the housing requires that the engine be removed and the crankcase disassembled.*

Removal

1 Set the bike on its centerstand. On EX models, remove the lower fairing (see Chapter 8).

17.16 The recessed side of the drive gear faces away from the oil pump – the circlip fits into the recess

18.2 Location of the oil pressure relief valve (arrowed)

19.3 Loosen the forward clutch cable nut to create slack

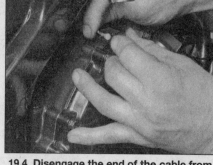

19.4 Disengage the end of the cable from the release lever

19.5a Remove the clutch cover bolts (arrowed) . . .

19.5b . . . take the cover off (tap it gently with a soft-faced hammer if it's stuck) . . .

19.5c . . . and note the location of the cover dowel

19.6a Loosen the spring bolts in a criss-cross pattern . . .

19.6b When spring tension is released, remove the springs and the spring plate

19.7 Remove the clutch pushrod from the hub, then remove the friction plates and metal plates

2 Drain the engine oil (see Chapter 1).
3 Completely loosen the forward adjustment nut on the clutch cable at its bracket on the clutch cover (see illustration).
4 Pull the cable out of the bracket, then detach the cable end from the lever (see illustration).
5 Remove the clutch cover bolts and take the cover off together with the release lever (see illustrations). If the cover is stuck, tap around its perimeter with a soft-faced hammer.
6 Loosen the clutch spring bolts in a criss-cross pattern (see illustration). To prevent the assembly from turning, thread one of the cover mounting bolts into the case and wedge a screwdriver between the bolt and the clutch housing. Remove the clutch springs, spring plate and bearing (see illustration).
7 Note the direction of the radial grooves in the friction plate, then remove the pushrod, friction plates and steel plates from the clutch housing (see illustration).
8 Remove the clutch hub nut, using either the special holding tool (Kawasaki tool no. 57001-305 or 1243) or a home-made equivalent (see Tool Tip) to prevent the clutch housing from

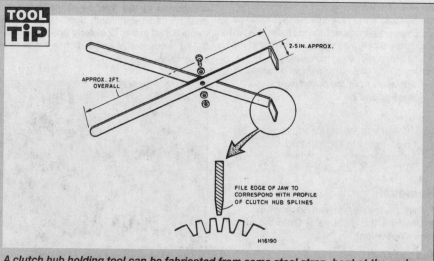

TOOL TiP

APPROX. 2FT. OVERALL

2·5 IN. APPROX.

FILE EDGE OF JAW TO CORRESPOND WITH PROFILE OF CLUTCH HUB SPLINES

H16190

A clutch hub holding tool can be fabricated from some steel strap, bent at the ends and bolted together in the middle.

19.9a Remove the nut and washer, then remove the clutch hub and thrust washer

turning. The nut is self-locking, so always renew it.

9 Remove the washer, clutch hub and thrust washer **(see illustrations)**.

Inspection

10 Examine the splines on both the inside and the outside of the clutch hub **(see illustration)**. If any wear is evident, renew the hub.

11 Measure the free length of the clutch springs **(see illustration)** and compare the results to this Chapter's Specifications. If the springs have sagged, or if cracks are noted, renew them as a set.

12 If the lining material of the friction plates smells burnt or if it is glazed, new parts are required. If the metal clutch plates are scored or discoloured, they must be renewed. Measure the thickness of each friction plate **(see illustration)** and compare the results to this Chapter's Specifications. If any friction plate is near the wear limit renew the whole set of friction plates.

13 Lay the metal and friction plates, one at a time, on a perfectly flat surface (such as a piece of plate glass) and check for warpage by trying to slip a 0.3 mm (0.012-in) feeler gauge between the flat surface and the plate

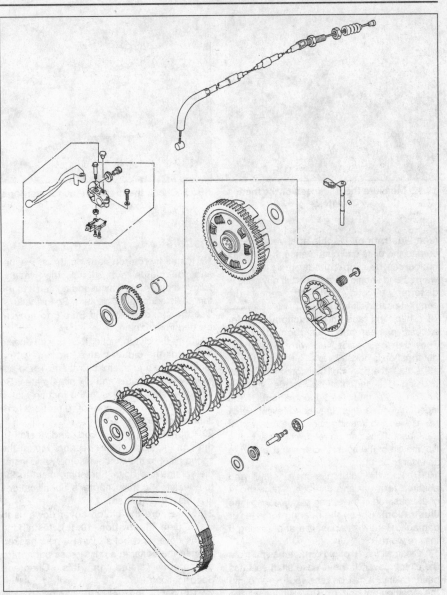

19.9b Exploded view of the clutch assembly

19.10 Check the clutch hub splines (arrowed) for wear and distortion

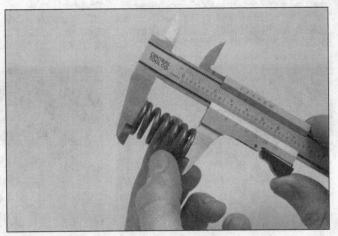

19.11 Measure the clutch spring free length

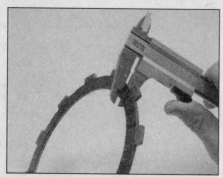

19.12 Measure the thickness of the friction plates

19.13 Check the metal plates for warpage

19.15 Check the slots on the clutch hub for indentations – if they're worn, the crankcase will have to be disassembled to remove the clutch hub

(see illustration). Do this at several places around the plate's circumference. If the feeler gauge can be slipped under the plate, it is warped and should be renewed. If any plate is distorted beyond the limit, renew the complete set of clutch plates.

14 Check the tabs on the friction plates for excessive wear and mushroomed edges. They can be cleaned up with a file if the deformation is not severe.

15 Check the edges of the slots in the clutch housing for indentations made by the friction plate tabs **(see illustration).** If the indentations are deep they can prevent clutch release, so the housing should be renewed. If the indentations can be removed easily with a file, the life of the housing can be prolonged to an extent.

16 Check the clutch spring plate and pushrod for wear and damage. Check the fit of the pushrod in the spring plate bearing **(see illustration).** Check the bearing for wear or damage. Renew the pushrod and bearing if they're worn.

17 Clean all traces of old gasket material from the clutch cover. If the release shaft seal has been leaking, it can be renewed by removing the positioning bolt on the outside of the housing and pulling out the shaft. The seal can then be pried out and a new one driven in, using a hammer and a socket with an outside diameter slightly smaller than that of the seal.

Installation

18 Install the clutch housing thrust washer and the clutch hub. Install the washer, followed by a new hub nut and tighten it to the torque listed in this Chapter's Specifications. Use the tool described in Step 8 to prevent the hub from turning.

19 Coat the clutch friction plates with engine oil. Install the clutch plates, starting with a friction plate and alternating them. There are seven friction plates and six steel plates. Be sure the radial grooves in the friction plates are pointed in the correct direction **(see illustration 19.7).**

20 Lubricate the pushrod and install it through the spring plate bearing. Mount the spring plate to the clutch assembly and install the springs and bolts, tightening them to the torque listed in this Chapter's Specifications in a criss-cross pattern.

21 Make sure the clutch cover dowel is in place **(see illustration 19.5c).** Install the clutch cover and bolts, using a new gasket. Tighten the bolts, in a criss-cross pattern, to the torque listed in this Chapter's Specifications.

22 Connect the clutch cable to the release lever and adjust the freeplay (see Chapter 1).

23 Fill the crankcase with the recommended type and amount of engine oil (see Chapter 1).

20 Clutch cable – replacement

1 Disconnect the upper end of the clutch cable from the lever (see Chapter 1).

2 Disconnect the clutch cable from the release lever (see Section 19).

3 Before removing the cable from the bike, tape the lower end of the new cable to the upper end of the old cable. Slowly pull the lower end of the old cable out, guiding the new cable down into position. Using this method will ensure the cable is routed correctly.

4 Lubricate the cable (see Chapter 1). Reconnect the ends of the cable by reversing the removal procedure, then adjust the cable following the procedure given in Chapter 1.

21 External gearchange mechanism – removal, inspection and installation

Gearchange lever and pedal – EX models

1 Set the bike on its centerstand.

2 Remove the gearchange pedal bolt **(see illustration).**

3 Remove the gearchange lever bolt **(see illustration).**

19.16 Check the pushrod and the bearing in the spring plate for wear and damage

21.2 Remove the gearchange pedal Allen bolt

21.3 Remove the pinch bolt from the bottom of the gearchange lever

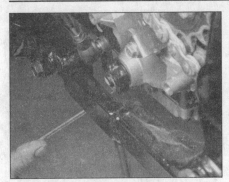

21.4 Remove the retaining clip from the gearchange lever shaft

21.5 Loosen the locknuts and turn the linkage rod to obtain a 90° angle at each end

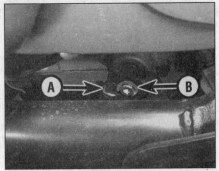

21.7 Remove the gearchange lever bolt (A) and the retaining clip (B)

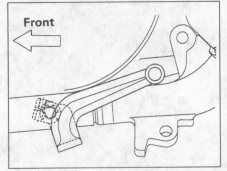

21.9 Correct fitted position of the gearchange lever – ER models

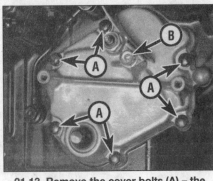

21.13 Remove the cover bolts (A) – the larger bolt (B) secures the bottom end of the chain inner guard

21.14 Compress the shift arm (A) to disengage it from the shift cam, and slide the shift shaft (B) out

4 To ease installation, make alignment marks on the gearchange lever shaft and the gearchange lever. Pry out the retaining clip and pull the lever off the shaft (see illustration).
5 Installation is the reverse of removal. The linkage shaft should be at 90° to the gearchange lever, as well as to the lever portion of the shift pedal. Adjust as needed with the nuts on the linkage shaft (see illustration).

Gearchange lever – ER models

6 Set the bike on its centerstand.
7 Remove the gearchange lever bolt (see illustration).
8 To ease installation, make alignment marks on the gearchange lever shaft and the gearchange lever. Pry out the retaining clip and pull the lever off the shaft.
9 Installation is the reverse of removal. Use the marks made on removal to install the lever at the correct angle (see illustration).

Gearchange mechanism – all models

10 Remove the gearchange lever as described above.
11 Remove the engine sprocket and the drive chain inner guard (see Chapter 6).
12 Disconnect the electrical connector from the neutral switch (see Chapter 9).
13 Remove the gearchange mechanism cover bolts and remove the cover (see illustration).

14 Compress the gearchange mechanism arm against the spring tension to disengage it from the selector drum cam (see illustration). Slide the shift mechanism out of the crankcase.
15 Remove the nut from the gear positioning lever (see illustration). Remove the locating washer, lever, spring and washer (see illustration).

Inspection

16 Check the gearchange shaft for bends and damage to the splines. If the shaft is bent, you can attempt to straighten it, but if the splines are damaged it will have to be renewed.
17 Check the condition of the gear positioning lever and spring, pin plate and

selector drum cam. Renew them if they are cracked or distorted.
18 Check the gearchange mechanism arm for cracks, distortion and wear. If any of these conditions are found, renew the gearchange mechanism. Make sure the return spring pin isn't loose. If it is, unscrew it, apply a non-permanent locking compound to the threads, then reinstall the pin and tighten it securely.
19 Check the condition of the seal in the cover. If it has been leaking, drive it out with a

21.15a Remove the nut (A) and detach the washer, gear positioning lever, spring and washer. Note return spring pin (B)

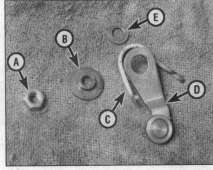

21.15b Details of the gear positioning lever

A Nut
B Washer (the collar fits inside the gear positioning lever hole)
C Spring
D Gear positioning lever
E Washer

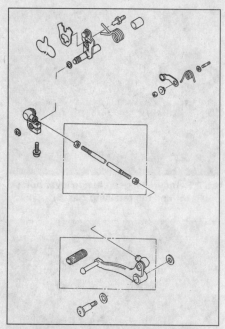

21.21 Gearchange mechanism
EX model gearchange lever shown

hammer and punch. Drive a new seal in with a socket.

Installation

20 Make sure the selector drum is in the neutral position, then assemble the gear positioning lever components and engage the lever's roller with the selector drum neutral detent. Tighten the gear positioning lever nut securely.

21 Slide the gearchange mechanism into place, compressing the arm against the spring to clear the selector drum. Make sure the springs are positioned correctly **(see illustration)**.

22 Apply high-temperature grease to the lip of the seal. Wrap the splines of the gearchange shaft with electrical tape, so the splines won't damage the seal as the cover is installed.

23 Carefully guide the cover into place and install the screws, tightening them securely. Remove the tape from the shaft splines.

24 Install the engine sprocket, chain inner guard and sprocket cover (see Chapter 6).

25 Install the gearchange lever (see above).

26 Check the engine oil level and add some, if necessary (see *Daily (pre-ride) checks*).

22 Crankcase – disassembly and reassembly

1 To examine and repair or renew the crankshaft, connecting rods, bearings, clutch housing, transmission components, balancer and starter motor clutch, the crankcase must be split into two parts.

2 Remove the clutch cover (see Section 19)

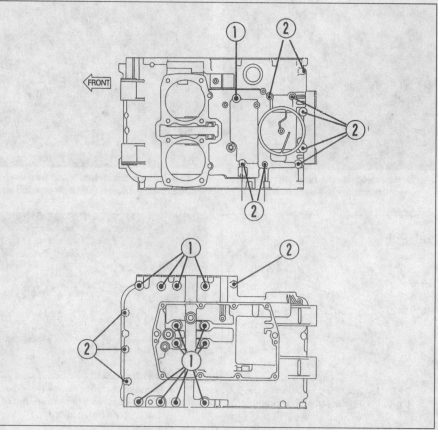

22.6a Loosen the small upper case bolts first, then the large bolt . . .

1 Large bolts (8 mm)   *2 Small bolts (6 mm)*

and the external gearchange mechanism (see Section 21).

3 Remove the water pump and coolant pipe (on the cylinder block) (see Chapter 3).

4 Remove the alternator cover (see Chapter 9).

Disassembly

5 If the crankcase is being separated to remove the crankshaft, remove the alternator rotor and the stator (see Chapter 9), cylinder head, cylinder block and pistons (see Sections 10, 13 and 14). Remove the clutch if

you are separating the crankcase halves to disassemble the transmission main drive shaft (see Section 19).

6 Remove the small upper crankcase half bolts, then the single large bolt **(see illustrations)**.

7 Turn the engine upside-down and remove the oil filter (see Chapter 1, if necessary).

8 Remove the oil pan (see Section 16) and retrieve the O-rings from the oil passages.

9 Remove the oil pump outer pipe and main oil pipe connecting pipe **(see illustrations)**.

22.6b . . . and place them in order in a holder (a piece of cardboard with holes punched in it works well)

22.9a Remove the mounting bolt and lift out the outer oil pipe

22.9b Remove the main oil pipe connecting bolt on the side of the case (arrowed) . . .

22.9c . . . and one in the oil pan (upper arrow), then disconnect the oil pipe from the engine (lower arrow)

22.10 The tightening sequence numbers for the large lower case bolts are cast into the case (arrowed)

10 Remove the small lower crankcase half bolts, then the large bolts (**see illustration 22.6a and the accompanying illustration**).

11 Carefully separate the crankcase halves. Pry ONLY in the areas indicated (**see illustrations**).

12 Separate the crankcase halves (**see illustration**).

13 Refer to Sections 23 through 31 for information on the internal components of the crankcase.

Reassembly

14 Remove all traces of sealant from the crankcase mating surfaces. Be careful not to let any fall into the case as this is done.

15 Check to make sure the two dowel pins are in place in their holes in the mating surface of the upper crankcase half (**see illustrations**). Pour some engine oil over the transmission gears, the crankshaft main bearings and the selector drum. Don't get any oil on the crankcase mating surface.

16 Apply a thin, even bead of Kawasaki Bond sealant (part no. 56019-120) to the indicated areas of the crankcase mating surfaces (**see illustration**).

Caution: Don't apply an excessive amount of sealant, and don't apply it next to the bearing inserts, as it will ooze out when the case halves are assembled and may obstruct oil passages and prevent the bearings from seating.

22.11a Pry only at the pry points; there's one on the end of the case (arrowed) . . .

22.11b . . . one on the clutch side (arrowed) . . .

22.11c . . . and one on the alternator side (arrowed)

22.12 Lift the lower case half off the upper case half

22.15a Note the location of the case dowels (arrowed) . . .

22.15b . . . there's one in each end of the case (arrowed)

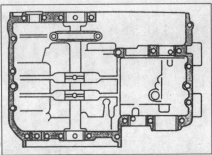

22.16 Spread a thin layer of gasket sealant on the mating surfaces, but don't place it too close to the crankshaft and balancer shaft bearing shells

22.17a When the selector drum is in neutral, the gear positioning lever fits into the slot in the selector cam (arrowed)

22.17b The selector forks should be in the Neutral position . . .

22.17c . . . and so should the fork slots in the gears (arrowed)

17 Check the position of the selector drum, selector forks and transmission shafts – make sure they're in the neutral position (**see illustrations**).

18 Carefully assemble the crankcase halves. While doing this, make sure the selector forks fit into their gear grooves, and guide the breather tube into its hole in the lower crankcase half (**see illustration**).

19 Install the lower crankcase half bolts and tighten them so they are just snug.

20 In two steps, tighten the larger bolts (8 mm), in the indicated sequence, to the torque listed in this Chapter's Specifications (**see illustration**).

21 Install the smaller (6 mm) bolts in the

22.18 Be sure both ends of the breather tube fit into their holes when the cases are assembled (transmission output shaft removed for clarity)

lower crankcase half (**see illustration 22.6a**), tightening them to the torque listed in this Chapter's Specifications.

22 Install the main oil connecting pipe (**see illustration 22.9b**). Use new O-rings coated lightly with engine oil.

23 Apply engine oil to both ends of the oil pump outer pipe, then install the ends in their holes (**see illustration 22.9a**). Apply non-permanent thread locking compound to the bolt that secures the outer pipe.

24 Install the oil pan (see Section 16).

25 Turn the case over and install the upper

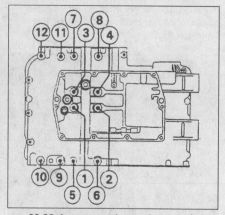

22.20 Lower crankcase 8 mm bolt tightening sequence

Sequence should also be cast in the crankcase (see illustration 22.10)

crankcase half bolts. Tighten the large (8 mm bolt) first, then tighten the others evenly to the torque listed in this Chapter's Specifications (**see illustration 22.6a**).

26 Turn the main drive shaft and the output shaft to make sure they turn freely. Also make sure the crankshaft turns freely.

27 The remainder of installation is the reverse of removal, with the following additions:

a) *Once the external gearchange mechanism is installed, move the transmission through all the gear positions and back to Neutral. Because the positive neutral finder locks out second gear when the output shaft isn't spinning, you'll have to spin the output shaft to change into second through sixth gears.*

b) *Be sure to refill the engine oil and coolant after assembly.*

23 Crankcase components – inspection and servicing

1 After the crankcases have been separated and the crankshaft, selector drum and forks and transmission components removed, the crankcases should be cleaned thoroughly with new solvent and dried with compressed air.

2 Remove any oil pipes that haven't already been removed. All oil passages and pipes should be blown out with compressed air (**see illustrations**).

23.2a Remove the oil line from the left front corner of the case . . .

23.2b . . . the line farther back along the left side . . .

23.2c . . . and the oil passage plug so all the lines and passages can be cleaned

23.3 The breather body is secured by the centre bolt (arrowed)

23.4 Small burrs can be removed from the gasket surfaces with a fine sharpening stone

23.5 Check both primary chain guides for wear (the lower one is shown here) and renew them if necessary

3 Remove the breather body **(see illustration)**. Inspect its O-ring; it's a good idea to install a new one.
4 All traces of old gasket sealant should be removed from the mating surfaces. Minor damage to the surfaces can be cleaned up with a fine sharpening stone **(see illustration)**. *Caution: Be very careful not to nick or gouge the crankcase mating surfaces or leaks will result. Check both crankcase sections very carefully for cracks and other damage.*

 HAYNES HiNT *Refer to Tools and Workshop Tips in the Reference section for gasket compound removal details.*

5 Check the primary chain guides for wear – one is in the upper case half and the other is in the lower case half **(see illustration)**. If they appear to be worn excessively, renew them.
6 Check the cam chain tensioner blade for wear. If it's worn, remove the lock-pin **(see illustration)**. The retaining pin **(see illustration)** and tensioner blade can be removed after the crankshaft has been removed (see Section 25).
7 If any damage is found that can't be repaired, renew the crankcase halves as a set.

24 Main and connecting rod bearings – general note

1 Even though main and connecting rod bearings are generally renewed during the engine overhaul, the old bearings should be retained for close examination as they may reveal valuable information about the condition of the engine.
2 Bearing failure occurs mainly because of lack of lubrication, the presence of dirt or other foreign particles, overloading the engine and/or corrosion. Regardless of the cause of bearing failure, it must be corrected before the engine is reassembled to prevent it from happening again.
3 When examining the bearings, remove the

23.6a Remove this lock-pin if you plan to remove the cam chain tensioner blade . . .

23.6b . . . after removing the crankshaft, pull out the retaining pin and remove the blade

main bearings from the case halves and the rod bearings from the connecting rods and caps and lay them out on a clean surface in the same general position as their location on the crankshaft journals. This will enable you to match any noted bearing problems with the corresponding side of the crankshaft journal.
4 Dirt and other foreign particles get into the engine in a variety of ways. It may be left in the engine during assembly or it may pass through filters or breathers. It may get into the oil and from there into the bearings. Metal chips from machining operations and normal engine wear are often present. Abrasives are sometimes left in engine components after reconditioning operations such as cylinder honing, especially when parts are not thoroughly cleaned using the proper cleaning methods. Whatever the source, these foreign objects often end up imbedded in the soft bearing material and are easily recognised. Large particles will not imbed in the bearing and will score or gouge the bearing and journal. The best prevention for this cause of bearing failure is to clean all parts thoroughly and keep everything spotlessly clean during engine reassembly. Frequent and regular oil and filter changes are also recommended.
5 Lack of lubrication or lubrication breakdown has a number of interrelated causes. Excessive heat (which thins the oil), overloading (which squeezes the oil from the bearing face) and oil leakage or throw off

(from excessive bearing clearances, worn oil pump or high engine speeds) all contribute to lubrication breakdown. Blocked oil passages will also starve a bearing and destroy it. When lack of lubrication is the cause of bearing failure, the bearing material is wiped or extruded from the steel backing of the bearing. Temperatures may increase to the point where the steel backing and the journal turn blue from overheating.
6 Riding habits can have a definite effect on bearing life. Full throttle low speed operation, or lugging (labouring) the engine, puts very high loads on bearings, which tend to squeeze out the oil film. These loads cause the bearings to flex, which produces fine cracks in the bearing face (fatigue failure). Eventually the bearing material will loosen in pieces and tear away from the steel backing. Short trip riding leads to corrosion of bearings, as insufficient engine heat is produced to drive off the condensed water and corrosive gases produced. These products collect in the engine oil, forming acid and sludge. As the oil is carried to the engine bearings, the acid attacks and corrodes the bearing material.
7 Incorrect bearing installation during engine assembly will lead to bearing failure as well. Tight fitting bearings which leave insufficient bearing oil clearances result in oil starvation. Dirt or foreign particles trapped behind a bearing insert result in high spots on the bearing which lead to failure.

25.2 Slip the clutch housing back-and-forth to expose the inner bearing sleeve (arrowed), then pull it out

25.3a Lift the clutch housing and transmission main drive shaft . . .

25.3b . . . and disengage the housing from the primary chain

8 To avoid bearing problems, clean all parts thoroughly before reassembly, double check all bearing clearance measurements and lubricate the new bearings with engine assembly lube or moly-based grease during installation.

---

25 Clutch housing and crankshaft – removal, inspection and installation

Clutch housing removal

1 If you haven't already done so, remove all clutch components from the housing (see Section 19).
2 Slide the clutch housing back and forth on the shaft within the limits allowed by the primary chain to expose the inner bearing **(see illustration)**. Pull the bearing out.
3 Lift the transmission main drive shaft and clutch housing from the case **(see illustration)**. Slip the transmission shaft out of the clutch housing and disengage the housing from the primary chain **(see illustration)**.

Crankshaft removal

4 If the cylinder head, block and pistons have not been removed, refer to Section 26 and remove the connecting rod caps.
5 Before removing the crankshaft check the

25.5 Measure the endplay with a feeler gauge inserted between the no. 2 crank journal and the case web – if the endplay isn't as listed in this Chapter's Specifications, the case halves must be renewed

endplay. This can be done with a dial gauge mounted in-line with the crankshaft, or feeler gauges inserted between the crankshaft and no. 2 crankcase main journal **(see illustration)**. Compare your findings with this Chapter's Specifications. If the endplay is excessive, the case halves must be renewed.
6 If the balancer shaft is still in place, turn the crankshaft and balancer shaft so that their alignment marks are facing each other and level with the crankcase mating surface **(see**

25.6 The crankshaft, primary chain and cam chain

illustration 27.2). Lift the crankshaft out, together with the cam chain and primary chain and set them on a clean surface **(see illustration)**.
7 The main bearing inserts can be removed from their saddles by pushing their centres to the side, then lifting them out **(see illustration)**. Keep the bearing inserts in order. The main bearing oil clearance should be checked, however, before removing the inserts (see Step 13).

Inspection

8 Check the clutch housing bearing for wear or damage **(see illustration)**. Renew the

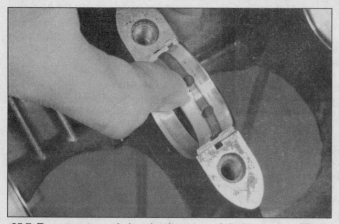

25.7 To remove a main bearing insert, push it sideways and lift it out

25.8 Inspect the bearing in the centre of the clutch housing – renew the clutch housing if it's worn or damaged

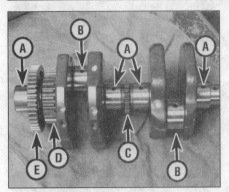

25.10 Inspect the crankshaft at the following points:

A *Main bearing journals*
B *Connecting rod journals*
C *Cam chain gear*
D *Primary chain gear*
E *Balancer gear*

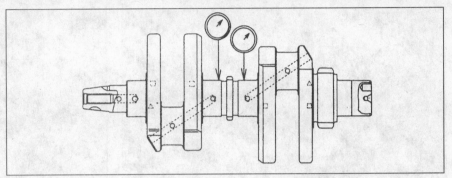

25.12 Crankshaft runout check points

clutch housing if necessary. Also inspect the slots in the housing (see Section 19).

9 If you haven't already done so, mark and remove the connecting rods from the crankshaft (see Section 26).

10 Clean the crankshaft with solvent, using a rifle-cleaning brush to scrub out the oil passages. If available, blow the crank dry with compressed air. Check the main and connecting rod journals for uneven wear, scoring and pits **(see illustration)**.

11 Check the balancer gear, cam chain gear and primary chain gear on the crankshaft for chipped teeth and other wear. If any undesirable conditions are found, renew the crankshaft. Check the chains as described in Section 28. Check the rest of the crankshaft for cracks and other damage. It should be magnafluxed to reveal hidden cracks – a Kawasaki dealer or motorcycle engineer will handle the procedure.

12 Set the crankshaft on V-blocks and check the runout with a dial gauge touching one of the centre main journals, comparing your findings with this Chapter's Specifications **(see illustration)**. Repeat the runout check against the other centre main journal. If the runout exceeds the limit, renew the crankshaft.

Main bearing selection

13 To check the main bearing oil clearance, clean off the bearing inserts (and reinstall them, if they've been removed from the case) and lower the crankshaft into the upper half of the case. Cut four pieces of Plastigauge (type HPG-1) and lay them on the crankshaft main journals, parallel with the journal axis **(see illustration)**.

14 Very carefully, guide the lower case half down onto the upper case half. Install the large (8 mm) bolts and tighten them, using the recommended sequence **(see illustration 22.20)**, to the torque listed in this Chapter's Specifications. Don't rotate the crankshaft!

15 Now, remove the bolts and carefully lift the lower case half off. Compare the width of the crushed Plastigauge on each journal to the scale printed on the Plastigauge envelope to obtain the main bearing oil clearance **(see illustration)**. Write down your findings, then remove all traces of Plastigauge from the journals, using your fingernail or the edge of a credit card.

16 If the oil clearance falls into the specified range, no bearing renewal is required (provided they are in good shape). If the clearance is more than the standard range, but within the service limit, renew the bearing inserts with inserts that have blue paint marks **(see illustration)**, then check the oil clearance once again (these are the thickest bearing

inserts, and may be thick enough to bring bearing clearance within the specified range). Always renew all of the inserts at the same time.

17 The clearance might be slightly greater than the standard clearance, but that doesn't matter, as long as it isn't greater than the maximum clearance or less than the minimum clearance.

18 If the clearance is greater than the service limit listed in this Chapter's Specifications, measure the diameter of the crankshaft journals with a micrometer **(see illustration)** and compare your findings with this Chapter's Specifications. Also, by measuring the diameter at a number of points around each journal's circumference, you'll be able to

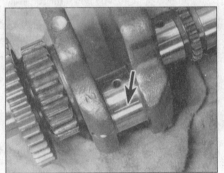

25.13 Lay the Plastigauge strips (arrowed) on the journals, parallel to the crankshaft centreline

25.15 Measuring the width of the crushed Plastigauge (be sure to use the correct scale – standard and metric are included)

25.16 Bearing thicknesses are identified by colour codes on the sides of the bearings

25.18 Measure the diameter of each crankshaft journal at several points to detect taper and out-of-round conditions

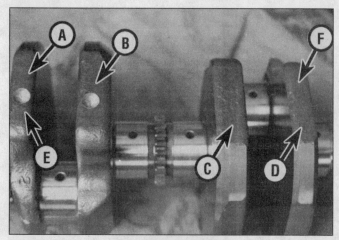

25.20 Use the marks (or absence of marks) on the crankshaft (this crankshaft has no marks) . . .

A   No. 1 main bearing journal mark
B   No. 2 main bearing journal mark
C   No. 3 main bearing journal mark
D   No. 4 main bearing journal mark
E   No. 1 connecting rod journal mark
F   No. 2 connecting rod journal mark

25.21 . . . in conjunction with the marks (or absence of marks) on the case (this case has no marks) . . .

A   No. 1 main bearing bore mark
B   No. 2 main bearing bore mark
C   No. 3 main bearing bore mark
D   No. 4 main bearing bore mark

determine whether or not the journal is out-of-round. Take the measurement at each end of the journal, near the crank throws, to determine if the journal is tapered.

19 If any crank journal has worn down past the service limit, renew the crankshaft.

20 If the diameters of the journals aren't less than the service limit but differ from the original markings on the crankshaft **(see illustration)**, apply new marks with a hammer and punch.

If the journal measures within the 'no mark' range listed in the Specifications, don't make any marks on the crank (there shouldn't be any marks there, anyway).

If the journal measures within the '1' mark range listed in the Specifications, make a '1' mark on the crank in the area indicated *(if it's not already there).*

21 Remove the main bearing inserts and assemble the case halves (see Section 22). Using a telescoping gauge and a micrometer, measure the diameters of the main bearing bores, then compare the measurements with the marks on the upper case half **(see illustration)**. Compare the bore measurements with those listed in this Chapter's Specifications. Also compare the bore measurements to the marks on crankcase to find out whether the marks are accurate.

22 Using the marks on the crank and the marks on the case, determine the bearing sizes required by referring to the accompanying bearing selection chart **(see illustration)**.

Installation

23 Separate the case halves once again. Clean the bearing saddles in the case halves, then install the bearing inserts in their webs in the case **(see illustration)**. The centre two bearing inserts have oil grooves. When installing the bearings, use your hands only – don't tap them into place with a hammer.

24 Lubricate the bearing inserts with engine assembly lube or moly-based grease.

25 You can install the connecting rods on the crankshaft at this point if the top end was removed from the engine (see Section 26).

26 Loop the camshaft chain and the primary chain over the crankshaft and lay them onto their gears.

27 Check to make sure the cam chain guide retaining pin and lock-pin are in position. If the connecting rods are in the engine, place

Crankshaft Main Bearing Insert Selection

Crankcase Main Bearing Bore Diameter Mark	Crankshaft Main Journal Diameter Mark	Bearing Insert*		
		Size Color	Part Number	Journal Nos.
O	1	Brown	92028-1102	2, 3
			92028-1274	1, 4
None	None	Blue	92028-1100	2, 3
			92028-1272	1, 4
O	None	Black	92028-1101	2, 3
None	1		92028-1273	1, 4

*The bearing inserts for Nos. 2 and 3 journals have oil grooves.

25.22 . . . to determine the proper main bearing sizes

25.23 Make sure the tabs in the bearing inserts (arrowed) fit into the notches in the web

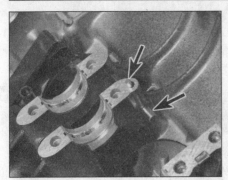

25.27 Before you install the crankshaft, check to be sure the cam chain guide retainer pin (lower arrow) is pushed all the way in and its lock-pin (upper arrow) is in place

25.30a The pin in the oil pump drive gear must engage the notch in the clutch housing (arrowed) . . .

25.30b . . . and the bevelled side of the clutch housing thrust washer must face toward the ball bearing on the transmission shaft

pieces of hose over the studs to protect the crankshaft **(see illustration)**.

28 Before installing the crankshaft, check that the balancer shaft gear alignment mark is level with the crankcase surface and facing the crankshaft location. Carefully lower the crankshaft into place so that the alignment mark on its balancer shaft drive gear meshes with the corresponding mark on the balancer shaft gear **(see illustration 27.2)**. If the connecting rods are in the engine, guide them onto the crankshaft journals.

29 Assemble the case halves (see Section 22) and check to make sure the crankshaft and the transmission shafts turn freely.

30 Install the oil pump drive gear and clutch housing. The pin in the gear must engage the notch in the housing **(see illustration)**. The bevelled side of the clutch housing thrust washer faces the ball bearing on the transmission main drive shaft **(see illustration)**.

26 Connecting rods and bearings
– removal, inspection, bearing selection and installation

Removal

1 Before removing the connecting rods from the crankshaft, measure the side clearance of

each rod with a feeler gauge **(see illustration)**. If the clearance on any rod is greater than that listed in this Chapter's Specifications, that rod will have to be renewed with a new one.

2 Using a centre punch, mark the position of each rod and cap, relative to its position on the crankshaft **(see illustration)**. The letter mark across the rod and cap indicates the connecting rod weight grade

3 Unscrew the bearing cap nuts, separate the cap from the rod, then detach the rod from the crankshaft **(see illustrations)**. If the cap is

26.1 Slip a feeler gauge blade between the connecting rod and crankshaft throw (arrowed) to check connecting rod side clearance

stuck, tap on the ends of the rod bolts with a soft-faced hammer to free them.

4 Separate the bearing inserts from the rods and caps, keeping them in order so they can be reinstalled in their original locations. Wash the parts in solvent and dry them with compressed air, if available.

Inspection

5 Check the connecting rods for cracks and other obvious damage. Lubricate the piston pin for each rod, install it in the proper rod and check for play **(see illustration)**. If it is loose,

26.2 Make number marks (arrowed) on the connecting rod and cap so they can be reassembled in their original positions, and note the relationship of the connecting rod to the crankshaft

26.3a Remove the connecting rod nuts (arrowed) . . .

26.3b . . . and take the cap off the studs

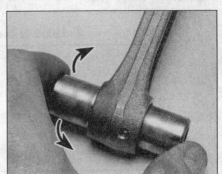

26.5 Checking the piston pin and connecting rod bore for wear

renew the connecting rod and/or the pin.

6 Refer to Section 24 and examine the connecting rod bearing inserts. If they are scored, badly scuffed or appear to have been seized, new bearings must be installed. Always renew the bearings in the connecting rods as a set. If they are badly damaged, check the corresponding crankshaft journal. Evidence of extreme heat, such as discoloration, indicates that lubrication failure has occurred. Be sure to thoroughly check the oil pump and pressure relief valve as well as all oil holes and passages before reassembling the engine.

7 If you are in doubt about the straightness of the connecting rods, have them checked for twisting and bending by a Kawasaki dealer or motorcycle engineer.

Bearing selection

8 If the bearings and journals appear to be in good condition, check the oil clearances as follows:

9 Start with the rod for the number one cylinder. Wipe the bearing inserts and the connecting rod and cap clean, using a lint-free cloth.

10 Install the bearing inserts in the connecting rod and cap. Make sure the tab on the bearing engages with the notch in the rod or cap.

11 Wipe off the connecting rod journal with a lint-free cloth. Lay a strip of Plastigauge (type HPG-1) across the top of the journal, parallel with the journal axis **(see illustration 25.13)**.

12 Position the connecting rod on the bottom of the journal, then install the rod cap and nuts. Tighten the nuts to the torque listed in this Chapter's Specifications, but don't allow the connecting rod to rotate at all.

13 Unscrew the nuts and remove the connecting rod and cap from the journal, being very careful not to disturb the Plastigauge. Compare the width of the crushed Plastigauge to the scale printed in the Plastigauge envelope **(see illustration 25.15)** to determine the bearing oil clearance.

14 If the clearance is within the range listed in this Chapter's Specifications and the bearings are in perfect condition, they can be reused. If the clearance is beyond the standard range, but within the service limit, renew the bearing inserts with inserts that have blue paint marks, then check the oil clearance once again (these are the thickest bearing inserts, and may be thick enough to bring bearing clearance with the specified range). Always renew all of the inserts at the same time.

15 The clearance might be slightly greater than the standard clearance, but that doesn't matter, as long as it isn't greater than the maximum clearance or less than the minimum clearance.

16 If the clearance is greater than the service limit listed in this Chapter's Specifications, measure the diameter of the connecting rod journal with a micrometer and compare your findings with this Chapter's Specifications. Also, by measuring the diameter at a number of points around the journal's circumference,

you'll be able to determine whether or not the journal is out-of-round. Take the measurement at each end of the journal to determine if the journal is tapered.

17 If any journal has worn down past the service limit, renew the crankshaft.

18 If the diameter of the journal isn't less than the service limit but differs from the original markings on the crankshaft **(see illustration 25.20)**, apply new marks with a hammer and punch.

If the journal measures within the 'no mark' range listed in this Chapter's Specifications, don't make any marks on the crank (there shouldn't be one there anyway).

If the journal measures within the 'O' mark range listed in this Chapter's Specifications, make a 'O' mark on the crank in the area indicated (if not already there).

19 Remove the bearing inserts from the connecting rod and cap, then assemble the cap to the rod. Tighten the nuts to the torque listed in this Chapter's Specifications.

20 Using a telescoping gauge and a micrometer, measure the inside diameter of the connecting rod **(see illustration)**. The mark on the connecting rod (if any) should coincide with the measurement, but if it doesn't, make a new mark **(see illustration)**.

If the inside diameter measures within the 'no mark' range listed in this Chapter's Specifications, don't make any mark on the rod (there shouldn't be one there anyway).

If the inside diameter measures within the 'O' mark range, make a 'O' mark on the rod (it should already be there).

21 By referring to the accompanying chart **(see illustration)**, select the correct connecting rod bearing inserts.

22 Repeat the bearing selection procedure for the remaining connecting rod.

Installation

23 Wipe off the bearing inserts, connecting rods and caps. Install the inserts into the rods and caps, using your hands only, making sure the tabs on the inserts engage with the notches in the rods and caps. When all the inserts are installed, lubricate them with engine assembly lube or moly-based grease. Don't get any lubricant on the mating surfaces of the rod or cap.

24 Assemble each connecting rod to its proper journal, making sure the previously applied matchmarks correspond to each other. Also, the letter present at the rod/cap seam on one side of the connecting rod is a weight mark. If new rods are being installed, they should both have the same letter on them to minimise vibration.

25 When you're sure the rods are positioned correctly, tighten the nuts to the torque listed in this Chapter's Specifications.

26 Turn the rods on the crankshaft. If either rod feels tight, tap on the bottom of the connecting rod cap with a hammer – this should relieve stress and free them up. If it doesn't, recheck the bearing clearance.

26.20a Assemble the connecting rod and measure the diameter of the bore with a telescoping gauge – then measure the gauge with a micrometer

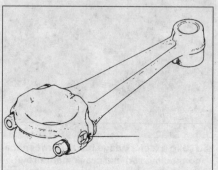

26.20b There's a letter that indicates weight grade on each connecting rod; a 'O' or the absence of an 'O' around the letter . . .

Connecting Rod Big End Bearing Insert Selection

Con-rod Big End Bore Diameter Mark	Crankpin Diameter Mark	Bearing Insert	
		Size Color	Part Number
O	O	Black	92028-1349
None	None	Black	92028-1349
O	None	Blue	92028-1348
None	O	Brown	92028-1350

26.21 . . . can be used, in conjunction with this chart, to determine the correct bearing inserts to install

27.2 Correct alignment of the marks on the balancer gear and crankshaft gear is essential to prevent severe engine vibration

27 As a final step, recheck the connecting rod side clearances (see Step 1). If the clearances aren't correct, find out why before proceeding with engine assembly.

27 Balancer shaft – removal, inspection, bearing selection and installation

Removal

1 Split the crankcases (see Section 22).
2 If you're only planning to remove the balancer (not the crankshaft), turn the crankshaft until the marks on the balancer and crankshaft gears are aligned (see illustration).
3 Lift the balancer shaft and gear out of the crankcase.

Inspection

4 Check the shaft and gear for wear and damage. Make sure the springs inside the gear are not broken. Renew the balancer shaft if you find any undesirable conditions.
5 Check the bearings for wear and for damage such as grooves, nicks or small bits of foreign material stuck in their surfaces (see illustrations). Renew them if they aren't in perfect condition.

27.13 There's a journal diameter mark (or no mark, as on this balancer) on each balancer weight; there's also a size mark for each bearing bore on the case ...

A   Left bearing bore size mark
B   Right bearing bore size mark

27.5a The balancer bearing inserts near the external oil line have oil grooves ...

Bearing selection

6 To check the balancer bearing oil clearance, clean off the bearing inserts (and reinstall them, if they've been removed from the case) and lower the balancer shaft into the upper half of the case. Cut two pieces of Plastigauge (type HPG-1) and lay them on the balancer journals, parallel with the journal axis.
7 Very carefully, guide the lower case half down onto the upper case half. Install the large (8 mm) bolts and tighten them, using the recommended sequence (see illustration 22.20), to the torque listed in this Chapter's Specifications. Don't rotate the balancer!
8 Now, remove the bolts and carefully lift the lower case half off. Compare the width of the crushed Plastigauge on each journal to the scale printed on the Plastigauge envelope to obtain the balancer bearing oil clearance. Write down your findings, then remove all traces of Plastigauge from the journals, using your fingernail or the edge of a credit card.
9 If the oil clearance falls into the specified range, no bearing renewal is required (provided they are in good shape). If the clearance is more than the standard range, but within the service limit, renew the bearing inserts with inserts that have blue paint marks (see illustration 27.15), then check the oil clearance once again (these are the thickest bearing inserts, and may be thick enough to bring bearing clearance within the specified range). Always renew all of the inserts at the same time.
10 The clearance might be slightly greater than the standard clearance, but that doesn't matter, as long as it isn't greater than the maximum clearance or less than the minimum clearance.
11 If the clearance is greater than the service limit listed in this Chapter's Specifications, measure the diameter of the balancer journals

27.5b ... while the inserts at the opposite end of the balancer are smooth

with a micrometer and compare your findings with this Chapter's Specifications. Also, by measuring the diameter at a number of points around each journal's circumference, you'll be able to determine whether or not the journal is out-of-round. Take the measurement at each end of the journal to determine if the journal is tapered.
12 If either balancer journal has worn down past the service limit, renew the balancer shaft.
13 If the diameters of the journals aren't less than the service limit but differ from the original markings on the balancer shaft (see illustration), apply new marks with a hammer and punch.
If the journal measures within the 'no mark' range listed in the Specifications, don't make any marks on the balancer (there shouldn't be any marks there, anyway).
If the journal measures within the 'O' mark range listed in the Specifications, make a 'O' mark on the balancer in the area indicated (if it's not already there).
14 Remove the balancer bearing inserts and assemble the case halves (see Section 22). Using a telescoping gauge and a micrometer, measure the diameters of the balancer bearing bores, then compare the measurements with the marks on the upper case half (see illustration 27.13). Compare the bore measurements with those listed in this Chapter's Specifications. Also compare the bore measurements to the marks on the crankcase to find out whether the marks are accurate.
15 Using the marks on the crank and the marks on the case, determine the bearing sizes required by referring to the accompanying bearing selection chart (see illustration).

Crankcase Bearing Inside Diameter Marking	Balancer Shaft Journal Diameter Marking	Bearing Insert		
		Size Color	Part Number	
			L. H.	R. H.
◯	◯	Brown	92028-1497	92028-1692
None	None	Blue	92028-1495	92028-1690
◯	None	Black	92028-1496	92028-1691
None	◯			

27.15 ... use them in conjunction with this table to select the correct bearing size

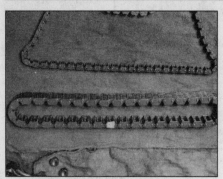

28.9a Check the cam chain (top) and primary chain (bottom) for wear and damage

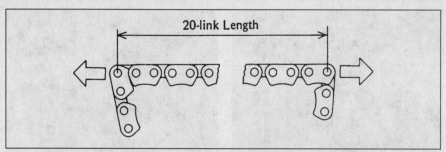

28.9b Measure the length of 20 links (21 pins) to check for chain stretch

Installation

16 Separate the case halves once again. Clean the bearing saddles in the case halves, then install the bearing inserts in their webs in the case **(see illustrations 27.5a and 27.5b)**. The bearing insert next to the oil line has an oil groove. When installing the bearings, use your hands only – don't tap them into place with a hammer.

17 Lubricate the bearing inserts with engine assembly lube or moly-based grease.

18 Carefully lay the balancer in the bearings. Be sure the ' – ' mark on the balancer gear aligns with the 'O' mark on the crankshaft gear **(see illustration 27.2)**. Incorrect alignment will cause severe engine vibration.

19 The remainder of installation is the reverse of the removal steps.

28 Primary chain, cam chain and guides – removal, inspection and installation

Removal

Primary chain and cam chain

1 Remove the engine (see Section 5).
2 Separate the crankcase halves (see Section 22).
3 Remove the crankshaft (see Section 25).
4 Remove the chains from the crankshaft.

Chain guides

5 The cam chain rear guide can be lifted from the cylinder block after the head has been removed (see Section 13).
6 The cam chain tensioner blade is fastened to the crankcase with a retaining pin and lock-pin **(see illustrations 23.6a and b)**. Pull out the lock-pin and push the retaining pin out, then lift out the blade.
7 The primary chain guide in the lower case half is secured by a bolt **(see illustration 23.5)**.
8 The primary chain guide in the upper case half is secured by two bolts.

Inspection

Primary chain and cam chain

9 The primary chain and camshaft chains are checked in a similar manner. Pull the chain tight to eliminate all slack and measure the length of twenty links, pin-to-pin **(see illustrations)**. Compare your findings to this Chapter's Specifications.
10 Also check the chains for binding and obvious damage.
11 If the twenty-link length is not as specified, or there is visible damage, renew the chain.

Chain guides

12 Check the guides for deep grooves, cracking and other obvious damage, renewing them if necessary.

Installation

13 Installation of these components is the reverse of the removal procedure. When installing the primary chain guides, apply a non-hardening thread locking compound to the threads of the bolts. Tighten the bolts to the torque listed in this Chapter's Specifications. Apply engine oil to the faces of the guides and to the chains.

29 Transmission shafts – removal and installation

Removal

1 Remove the engine and clutch, then separate the crankcase halves (see Sections 5, 19 and 22).
2 If you suspect that the gearbox is worn you can measure the backlash present between each set of gears; a maximum backlash figure is given for EX models in the Specifications at the beginning of this Chapter. To measure backlash, mount a dial gauge with the plunger of the indicator touching a tooth on one of the gears, then move the gear back and forth within its freeplay, holding its companion gear stationary. Check each set of gears, recording the measurements, and compare the results to this Chapter's Specifications. If the backlash between any pair of gears exceeds the limit, renew both gears (see Section 30).
3 The output shaft can simply be lifted out of the upper half of the case **(see illustration)**. The main drive shaft **(see illustration)** is removed together with the clutch housing (see Section 25). If they are stuck, use a soft-faced

29.3a The output shaft (arrowed) can simply be lifted out . . .

29.3b . . . the main drive shaft is removed together with the clutch housing

29.5 At each end of the shafts there's a set pin for the small bearing and a set ring for the large bearing

29.6a The hole in the small bearing (arrowed) . . .

29.6b . . . must fit over the set pin (lower arrow) – the groove in the large bearing must fit over the set ring (upper arrow) . . .

29.6c . . . if the bearings are correctly installed, they will fit into their saddles with no gap between the bearing and case

hammer and gently tap on the bearings on the ends of the shafts to free them.

4 Refer to Section 30 for information pertaining to transmission shaft service and Section 31 for information pertaining to the selector drum and forks.

Installation

5 Check to make sure the set pins and rings are present in the upper case half, where the shaft bearings seat (see illustration).

6 Carefully lower each shaft into place. The holes in the needle bearing outer races must engage with the set pins, and the grooves in the ball bearing outer races must engage with the set rings (see illustrations).

7 The remainder of installation is the reverse of removal.

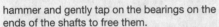

30 Transmission shafts – disassembly, inspection and reassembly

Note: When disassembling the transmission shafts, place the parts on a long rod or thread a wire through them to keep them in order and facing the proper direction.

1 Remove the shafts from the case (see Section 29).

Main drive shaft

Disassembly

2 All of the main drive shaft parts slide off the shaft except first gear, which is integral with

the shaft, and the ball bearing, which is a press fit (see illustration).

3 Each freewheeling gear is secured with a toothed washer and circlip. Use circlip pliers to remove the circlips.

Caution: There are two sizes of circlip, with only a small difference between them. Be sure to keep the snap rings in their original locations and to renew them with ones of the same size.

4 To disassemble the main drive shaft, refer to the accompanying sequence (see illustrations).

Inspection

5 Wash all of the components in clean solvent and dry them off. Rotate the ball bearing on the shaft, feeling for tightness,

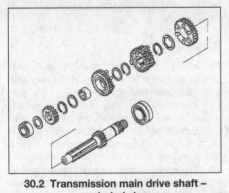

30.2 Transmission main drive shaft – exploded view

30.4a Remove the bearing plug . . .

30.4b . . . the outer bearing, inner bearing and spacer (arrowed) . . .

30.4c . . . slide off second gear . . .

30.4d . . . remove the circlip and toothed washer, then slide off sixth gear . . .

30.4e . . . slide off the sixth gear bushing and toothed washer . . .

30.4f . . . then remove the circlip . . .

30.4g . . . slide the third-fourth gear cluster off the shaft . . .

30.4h . . . remove the circlip and toothed washer . . .

30.4i . . . slide off fifth gear . . .

30.4j . . . and the fifth gear bushing (if equipped)

30.8 If the gear dogs and dog holes (arrowed) show signs of excessive wear, renew the gears as a set

rough spots and excessive looseness and listening for noises. If any of these conditions are found renew the bearing. This will require the use of an hydraulic press or a bearing puller setup. If you don't have access to these tools, take the shaft and bearing to a Kawasaki dealer and have them press the old bearing off the shaft and install the new one.

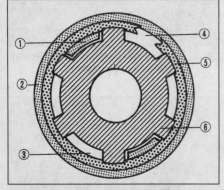

30.10 The teeth of the toothed washers should not be aligned with the gap in the circlip; the gap in the circlip should be centred within a shaft groove

1 Teeth of toothed washer
2 Toothed washer
3 Shaft groove
4 Gap in circlip
5 Circlip
6 Shaft

6 Measure the selector fork groove between third and fourth gears. If the groove width exceeds the figure listed in this Chapter's Specifications, renew the third/fourth gear assembly, and also check the third/fourth gear selector fork (see Section 31).

7 Check the gear teeth for cracking and other obvious damage. Check the sixth gear bushing and the surface in the inner diameter of sixth gear (and the fifth gear bushing, if equipped) for scoring or heat discoloration. If the gear or bushing is damaged, renew it.

8 Inspect the dogs and the dog holes in the gears for excessive wear (see illustration). Renew the paired gears as a set if necessary.

30.11a If the main drive shaft fifth gear has a separate bushing, install it so its oil hole lines up with the hole in the shaft

9 Check the needle bearing and outer race for wear or heat discoloration and renew them if necessary.

Reassembly

10 During reassembly, always use new circlips and align the opening of the ring with a spline groove (see illustration).

11 To reassemble the main drive shaft, refer to the accompanying illustrations. Lubricate the components with engine oil before assembling them (see illustrations).

12 Check the assembled main drive shaft to make sure all parts are installed correctly (see illustration).

30.11b Install fifth gear with its dogs facing away from first gear; install a toothed washer and secure it with a circlip

30.11c Install the third-fourth gear cluster with third gear (the smaller gear) toward fifth gear

30.11d Install a circlip in the next shaft groove . . .

30.11e . . . and place a toothed washer against it

30.11f . . . Align the oil hole in the sixth gear bushing with the oil hole in the shaft, then slide the bushing down against the toothed washer

30.11g Install sixth gear with its flat side away from fourth gear and place a toothed washer next to it . . .

30.11h . . . then secure the gear and washer with a circlip

30.11i Install second gear . . .

30.11j . . . its spacer . . .

30.11k . . . the bearing . . .

30.11l . . . the bearing outer race . . .

30.11m . . . and the plug

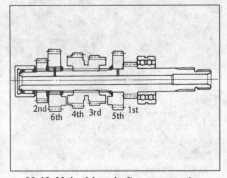

30.12 Main drive shaft components – assembled view

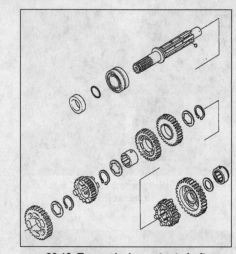

30.13 Transmission output shaft

30.15a Pull off the bearing outer race . . .

30.15b . . . the bearing and spacer (arrowed)

Output shaft

Disassembly

13 All of the output shaft parts slide off the shaft except the ball bearing, which is a press fit **(see illustration)**.

14 Each freewheeling gear is secured with a toothed washer and circlip. Use circlip pliers to remove the circlips.

15 To disassemble the output shaft, refer to the accompanying sequence **(see illustrations)**. Fifth gear is secured to the shaft by three steel balls, installed in channels

30.15c Slide first gear off the shaft

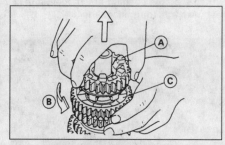

30.15d The next gear on the output shaft is fifth gear . . .

in the gear, which must be spun outward by centrifugal force. To do this, spin the shaft

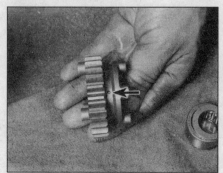

30.15e . . . it contains three steel balls (arrowed) . . .

30.15f . . . which locate in these slots (arrowed)

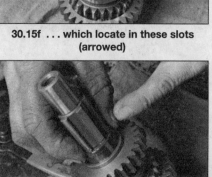

30.15g Removing the 5th gear from the output shaft

Position the output shaft shaft vertically with the 5th gear (A) uppermost. Spin the output shaft (B) whilst holding 3rd gear (C) and pulling up on the 5th gear (A)

30.15h Remove the circlip and toothed washer, then slide third gear off the shaft . . .

30.15i . . . this will expose the bushing shared by third and fourth gears . . .

30.15j . . . slide off the bushing and fourth gear

30.15k Remove the toothed washer, then the circlip . . .

30.15l . . . and slide sixth gear off the shaft

30.15m Remove the circlip . . .

30.15n . . . and the toothed washer . . .

30.15o . . . and slide second gear off the shaft

30.15p Pull the oil seal off the bearing collar

with one hand, and at the same time, lift the gear with the other hand. This may take several tries.

Inspection

16 Refer to Steps 5 through 9 for the inspection procedures. They are the same, except that when checking the selector fork groove width you'll be checking it on fifth gear and sixth gear.

Reassembly

17 Reassembly is basically the reverse of the disassembly procedure (see illustrations), but take note of the following points:

a) *Always use new circlips and align the opening of the ring with a spline groove (see illustration 30.10).*

30.15q If the bearing is worn or damaged, place it in a bearing splitter, press it off the shaft and press a new one on (or have the job done by a motorcycle dealer)

30.17a Stand the shaft on its ball bearing end . . .

30.17b . . . and install second gear (flat side toward bearing), then secure it with a toothed washer and circlip

30.17c Install sixth gear with its fork groove away from second gear

30.17d Install a circlip in the groove farthest down the shaft . . .

30.17e . . . place a toothed washer next to it . . .

30.17f . . . install fourth gear . . .

30.17g . . . and its bushing (align BOTH oil holes in the bushing with those in the shaft)

30.17h Install third gear . . .

30.17i . . . install a toothed washer next to it . . .

30.17j . . . and secure them with a circlip; the slots in the shaft (arrowed) . . .

30.17k . . . must align with the balls in fifth gear (arrowed) when it's installed

30.17l Install first gear and its spacer . . .

30.17m . . . the bearing . . .

30.17n . . . and the bearing outer race – the assembled output shaft should look like this . . .

30.17o . . . don't forget the seal on the other end of the shaft

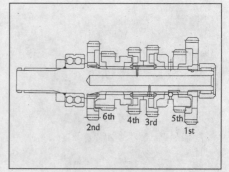

30.17p Output shaft details

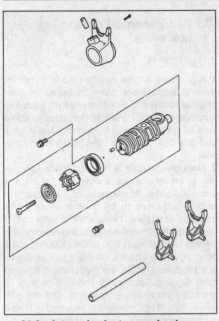

31.2a Internal selector mechanism –
exploded view

b) When installing the bushing for third and
fourth gear, align the oil hole in the
bushing with the hole in the shaft.
c) When installing fifth gear, don't use
grease to hold the balls in place – to do
so would impair the positive neutral finder
mechanism. Just set the balls in their
holes (the holes that they can't pass

31.3 Remove the selector drum bearing
retainer bolts (arrowed)

31.5a . . . and slide the selector drum out
of the fork and case

31.2b Note the positions of the selector
forks on the shaft, then slide out the shaft
and remove the forks

through), keep the gear in a vertical
position and carefully set it on the shaft
(engine oil will help keep them in place).
The spline grooves that contain the holes
with the balls must be aligned with the
slots in the shaft spline grooves.
d) Lubricate the components with engine oil
before assembling them.

31 Selector drum and forks –
removal, inspection and
installation

Removal

1 Remove the engine and separate the
crankcase halves (see Sections 5 and 22).

31.4 Remove the cotter pin (split pin) and
guide pin (arrowed) . . .

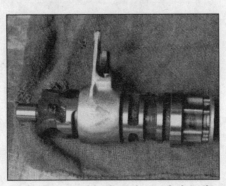

31.5b Reassemble the selector fork to the
drum

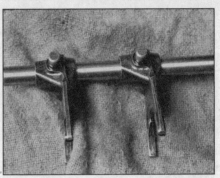

31.2c It's a good idea to reassemble the
forks to the shaft temporarily so you don't
forget how they go

2 Support the selector forks and pull the
selector rod out (see illustrations).
3 Remove the selector drum bearing retaining
bolts (see illustration).
4 Remove the cotter pin (split pin) and pull
out the guide pin (see illustration).
5 Pull the selector drum out of the case far
enough to remove the third/fourth selector
fork (see illustration), then slide the selector
drum out of the case (see illustration).

Inspection

6 Check the edges of the grooves in the drum
for signs of excessive wear. Measure the
widths of the grooves and compare your
findings to this Chapter's Specifications.
Check the holder and bearing on the end of
the selector drum for wear and damage. If
undesirable conditions are found, remove the
holder screw and renew the holder and
bearing.
7 Check the selector forks for distortion and
wear, especially at the fork ears. Measure the
thickness of the fork ears and compare your
findings with this Chapter's Specifications
(see illustration). If they are discoloured or
severely worn they are probably bent. If
damage or wear is evident, check the selector
fork groove in the corresponding gear as well.
Inspect the guide pins and the shaft bore for
excessive wear and distortion and renew any
defective parts.
8 Check the selector fork shafts for evidence
of wear, galling and other damage. Make sure

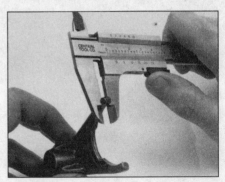

31.7 Measure the thickness of the selector
fork ears

the selector forks move smoothly on the shafts. If the shafts are worn or bent renew them.

Installation

9 Installation is the reverse of removal, noting the following points:
 a) Install the selector drum part-way into the case and install the third/fourth selector fork (the long end goes onto the drum first).
 b) Be sure to use a new cotter pin (split pin) and install it correctly (see illustration 31.4).
 c) Lubricate all parts with engine oil before installing them.
 d) Apply a non-permanent locking agent to the threads of the bearing retainer bolts and tighten them securely.

32 Initial start-up after overhaul

1 Make sure the engine oil level and coolant level are correct (see Daily (pre-ride) checks).
2 Remove the fuel tank (see Chapter 4). Pull the plug caps off the spark plugs and insert a spare spark plug into each cap. Position the spare plugs so that their bodies are earthed (grounded) against the engine – this is important to prevent damage to the ignition system.
3 Turn the ignition switch ON and the engine stop switch to the RUN position. Crank the engine over with the starter until the oil pressure warning light goes off (which indicates that oil pressure exists). Turn the ignition OFF. Remove the spare spark plugs and reconnect the plug caps.
4 Install the fuel tank (see Chapter 4) and turn the fuel tap to ON or RES, as appropriate.
5 Operate the choke, then start the engine and allow it to run at a moderately fast idle until it reaches operating temperature. Stop the engine.

 Warning: If the oil pressure warning light doesn't go off, or it comes on while the engine is running, stop the engine immediately.

6 Check carefully that there are no oil or coolant leaks and make sure the transmission and controls, especially the brakes, function properly before road testing the machine. Refer to Section 33 for the recommended running-in procedure.
7 Upon completion of the road test, and after the engine has cooled down completely, recheck the valve clearances (see Chapter 1) and check the engine oil and coolant levels (see Daily (pre-ride) checks).

33 Recommended running-in procedure

1 Any rebuilt engine needs time to break-in, even if parts have been installed in their original locations. For this reason, treat the machine gently for the first few miles to make sure oil has circulated throughout the engine and any new parts installed have started to seat.
2 Even greater care is necessary if the engine has been rebored or a new crankshaft has been installed. In the case of a rebore, the engine will have to be broken in as if the machine were new. This means greater use of the transmission and a restraining hand on the throttle until at least 500 miles (800 km) have been covered. There's no point in keeping to any set speed limit – the main idea is to keep from lugging (labouring) the engine and to gradually increase performance until the 500 mile (800 km) mark is reached. These recommendations can be lessened to an extent when only a new crankshaft is installed. Experience is the best guide, since it's easy to tell when an engine is running freely.
3 If a lubrication failure is suspected, stop the engine immediately and try to find the cause. If an engine is run without oil, even for a short period of time, severe damage will occur.

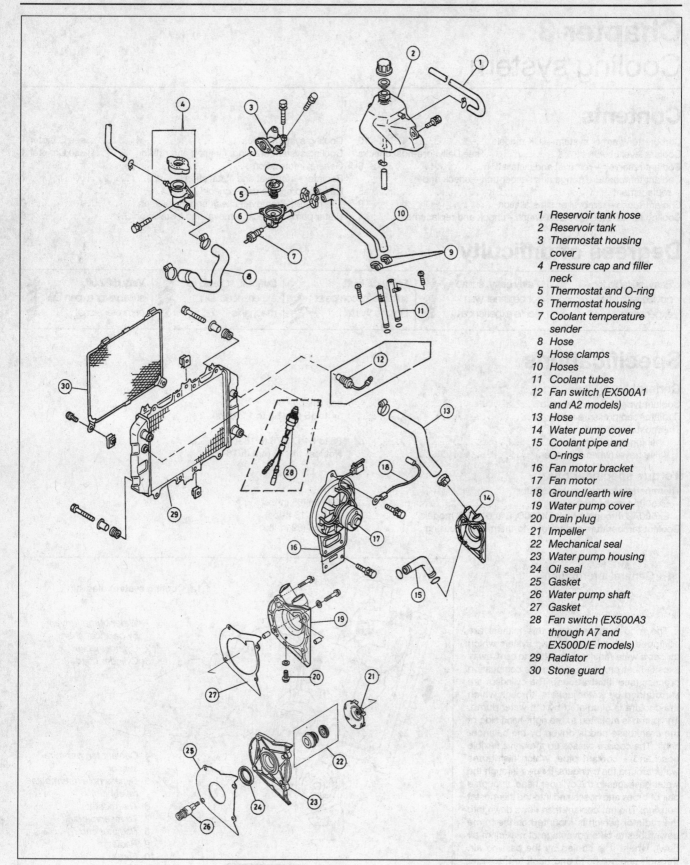

1 Reservoir tank hose
2 Reservoir tank
3 Thermostat housing
   cover
4 Pressure cap and filler
   neck
5 Thermostat and O-ring
6 Thermostat housing
7 Coolant temperature
   sender
8 Hose
9 Hose clamps
10 Hoses
11 Coolant tubes
12 Fan switch (EX500A1
   and A2 models)
13 Hose
14 Water pump cover
15 Coolant pipe and
   O-rings
16 Fan motor bracket
17 Fan motor
18 Ground/earth wire
19 Water pump cover
20 Drain plug
21 Impeller
22 Mechanical seal
23 Water pump housing
24 Oil seal
25 Gasket
26 Water pump shaft
27 Gasket
28 Fan switch (EX500A3
   through A7 and
   EX500D/E models)
29 Radiator
30 Stone guard

1.1b Exploded view of cooling system – EX models

Chapter 3
Cooling system

Contents

Degrees of difficulty

Easy, suitable for novice with little experience	Fairly easy, suitable for beginner with some experience	Fairly difficult, suitable for competent DIY mechanic	Difficult, suitable for experienced DIY mechanic	Very difficult, suitable for expert DIY or professional

Specifications

General
Coolant type and mixture ratio	see Chapter 1
Radiator cap pressure rating	14 to 18 psi (1.0 to 1.2 Bars)
Thermostat rating	
Opening temperature	80 to 84°C (176 to 183°F)
Valve travel (when fully open)	Not less than 8 mm (5/16-in)

Torque specifications
Thermostatic fan switch-to-radiator	
EX500A1 and A2 models	7.4 Nm (65 in-lbs)
EX500A3 through A7, all EX500D, E and all ER models	18 Nm (13 ft-lbs)
Coolant temperature sender unit-to-thermostat housing	7.8 Nm (69 in-lbs)

1 General information

The models covered by this manual are equipped with a liquid cooling system which utilises a water/antifreeze mixture to carry away excess heat produced during the combustion process **(see illustrations)**. The cylinders are surrounded by water jackets, through which the coolant is circulated by the water pump. The pump is mounted to the right-hand side of the crankcase and is driven by the balancer shaft. The coolant passes up through a flexible hose and a coolant pipe, which distributes water around the cylinders. It flows through the water passages in the cylinder head, through a pair of tubes and hoses and into the thermostat housing. The hot coolant then flows down into the radiator (which is mounted on the frame downtubes to take advantage of maximum air flow), where it is cooled by the passing air, through another hose and back to the water pump, where the cycle is repeated.

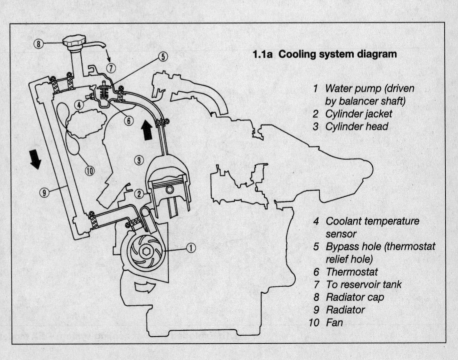

1.1a Cooling system diagram

1 Water pump (driven by balancer shaft)
2 Cylinder jacket
3 Cylinder head
4 Coolant temperature sensor
5 Bypass hole (thermostat relief hole)
6 Thermostat
7 To reservoir tank
8 Radiator cap
9 Radiator
10 Fan

1 Reservoir tank
2 Radiator pressure cap
3 Filler neck
4 Radiator top hose
5 Thermostat cover
6 O-rings
7 Thermostat
8 Thermostat housing
9 Temperature sender unit
10 Coolant tubes
11 O-rings
12 Radiator covers
13 Radiator
14 Stone guard
15 Fan switch
16 Fan motor
17 Radiator bottom hose
18 Water pump cover
19 Coolant pipe and O-rings
20 Drain plug
21 Gaskets
22 Impeller
23 Mechanical seal
24 Water pump housing
25 Oil seal
26 Water pump shaft

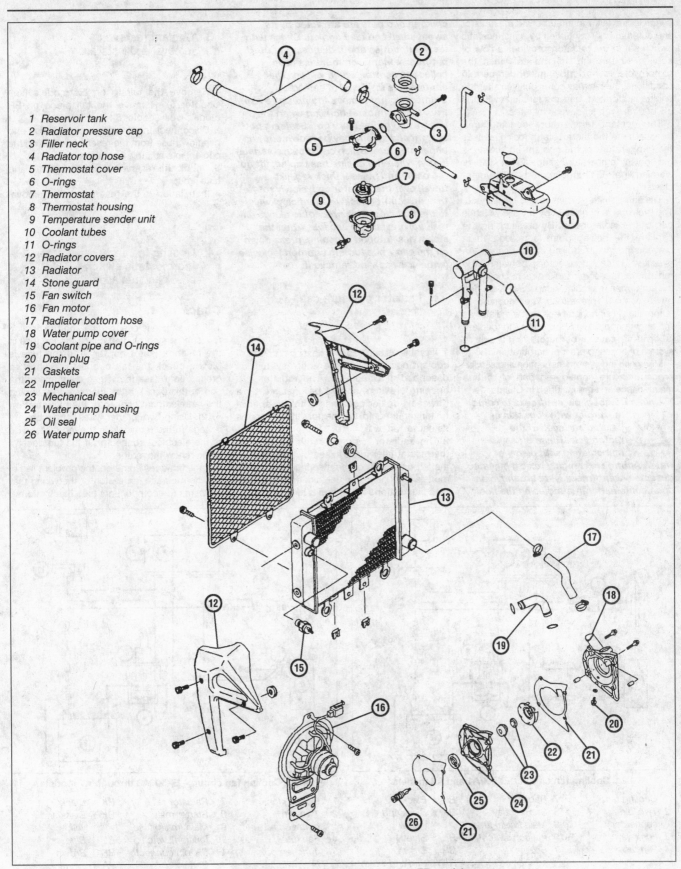

1.1c Exploded view of cooling system – ER models

An electric fan, mounted behind the radiator and automatically controlled by a thermostatic switch set in the radiator, provides a flow of cooling air through the radiator when the motorcycle is not moving. Under certain conditions, the fan may come on even after the engine is stopped, and the ignition switch is off, and may run for several minutes.

The coolant temperature sending unit, threaded into the thermostat housing, senses the temperature of the coolant and controls the coolant temperature gauge (EX models) or warning light (ER models) on the instrument cluster.

The entire system is sealed and pressurised. The pressure is controlled by a valve which is part of the radiator cap. By pressurising the coolant, the boiling point is raised, which prevents premature boiling of the coolant. An overflow hose, connected between the radiator and reservoir tank, directs coolant to the tank when the radiator valve is opened by excessive pressure. The coolant is automatically siphoned back to the radiator as the engine cools. On UK models, hot coolant is diverted to the carburettors through a system of hoses to prevent carburettor icing.

Many cooling system inspection and service procedures are considered part of routine maintenance and are included in Chapter 1.

⚠ **Warning:** *Do not allow antifreeze to come in contact with your skin or painted surfaces of the motorcycle. Rinse off spills immediately with plenty of water. Antifreeze is highly toxic if ingested. Never leave antifreeze lying around in an open container or in puddles on the floor;*

children and pets are attracted by its sweet smell and may drink it. Check with local authorities about disposing of used antifreeze. Many communities have collection centres which will see that antifreeze is disposed of safely.
Caution: Do not remove the pressure cap from the thermostat housing when the engine and radiator are hot. Scalding hot coolant and steam may be blown out under pressure, which could cause serious injury. When the engine has cooled, lift up the panel and place a thick rag, like a towel, over the radiator cap; slowly rotate the cap counterclockwise (anticlockwise) to the first stop. This procedure allows any residual pressure to escape. When the steam has stopped escaping, press down on the cap while turning counterclockwise (anticlockwise) and remove it.

2 Radiator pressure cap – check

1 If problems such as overheating and loss of coolant occur, check the entire system as described in Chapter 1. The radiator cap opening pressure should be checked by a Kawasaki dealer equipped with the special tester required to do the job. If the cap is defective, renew it.
2 The radiator cap is combined in the thermostat/filler neck assembly, located on the left-hand side of the steering head on EX models and under the fuel tank on ER models **(see illustrations 24.7a and b in Chapter 1)**.

3 Coolant reservoir – removal and installation

1 Remove the fairing on EX models (see Chapter 8). Remove the tail piece on ER models (see Chapter 8).
2 Disconnect the coolant breather hose and overflow hose from the reservoir, catching the coolant in a suitable container.
3 Unbolt the reservoir from the bracket and take it out.
4 Installation is the reverse of the removal steps.

4 Cooling fan and thermostatic switch – check and replacement

Check

1 If the engine is overheating and the cooling fan isn't coming on, first check the fan fuse in the fusebox (see Chapter 9). If the fuse is blown, check the fan circuit for a short to ground/earth (see the Wiring diagrams at the end of this book). If the fuse is good, unplug the fan electrical connector **(see illustration 4.12)**. Using two jumper wires, apply battery voltage to the terminals in the fan motor side of the electrical connector. If the fan doesn't work, renew the motor.
2 If the fan does come on, the problem lies in the thermostatic fan switch or the wiring that connects the components **(see illustrations)**.

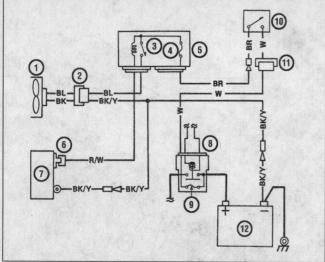

4.2a Cooling fan circuit – EX500A1 and A2 models

1 *Cooling fan*	7 *Radiator*	BK	*Black*
2 *Two-pin connector*	8 *Starter relay*	BK/Y	*Black and yellow*
3 *Fan relay*	9 *Main (main) fuse*		
4 *Fan fuse*	10 *Ignition switch*	BL	*Blue*
5 *Junction box*	11 *Six-pin connector*	BR	*Brown*
6 *Fan switch*	12 *Battery*	R/W	*Red and white*
		W	*White*

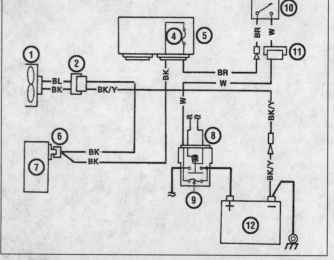

4.2b Cooling fan circuit – EX500A3 through A7 models

1 *Cooling fan*	7 *Radiator*	BK	*Black*
2 *Two-pin connector*	8 *Starter relay*	BK/Y	*Black and yellow*
4 *Fan fuse*	9 *Main (main) fuse*		
5 *Junction box*	10 *Ignition switch*	BL	*Blue*
6 *Fan switch*	11 *Six-pin connector*	BR	*Brown*
	12 *Battery*	W	*White*

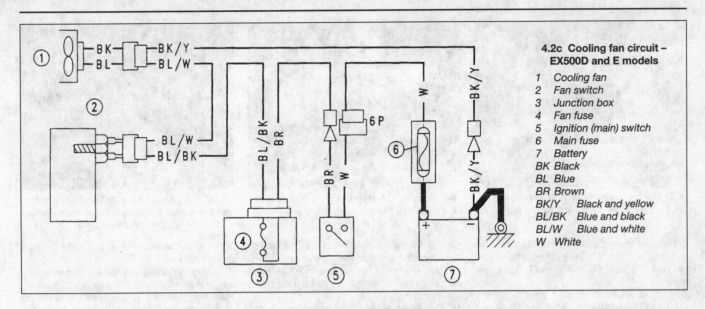

4.2c Cooling fan circuit – EX500D and E models

1 Cooling fan
2 Fan switch
3 Junction box
4 Fan fuse
5 Ignition (main) switch
6 Main fuse
7 Battery
BK   Black
BL   Blue
BR   Brown
BK/Y   Black and yellow
BL/BK   Blue and black
BL/W   Blue and white
W   White

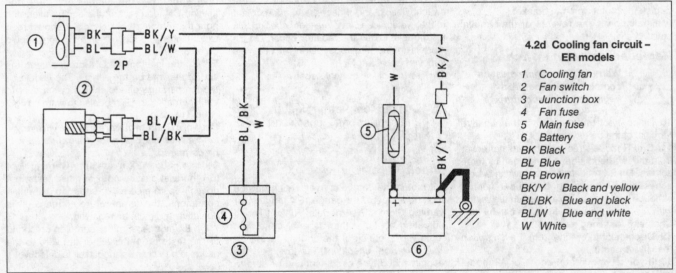

4.2d Cooling fan circuit – ER models

1 Cooling fan
2 Fan switch
3 Junction box
4 Fan fuse
5 Main fuse
6 Battery
BK   Black
BL   Blue
BR   Brown
BK/Y   Black and yellow
BL/BK   Blue and black
BL/W   Blue and white
W   White

Remove the jumper wires and reconnect the electrical connector to the fan.

a) If you're working on an EX500A1 or A2 model (with a single-wire fan switch harness), unplug the electrical connector to the fan switch, attach a jumper wire to the harness side of the connector and ground/earth the other end of the jumper wire. If the fan comes on, the circuit to the motor is good, and the thermostatic fan switch is defective (see Step 10).

b) If you're working on a later model (with a double-wire fan switch connector), unplug the connector. Connect the terminals in the harness side of the connector together with a jumper wire. If the fan comes on, the circuit to the motor is good and the switch is defective.

3 If you're working on an EX500A1 or A2 model and the fan still doesn't work, place your hand on the junction box. Repeatedly touch the jumper wire to ground/earth again – if you feel a clicking inside the junction box, the relay is probably good. If it's not clicking, check the wiring from the thermostatic fan switch to the junction box. If it is clicking, check the wiring from the junction box to the fan motor. If the wiring checks out okay, the fan relay is likely the problem, in which case the junction box must be renewed (the relays aren't available individually). Complete junction box testing, including the fan relay, is included in Chapter 9.

4 If you're working on a later model and the fan still doesn't work, refer to the wiring diagrams at the end of Chapter 9 and check the wiring back to the battery.

Replacement – fan motor

 Warning: The engine must be completely cool before beginning this procedure.

5 Disconnect the cable from the negative terminal of the battery. Remove the radiator (see Section 7).

6 Remove the three bolts securing the fan bracket to the radiator (see illustration). On A1 and A2 models, note which bolt secures the fan motor ground/earth wire. Separate the fan and bracket from the radiator.

4.6 Remove the fan bracket-to-radiator bolts and separate the fan from the radiator

4.7 The fan blade assembly is retained to the motor shaft by a single nut

4.8 Remove the three screws that secure the motor to the bracket, then detach the motor

4.12 Disconnect the electrical connector and unscrew the switch from the radiator (later model shown)

7 Remove the nut that retains the blades to the fan motor shaft **(see illustration)** and remove the fan blade assembly from the motor.

8 Remove the screws that attach the fan motor to the bracket **(see illustration)** and detach the motor from the bracket.

9 Installation is the reverse of the removal steps.

Replacement - fan switch

 Warning: The engine must be completely cool before beginning this procedure.

10 Disconnect the cable from the negative terminal of the battery.

11 On ER models remove the radiator cover from the left-hand side; it is retained by three screws. On EX models, the fan switch is best accessed by removing the upper fairing, although you may be able to reach the switch with the fairing in place if you're careful (see Chapter 8 for fairing removal).

12 Disconnect the wiring from the fan switch **(see illustration)**.

13 If you're working on an A1 or A2 model with a single-wire fan switch harness, don't place Teflon tape or silicone sealer on the switch threads. On all other models, prepare the new switch by wrapping the new threads with Teflon tape or by coating the threads with RTV sealant.

14 Unscrew the switch from the right-hand

side of the radiator (A1 and A2 models) or from the left-hand side (later models).

15 Quickly install the new switch, tightening it to the torque listed in this Chapter's Specifications.

16 Connect the electrical connector to the switch. Check, and if necessary, add coolant to the system (see *Daily (pre-ride) checks*). On ER models, install the radiator cover. On EX models install the upper fairing if this was removed (see Chapter 8).

17 Reconnect the battery negative lead.

5 Coolant temperature gauge and sender unit – check and replacement

Check

1 If the engine has been overheating but the coolant temperature gauge (EX models) or warning light (ER models) hasn't been indicating a hotter than normal condition, begin with a check of the coolant level (see *Daily (pre-ride) checks*). If it's low, add the recommended type of coolant and be sure to locate the source of the leak. On ER models check that the warning light bulb hasn't blown (see Chapter 9); the bulb should illuminate when the ignition is switched on but go off as soon as the engine is started.

2 Remove the seat and the fuel tank (see Chapter 4).

3 Remove the upper fairing on EX models (see Chapter 8).

4 Locate the coolant temperature sender unit, which is screwed into the thermostat housing **(see illustrations)**. Disconnect the electrical connector from the sender unit, turn the ignition ON (don't crank the engine over) and note the temperature gauge – it should read Cold. On ER models the warning light should be out.

5 With the ignition still ON, ground/earth the end of the wire on the engine. The needle on the temperature gauge should swing over to the Hot mark. On ER models the warning light should come on.

Caution: Don't ground/earth the wire any longer than necessary or the gauge may be damaged.

6 If the gauge (EX models) or warning light (ER models) passes both of these tests, but doesn't operate correctly under normal riding conditions, the temperature sender unit is defective and must be renewed.

7 On EX models, if the gauge didn't respond to the tests properly, either the wire to the gauge is bad or the gauge itself is defective.

Replacement

Sender unit

 Warning: The engine must be completely cool before beginning this procedure.

8 Prepare the new sender unit by wrapping the threads with Teflon tape or coating them with silicone sealant. Disconnect the electrical connector from the sender unit.

9 Unscrew the sender unit from the thermostat housing and quickly install the new unit, tightening it to the torque listed in this Chapter's Specifications.

10 Connect the electrical connector to the sender unit. Check, and if necessary, add coolant to the system (see Chapter 1).

Coolant temperature gauge/warning light

11 Refer to Chapter 9 for the coolant temperature gauge or warning light bulb renewal procedure.

5.4a The coolant temperature sender (arrowed) is located at the bottom of the thermostat housing on EX models

5.4b Coolant temperature sender (arrowed) – ER models

6.5a Remove the thermostat housing bolts (arrowed); the forward bolt secures a ground/earth wire

6.5b Unbolt the thermostat housing from the filler neck

6.6a Remove the three bolts and lift off the thermostat cover; note the earth wire

6 Thermostat – removal, check and installation

Warning: The engine must be completely cool before beginning this procedure.

Removal

1 If the thermostat is functioning properly, the coolant temperature gauge should rise to the normal operating temperature quickly and then stay there, only rising above the normal position occasionally when the engine gets abnormally hot. If the engine does not reach normal operating temperature quickly, or if it overheats, the thermostat should be removed and checked, or renewed.

2 Refer to Chapter 1 and drain the cooling system.

3 Remove the seat and the fuel tank (see Chapter 4). Disconnect the battery negative lead.

4 Remove the fairing on EX models (see Chapter 8).

5 If the thermostat housing is to be removed, disconnect all hoses from the thermostat housing having taken note of their positions. Unbolt the thermostat housing from the frame on EX models (see illustration); the forward

bolt also secures a ground/earth wire. On ER models, remove the bolt which retains the coolant tubes to the thermostat and the two bolts which retain the filler neck to the housing (see illustration).

6 Remove the three bolts to access the thermostat (see illustration) and on ER models disconnect the hose from the filler neck. Lift out the thermostat (see illustration).

7 Check the cover O-ring and renew it if its condition is in doubt. It's a good idea to renew the O-ring as a matter of course.

8 If required, the radiator cap, filler neck can be detached from the thermostat housing by removing the two bolts (see illustration 6.5b). Always renew the O-ring between the filler neck and thermostat housing if the two components have been separated.

Check

9 Remove any coolant deposits, then visually check the thermostat for corrosion, cracks and other damage. If it was open when it was removed, the thermostat is defective.

10 To check the thermostat operation, submerge it in a container of water along with a thermometer. The thermostat should be suspended so it does not touch the sides of the container (see illustration).

Warning: Antifreeze is poisonous. Do not use a cooking pan to test the thermostat.

11 Gradually heat the water in the container with a hot plate or stove and check the temperature when the thermostat first starts to open.

12 Compare the opening temperature to the values listed in this Chapter's Specifications.

13 Continue heating the water until the valve is fully open.

14 Measure how far the thermostat valve has opened and compare to the value listed in this Chapter's Specifications.

15 If these specifications are not met, or if the thermostat doesn't open while the water is heated, renew it.

Installation

16 On EX models install the thermostat into the housing with the relief hole positioned outward, away from the bike. On ER models install the thermostat so that the relief hole is at the rear (see illustration).

17 Install a new O-ring in the groove in the thermostat cover.

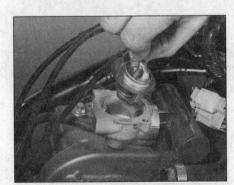

6.6b Lift out the thermostat

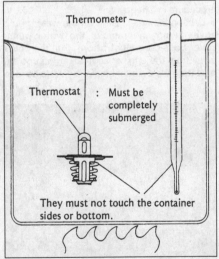

6.10 Thermostat test set-up

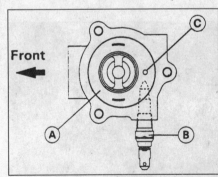

6.16 Install the thermostat (A) so that it doesn't foul the sender unit (B) and so that its relief hole (C) is at the rear - ER models

18 Place the cover on the housing and install the bolts, tightening them securely.

19 The remainder of installation is the reverse of the removal steps. Fill the cooling system with the recommended coolant (see Chapter 1).

7 Radiator – removal and installation

Warning: The engine must be completely cool before beginning this procedure.

1 Set the bike on its centerstand.

2 On EX models, remove the upper fairing (and lower fairing, if equipped) (see Chapter 8).

3 On ER models, remove the radiator covers from each side of the radiator; each cover is retained by three screws.

4 Drain the cooling system (see Chapter 1).

5 Disconnect the fan switch connector **(see illustration 4.12)**. Disconnect the ground/earth wire for the fan switch (EX500A1 and A2 models).

6 Loosen the radiator hose clamps. Work the hoses free from the fittings, taking care not to damage the fittings in the process.

7 Remove the stone shield from the radiator **(see illustration)**.

8 Remove the radiator mounting bolts **(see illustration)**. Take the radiator out.

9 Inspect the mounting bushings. Renew them if they're cracked or deteriorated.

7.5 The stone shield is secured by screws at the bottom and clips at the top (arrowed)

10 Installation is the reverse of the removal steps, with the following additions:

a) Don't forget to connect the fan switch ground/earth wire (if equipped).

b) On all models, fill the cooling system with the recommended coolant (see Chapter 1).

8 Water pump – check, removal and installation

⚠ **Warning: The engine must be completely cool before beginning this procedure.**

Check

1 Visually check the area around the water pump for coolant leaks. Try to determine if the leak is simply the result of a loose hose clamp or deteriorated hose.

2 Set the bike on its centerstand.

3 Remove the lower fairing on EX models (see Chapter 8).

4 Drain the engine coolant following the procedure in Chapter 1.

5 Loosen the hose clamp on the water pump cover fitting and remove the water pump cover bolts **(see illustration)**. Pull the cover away from the engine, separating the coolant pipe from the cylinder block as you do so (see

7.8 Remove the radiator mounting bolts

illustration). Retrieve the two cover dowels if they are loose.

6 Try to wiggle the pump impeller back-and-forth and in-and-out **(see illustration)**. If you can feel movement, the water pump must be renewed.

7 Check the impeller blades for corrosion. If they are heavily corroded, renew the water pump and flush the system thoroughly (it would also be a good idea to check the internal condition of the radiator).

8 If the cause of the leak was just a defective cover gasket, remove the old gasket and install a new one.

Removal

9 Drain the coolant and remove the cover (if it hasn't already been removed); see Step 5.

10 Drain the engine oil (see Chapter 1).

11 Shift the transmission into first gear and press the rear brake pedal to keep the engine from turning.

12 Unscrew the impeller in a clockwise direction and take it off the shaft **(see illustration)**.

13 Take the water pump housing and gasket off the engine.

14 Turn the water pump shaft clockwise to remove it (if necessary).

15 Remove the gasket from the water pump housing and pry out the oil seal **(see illustration)**.

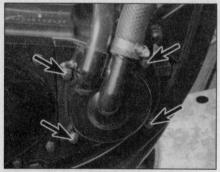

8.5a Remove the cover bolts (arrowed) . . .

8.5b . . . and lift the cover from the engine

8.6 If you can wiggle the impeller or pull it in-and-out, the pump is defective

8.12 Turn the impeller clockwise to remove it from the shaft

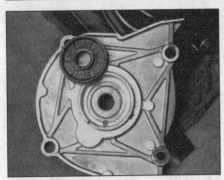

8.15 Pry the oil seal out of the housing

8.18 Install a new oil seal and gasket

8.19 Position the housing on the engine, install a new gasket and the dowels (arrowed)

16 Check all parts for wear and damage and renew as necessary.

17 If the mechanical seal set in the cover needs to be renewed, have it pressed out and a new one pressed in by a Kawasaki dealer.

Installation

18 Install a new oil seal and gasket on the inner side of the pump housing **(see illustration)**.

19 Install the pump housing on the engine. Install the dowels (if they were removed), the shaft (if removed), a new cover gasket and the impeller **(see illustration)**. Turn the impeller counterclockwise (anticlockwise) to tighten it.

8.20 The lower right cover bolt (arrowed) is the only one with a washer

20 Use a new O-ring at the joint between the coolant pipe and the cylinder block when installing the pump cover. When installing the cover bolts, note that the lower right-hand bolt is the only one with a washer **(see illustration)**.

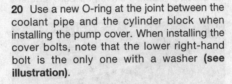

9 **Coolant tubes –** removal and installation

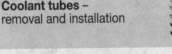

Warning: The engine must be completely cool for this procedure.

9.3a Remove the screws that secure the tubes

EX models

1 Remove the seat (see Chapter 8) and fuel tank (see Chapter 4).
2 Drain the cooling system (see Chapter 1).
3 Remove the screws that secure the tubes to the engine **(see illustration)**. Pull the tubes out of the engine **(see illustration)**.
4 Remove the O-ring from each tube with a pointed tool **(see illustration)**. Lightly coat new O-rings with high-temperature grease and install them on the tubes.
5 If the tubes are being removed to provide access for other work, suspend them from the handlebars with their ends up **(see illustration)**.
6 Installation is the reverse of the removal steps.

ER models

7 Remove the seat (see Chapter 8) and fuel tank (see Chapter 4). Where fitted, remove the vacuum switch valve and its hoses from the air suction valves – this will give improved access.
8 Drain the cooling system (see Chapter 1).
9 Remove the bolt which retains the coolant tubes to the thermostat housing and separate the two components, noting the O-ring. Remove the two bolts which retain the coolant

9.3b Pull the tubes out

9.4 Remove the O-rings with a pointed tool

9.5 Suspending the tubes from the handlebars will keep coolant from leaking out

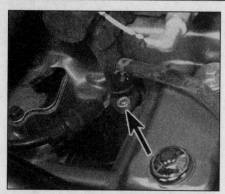

9.9 Coolant tube retaining bolts (arrowed)

tubes to the engine **(see illustration)**. Pull the coolant tubes out of the engine.

10 Remove the O-ring from each tube end with a pointed tool. Lightly coat new O-rings with high-temperature grease and install them on the tubes.

11 Installation is the reverse of the removal steps.

10 Carburettor warmer system – UK models

Note: *This system is not fitted to UK EX500A1 and A2 models.*

1 Hot coolant is routed through the carburettor bodies via small-bore coolant pipes. The cooling circuit connects to the main cooling system at the water pump pipe union (EX models) or at top of the radiator on the right-hand side on ER models **(see illustration)** and to the coolant tubes on the valve cover **(see illustration 9.9)**.

2 A valve is located in the coolant pipe from the right-hand carburettor **(see illustration)** and a filter is located in the coolant pipe between the left-hand carburettor and the coolant tubes **(see illustration)**. The filter should be checked at the appropriate service interval (see Chapter 1, Section 24).

3 If the coolant pipes are disturbed for any reason, such as carburettor removal, clamp them to avoid coolant loss (see *Tools and Workshop Tips* in the Reference section).

10.1 Carburettor warmer circuit valve (ER models)

10.2a Valve location (EX models)

10.2b Filter location

Chapter 4
Fuel and exhaust systems

Contents

Degrees of difficulty

Easy, suitable for novice with little experience		Fairly easy, suitable for beginner with some experience		Fairly difficult, suitable for competent DIY mechanic		Difficult, suitable for experienced DIY mechanic		Very difficult, suitable for expert DIY or professional	

Specifications

Fuel tank

Fuel tank overall capacity
    EX models . . . . 18 lit (4.8 US gal, 4.0 Imp gal)
    ER models . . . . 16 lit (3.5 Imp gal)
Fuel tank reserve capacity
    EX models . . . . 2.2 lit (0.58 US gal, 0.48 Imp gal)
    ER models . . . . 4 lit (0.88 Imp gal)
Fuel grade . . . . Unleaded or low-lead (subject to local regulations), minimum octane rating 91 RON

Carburettors – EX models

Carburettor type . . . . Keihin CVK34 (two)
Main jet 130
Main air jet 100
Jet needle N36N
Pilot jet 35
Pilot air jet 130
Pilot screw setting . . . . $2 \pm 1/4$ turns out
Starter jet 50
Float height . . . . 17 ± 2 mm (0.669 ± 0.08 in)
Fuel level (in relation to mating surface) . . . . 0.5 mm (0.02 in) below to 1.5 mm (0.06 in) above
Idle speed . . . . see Chapter 1

Carburettors – ER models

Carburettor type . . . . Keihin CVK34 (two)
Main jet . . . . 105 or 102
Main air jet 100
Jet needle . . . . N2WZ or N4BE
Pilot jet 35
Pilot air jet 130
Pilot screw setting . . . . $1 1/4 \pm 1/4$ turns out
Starter jet 55
Float height . . . . 17 ± 2 mm (0.669 ± 0.08 in)
Fuel level (in relation to mating surface) . . . . 0.5 mm (0.02 in) below to 1.5 mm (0.06 in) above
Idle speed . . . . see Chapter 1

2.5 Push the lines off the fittings with a screwdriver; if you pull on them, they'll tighten on the fittings and be hard to remove

2.7 Inspect the lines under the tank

1 General information

The fuel system consists of the fuel tank, the fuel filter, fuel tap, the carburettors and the connecting lines, hoses and control cables.

The carburettors used on these motorcycles are two constant vacuum Keihins with butterfly-type throttle valves. For cold starting, an enrichment circuit is actuated by a cable and the choke lever mounted on the left-hand handlebar. On UK models, hot coolant is diverted to the carburettors through a system of hoses to prevent carburettor icing. The carburettor warmer system is covered in Chapter 3.

The exhaust system is a twin pipe design with a crossover pipe.

Many of the fuel system service procedures are considered routine maintenance items and for that reason are included in Chapter 1.

2 Fuel tank –
removal and installation

Warning: Gasoline (petrol) is extremely flammable, so take extra precautions when you work on any part of the fuel system. Don't smoke or allow open flames or bare light bulbs near the work area, and don't

work in a garage where a natural gas-type appliance (such as a water heater or clothes dryer) is present. If you spill any fuel on your skin, rinse it off immediately with soap and water. When you perform any kind of work on the fuel system, wear safety glasses and have a fire extinguisher suitable for a Class B type fire (flammable liquids) on hand.

1 The fuel tank is held in place at the forward end by two cups, one on each side of the tank, which slide over two rubber dampers on the frame. The rear of the tank is fastened to a bracket by a bolt and rubber insulator, which fit through a flange projecting from the tank.

Removal and installation - EX models

Note: *Refer to Chapter 1, Section 22 for information on the fuel tap and its filter.*

2 Remove the seat and disconnect the cable from the negative terminal of the battery.

3 Remove the side covers (see Chapter 8). Remove the upper fairing rear mounting screw on each side (see Chapter 8) and prop the fairing ends out of the way with blocks of wood.

4 Remove the bolt securing the rear of the tank to the bracket. **Note:** *If you're going to remove the tank bracket for access to other parts, leave it attached to the tank. Remove the four bracket bolts instead.*

5 Make sure the fuel tap is in the ON or RES position, not PRI. Lift the rear of the tank up, slide back the hose clamps and push the fuel and vacuum lines **(see illustration)** off the fuel

tap. Mark and disconnect the breather hose and, on California models, the evaporative emission control system hoses from the tank.

6 Slide the tank to the rear to disengage the front of the tank from the rubber dampers, then carefully lift the tank away from the machine.

7 Before installing the tank, check the condition of the rubber mounting dampers and the hoses on the underside of the tank – if they're hardened, cracked, or show any other signs of deterioration, renew them **(see illustration)**.

8 When installing the tank, reverse the above procedure. Make sure the tank seats properly and does not pinch any control cables or wires.

> **HAYNES HiNT** *If difficulty is encountered when trying to slide the tank cups onto the dampers, a small amount of liquid soap or silicone spray should be used to lubricate them.*

Removal and installation - ER models

Note: *Refer to Chapter 1, Section 22 for information on the fuel filters set in the base of the tank.*

9 Remove the seat and both side covers (see Chapter 8).

10 Make sure that the fuel tap is in the ON or RES positions, not PRI. Remove the two bolts to free the fuel tap from the frame **(see illustration)**. Identify the fuel hose which runs to the carburettors and detach it from the tap, then detach the vacuum hose from the tap **(see illustration)**. Do not detach either of the two fuel delivery pipes from the tank.

11 Remove the bolt securing the rear of the tank to the bracket **(see illustration)**. Lift the tank up at the rear and disconnect the breather hose from the base of the tank, where fitted. On A2 and A3 models and all C models, trace the fuel level sender wiring to the block connector and disconnect it. Slide the tank to the rear to disengage the front of the tank from the rubber dampers, then carefully lift the tank away from the machine,

2.10a The fuel tap is retained by two bolts (arrows)

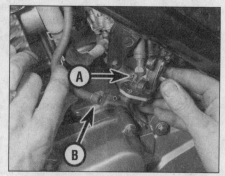

2.10b Disconnect the fuel pipe to the carburettors (A) and the vacuum pipe (B)

2.11 Tank rear mounting bolt

complete with the fuel tap. Note that the tap will pass between the engine and frame tube but is a tight fit on models equipped with a carburettor warmer circuit.

12 Before installing the tank, check the condition of the rubber mounting dampers and the hoses on the underside of the tank – if they're hardened, cracked, or show any other signs of deterioration, renew them.

13 When installing the tank, reverse the above procedure and, where fitted, ensure that the fuel level sender wiring and the breather hose are clipped to the underside of the tank. Check that the tank seats properly and does not pinch any control cables or wires.

Fuel tank repairs – all models

14 All repairs to the fuel tank should be carried out by a professional who has experience in this critical and potentially dangerous work. Even after cleaning and flushing of the fuel system, explosive fumes can remain and ignite during repair of the tank.

15 If the fuel tank is removed from the vehicle, it should not be placed in an area where sparks or open flames could ignite the fumes coming out of the tank. Be especially careful inside garages where a natural gas-type appliance is located, because the pilot light could cause an explosion.

3 Fuel level sender unit – removal and installation

1 ER500A2, A3 and all 500C models have a fuel level sender unit in the base of the fuel tank and a fuel gauge incorporated in the instrument cluster.

2 Remove the fuel tank as described in Section 2. Drain the fuel by disconnecting the two fuel pipes from the tap and directing their ends into a container suitable for holding petrol (gasoline).

3 Where fitted, unclip the catch tray from the base of the sender unit. Remove the four bolts to free the sender from the fuel tank. Be very careful not to bend the arm of the sender as the float is manoeuvred out of the tank.

4 No specific test data is available for checking the function of the sender unit, although the gauge can be checked as described in Chapter 9, Section 16.

5 Installation is a reverse of the removal procedure, noting that a new gasket must be used between the sender and tank surfaces.

4 Idle fuel/air mixture adjustment – general information

1 Due to the increased emphasis on controlling motorcycle exhaust emissions in certain countries, governmental regulations

have been formulated which directly affect the carburetion settings. In these markets, the carburettors have a metal sealing plug pressed into the hole over the pilot screw (which controls the idle fuel/air mixture) on each carburettor, so they can't be tampered with. These should only be removed in the event of a complete carburettor overhaul, and even then the screws should be returned to their original settings and new sealing plugs fitted.

2 The pilot screws on other models are accessible, but adjustment should be left to a Kawasaki dealer or fuel systems expert. Do not tamper with the pilot screw setting unnecessarily, only make adjustment if the engine runs extremely rough at idle or continually stalls.

3 Refer to Section 7 for pilot screw removal and installation details. If the pilot screws are renewed, they must be set to the number of turns out given in the Specifications at the beginning of this Chapter and then a djusted by a Kawasaki dealer or fuel systems expert.

5 Carburettor overhaul – general information

1 Poor engine performance, hesitation, hard starting, stalling, flooding and backfiring are all signs that major carburettor maintenance may be required.

2 Keep in mind that many so-called carburettor problems are really not carburettor problems at all, but mechanical problems within the engine or malfunctions within the ignition system. Try to establish for certain that the carburettors are in need of a major overhaul before beginning.

3 Check the fuel filter(s), the fuel lines, the tank breather pipe, the inlet manifold hose clamps, the vacuum hoses, the air filter element, the cylinder compression, the spark plugs, the air suction system (US models only) and the carburettor synchronisation before assuming that a carburettor overhaul is required. Also make sure that the end of the carburettor vent tube is not placed near the air inlet. This will cause fuel starvation, resulting in poor performance above 3,500 rpm and a maximum engine speed of 5,000 rpm.

4 Most carburettor problems are caused by dirt particles, varnish and other deposits which build up in and block the fuel and air passages. Also, in time, gaskets and O-rings shrink or deteriorate and cause fuel and air leaks which lead to poor performance.

5 When the carburettor is overhauled, it is generally disassembled completely and the parts are cleaned thoroughly with a carburettor cleaning solvent and dried with filtered, unlubricated compressed air. The fuel and air passages are also blown through with compressed air to force out any dirt that may have been loosened but not removed by the solvent. Once the cleaning process is

complete, the carburettor is reassembled using new gaskets, O-rings and, generally, a new inlet needle valve and seat.

6 Before disassembling the carburettors, make sure you obtain all the necessary O-rings and gaskets, some carburettor cleaner, a supply of rags, some means of blowing out the carburettor passages and a clean place to work. It is recommended that only one carburettor be overhauled at a time to avoid mixing up parts.

6 Carburettors – removal and installation

> ⚠️ *Warning: Gasoline (petrol) is extremely flammable, so take extra precautions when you work on any part of the fuel system. Don't smoke or allow open flames or bare light bulbs near the work area, and don't work in a garage where an appliance fueled by natural gas is present (such as a water heater or clothes dryer). If you spill any fuel on your skin, rinse it off immediately with soap and water. When you perform any kind of work on the fuel system, wear safety glasses and have a fire extinguisher suitable for a class B type fire (flammable liquids) on hand.*

Removal

1 Remove the fuel tank (see Section 2). On ER models also remove the tank mounting bracket.

2 If you are working on a US model or any ER500C model, remove the vacuum switching valve from the air suction system (see Chapter 1). On UK models, where fitted, disconnect the carburettor warmer pipes and clamp them to avoid coolant loss (see Tools and Workshop Tips in the Reference section).

3 Disconnect the choke cable from the carburettor assembly (see Section 10).

4 Loosen the lockwheel on the throttle cable adjuster at the handlebar and turn the adjuster in all the way.

5 Loosen the clamp screws on the inlet manifolds (the rubber tubes that connect the carburettors to the engine) **(see illustration)**.

6.5 Loosen the clamps on the intake manifold tubes

6.7a Pull the spring bands back, toward the air cleaner housing – EX models

6.7b Loosen the clamps on the air inlet tubes – ER models

6.8 Gently work the air inlet tubes on the air box free of the carburettors, then detach the carburettors from the intake manifold tubes

6.14a Route the carburettor vent tube (arrowed) so it won't be pinched when the tank is installed . . .

6.14b . . . and be careful not to place its end near the air intake (arrowed); this will cause fuel starvation

6 Mark and disconnect the vacuum hose(s) from the carburettors (see Chapter 1, Section 6).

7 On EX models, slide the spring bands on the air inlet ducts away from the carburettors **(see illustration)**. On ER models, loosen the clamp screws on the air inlet ducts **(see illustration)**.

8 Pull the carburettor assembly clear of the air box tubes **(see illustration)**. Raise the assembly up far enough to disconnect the throttle cables from the throttle pulley, then remove the carburettors from the machine.

9 After the carburettors have been removed, stuff clean rags into the inlet manifold tubes to prevent the entry of dirt or other objects.

Installation

10 Position the assembly over the inlet manifold tubes. Lightly lubricate the ends of the throttle cables with multi-purpose grease and attach them to the throttle pulley. Make sure the accelerator and decelerator cables are in their proper positions.

11 Tilt the front of the assembly down and insert the fronts of the carburettors into the inlet manifold tubes. Push the assembly forward and tighten the clamps.

12 Make sure the ducts from the air cleaner housing are seated properly, then slide the spring bands into position (EX models) or tighten the clamp screws (ER models).

13 Connect the choke cable to the assembly and adjust it (see Section 10).

14 The remainder of installation is the reverse of the removal steps, with the following additions:

a) On EX models, be sure the vent tube is routed next to the wiring harness so it isn't pinched **(see illustration)**. Don't place the end of the vent tube near the air inlet **(see illustration)** or fuel starvation will occur, resulting in poor performance above 3,500 rpm and failure to rev past 5,000 rpm.

b) Adjust the throttle grip freeplay (see Chapter 1).

c) Check for fuel leaks.

d) Check and, if necessary, adjust the idle speed and carburettor synchronisation (see Chapter 1).

e) On UK models, if applicable, check and top up the coolant level – see Daily (pre-ride) checks.

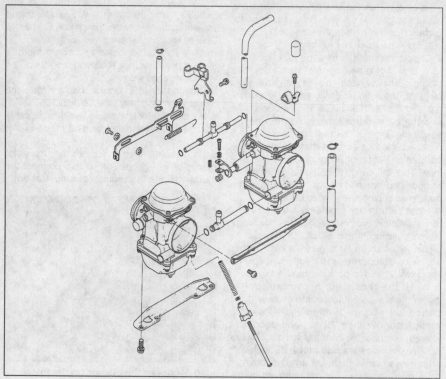

7.2a Carburettor mounting details – EX models (ER models similar)

7.2b Lower mounting bracket screws (lower arrows) and upper bracket (upper arrow)

7.2c Upper mounting bracket screws (arrowed) on each carburettor

7.3a Each carburettor top cover is secured by four screws (arrowed); note the choke cable bracket

7 Carburettors – disassembly, cleaning and inspection

⚠️ **Warning: Gasoline (petrol) is extremely flammable, so take extra precautions when you work on any part of the fuel system. Don't smoke or allow open flames or bare light bulbs near the work area, and don't work in a garage where an appliance fuelled by natural gas is present (such as a water heater or clothes dryer). If you spill any fuel on your skin, rinse it off immediately with soap and water. When you perform any kind of work on the fuel system, wear safety glasses and have a fire extinguisher suitable for a class B type fire (flammable liquids) on hand.**

Disassembly

1 Remove the carburettors from the machine as described in Section 6. Set the assembly on a clean working surface. **Note:** *Unless the O-rings on the fuel and vent fittings between the carburettors are leaking, don't detach the carburettors from their mounting brackets. Also, work on one carburettor at a time to avoid getting parts mixed up.*

2 If the carburettors must be separated from each other (during a complete overhaul, for example) remove the idle adjusting screw assembly **(see illustration)**, being careful not to lose the spring and washer on the end of the screw. Disconnect the fuel hoses. Remove the choke linkage rod spring and choke linkage rod by removing the screw and plastic washers (two washers, one on each side of the lever) then remove the screws securing the upper and lower mounting plates to the carburettors **(see illustrations)**. Mark the position of each carburettor and gently separate them, noting how the throttle linkage is connected, and being careful not to lose any springs or fuel and vent

fittings that are present between the carburettors.

3 Remove the four screws securing the top cover to the carburettor body **(see**

illustration). Lift the cover off and remove the piston spring **(see illustration)**.

4 Peel the diaphragm away from its groove in the carburettor body, being careful not to tear it.

1   Screw
2   Spring washer
3   Washer
4   Top cover
5   Piston spring
6   Spring seat
7   Jet needle
8   Diaphragm/ vacuum piston assembly
9   Needle jet
10 Needle jet holder/air bleed pipe
11 Main jet
12 Pilot jet
13 Float assembly
14 Pivot pin
15 Fuel inlet valve needle
16 Clip
17 O-ring
18 Float bowl
19 Drain screw
20 O-ring
21 Screw
22 Spring washer
23 Sealing plug (US models only)
24 Pilot screw
25 Spring
26 Washer
27 O-ring
28 Choke plunger
29 Spring
30 Nut
31 Cap

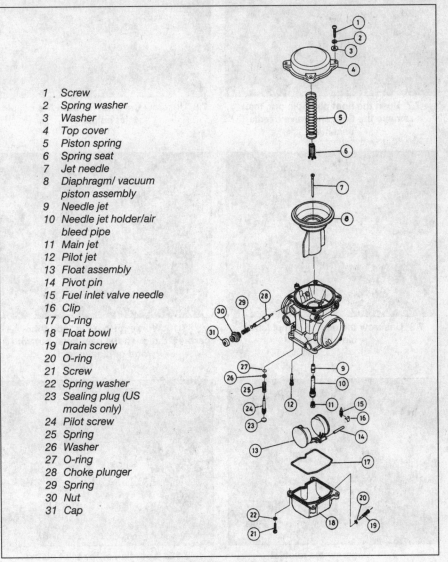

7.3b Carburettor - exploded view

7.4 Remove the diaphragm/piston assembly from the carburettor body

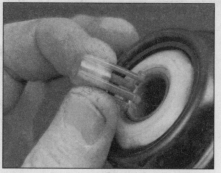

7.5a Remove the vacuum piston spring seat from the piston

7.5b Remove the needle from the piston

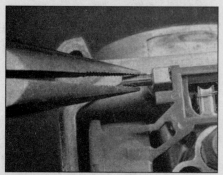

7.7 Push the float pivot pin out, then remove the float and valve needle assembly

7.8 Unscrew the main jet from the needle jet holder

Lift out the diaphragm/piston assembly (see illustration).

5 Remove the piston spring seat and separate the needle from the piston (see illustrations).

6 Remove the four screws retaining the float bowl to the carburettor body, then detach the bowl (see illustration 7.3b).

7 Push the float pivot pin out and detach the float (and fuel inlet valve needle) from the carburettor body (see illustration). Detach the valve needle from the float.

8 Unscrew the main jet from the needle jet holder (see illustration).

9 Unscrew the needle jet holder/air bleed pipe (see illustration).

10 Using a wood or plastic tool, push the needle jet out of the carburettor body (see illustration).

11 Using a small, flat-bladed screwdriver, remove the pilot jet (see illustration).

12 The pilot (idle mixture) screw is located in the bottom of the carburettor body (see illustration). On US models, this screw is hidden behind a plug which will have to be removed if the screw is to be taken out. The usual way to do this is to drill a hole in the plug, then pry it out. To avoid the risk of drilling into the screw, you can also drill a very small hole above the plug, then insert a hooked tool into the hole and push the plug out (see illustration). On all models, turn the pilot screw in, counting the number of turns

7.9 Unscrew the needle jet holder/air bleed pipe

7.10 Working from the top of the carburettor, push the needle jet out with a wood or plastic tool

7.11 Unscrew the pilot jet

7.12a Location of the pilot screw (arrowed)

7.12b One way to remove the sealing plug is to drill a very small hole above it (left arrow), then reach into the hole with a hooked tool and push out the plug (right arrow)

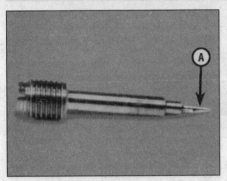

7.17 Check the tapered portion of the pilot screw (A) for wear or damage

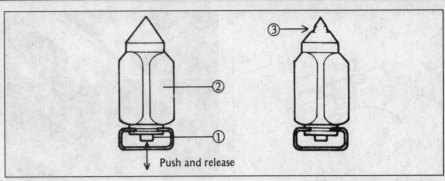

7.22 Check the tip of the fuel inlet valve needle for grooves or scratches - also make sure the rod in the end of the needle pops back out quickly after it's pushed in

Push and release

1 Rod   2 Valve needle   3 Groove in tip

until it bottoms lightly. Record that number for use when installing the screw. Now remove the pilot screw along with its spring, washer and O-ring.

13 The choke plunger can be removed by unscrewing the nut that retains it to the carburettor body **(see illustration 7.3b)**, if the carburettors have not been separated from each other (see Step 2).

Cleaning

Caution: Use only a carburettor cleaning solution that is safe for use with plastic parts (be sure to read the label on the container).

14 Submerge the metal components in the carburettor cleaner for approximately thirty minutes (or longer, if the directions recommend it).

15 After the carburettor has soaked long enough for the cleaner to loosen and dissolve most of the varnish and other deposits, use a brush to remove the stubborn deposits. Rinse it again, then dry it with compressed air. Blow out all of the fuel and air passages in the main and upper body.

Caution: Never clean the jets or passages with a piece of wire or a drill bit, as they will be enlarged, causing the fuel and air metering rates to be upset.

Inspection

16 Check the operation of the choke plunger. If it doesn't move smoothly, renew it, along with the return spring.

17 Check the tapered portion of the pilot screw for wear or damage **(see illustration)**. Renew the pilot screw if necessary.

18 Check the carburettor body, float bowl and top cover for cracks, distorted sealing surfaces and other damage. If any defects are found, renew the faulty component, although renewal of the entire carburettor will probably be necessary (check with your parts supplier for the availability of separate components).

19 Check the diaphragm for splits, holes and general deterioration. Holding it up to a light will help to reveal problems of this nature.

20 Insert the vacuum piston in the carburettor body and see that it moves up-and-down smoothly. Check the surface of the piston for wear. If it's worn excessively or

doesn't move smoothly in the bore, renew the carburettor.

21 Check the jet needle for straightness by rolling it on a flat surface (such as a piece of glass). Renew it if it's bent or if the tip is worn.

22 Check the tip of the fuel inlet valve needle. If it has grooves or scratches in it, it must be renewed. Push in on the rod in the other end of the needle, then release it – if it doesn't spring back, renew the valve needle **(see illustration)**.

23 Check the O-rings on the float bowl and the drain plug (in the float bowl). Renew them if they're damaged.

24 Operate the throttle shaft to make sure the throttle butterfly valve opens and closes smoothly. If it doesn't, renew the carburettor.

25 Check the floats for damage. This will usually be apparent by the presence of fuel inside one of the floats. If the floats are damaged, they must be renewed.

---

8 Carburettors – reassembly and fuel level adjustment

Caution: When installing the jets, be careful not to over-tighten them – they're made of soft material and can strip or shear easily.

Note: *When reassembling the carburettors, be sure to use all new O-rings and gaskets.*

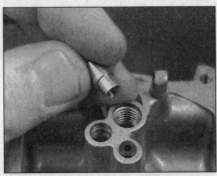

8.4 Install the needle jet, small diameter end first

Reassembly

1 If the choke plunger was removed, install it in its bore, followed by its spring and nut. Tighten the nut securely and install the cap.

2 Install the pilot screw (if removed) along with its spring, washer and O-ring, turning it in until it seats lightly. Now, turn the screw out the number of turns that was previously recorded. If you're working on a US model, install a new metal sealing plug in the hole over the screw; apply a little bonding agent around the circumference of the plug after it has been seated.

3 Install the pilot jet, tightening it securely.

4 Turn the carburettor body upside-down and install the needle jet into its hole, small diameter first **(see illustration)**.

5 Install the needle jet holder/air bleed pipe, tightening it securely.

6 Install the main jet into the needle jet holder/air bleed pipe, tightening it securely.

7 Drop the jet needle down into its hole in the vacuum piston and install the spring seat over the needle. Make sure the spring seat doesn't cover the hole at the bottom of the vacuum piston – reposition it if necessary.

8 Install the diaphragm/vacuum piston assembly into the carburettor body. Lower the spring into the piston. Seat the bead of the diaphragm into the groove in the top of the carburettor body, making sure the diaphragm isn't distorted or kinked **(see illustration)**.

8.8 Make sure the bead of the vacuum diaphragm seats in its groove, and that the diaphragm isn't distorted

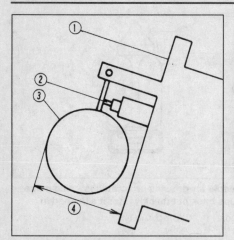

8.10 Float height adjustment details

1 *Carburettor body*   3 *Float*
2 *Float valve needle rod* 4 *Float height*

This isn't always an easy task. If the diaphragm seems too large in diameter and doesn't want to seat in the groove, place the top cover over the carburettor diaphragm, insert your finger into the throat of the carburettor and push up on the vacuum piston. Push down gently on the top cover – it should drop into place, indicating the diaphragm has seated in its groove.

9 Install the top cover, tightening the screws securely. If you're working on the right-hand carburettor, don't forget to install the choke cable bracket on the corner.

10 Invert the carburettor. Attach the fuel inlet valve needle to the float. Set the float into position in the carburettor, making sure the valve needle seats correctly. Install the float pivot pin. To check the float height, hold the carburettor so the float hangs down, then tilt it back until the valve needle is just seated (the rod in the end of the valve shouldn't be compressed). Measure the distance from the carburettor body to the top of the float **(see illustration)** and compare your measurement to the float height listed in this Chapter's Specifications. If it isn't as specified, carefully bend the tang that contacts the valve needle up or down until the float height is correct.

11 Install the O-ring into the groove in the float bowl. Place the float bowl on the carburettor and install the screws, tightening them securely.

12 If the carburettors were separated, install new O-rings on the fuel and vent fittings. Lubricate the O-rings on the fittings with a light film of oil and install them into their respective holes, making sure they seat completely **(see illustration 7.2a)**.

13 Position the coil springs between the carburettors, gently push the carburettors together, then make sure the throttle linkages are correctly engaged. Check the fuel and vent fittings to make sure they engage properly also.

14 Install the upper and lower mounting plates and install the screws, but don't tighten

8.15 Make sure to install a plastic washer on each side of the choke linkage rod when installing the screws

them completely yet. Set the carburettors on a sheet of glass, then align them with a straight-edge placed along the edges of the bores. When the centrelines of the carburettors are both in horizontal and vertical alignment, tighten the mounting plate screws securely.

15 Install the choke linkage rod, making sure it engages correctly with both choke plungers. Position a plastic washer on each side of the choke linkage rod **(see illustration)** and install the screws, tightening them securely. Install the return spring, then make sure the choke mechanism operates smoothly.

16 Install the throttle linkage springs **(see illustration)**. Visually synchronise the throttle butterfly valves, turning the adjusting screws on the throttle linkage, if necessary, to equalise the clearance between the butterfly valve and throttle bore of each carburettor. Check to ensure the throttle operates smoothly.

Fuel level adjustment

⚠ *Warning: Gasoline (petrol) is extremely flammable, so take extra precautions when you work on any part of the fuel system. Don't smoke or allow open flames or bare light bulbs near the work area, and don't work in a garage where an appliance fuelled by natural gas is present (such as a water heater or clothes dryer). If you spill any fuel on your skin, rinse it off immediately with soap and water. When you perform any kind of work on the fuel system, wear safety glasses and have a fire extinguisher suitable for a class B type fire (flammable liquids) on hand.*

17 Lightly clamp the carburettor assembly in the jaws of a vice. Make sure the vice jaws are lined with wood. Set an auxiliary fuel tank next to the vice, but at an elevation that is higher than the carburettors (resting on a box, for example). Connect a hose from the fuel tank to the fuel inlet fitting on the carburettor assembly.

18 Attach Kawasaki service tool no. 57001-1017 to the drain fitting on the bottom of one of the carburettor float bowls (both will be checked) **(see illustration)**. This is a clear

8.16 Install the throttle linkage springs

plastic tube graduated in millimetres. An alternative is to use a length of clear plastic tubing and an accurate ruler. Hold the graduated tube (or the free end of the clear plastic tube) against the carburettor body, as shown in the accompanying illustration. If the Kawasaki tool is being used, raise the zero mark to a point several millimetres above the bottom edge of the carburettor main body. If a piece of clear plastic tubing is being used, make a mark on the tubing at a point several millimetres above the bottom edge of the carburettor main body.

19 Unscrew the drain screw at the bottom of the float bowl a couple of turns, then let fuel flow into the tube. Wait for the fuel level to stabilise, then slowly lower the tube until the zero mark is level with the bottom edge of the carburettor body. **Note:** *Don't lower the zero mark below the bottom edge of the carburettor then bring it back up – the reading won't be accurate.*

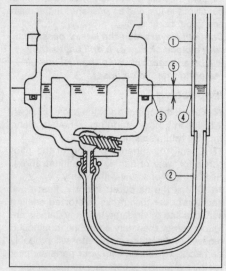

8.18 Checking the fuel level in a carburettor

1 *Kawasaki tool no. 57001-1017*
2 *Fuel hose*
3 *Bottom edge of carburettor body*
4 *Zero line*
5 *Fuel level*

20 Measure the distance between the mark and top of the fuel level in the tube or gauge. This distance is the fuel level – write it down on a piece of paper, screw in the drain screw, close off the fuel supply, then move on to the next carburettor and check it the same way.

21 Compare your fuel level readings to the value listed in this Chapter's Specifications. If the fuel level in either carburettor is not correct, remove the float bowl and bend the tang up or down (see Step 10), as necessary, then recheck the fuel level. **Note:** *Bending the tang up increases the float height and lowers the fuel level – bending it down decreases the float height and raises the fuel level.*

22 After the fuel level for each carburettor has been adjusted, install the carburettor assembly (see Section 6).

9 Throttle cables – removal, installation and adjustment

Removal

1 Remove the fuel tank (see Section 2).

2 Cut the tie wrap that secures the cables to the wiring harness **(see illustration)**.

3 Loosen the accelerator cable lockwheel and screw the cable adjuster in.

4 Remove the cable/switch housing screws and detach the housing from the handlebar **(see illustration)**.

5 Detach the cables from the cable/switch housing, then lift them out of their grooves in the throttle pulley, align the cables with the pulley slots and slip the cable ends out of the throttle pulley **(see illustration)**.

6 Detach the decelerator and accelerator cables from the throttle pulley at the carburettor assembly (see Chapter 1, Section 18).

7 Remove the cables, noting how they are routed.

Installation

8 Route the cables into place. Make sure they

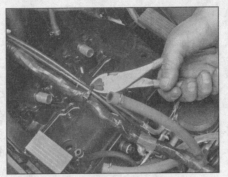

9.2 Cut the tie wrap that secures the cables to the wiring harness

don't interfere with any other components and aren't kinked or bent sharply.

9 Lubricate the end of the accelerator cable with multi-purpose grease and connect it to the throttle pulley at the carburettor. Pass the inner cable through the slot in the bracket, then seat the cable housing in the bracket.

10 Repeat the previous step to connect the decelerator cable.

11 Attach the rear half of the cable/switch housing to the handlebar, seating the decelerator cable in the groove in the housing as it's installed **(see illustration)**. Hook the decelerator cable to the throttle pulley.

12 Hold the rear half of the cable/switch housing to the handlebar and hook the accelerator cable to the throttle pulley, then push the accelerator cable guide into place, making sure it's correctly engaged with the housing **(see illustration)**.

13 Install the front half of the cable/switch housing, making sure the housing halves mate together and align correctly with the handlebar. Install the screws and tighten them securely.

14 Install a new tie wrap to secure the cables to the wiring harness.

Adjustment

15 Follow the procedure outlined in Chapter 1, Section 18, to adjust the cables.

16 Turn the handlebars back and forth to

9.4 Detach the cable/switch housing from the handlebar

make sure the cables don't cause the steering to bind.

17 Operate the throttle and check the cable action. The cables should move freely and the throttle pulley at the carburettor should move back and forth in response to both acceleration and deceleration. If the cables don't operate properly, find and fix the problem before you put the fuel tank back on.

18 Install the fuel tank.

19 Start the engine. With the engine idling, turn the handlebars all the way to left and right while listening and watching the tachometer for changes in idle speed. If idle speed increases as the handlebars turn, the cables are improperly routed. This is dangerous. Find the problem and fix it before riding the bike.

10 Choke cable – removal, installation and adjustment

Removal

1 Remove the seat (see Chapter 8) and fuel tank (see Section 2). Cut the tie wrap that secures the choke and throttle cables to the wiring harness **(see illustration 9.2)**.

2 Pull the choke cable casing away from its mounting bracket at the carburettor and pass

9.5 Lift the inner cables out of their grooves and slip them out of the pulley slots

9.11 Route the decelerator cable through the guide in the cable/switch housing

9.12 Hold the rear half of the housing in place and install the accelerator cable

10.2 Separate the choke cable housing from the bracket at the carburettor

10.3 The choke cable/switch housing is held together by screws (arrowed)

10.6 The cable housing should be securely seated in the bracket

the inner cable through the opening in the bracket **(see illustration)**. Detach the cable end from the choke lever by the right-hand carburettor.

3 Remove the two screws securing the choke cable/switch housing halves to the left-hand handlebar **(see illustration)**. Pull the front half of the housing off and separate the choke cable from the lever.

4 Remove the cable, noting how it's routed.

Installation

5 Route the cable into position. Connect the upper end of the cable to the choke lever. Place the housing up against the handlebar, making sure the housing halves align correctly with each other and the handlebar. Install the screws, tightening them securely.

11.5 The housing side covers are secured by screws

6 Connect the lower end of the cable to the choke lever. Pull back on the cable casing and connect it to the bracket on the right-hand carburettor **(see illustration)**.

Adjustment

7 Refer to Chapter 1, Section 18 for cable adjustment procedures.

8 Install the fuel tank and all of the other components that were previously removed. Renew the cut tie wrap.

11 Air filter housing – removal and installation

EX models

1 Remove the seat (see Chapter 8). Disconnect the cables from the battery (negative cable first), then remove the battery (see Chapter 9).

2 Remove the fuel tank and fuel tank bracket (see Section 2).

3 Remove the side covers (see Chapter 8).

4 Disconnect the junction box wiring then remove the junction box bracket (see Chapter 9).

5 Remove both side covers from the air cleaner housing **(see illustration)**.

6 If you're working on a US model, disconnect the large air suction hose from the front of the air filter housing.

7 Slide the spring bands that attach the ducts

to the carburettors toward the air filter housing.

8 Disconnect the crankcase breather hose from the engine.

9 Lift the air filter housing up and out of the frame.

10 Installation is the reverse of removal.

ER models

11 Remove the air filter element as described in Chapter 1, Section 21.

12 Refer to Section 6 of this Chapter and remove the carburettors.

13 The air filter housing can now be manoeuvred forwards and upwards out of the frame.

12 Exhaust system – removal and installation

EX models

1 Remove the lower fairing (see Chapter 8).

2 Drain the coolant (see Chapter 1).

3 Remove the radiator (see Chapter 3).

4 Remove the nuts that secure the exhaust pipe holders to the cylinder head, then remove the holders **(see illustration)**.

5 Loosen the clamp that secures the crossover pipe **(see illustration)**.

6 If you plan to separate the mufflers from the pipes, loosen the clamps **(see illustration)**.

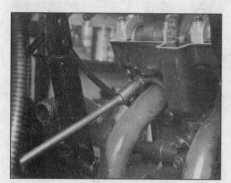

12.4 Remove the nuts and holders from the cylinder head studs

12.5 Loosen the crossover clamp

12.6 Loosen the muffler clamps if you plan to separate the mufflers from the pipes

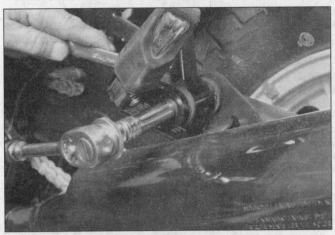

12.7 Remove the muffler mounting bolts at the rear footrests

12.9 The gaskets at the cylinder head should be renewed whenever the pipes are removed

12.10 The holder halves are notched so they form a flush surface when assembled correctly

12.11 Remove the nuts and holders from the cylinder head

7 Remove the muffler mounting bolts at the footrest brackets **(see illustration)**.

8 Pull the exhaust system forward, separate the right-hand side pipe from the left-hand side pipe and remove the system from the machine.

9 Remove the gaskets from the cylinder head **(see illustration)**.

10 Installation is the reverse of removal, with the following additions:

a) Install new gaskets at the cylinder head.

b) Be sure the holders overlap correctly **(see illustration)**.

c) Tighten all exhaust fasteners securely once the system is fully in place, then tighten them again once the engine has been run and allowed to cool down.

ER models

11 Remove the nuts that secure the exhaust pipe holders to the cylinder head, then remove the holders **(see illustration)**.

12 Support the exhaust system, then remove the bolt beneath the rider's footrest which secures the system to the frame, followed by

the bolt at rear which secures the system to the footrest bracket **(see illustrations)**. Manoeuvre the exhaust system off the cylinder head studs, being careful not to damage the radiator.

13 Check the rubber mountings set in exhaust system mounting points and renew them if they are damaged or perished. Remove the old gasket rings from the cylinder head and fit new ones.

14 Installation is the reverse of removal, with the following additions:

a) Install new gaskets at the cylinder head.

b) Be sure the holders overlap correctly **(see illustration 12.10)**.

c) Tighten all exhaust fasteners securely once the system is fully in place, then tighten them again once the engine has been run and allowed to cool down.

12.12a Exhaust system mounting bolts at the frame . . .

12.12b . . . and the footrest bracket

13.1 Location of the air switching valve

13 Air switching valve – operational test

1 The air switching valve is part of the air suction system used on US models and ER500C models **(see illustration)**. Checking procedures for the reed valves are described in Chapter 1, Section 4. If you suspect the switching valve has failed (for example if the bike runs poorly at low speed or backfires during deceleration) test it as follows:

2 Remove the valve and its hoses from the motorcycle (see the illustrations which accompany Section 7 in Chapter 1).

3 Connect a vacuum gauge to one end of the vacuum line that branches out from the T-fitting. Connect a vacuum pump to the other end **(see illustration)**.

4 Try to blow air into the large air hose. It should flow easily when there's no vacuum applied to the vacuum line.

5 Operate the vacuum pump and raise vacuum to 430 to 490 mm Hg (17 to 19 in Hg). The valve should close, making it impossible to blow air into the hose.

6 If the valve doesn't perform as described, renew it.

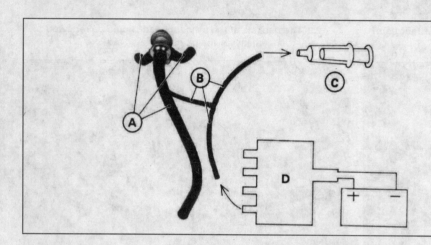

13.3 Air switching valve test setup

a Air hose
b Vacuum line
c Syringe (part of Kawasaki special tool) or hand vacuum pump
d Vacuum gauge set (part of Kawasaki special tool 57001-1198) or standard vacuum gauge

Chapter 5
Ignition system

Contents

Degrees of difficulty

Easy, suitable for novice with little experience	Fairly easy, suitable for beginner with some experience	Fairly difficult, suitable for competent DIY mechanic	Difficult, suitable for experienced DIY mechanic	Very difficult, suitable for expert DIY or professional

Specifications

Spark plug
Plug type and gap .... see Chapter 1
Plug cap resistance
  EX500A models .... not available
  EX500D, E and ER models .... 3.75 to 6.25 K-ohms

Ignition HT coils
EX500A models
  Primary resistance .... 2.2 to 3.9 ohms
  Secondary resistance .... 10 to 16 K-ohms
EX500D, E and ER models
  Primary resistance .... 2.3 to 3.5 ohms
  Secondary resistance .... 12 to 18 K-ohms

Pickup coil resistance
EX500A models .... 400 to 490 ohms
EX500D, E and ER models .... 360 to 540 ohms

Ignition timing
All models (non adjustable) .... 10° BTDC @ 1200 rpm to 37.5° BTDC @ 10,000 rpm

1 General information

This motorcycle is equipped with a battery operated, fully transistorised, breakerless ignition system. The system consists of the following components:
  Pickup coil(s)
  IC igniter unit
  Battery and fuse
  Ignition HT coils
  Spark plugs
  Stop and ignition (main) switches
  Primary and secondary circuit wiring
The transistorised ignition system functions on the same principle as a conventional DC ignition system with the pickup coil(s) and igniter performing the tasks previously associated with the contact breaker points and mechanical advance system. As a result, adjustment and maintenance of ignition components is eliminated (with the exception of the spark plugs).

Because of their nature, the individual ignition system components can be checked but not repaired. If ignition system troubles occur, and the faulty component can be isolated, the only cure for the problem is to renew the part. Keep in mind that most electrical parts, once purchased, can't be returned. To avoid unnecessary expense, make very sure the faulty component has been positively identified before buying a new part.

2 Ignition system – check

 Warning: Because of the very high voltage generated by the ignition system, extreme care should be taken when these checks are performed. On no account should the ignition be switched on whilst the plugs or plug caps are being held. Shocks from the HT circuit can be most unpleasant. Secondly, it is vital that the engine is not turned over or run with either of the plug caps removed, and that the plugs are soundly earthed (grounded) when the system is checked for sparking.

The ignition system components can be seriously damaged if the HT circuit becomes isolated.

1 If the ignition system is the suspected cause of poor engine performance or failure to start, a number of checks can be made to isolate the problem.

2 Make sure the ignition stop switch is in the RUN or ON position.

Engine will not start

3 Remove the fuel tank (see Chapter 4). Disconnect one of the spark plug leads, connect the lead to a spare spark plug and lay the plug on the engine with the threads contacting the engine. If it's necessary to hold the spark plug, use an insulated tool **(see illustration)**. Crank the engine over and make sure a well-defined, blue spark occurs between the spark plug electrodes. Before proceeding further, turn the ignition OFF.

⚠️ *Warning: DO NOT remove one of the spark plugs from the engine to perform this check – atomised fuel being pumped out of the open spark plug hole could ignite, causing severe injury!*

4 If no spark occurs, the following checks should be made:

5 Unscrew one of the spark plug caps from its plug lead and check the cap resistance with an ohmmeter **(see illustration)**. If the resistance is infinite, renew it; the reading should correspond with that given in the Specifications. Repeat this check on the other plug cap.

6 Make sure all electrical connectors are clean and tight. Refer to the wiring diagrams at the end of this book and check all wires for shorts, opens and correct installation.

7 Check the battery voltage with a voltmeter (see Chapter 9). If the voltage is less than 12-volts recharge the battery.

8 Check the ignition fuse and the fuse connections. If the fuse is blown, renew it; if the connections are loose or corroded, clean or repair them.

9 Refer to Section 3 and check the ignition HT coil primary and secondary resistance.

10 Refer to Section 4 and check the pick-up coil resistance.

11 If the preceding checks produce positive results but there is still no spark at the plug, have the IC igniter checked by a Kawasaki dealer.

Engine starts but misfires

12 If the engine starts but misfires, make the following checks before deciding that the ignition system is at fault.

13 The ignition system must be able to produce a spark which is capable of jumping a particular size gap. A healthy system should produce a spark capable of jumping at least 7 mm (EX500A), 6 mm (EX500D and E) or 8 mm (ER500). A simple testing tool can be made to test the minimum gap across which the spark will jump (see **Tool Tip**) or alternatively it is possible to buy an ignition spark gap tester tool and some of these tools are adjustable to alter the spark gap.

14 Connect one of the spark plug leads to the protruding test fixture electrode, then attach the fixture's alligator clip to a good engine ground/earth **(see illustration)**.

15 Crank the engine over (it may start and run on the remaining cylinder) and see if well-defined, blue sparks occur between the test fixture electrodes. If the minimum spark gap test is positive, the ignition coil for that cylinder is functioning properly. Repeat the check on the spark plug wire that is connected to the other coil. If the spark will not jump the gap during either test, or if it is weak (orange coloured), refer to Steps 5 through 11 of this Section and perform the component checks described.

---

3 Ignition HT coils – check, removal and installation 🔧

Check

1 In order to determine conclusively that the ignition coils are defective, they should be tested by a Kawasaki dealer equipped with the Electro Tester.

2 However, the coils can be checked visually (for cracks and other damage) and the primary

TOOL TiP

A simple spark gap testing tool can be made from a block of wood, a large alligator clip and two nails, one of which is fashioned so that a spark plug cap or bare HT lead end can be connected to its end. Make sure the gap between the two nail ends is the same as specified.

and secondary coil resistances can be measured with an ohmmeter. If the coils are undamaged, and if the resistances are as specified, they are probably capable of proper operation.

3 To check the coils for physical damage, they must be removed (see Step 9). To check the resistances, simply remove the fuel tank (see Chapter 4), unplug the primary circuit electrical connectors from the coil(s) and remove the spark plug lead from the plug that is connected to the coil being checked. Mark the locations of all wires before disconnecting them.

4 To check the coil primary resistance, attach one ohmmeter lead to one of the primary terminals and the other ohmmeter lead to the other primary terminal **(see illustration)**.

5 Place the ohmmeter selector switch in the ohms (Ω) x 1 position and compare the measured resistance to the value listed in this Chapter's Specifications.

6 If the coil primary resistance is as specified, check the coil secondary resistance by disconnecting the meter leads from the primary terminals and attaching one of them to the spark plug lead terminal and the other to either of the primary terminals **(see**

2.3 With the wire attached, ground a spark plug to the engine and operate the starter - bright blue sparks should be visible

2.5 Unscrew the spark plug caps from the plug wires and measure their resistance with an ohmmeter

2.14 Connect the tester to a good earth and attach one of the spark plug leads - when the engine is cranked, sparks should jump the gap between the nails

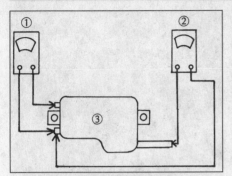

3.4 Ignition coil test

1 *Measure primary winding resistance*
2 *Measure secondary winding resistance*
3 *Ignition coil*

3.10a Right-hand HT coil (cyl no. 2) – EX models

3.10b Left-hand HT coil (cyl no. 1) – EX models

illustration 3.4). Note that the spark plug cap must be unscrewed from the lead before making this test.

7 Place the ohmmeter selector switch in the K-ohms (KΩ) position and compare the measured resistance to the values listed in this Chapter's Specifications.

8 If the secondary resistance is not as specified, unscrew the spark plug lead retainer from the coil, detach the lead and check the resistance again. If it is now within specifications, the lead is broken internally. If the secondary resistance is still not as specified, the coil is probably defective and should be renewed.

Removal and installation

9 To remove the coils, refer to Chapter 4 and remove the fuel tank, then disconnect the spark plug leads from the plugs. After labelling them with tape to aid in reinstallation, unplug the coil primary circuit electrical connectors.

10 Support the coil with one hand and remove the coil mounting bolts **(see illustrations)**, then withdraw the coil from its bracket. Retrieve the collar from each mounting point.

11 Installation is the reverse of removal. Make sure the primary circuit electrical connectors are attached to the proper terminals. If you forgot to mark the wires refer to the wiring diagrams at the end of Chapter 9 for identification.

3.10c Right-hand HT coil (cyl no. 2) – ER models

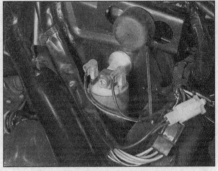

3.10d Left-hand HT coil (cyl no. 1) – ER models

2 Using a multimeter set to the ohms scale, measure the pick-up coil resistance on the engine side of the wire connector and compare the result to the value given in the Specifications. On EX500A models, connect the meter probes between the black and yellow wire terminals of the connector for one coil, then repeat the test between the blue and black/white wire terminals for the other coil. On EX500D, E and ER models, simply connect the meter probes between the black and yellow wire terminals.

3 Now set the ohmmeter on the highest resistance range. Measure the resistance between a good ground/earth and each terminal in the electrical connector. The meter should read infinity.

4 If the pick-up coils fail either of the above

tests, they must be renewed, although check first that the fault is not caused by corrosion in the connector or a broken wire.

Removal

5 Remove the alternator cover (see Chapter 9).

6 Unscrew the pick-up coil mounting screws and remove the pick-up coil(s) **(see illustrations)**. Remove the wiring harness retainer, slip the grommet out of its slot and remove the pick-up coil(s) together with the wiring.

Installation

7 Position the pick-up coil(s) in the alternator cover and install the screws, tightening them securely. Apply a small amount of silicone

---

4 Pick-up coil(s) – check, removal and installation

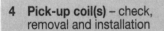

Check

1 Follow the pick-up coil wiring harness from the point where it leaves the alternator cover to the electrical connector, then disconnect the connector for the pick-up coil(s) **(see illustration)**. EX500A models have two pick-up coils and the connector will contain four wires, whereas EX500D, E and ER models have a single pick-up coil with two wires leading to the connector.

4.1 The pick-up coil wiring harness leaves the alternator cover at this grommet (arrowed)

4.6a Pick-up coil screws (upper arrows) and wiring clip (lower arrow) – EX500A

4.6b Pick-up coil screws (arrowed) – EX500D, E and ER500

5.2a IC igniter location – EX500A

5.2b IC igniter location – EX500D and E

sealant to the grommet on the wiring harness and seat the grommet securely in the notch in the alternator cover **(see illustration 4.1)**.
8 Install the alternator cover and reconnect the electrical connector.

5 IC igniter – removal, check and installation

⚠️ **Warning: The ignition must be switched OFF before disconnecting the IC igniter.**

Removal

1 Remove the right-hand side cover on EX models (see Chapter 8). On ER models, remove the seat (see Chapter 8).
2 Disconnect the electrical connector and remove the igniter mounting bolts **(see illustrations)**. Take the igniter out.

Check

3 It is recommended that the motorcycle is taken to a Kawasaki dealer for testing of the IC igniter. Not only is it a very expensive unit which could be damaged by inadvertently applying the wrong test connections, but

5.2c IC igniter location – ER500

often the best way to test the unit is by the substitution of a known good igniter from another bike. Note that it is very rare for the igniter to fail and it should last the life of the motorcycle; you are advised to check all other components in the ignition system before having the igniter tested.

Installation

4 Installation is the reverse of the removal steps.

6 Ignition timing – check

General information

1 Since no provision exists for adjusting the ignition timing and since no component is subject to mechanical wear, there is no need for regular checks; only if investigating a fault such as a loss of power or a misfire, should the ignition timing be checked.
2 The ignition timing can only be checked while the engine is running using a stroboscopic (timing) lamp. The inexpensive neon lamps should be adequate in theory, but

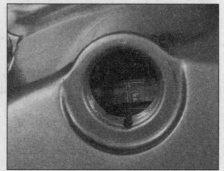

6.6 The F mark should align with the notch in the cover

in practice may produce a pulse of such low intensity that the timing mark remains indistinct. If possible, one of the more precise xenon tube lamps should be used, powered by an external source of the appropriate voltage. **Note:** *Do not use the machine's own battery as an incorrect reading may result from stray impulses within the machine's electrical system.*

Check

3 Warm the engine up to normal operating temperature then stop it.
4 Unscrew the inspection cap from the top of the alternator cover. Recover the cap sealing ring. The timing mark is stamped on the periphery of the alternator rotor and can be seen if the engine is rotated by removing the centre cap from the cover and rotating the crankshaft (turn the engine in the normal direction of opporation, ie clockwise as viewed from the left-hand side of the bike). The ignition timing mark is represented by the letter F, ignore the T mark which denotes TDC. Refit the centre cap when you have familiarised yourself with the correct timing mark.
5 Connect the timing light to the No. 1 (left) cylinder HT lead as described in the manufacturer's instructions. Start the engine and aim the light at the inspection hole.
6 With the machine idling at 1500 rpm or less and the strobe aimed at the timing marks, the F mark should align with the index mark, in the form of a notch in the bottom of the cover hole **(see illustration)**.
7 As already stated, there is no means of adjustment of the ignition timing on these machines. If the ignition timing is incorrect one of the ignition system components is at fault, and system must be tested as described in the preceding Sections of this Chapter.
8 Stop the engine and turn the ignition OFF when the test is complete. Disconnect the stroboscope. Refit the inspection cap.

Chapter 6
Frame, suspension and final drive

Contents

Degrees of difficulty

Easy, suitable for novice with little experience	**Fairly easy,** suitable for beginner with some experience	**Fairly difficult,** suitable for competent DIY mechanic	**Difficult,** suitable for experienced DIY mechanic	**Very difficult,** suitable for expert DIY or professional

Specifications

Front forks

Oil capacity, level and type	see Chapter 1	
Spring length:	**Standard**	**Minimum**
EX500A models	516.7 mm (20.34 in)	506 mm (19.92 in)
EX500D and E models	434.5 mm (17.11 in)	425 mm (16.73 in)
ER500A models	429.5 mm (16.91 in)	420 mm (16.54 in)
ER500C1 and C3 models	338.5 mm (13.33 in)	332 mm (13.07 in)
ER500C4 and C5 models	438.5 mm (17.26 in)	430 mm (16.93 in)

Rear shock absorber

Rear spring preload – EX models	
Standard setting	Compressed to 17 mm (0.669 in) less than free length
Range	7 to 27 mm (0.275 to 1.06 in) less than free length

Drive chain

Chain slack, wear limit and lubricant	see Chapter 1
Chain size	520 O-ring
No. of links	
EX models	104
ER models	106

Sprockets

Rear sprocket runout (maximum)	0.5 mm (0.020 in)
Sprocket sizes	
EX500A1, A2, A3 models	17T (front), 42T (rear)
EX500A4, A5, A6, A7 models	16T (front), 42T (rear)
EX500D and E models	16T (front), 41T (rear)
ER models	17T (front), 42T (rear)

Torque specifications

Footrest bracket bolts
   ER models . . . . 34 Nm (25 ft-lbs)
   EX models . . . . 25 Nm (25 ft-lbs)
Brake pedal pivot bolt . . . . 8.8 Nm (78 in-lbs)
Centerstand and sidestand bolts
   EX500A models . . . . not available
   EX500D, E models and ER models . . . . 44 Nm (33 ft-lbs)
Handlebar grip-to-upright bolts – EX models . . . . 23 Nm (16.5 ft-lbs)
Handlebar upright-to-upper triple clamp bolts – EX models . . . . 23 Nm (16.5 ft-lbs)
Handlebar clamp bolts – ER models . . . . 23 Nm (16.5 ft-lbs)
Damper rod bolt
   EX500A models . . . . 29 Nm (22 ft-lbs)
   EX500D, E models and ER models . . . . 20 Nm (14.5 ft-lbs)
Steering stem bolt
   EX500A models . . . . 47 Nm (35 ft-lbs)
   EX500D, E models and ER models . . . . 44 Nm (33 ft-lbs)
Steering bearing adjuster nut
   EX500A . . . . 7.4 Nm (65 in-lbs)
   EX500D and E models . . . . 4.9 Nm (43 in-lbs or finger-tight)
   ER models . . . . 4.9 Nm (43 in-lbs or finger-tight)
Fork upper triple clamp bolts . . . . 20 Nm (14.5 ft-lbs)
Fork lower triple clamp bolts
   EX500A models and ER models . . . . 29 Nm (22 ft-lbs)
   EX500D and E models . . . . 34 Nm (25 ft-lbs)
Rear shock absorber mounting bolts/nuts
   EX500A models . . . . 49 Nm (36 ft-lbs)
   EX500D and E models . . . . 59 Nm (43 ft-lbs)
   ER models . . . . 34 Nm (25 ft-lbs)
Rear suspension linkage pivot bolt nuts – EX models
   EX500A models . . . . 49 Nm (36 ft-lbs)
   EX500D and E models . . . . 59 Nm (43 ft-lbs)
Swingarm pivot shaft nut . . . . 88 Nm (65 ft-lbs)
Rear sprocket-to-wheel coupling nuts
   EX500A models and ER models . . . . 74 Nm (54 ft-lbs)
   EX500D and E models . . . . 59 Nm (43 ft-lbs)
Engine sprocket holding plate bolts – EX models . . . . 9.8 Nm (87 in-lbs)
Engine sprocket nut – ER models . . . . 125 Nm (94 ft-lbs)

1 General information

The machines covered by this manual use a full cradle frame, constructed of steel square tubing on EX models and steel round tubing on ER models. The right-hand downtube is detachable, which allows for easy engine removal.

3.1 The footrests are secured to their brackets by C-clips (rider's right footrest shown)

The front forks are of the conventional coil spring, hydraulically damped telescopic type.

The rear suspension on EX models uses Kawasaki's Uni-Trak design, which consists of a single shock absorber, a rocker arm, two tie-rods and a square-section aluminium swingarm. ER models use a traditional rear suspension set up, with two shock absorbers linked to a square-section aluminium swingarm

The final drive uses an endless chain (which means it doesn't have a master link). A rubber damper is installed between the rear wheel coupling and the wheel.

2 Frame – inspection and repair

1 The frame should not require attention unless accident damage has occurred. In most cases, frame renewal is the only satisfactory remedy for such damage. A few frame specialists have the jigs and other equipment necessary for straightening the frame to the required standard of accuracy, but even then there is no simple way of assessing to what extent the frame may have been over stressed.

2 After the machine has accumulated a lot of miles, the frame should be examined closely for signs of cracking or splitting at the welded joints. Rust can also cause weakness at these joints. Loose engine mount bolts can cause ovaling or fracturing of the mounting tabs. Minor damage can often be repaired by welding, depending on the extent and nature of the damage.

3 Remember that a frame which is out of alignment will cause handling problems. If misalignment is suspected as the result of an accident, it will be necessary to strip the machine completely so the frame can be thoroughly checked.

3 Footrests and brackets – removal and installation

EX models

Rider's right-hand side footrest

1 If it's only necessary to detach the footrest from the bracket, pry the C-clip off the pivot pin **(see illustration)**, slide out the pin and detach the footrest from the bracket. Be careful not to lose the spring. Installation is

the reverse of removal, but be sure to install the spring correctly.

2 If it's necessary to remove the entire bracket from the frame, unplug the electrical connector for the rear brake light switch.

3 Remove the cotter pin (split pin) from the clevis pin that attaches the brake pedal to the brake rod, then remove the clevis pin (see Chapter 7).

4 Remove the bolts that secure the bracket to the frame, then detach the footrest and bracket.

5 Installation is the reverse of removal.

Rider's left-hand side footrest

6 If it's only necessary to detach the footrest from the bracket, pry the C-clip off the pivot pin **(see illustration 3.1)**, slide out the pin and detach the footrest from the bracket.

7 If it's necessary to remove the entire bracket from the frame, remove the gearchange lever (see Chapter 2).

8 Remove the bracket bolts **(see illustration)** and remove the bracket from the frame.

9 Installation is the basically the reverse of removal. Apply a thin coat of grease to the shift pedal pivot bolt, and be sure to line up the matchmarks on the gearchange lever and gearchange shaft. The link rod should be parallel to the gearchange lever.

Passenger footrests and brackets (either side)

10 If it's only necessary to detach the footrest from the bracket, pry the C-clip off the pivot pin **(see illustration 3.1)**, slide out the pin and detach the footrest from the bracket.

11 If it's necessary to remove the entire bracket, unscrew the bolt and detach the bracket from the frame.

12 Installation is the reverse of removal.

ER models

Rider and passenger footrests

13 If it's only necessary to detach the footrest from the bracket, pry the C-clip off

the pivot pin **(see illustration 3.1)**, slide out the pin and detach the footrest from the bracket. Installation is the reverse of removal. Don't forget the washer between the footrest and its bracket.

Footrest brackets

14 The left-hand footrest bracket is simply secured to the frame by two bolts.

15 If removal of the right-hand footrest bracket is required, first remove the silencer mounting bolt at the rear; place a support under the silencer to prevent strain on the other exhaust system mountings. Refer to Chapter 7, Section 13 and disconnect the brake rod from the brake cam. Remove the two footrest bracket bolts and ease the bracket away from the frame to enable the brake light switch spring and brake pedal return spring to be disconnected. Remove the footrest bracket and brake pedal/rod from the motorcycle.

16 If necessary remove the brake pedal pivot bolt and washer to separate the pedal from the footrest bracket.

17 Installation is a reverse on the removal procedure. Tighten the footrest mounting bolts and brake pedal pivot bolt to the specified torque. If the right-hand bracket was disturbed, set up the brake pedal height and pedal freeplay as described in Chapter 1.

---

4 Centerstand and sidestand – removal and installation

Centerstand

1 Support the bike securely on its sidestand or on an auxiliary stand. Using a pair of strong pliers, disconnect the stand return spring at one end.

2 On EX models the centerstand pivots on two bolts with nuts attached to the frame **(see illustration)**. Hold the nut on the inside of the frame tube and unscrew the bolt. On

3.8 The rider's left side footrest bracket is secured by two bolts (arrowed)

installation, apply grease to the pivot bolt shank. Tighten the pivot bolts to the specified torque, where given. Reconnect the return spring.

3 On ER models the centerstand pivots on a single throughbolt and nut. Hold the nut on the right-hand side of the bike and unscrew the bolt. On installation, apply grease to the pivot bolt shank and don't omit the stopper plate on the right-hand side as the pivot bolt is inserted. Tighten the pivot bolt to the specified torque. Reconnect the return spring.

4 Make sure the return spring is in good condition. A broken or weak spring is an obvious safety hazard. On EX models the return spring must be positioned with its longer end upwards.

Sidestand

5 Support the bike securely on its centerstand. Using a pair of strong pliers, disconnect the stand return spring at one end.

6 Hold the nut on the inside of the sidestand bracket and unscrew the bolt **(see illustration)**. On installation, apply grease to the pivot bolt shank. Tighten the pivot bolt to the specified torque, where given. Reconnect the return spring.

7 Make sure the return spring is in good condition. A broken or weak spring is an obvious safety hazard. On EX models the

4.2 The centerstand is secured by pivot bolts (arrowed) – EX models

4.6 The sidestand is secured by two bolts (arrowed); the long end of the spring is upward when the stand is down

5.1a Remove the plugs (right arrow) and the bolts beneath them (left arrow) . . .

5.1b . . . and lift the handlebar off

5.2a To detach a handlebar grip, remove the plug (arrowed) . . .

return spring must be positioned with its longer end upwards.

8 The sidestand switch is also fitted to the stand mounting bracket. Check that the switch is free from oil and road dirt; if its operation is stiff spray the switch plunger with a water dispersant aerosol. If the switch is faulty refer to the testing procedure in Chapter 9.

5 Handlebars –
removal and installation

EX models

Removal

1 The handlebars are individual assemblies that slip over the tops of the fork tubes, each being retained to the triple clamp by two Allen-head bolts. If the handlebars must be removed for access to other components, such as the forks or the steering head, simply remove the bolts and slip the handlebar(s) off the fork tubes **(see illustrations)**. It's not necessary to disconnect the cables, wires or hoses, but it is a good idea to support the assembly with a piece of wire or rope, to avoid unnecessary strain on the cables, wires and (on the right-hand side) the brake hose.

2 To remove the grip portion of the handlebar, refer to Chapter 7 for the master cylinder removal procedure and Chapter 4 for the throttle cable/switch housing and choke

cable/switch housing removal procedures. Remove the plug and the bolt behind it **(see illustrations)**, then detach the grip from the handlebar upright.

3 Check the handlebars for cracks and distortion and renew them if any undesirable conditions are found.

Installation

4 Installation is the reverse of the removal steps. Tighten the bolts to the torques listed in this Chapter's Specifications.

ER models

Removal

5 If the handlebars are being removed for access to the front forks or steering head, it's not necessary to disconnect any of the cables, switches or hydraulic brake hose; just support the handlebar so that there is no strain on its cables/wiring and so that the brake master cylinder is kept upright. If complete removal is required, remove the throttle and choke cables with the handlebar switches (Chapter 4), the clutch cable (Chapter 2), and the brake master cylinder (Chapter 7) – there is no need to disconnect the hydraulic hose from the master cylinder.

6 Remove the four bolts **(see illustration 5.8a)** to free the handlebar clamps and lift the handlebars off the triple clamp.

7 If the handlebar grips require renewal, remove the screw from the end of the handlebar, withdraw the end weight, rubber damper and circlip. The right-hand grip/throttle

twistgrip will slip off the handlebar end, whereas the left-hand grip is bonded in place and must be cut off. If fitting a new left-hand grip degrease the handlebar end and bond the grip in place with adhesive. Apply grease to the inside of the throttle twistgrip when fitting the right-hand grip on the handlebar. Assemble the end weight components and apply thread locking compound to the threads of the retaining screw.

Installation

8 Place the handlebar in the triple clamp holders and fit the clamps so that the arrow on their top points forwards **(see illustration)**. Position the handlebar so that the punch mark aligns with the clamp join at the rear **(see illustration)**, then fully tighten both front bolts, followed by the rear bolts to the specified torque; the gap between the clamp rear face and triple clamp is intentional.

9 If removed install the brake master cylinder, clutch cable, throttle and choke cables, and handlebar switches.

6 Forks – removal and installation

Removal

1 Set the bike on its centerstand and place a support under the engine to prevent the bike toppling forwards.

5.2b . . . and remove the bolt behind it

5.8a Arrow mark on clamp must face forwards

5.8b Punch mark (arrowed) on handlebar must align with clamp rear joint

6.9a Upper triple clamp bolt (arrowed) . . .

6.9b . . . lower triple clamp bolt (arrowed) – EX models

6.9c Upper triple clamp bolt (arrowed) . . .

6.9d . . . and lower triple clamp bolt – ER models

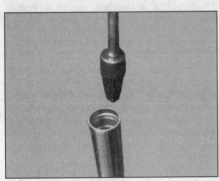

7.4a Insert the tool down through the fork tube to engage the damper rod head

2 Remove the fuel tank on EX models (see Chapter 4)

3 Remove the upper fairing on EX models (see Chapter 8).

4 Unbolt the brake caliper and hang it from the bike with a piece of rope or wire (see Chapter 7).

5 Remove the wheel (see Chapter 7).

6 Remove the front mudguard (see Chapter 8).

7 Remove the handlebars (see Section 5). Support them so the cables, wires and brake hose aren't strained or kinked.

8 Remove any wiring harness clamps or straps from the fork tubes.

9 Loosen the fork upper and lower triple clamp bolts **(see illustrations)**, then twist the fork tubes and slide them downward and out of the triple clamps.

Installation

10 Slide each fork leg into the lower triple clamp.

11 Slide the fork legs up, installing the tops of the tubes into the upper triple clamp. On EX models the fork tubes must extend 15 mm (0.6 in) above the top surface of the upper triple clamp. On ER models the fork tubes must be level with the top surface of the upper triple clamp.

12 The remainder of installation is the reverse of the removal procedure. Be sure to tighten the triple clamp bolts to the torque listed in this Chapter's Specifications. Tighten the caliper mounting bolts to the torque listed in the Chapter 7 Specifications.

13 Pump the front brake lever several times to bring the pads into contact with the discs.

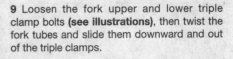

7 Forks – disassembly, inspection and reassembly

Disassembly

1 Remove the forks following the procedure in Section 6. Work on one fork leg at a time to avoid mixing up the parts.

2 Remove the retaining ring, top plug (spacer and spring seat on EX500D, E and ER models) and fork spring (see Chapter 1, Section 31).

3 Invert the fork assembly over a container and allow the oil to drain out. Pump the fork to expel the oil.

4 Prevent the damper rod from turning using a holding handle (Kawasaki tool no. 57001-183) and adapter (Kawasaki tool no. 57001-1057) or equivalents **(see illustrations)**. Unscrew the Allen bolt at the bottom of the outer tube and retrieve the copper washer **(see illustration)**.

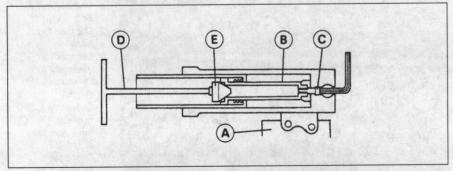

7.4b Kawasaki service tool engaged with the damper rod head

A	Fork outer tube held in vice
B	Damper rod
C	Damper rod Allen bolt
D	Tool holding handle
E	Tool adapter

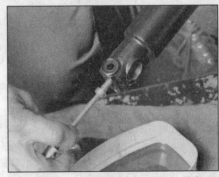

7.4c Remove the damper rod bolt with an Allen key

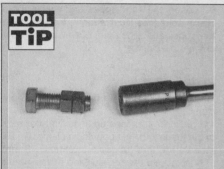

If you don't have access to the Kawasaki special tool, you can fabricate your own using a bolt with a head that fits inside the damper rod, two nuts, a socket (to fit on the nuts), a long extension and a ratchet. Thread the two nuts onto the bolt and tighten them against each other. Insert the assembly into the socket and tape it into place. Now, insert the tool into the fork tube and engage the bolt head into the round hole in the damper rod.

7.5 Remove the damper rod and rebound spring from the inner tube

7.6 Pry the dust seal out of the outer tube with a small screwdriver

7.7a Pry the retaining ring (arrowed) out of its groove . . .

5 Tip out the damper rod and the rebound spring **(see illustration)**.
6 Pry the dust seal from the outer tube **(see illustration)**. If required, ease the fork tube protectors off the outer tube.
7 Pry the retaining ring from its groove in the outer tube **(see illustrations)**.
8 Hold the outer tube and yank the inner tube upward, repeatedly (like a slide-hammer), until the seal and outer tube guide bushing pop loose.
9 Slide the seal, washer and outer tube guide bushing from the inner tube **(see illustration)**.
10 Invert the outer tube and remove the damper rod base **(see illustration)**.

Inspection

11 Clean all parts in solvent and blow them dry with compressed air, if available. Check the inner and outer fork tubes, the guide bushings and the damper rod for score marks, scratches, flaking of the chrome and excessive or abnormal wear. Look for dents in the tubes and renew them if any are found. Check the fork seal seat for nicks, gouges and scratches. If damage is evident, leaks will occur around the seal-to-outer tube junction. Renew worn or defective parts.
12 If you suspect that the forks tubes are bent or if the bike has been involved in an accident, have the fork inner tubes checked for runout by a suspension specialist.

> ⚠ *Warning: If either fork tube is bent, it should not be straightened; renew it.*

13 Measure the overall length of the long fork spring and check it for cracks and other damage. Compare the length to the minimum length listed in this Chapter's Specifications. If it's defective or sagged, renew both fork springs. Never renew the spring in one leg only.

Reassembly

14 If it's necessary to renew the inner guide bushing (the one that's on the bottom of the inner tube), pry it apart at the slit and slide it off. Make sure the new one seats properly.
15 Place the rebound spring over the damper rod and slide the rod assembly into the inner fork tube until it protrudes from the lower end of the tube.

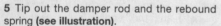

7.7b . . . and slide it off the inner fork tube

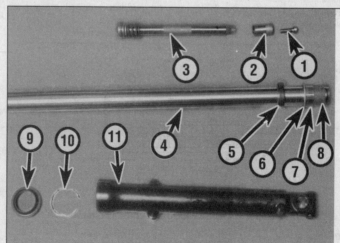

1 Damper rod bolt
2 Damper rod base
3 Damper rod
4 Inner fork tube
5 Oil seal
6 Washer
7 Outer fork tube bushing
8 Inner fork tube bushing
9 Dust seal
10 Retaining ring
11 Outer fork tube

7.9 Fork details

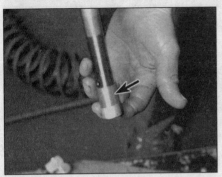

7.10 Dump the damper rod base (arrowed) out of the fork tube and put it back on the damper rod

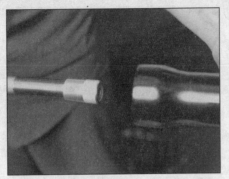

7.16 Assemble the damper rod into the inner fork tube . . .

7.17a . . . then install the assembly into the outer fork tube . . .

16 Install the damper rod base onto the end of the damper rod (see illustration).

17 Insert the inner tube/damper rod assembly into the outer tube (see illustration) until the Allen-head bolt (with copper washer) can be threaded into the damper rod from the lower end of the outer tube (see illustrations). **Note:** *Apply a non-permanent thread locking compound to the threads of the bolt. Keep the two tubes fairly horizontal so the damper rod base doesn't fall off. Using the tool described in Step 4, hold the damper rod and tighten the Allen bolt to the torque listed in this Chapter's Specifications.*

18 Slide the outer guide bushing down the inner tube. The slit in the bushing must point to the left or right – not to the front or rear.

Using a special bushing driver (Kawasaki tool no. 57001-1219) or equivalent and a used guide bushing placed on top of the guide bushing being installed, drive the bushing into place until it is fully seated (see illustration). If you don't have access to one of these tools, it is highly recommended that you take the assembly to a Kawasaki dealer or suspension specialist to have this done. It is possible, however, to drive the bushing into place using a section of tubing and an old guide bushing (see illustration). Wrap tape around the ends of the tubing to prevent it from scratching the fork tube.

19 Slide the washer down the inner tube, into position over the guide bushing.

20 Lubricate the lips and the outer diameter

of the fork seal with the recommended fork oil (see Chapter 1) and slide it down the inner tube, with the lips facing down (see illustration). Drive the seal into place using either the special seal driver described above or a length of tubing (see illustrations). If you

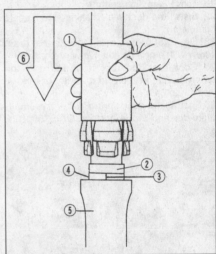

7.18a The Kawasaki service tool for installing the outer guide bushing

1	Tool no. 57001-1219	4	New guide bushing
2	Used bushing	5	Outer tube
3	Slit	6	Tap downward

7.17b . . . place a new washer on the damper rod bolt . . .

7.17c . . . and thread it into the damper rod (arrowed)

7.18b If you don't have the proper tool a section of pipe can be used as a driver

7.20a Press the oil seal into the fork outer tube as far as you can with finger pressure . . .

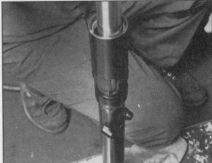

7.20b . . . then use a seal driver to seat it in the outer fork tube

7.21 Install the retaining ring

8.6a Remove the steering stem bolt . . .

8.6b . . . and the upper triple clamp

are very careful, the seal can be driven in with a hammer and a drift punch. Work around the circumference of the seal, tapping gently on the outer edge of the seal until it's seated, but be careful you don't distort the seal.

21 Install the washer and the retaining ring, making sure the ring is completely seated in its groove **(see illustration)**.

22 Install the dust seal, making sure it seats completely.

23 On EX500A models, install the drain screw with a new gasket, if it was removed.

24 Compress the fork fully and add the recommended type and quantity of fork oil (see Chapter 1).

25 Install the fork spring, with the small-diameter end at the bottom. On EX500D, E

and ER models install the spring seat and spacer.

26 Check the O-ring on the top plug, then coat it with a thin layer of multi-purpose grease. Install the top plug, push it down against the spring pressure, install the retaining ring and slowly release the top plug.

27 Install the fork by following the procedure outlined in Section 6. If you won't be installing the fork right away, store it in an upright position to prevent leakage.

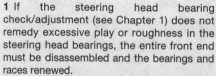

8 Steering head bearings – renewal

1 If the steering head bearing check/adjustment (see Chapter 1) does not remedy excessive play or roughness in the steering head bearings, the entire front end must be disassembled and the bearings and races renewed.

2 Remove the fuel tank (see Chapter 4).

3 On EX models, remove the upper fairing and lower fairing (see Chapter 8).

4 Remove the handlebars (see Section 5) and front forks (see Section 6).

5 Unbolt the horn bracket from the steering head (see Chapter 9).

6 Remove the steering stem bolt **(see illustration)**, then lift off the upper triple clamp (sometimes called the fork bridge or crown or yoke) **(see illustration)**.

7 Support the steering stem from the bottom so it doesn't fall out of the frame during the next steps.

8 Remove the bearing adjuster nut with a C-spanner.

9 Remove the dust cover and upper inner race from the upper bearing, then remove the 19 ball bearings **(see illustrations)**.

10 Lower the steering stem just far enough to expose the lower ball bearing **(see illustration)**. If it's stuck, gently tap on the top of the steering stem with a plastic mallet or a hammer and a wood block. **Note:** *Ball bearings may fall out when the steering stem is lowered. Position your hands so you can catch them. There are 20 ball bearings in the lower bearing.*

Inspection

11 Clean all the parts with solvent and dry them thoroughly, using compressed air, if available. Wipe the old grease out of the frame steering head and bearing races.

12 Examine the lower bearing inner race on the steering stem and the upper and lower bearing outer races in the steering head for cracks, dents, and pits **(see illustration)**. If even the slightest amount of wear or damage is evident, the races should be renewed.

13 Check the ball bearings for wear. Renew any defective parts. If a new bearing is required, renew both of them as a set.

14 To remove the races, drive them out of the steering head with a brass drift **(see**

8.9a After removing the dust cover, lift out the upper bearing inner race . . .

8.9b . . . and the 19 ball bearings

8.10 When you lower the steering stem, some ball bearings (arrowed) will fall out, so be ready to catch them

8.12 Check the lower bearing inner race on the steering stem (arrowed)

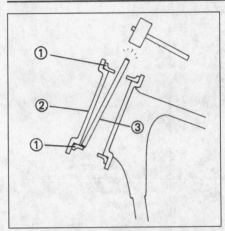

8.14a Drive out the outer races with a hammer and brass drift

1 *Outer races*   3 *Brass drift*
2 *Steering head*

illustration). A slide-hammer with the proper internal-jaw puller will also work. When installing the races, coat them with oil and tap them gently into place with a bearing driver **(see illustration)** or a large socket. The bearing driver or socket must bear only on the outer rim of the race – do not strike the bearing surface or the race will be damaged.

 Installation of new bearing outer races is made much easier if the races are left overnight in the freezer. This causes them to contract slightly making them a looser fit.

15 To remove the lower bearing inner race from the steering stem, use a bearing puller with adapter to clamp below the inner race **(see illustration)**. Don't remove this bearing unless it, or the grease seal underneath, must be renewed. If care is taken, you can use two large flat-bladed screwdrivers to work the bearing evenly off its seat.

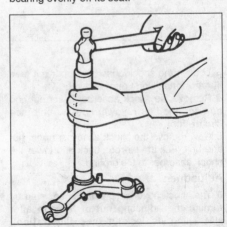

8.18 Drive the lower bearing inner race on with a suitable length of tubing

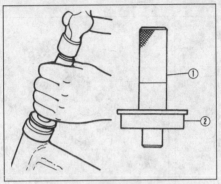

8.14b Drive in new outer races with a bearing driver or a socket the same diameter as the bearing race

1 *Bearing driver handle*   2 *Bearing driver*

16 Check the grease seal under the lower bearing and renew it if necessary. Note that there is a washer between the grease seal and the steering stem/lower triple clamp.
17 Inspect the steering stem/lower triple clamp for cracks and other damage. Do not attempt to repair any steering components. Renew them if defects are found.

Installation

18 Install the washer, grease seal and new lower bearing inner race onto the steering stem (if they were removed). Coat the race with oil and drive it onto the steering stem using a length of tubing which fits over the steering stem and bears only on the inner race's inner edge and not on its bearing surface **(see illustration)**. The end of the tubing must be square and filed smooth. Drive the bearing race on until it is fully seated.
19 Coat both bearing outer races in the steering head with a thick layer of grease **(see illustration)**.
20 Coat 20 ball bearings with grease and stick them to the lower bearing outer race in the steering head **(see illustration)**.
21 Carefully insert the steering stem/lower triple clamp into the frame head, making sure you don't displace any of the ball bearings.
22 Hold the steering stem in place and install 19 ball bearings in the upper bearing outer

8.19 Smear a thick layer of grease onto the lower inner race to hold the ball bearings in place . . .

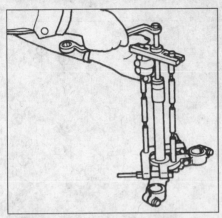

8.15 Remove the steering stem bearing inner race with a puller

race **(see illustration 8.9b)**. Install the upper inner race and dust cover. Thread the bearing adjuster nut, chamfered or recessed side down, onto the steering stem, securing it hand-tight. Rotate the lower triple clamp from lock to lock and check that it moves smoothly.
23 Tighten the bearing adjuster nut to the torque listed in this Chapter's Specifications.
24 Again turn the lower triple clamp back and forth. It should turn easily (without binding and without looseness).
25 Install the upper triple clamp on the steering stem. Install the bolt, tightening it to the torque listed in this Chapter's Specifications.
26 The remainder of installation is the reverse of removal.
27 Prior to installing the fuel tank, check steering head bearing adjustment and correct it if necessary (see Chapter 1).

9 Rear shock absorber(s) – removal, adjustment and installation

EX models
Removal
1 Set the bike on its centerstand.
2 Remove the side covers.

8.20 . . . then stick 20 steel balls into place in the grease

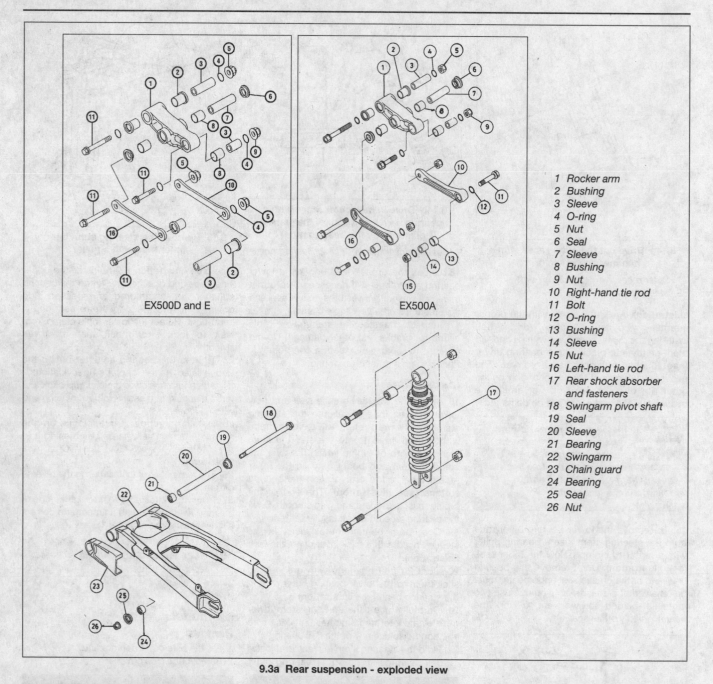

1 Rocker arm
2 Bushing
3 Sleeve
4 O-ring
5 Nut
6 Seal
7 Sleeve
8 Bushing
9 Nut
10 Right-hand tie rod
11 Bolt
12 O-ring
13 Bushing
14 Sleeve
15 Nut
16 Left-hand tie rod
17 Rear shock absorber
   and fasteners
18 Swingarm pivot shaft
19 Seal
20 Sleeve
21 Bearing
22 Swingarm
23 Chain guard
24 Bearing
25 Seal
26 Nut

EX500D and E

EX500A

9.3a Rear suspension - exploded view

9.3b Loosen the upper nut (arrowed) and bolt, but don't remove them at this stage

9.4 Remove the shock absorber lower nut and bolt (left arrow) and tie-rod nut and bolt (right arrow)

3 Loosen the shock absorber upper nut **(see illustrations)**. Don't remove it yet.

4 Remove the shock absorber lower nut and bolt and the tie-rod lower nut and bolt **(see illustration)**.

5 Now remove the shock absorber upper nut and bolt. Pull the tie-rods back and lower the shock absorber to the ground.

Adjustment

6 The shock absorber preload is adjusted by turning the adjusting nut at the top after slackening its locknut **(see illustration)**. Compressing the spring (turning the adjusting nut down) increases the preload, while turning the nut upward decreases it.

9.6 Spring preload locknut and adjusting nut (arrowed)

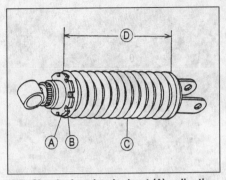

9.7 Shock absorber locknut (A), adjusting nut (B), spring (C) and spring length (D)

9.10a Shock upper mounting nut, spring washer and plain washer

9.10b Shock lower mounting nut and bolt on right side

9.10c Shock lower mounting bolt on left side

9.13 Preload adjuster collar

7 Note that preload is set with the shock removed from the bike. Back off the locknut and unscrew the adjusting nut until the spring is untensioned (free of any preload). Measure the spring's overall length to obtain the 'free length'. Now turn the adjusting nut down towards the spring until you reach the spring length required **(see illustration)**. Refer to the Specifications for details of the standard amount of preload and the preload range; preload is expressed in terms of the amount of spring compression from its free length.

Installation

8 Installation is the reverse of the removal procedure. Tighten the shock absorber and tie-rod nuts to the torque values listed in this Chapter's Specifications.

ER models

Removal

9 Set the bike on its centerstand. If both shock absorbers are being removed, place a support under the rear of the engine to prevent the bike toppling backwards. With the weight of the bike off the rear wheel place a wood block between the rear tyre and ground to prevent the rear wheel dropping with the shock absorbers are removed.

10 Remove one shock at a time. Remove the

domed nut with spring washer and plain washer from the shock upper mounting **(see illustration)**. Remove the nut and bolt from the shock lower mounting on the right-hand side **(see illustration)** or the bolt from the shock lower mounting on the left-hand side **(see illustration)**. Move the shock rearwards off its lower mounting point and pull it off its stud mounting at the top.

11 There are no replacement parts available for the shock absorbers. If they are leaking damping fluid or are damaged in any way they must be renewed as a pair. Note that new rubber bushes for the mounting eyes can be obtained and that a drawbolt tool will have to be used to remove and install them.

10.3 Remove the tie-rod upper bolts (arrowed) and nuts

Installation

12 Install the shock absorbers in a reverse of the removal procedure, noting the torque values listed in this Chapter's Specifications.

Adjustment

13 The shock absorbers are adjustable for spring preload. Use the C-spanner provided in the bike's toolkit to turn the slotted preload adjuster ring **(see illustration)**. There are five preload positions, position no. 5 gives the most preload and harder ride and position no. 1 the least preload and softer ride. Kawasaki recommend position no. 2 as standard.

---

10 Rear suspension linkage – removal, check and installation (EX models)

1 Set the bike on its centerstand.

Tie-rod(s)

2 Remove the tie-rod lower nut and bolt **(see illustration 9.4)**.

3 On EX500A models, remove the nut(s) and bolt(s) that secure the tie-rods to the swingarm and remove the tie-rod(s) **(see illustration)**. On EX500D and E models, remove the nut and throughbolt which secure the tie-rods to the swingarm and remove the tie-rods.

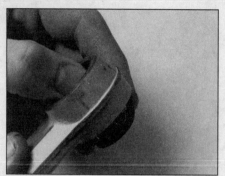

10.4 Push the sleeve out of the end of the tie-rod and remove the O-rings

10.10 Loosen the rocker arm pivot bolt nut, but don't remove it at first

10.15a To check the condition of the bushings, push the sleeves out of the rocker arm

4 On EX500A models, push the sleeve out of the tie-rod **(see illustration)**. Check the O-rings for cracking and general deterioration and renew them if necessary. Check the bushing in the tie-rod and the outer surface of the sleeve for wear, renewing them if necessary (see Step 16 below for bushing renewal). Apply a thin coat of moly-based grease to the bushing and sleeve and install the sleeve in the bushing. Press the O-rings into place around the sleeve.

5 On EX500D and E models, there are no bushings in the upper ends of the tie-rods. Instead the swingarm mounting contains two headed bushings, an inner sleeve and an O-ring at each end **(see illustration 9.3a)**. Slip out the inner sleeve and wipe all old grease off the sleeve and bushings set in the swingarm. Refit the sleeve and feel for any freeplay between the two components – if freeplay is evident, the bushings and sleeve should be renewed (see Step 16 below for bushing renewal). If the O-rings are damaged they must be renewed. Apply a thin coat of moly-based grease to the bushings and sleeve and install the sleeve in the bushings. Press the O-rings into place around the sleeve.

6 Installation is the reverse of the removal steps.

7 Tighten the nuts and bolts to the torque listed in this Chapter's Specifications.

Rocker arm

8 Remove the shock absorber lower nut and tie-rod nut, but not the bolts **(see illustration 9.4)**.

9 Support the swingarm with a jack and remove the shock absorber and tie-rod bolts.

10 Loosen the rocker arm nut **(see illustration)**, but don't remove the bolt yet.

11 Remove the exhaust pipes (see Chapter 4).

12 Support the bike on an auxiliary stand so the centerstand can be retracted.

 Warning: Whatever you use to support the bike must be stable enough so the machine can't fall on you during this procedure. It's a good idea to have an assistant ready to steady the bike.

13 Retract the centerstand.

14 Remove the nut and pull out the rocker arm pivot bolt **(see illustration 10.10)**. Detach the rocker arm from the frame.

15 Push the sleeves out of the rocker arm **(see illustration)**. Check the bushings for dryness and discoloration. If necessary, pry out the grease seals or O-rings **(see illustration)**, clean the bushings with solvent, dry and repack them with moly-based grease.

16 If the bushings are deteriorated, drive them out of the rocker arm with a hammer and punch **(see illustration)**. Install new bushings by driving them in with a hammer and a socket of the appropriate size **(see illustration)**.

17 Coat the bearings with grease, install the grease seals and slide the bushings into place.

18 The remainder of installation is the reverse of the removal procedure.

19 Tighten the linkage pivot bolt nuts to the torque values listed in this Chapter's Specifications.

11 Swingarm bearings – check

1 Refer to Chapter 7 and remove the rear wheel, then refer to Section 9 and remove the rear shock absorber(s).

2 Grasp the rear of the swingarm with one hand and place your other hand at the junction of the swingarm and the frame. Try to move the rear of the from side-to-side. Any wear (play) in the bearings should be felt as movement between the swingarm and the frame at the front. The swingarm will actually be felt to move forward and backward at the front (not from side-to-side). If any play is noted, the bearings should be renewed (see Section 13).

3 Next, move the swingarm up and down through its full travel. It should move freely, without any binding or rough spots. If it does not move freely, refer to Section 13 for servicing procedures.

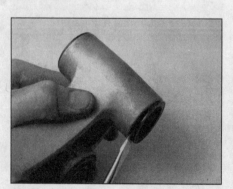

10.15b Pry out the grease seals for access to the bushings

10.16a To replace the bushings, knock them out with a hammer and punch . . .

10.16b . . . then drive the new ones in with a socket that just fits into the bore of the rocker arm

12.4a Remove the plastic cap from the pivot shaft head . . .

12.4b . . . and the pivot shaft nut

12.6 Pull the pivot shaft out

12 Swingarm – removal and installation

1 Raise the bike and set it on its centerstand.
2 Remove the rear wheel (see Chapter 7).
3 On EX500A and ER models, detach the brake torque link from the swingarm; it is retained by an R-pin, nut and bolt. On EX500D and E models, slip the rear brake hose out of its guide on the swingarm. On all models remove the chain guard.
4 Pry the swingarm pivot shaft caps out from each side of the frame **(see illustration)**. Remove the swingarm pivot nut **(see illustration)**.
5 On EX models, support the swingarm with a jack and detach the tie-rods and the shock absorber from the rocker arm **(see illustration 9.4)**.
6 On all models, support the swingarm and pull the pivot shaft out **(see illustration)**. Remove the swingarm and separate it from the drive chain. On EX models, if necessary, remove the bolts(s) and detach the tie-rods from the swingarm.
7 Check the pivot bearings in the swingarm for dryness or deterioration **(see illustration)**. If they're in need of lubrication or renewal refer to Section 13.
8 Installation is the reverse of the removal procedure, with the following additions:
a) *Don't forget to loop the drive chain around the swingarm as it is being installed.*

b) *Be sure the bearing seals are in position before installing the pivot shaft.*
c) *Tighten the pivot shaft nut and the suspension mounting bolts/nuts to the torque values listed in this Chapter's Specifications.*
d) *If the torque link was separated from the swingarm on EX500A and ER models don't forget to install the R-pin in the bolt hole.*
e) *Adjust the chain as described in Chapter 1.*

13 Swingarm bearings – renewal

Note: *Bearing removal requires the use of a slide-hammer with internal expanding adapter. If this tool is not available have the bearings renewed by a Kawasaki dealer.*

1 The two needle-roller bearings are a press fit in the swingarm. Do not remove the bearings unless they are to be renewed.
2 Remove the swingarm (see Section 12).
3 Slide the inner sleeve out **(see illustration)**.
4 Pry out the seals **(see illustration)**.
5 Use a slide-hammer with an internal expanding adapter to pull the bearings out of the swingarm. Prior to disturbing the bearings, measure and note down their installed depth in the swingarm (ie the distance from the end of the swingarm to the outer edge of the bearing.

12.7 There's a needle bearing in each side of the swingarm (sleeve and seal removed for clarity)

6 New bearings should be driven into the swingarm using a piece of tubing which bears only on the outer edge of the bearing and not on the rollers. Install the bearing to the previously noted depth; on ER models Kawasaki specify a depth of 6 mm **(see illustration)**.

14 Drive chain – removal, cleaning and installation

Removal – endless type chain

Note: *An endless chain has no riveted (soft) link – all links and pins are the same. The chain*

13.3 Slide the sleeve out of the front of the swingarm

13.4 Pry the seals out with a screwdriver

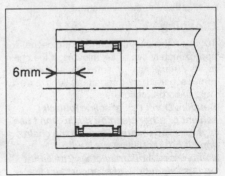

13.6 Swingarm bearing installed depth – ER models

6mm

14.1 Remove the screws (arrowed) and detach the chainguard

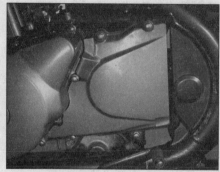

14.2 Engine sprocket cover bolts

fitted as original equipment and supplied as a spare part from Kawasaki dealers is of the endless type.

1 Remove the chainguard **(see illustration)**.
2 Remove the bolts securing the engine sprocket cover to the engine case **(see illustrations)**. Slide the sprocket cover off.
3 Remove the rear wheel (see Chapter 7).
4 Lift the chain off the engine sprocket.
5 Detach the swingarm from the frame by following the first few Steps of Section 12. Pull the swingarm back far enough to allow the chain to slip between the frame and the front of the swingarm.

Removal – riveted link chain

Note: *The riveted (soft) link can be identified by its identification markings on the side plate and usually slightly different colour. Also the staked ends of the link's two pins look as if they have been deeply centre-punched, instead of peened over as with all other pins.*

6 Locate the joining link in a suitable position to work on by rotating the back wheel; midway between the sprockets is ideal.
7 Slacken the drive chain as described in Chapter 1.
8 Split the chain at the joining link using an approved chain breaker tool intended for motorcycle use. There are a number of types available for motorcycle use and it is important to follow carefully the instructions supplied with the tool – see *Tools and Workshop Tips* in the Reference section for a typical example.
9 Remove the chain from the bike, noting its routing through the swingarm.

Cleaning

10 Soak the chain in paraffin (kerosene) for approximately five or six minutes. If the chain is very dirty, use a soft-bristled brush to remove caked-on deposits, taking care to wear hand protection.
Caution: Don't use gasoline (petrol), solvent or other cleaning fluids. Don't use high-pressure water. Remove the chain, wipe it off, then blow dry it with compressed air immediately. The entire process shouldn't take longer than ten minutes – if it does, the O-rings in the chain rollers could be damaged.

Installation – endless chain

11 Installation is the reverse of the removal procedure, with the following additions:
a) *Tighten the suspension fasteners to the torque values listed in this Chapter's Specifications.*
b) *Tighten the rear axle nut to the torque listed in the Chapter 7 Specifications.*
c) *Adjust and lubricate the chain following the procedure described in Chapter 1.*

Installation – riveted link chain

 Warning: NEVER install a drive chain which uses a clip-type master (split) link. If you do not have access to a chain riveting tool, have the chain fitted by a Kawasaki dealer.

12 Remove the engine sprocket cover and chainguard as described in Steps 1 and 2.
13 Thread the chain into position, making sure that it takes the correct route around the swingarm and sprockets and leave the two ends in a convenient place to work on. Obtain a new soft link – never attempt to reuse an old link.
14 Install the new soft link complete with an O-ring on each of its pins through the chain ends from the inside of the chain. Install an O-ring over the pin ends and fit the side plate with its identification marks facing out; use the chain tool to press the side plate into position.
15 Stake the new link pins using the chain riveting tool, following carefully the instructions of both the chain manufacturer and the tool manufacturer. Refer to *Tools and Workshop Tips*

15.4 Check the runout of the rear sprocket with a dial gauge

in the Reference section for chain riveting details using a typical commercially available tool.
16 After riveting, check the soft link pin ends for any signs of cracking. If there is any evidence of cracking, the soft link, O-rings and side plate must be removed and the procedure repeated with a new soft link.
17 Install the chainguard and sprocket cover in a reverse of the removal procedure. Adjust and lubricate the chain as described in Chapter 1.

15 Sprockets – check and replacement

Check

1 Set the bike on its centerstand.
2 Whenever the drive chain is inspected, the sprockets should be inspected also. If you are renewing the chain, renew the sprockets as well. Likewise, if the sprockets are in need of renewal, install a new chain also.
3 Remove the engine sprocket cover. Check the wear pattern on both sprockets **(see illustration 9.2 in Chapter 1)**. If the sprocket teeth are worn excessively, renew the chain and sprockets.
4 The rear sprocket can be checked for warpage by measuring its runout with a dial gauge. Attach the dial gauge to the swingarm, with the plunger of the gauge touching the sprocket near its outer diameter **(see illustration)**. Turn the wheel and measure the runout. If the runout exceeds the maximum runout listed in this Chapter's Specifications, renew the rear sprocket. As stated before, it's a good idea to renew the chain and the sprockets as a set.

Removal and installation – front sprocket

5 Remove the bolts securing the engine sprocket cover to the engine case **(see illustrations 14.2a and b)**. Slide the sprocket cover off.
6 On EX models remove the two bolts which retain the sprocket, then rotate the retaining plate so that it clears the shaft splines and draw it off the shaft **(see illustrations)**. On ER

15.6a Remove the engine sprocket holding plate bolts

15.6b Pull the holding plate off the shaft

15.6c Flatten back the lockwasher tab and unscrew the sprocket nut

models, flatten back the lockwasher tab, then unscrew the sprocket retaining nut (see illustration). On all models, to stop the shaft rotating as the bolts or nut is slacken, have an assistant sit on the bike, with the rear wheel in contact with the ground, and apply the rear brake.

7 Refer to Chapter 1 and slacken off the drive chain adjusters to create slack in the chain. Pull the sprocket off the shaft splines and disengage it from the chain (see illustration). If necessary, unbolt the internal chain guard to extra clearance (see illustration).

8 When installing the engine sprocket on EX models, engage it with the chain, making sure the IN mark, or recess, faces the engine case. Install the holding plate, rotating it in the shaft groove so the bolt holes align. Apply a non-hardening thread locking compound to the bolts, then tighten the bolts to the torque listed in this Chapter's Specifications.

9 When installing the engine sprocket on ER models, engage it with the chain so that the OUTSIDE marking on the sprocket faces outwards. Fit a new lockwasher to the shaft. Apply engine oil to the shaft threads and to the flanged face of the nut, then thread the nut into place. Tighten the nut to the torque listed in this Chapter's Specifications, then bend a portion of the lockwasher fully up against one flat of the nut.

10 Refer to Chapter 1 and adjust the drive chain.

11 Install the engine sprocket cover.

Removal and installation – rear sprocket

12 Remove the rear wheel (see Chapter 7).

13 Unscrew the nuts holding it to the wheel coupling and lift the sprocket off (see illustration). When installing the sprocket, apply a non-hardening thread locking compound to the threads of the studs.

15.7a Slide the sprocket off the shaft and separate it from the chain

Tighten the nuts to the torque listed in this Chapter's Specifications.

14 Also, check the condition of the rubber damper under the rear wheel coupling (see Section 16).

15 Install the rear wheel (see Chapter 7).

15.7b If necessary, unbolt and remove the internal chain guard

15.13 Remove these nuts to separate the sprocket from the coupling

16.2 Lift the sprocket and coupling from the rear wheel

16.3a Pull the damper out of the recesses . . .

16.3b . . . and separate it from the wheel

16.5 The damper should look like this when it's installed

16 Rear wheel coupling/rubber damper – check and replacement

1 Remove the rear wheel (see Chapter 7).
2 Lift the sprocket/rear wheel coupling and collar from the wheel (see illustration).
3 Lift the rubber damper from the wheel (see illustrations) and check it for cracks, hardening and general deterioration. Renew it if necessary.
4 Checking and renewal procedures for the coupling bearing are similar to those described for the wheel bearings. Refer to Chapter 7.
5 Installation is the reverse of the removal procedure (see illustration).

Chapter 7
Brakes, wheels and tyres

Contents

Degrees of difficulty

Easy, suitable for novice with little experience	**Fairly easy,** suitable for beginner with some experience	**Fairly difficult,** suitable for competent DIY mechanic	**Difficult,** suitable for experienced DIY mechanic	**Very difficult,** suitable for expert DIY or professional 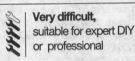

Specifications

Front and rear disc brake

Brake fluid type . . . . DOT 4
Brake pad minimum thickness . . . . 1.0 mm (0.04 in)
Disc thickness – EX500A models
   Standard . . . . 3.8 to 3.9 mm (0.150 to 0.153 in)
   Minimum* . . . . 3.5 mm (0.138 in)
Disc thickness – EX500D and ER models
   Standard . . . . 4.8 to 5.2 mm (0.189 to 0.205 in)
   Minimum . . . . 4.5 mm (0.177 in)
Disc thickness – EX500E models
   Front – standard . . . . 3.8 to 4.2 mm (0.150 to 0.165 in)
      Minimum . . . . 3.5 mm (0.138 in)
   Rear – standard . . . . 4.8 to 5.2 mm (0.189 to 0.205 in)
      Minimum . . . . 4.5 mm (0.177 in)
Disc runout (maximum) . . . . 0.3 mm (0.012 in)
Rear brake pedal position . . . . see Section 6

Rear drum brake (EX500A and ER models)

Brake shoe lining minimum thickness . . . . 2.0 mm (0.08 in)
Brake drum diameter
   Standard . . . . 160.00 to 160.16 mm (6.299 to 6.305 in)
   Maximum . . . . 160.75 mm (6.238 in)
Brake cam diameter
   Standard . . . . 16.975 to 16.984 mm (0.667 to 0.668 in)
   Minimum . . . . 16.88 mm (0.665 in)
Cam hole diameter in brake panel
   Standard . . . . 17.00 to 17.03 mm (0.669 to 0.670 in)
   Maximum . . . . 17.15 mm (0.675 in)
Brake pedal position and pedal freeplay . . . . see Chapter 1

Wheels and tyres

Wheel runout
   Axial (side-to-side) . . . . 0.5 mm (0.020 in)
   Radial (out-of-round) . . . . 0.8 mm (0.031 in)
Axle runout . . . . 0.2 mm (0.007 in) per 100 mm (3.94 in) of axle length
Tyre pressures and tread depth . . . . see Daily (pre-ride) checks

Wheels and tyres (continued)

Front tyre size
   EX500A models 100/90-16 54H
   EX500D, E and ER models 110/70-17 54H
Rear tyre size
   EX500A models 120/90-16 63H
   EX500D and ER models 130/70-17 62H

Torque specifications

Caliper mounting bolts
   EX500A models . . . . 32 Nm (24 ft-lbs)
   EX500D and E models . . . . 25 Nm (18 ft-lbs)
   ER models . . . . 34 Nm (25 ft-lbs)
Banjo fitting bolts . . . . 25 Nm (18 ft-lbs)
Brake disc-to-wheel bolts
   EX500A, D, E and ER models . . . . 23 Nm (16.5 ft-lbs)
   EX500E models
     Front discs . . . . 27 Nm (20 ft-lbs)
     Rear disc . . . . 23 Nm (16.5 ft-lbs)
Front master cylinder mounting bolts
   EX500A and ER models . . . . 11 Nm (95 in-lbs)
   EX500D and E models . . . . 8.8 Nm (78 in-lbs)
Rear master cylinder mounting bolts (EX500D and E) . . . . 23 Nm (16.5 ft-lbs)
Rear master cylinder fluid reservoir bolt (EX500D and E) . . . . 6.9 Nm (61 in-lbs)
Front brake lever pivot pin locknut . . . . 5.9 Nm (52 in-lbs)
Rear brake pivot bolt (EX500D, E and ER models) . . . . 8.8 Nm (78 in-lbs)
Front axle nut . . . . 88 Nm (65 ft-lbs)
Front axle clamp bolt
   EX500A models . . . . 29 Nm (22 ft-lbs)
   EX500D, E and ER models . . . . 20 Nm (14.5 ft-lbs)
Rear axle nut
   EX models . . . . 110 Nm (80 ft-lbs)
   ER models . . . . 98 Nm (72 ft-lbs)
Torque link nut
   EX500A models . . . . 29 Nm (22 ft-lbs)
   ER models . . . . 34 Nm (25 ft-lbs)

1 General information

EX500E models are equipped with twin front disc brakes – all other models covered in this manual are equipped with a single front disc brake. The brakes are hydraulically operated with two-piston, sliding calipers. The caliper is mounted on the left hand fork leg on EX500A and ER models and on the right hand fork left on EX500D models. EX500A and ER models use a drum rear brake and EX500D and E models use an hydraulic rear disc brake of the single piston sliding caliper type.

All models are equipped with cast aluminium wheels, which require very little maintenance and allow tubeless tyres to be used.

Caution: Disc brake components rarely require disassembly. Do not disassemble components unless absolutely necessary. If any hydraulic brake line connection in the system is loosened, the entire system should be disassembled, drained, cleaned and then properly filled and bled upon reassembly. Do not use solvents on internal brake components. Solvents will cause seals to swell and distort. Use only clean brake fluid or alcohol for cleaning. Use care when working with brake fluid as it can injure your eyes and it will damage painted surfaces and plastic parts.

2 Brake pads – renewal

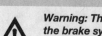

⚠️ *Warning: The dust created by the brake system may contain asbestos, which is harmful to your health. Never blow it out with compressed air and don't inhale any of it. An approved filtering mask should be worn when working on the brakes.*

1 1 Set the bike on its centerstand.
2 Remove the caliper mounting bolts **(see illustration)**. Slide the caliper and pads off the

2.2a Remove the front caliper mounting bolts (arrowed) and support the caliper so it doesn't hang by the brake hose

2.2b Rear caliper mounting bolts (arrowed)

2.3a Pull out the R-pin . . .

2.3b . . . and withdraw the pad pin

2.3c Remove the inner pad as described . . .

disc. Support the caliper with rope or wire so it doesn't hang by the brake hose.

3 On EX500E models, to remove the front brake pads, first pull out the R-pin, noting how it fits, then withdraw the pad pin (**see illustrations**). Pivot the inner pad out of the caliper and remove it, then lift out the outer pad (**see illustrations**). Note the location of the shim on the back of the inner pad (**see illustration**).

4 On all other models, push the caliper bracket in (towards the piston) until the pins on the bracket clear the holes in the pad backing plate, then remove the inner pad (**see illustration**). Remove the outer brake pad from the caliper (**see illustration**).

5 To remove the rear brake pads on all models, follow the procedure in Step 4.

6 Remove the anti-rattle spring (**see illustration**). If it appears damaged, renew it.

7 On the front caliper check the pad support clips on the caliper bracket. If they are missing or distorted, renew them. Note that on EX500E models, only one support clip is fitted.

8 Check the condition of the brake pads and measure the thickness of their friction material (see Chapter 1, Section 11). If either pad is worn down to, or beyond, the wear limit, fouled with oil or grease, or heavily scored or damaged by dirt and debris, both pads must be renewed as a set. On EX500E models, the pads in both front calipers should be renewed as a set. Note that is not possible to degrease the friction material; if the pads are contaminated in any way they must be renewed.

9 If you are installing new brake pads you will need to push the piston(s) back into the caliper to make room for the increased thickness of the new pads. Remove the cap from the master cylinder reservoir and siphon out some fluid. Push the pistons(s) equally into the caliper as far as possible, while checking the master cylinder reservoir to make sure it doesn't overflow. If you can't depress the piston(s) with thumb pressure, try using a C-clamp (G-clamp). Install the anti-rattle spring in the caliper (**see illustrations overleaf**).

10 On EX500E models, install the outer pad

2.3d . . . then lift out the outer pad

2.3e Note the location of the shim (arrowed)

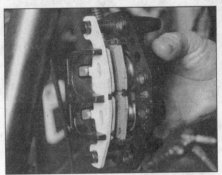

2.4a Slide the caliper bracket toward the pistons so it clears the inner pad, then remove the pad

2.4b Disengage the clips on the outer pad from the caliper and remove the pad

2.6a Remove the anti-rattle spring (front caliper)

2.6b Remove the anti-rattle spring (rear caliper)

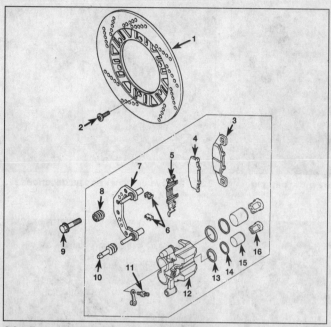

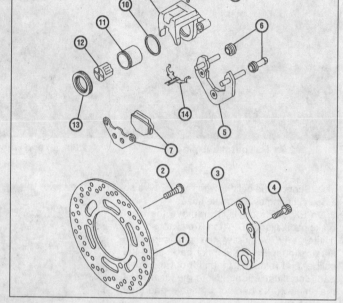

2.9a Front brake – exploded view (EX500A and D and all ER models)

1 Brake disc	9 Caliper mounting bolt
2 Allen bolt	10 Boot
3 Inner pad	11 Bleed valve and cap
4 Outer pad	12 Caliper
5 Anti-rattle spring	13 Piston fluid seals
6 Pad support clips	14 Piston dust seals
7 Caliper bracket and slider pins	15 Pistons
8 Boot	16 Piston inserts

2.9b Rear brake – exploded view

1 Brake disc	8 Caliper body
2 Allen bolt	9 Bleed valve and cap
3 Caliper support bracket	10 Piston fluid seal
4 Caliper mounting bolt	11 Piston
5 Caliper bracket and slider pins	12 Piston insert
6 Boots	13 Piston dust seal
7 Brake pads	14 Anti-rattle spring

in the caliper, ensuring it fits correctly against the tab, then install the inner pad **(see illustration)**. Secure the pads with the pad pin, then fit the R-pin.

11 On all other models, install both pads in the caliper and pull the caliper bracket out, so the pins on the bracket engage with the holes in the pad backing plate. **Note:** *If the caliper bracket doesn't slide easily in the caliper its pins may be corroded or in need of lubrication – refer to Section 3 for details.*

12 To install the rear brake pads on all models, follow the procedure in Step 11.

13 Install the caliper, tightening the mounting bolts to the torque listed in this Chapter's specifications.

14 Top up the master cylinder reservoir if necessary and install the diaphragm and cap (see *Daily (pre-ride) checks*).

15 Operate the brake lever (front) or pedal (rear) several times to bring the pads into contact with the disc. Check the operation of the brakes carefully before riding the motorcycle.

---

3 Brake caliper – removal, overhaul and installation

⚠️ *Warning: If a caliper indicates the need for an overhaul (usually due to leaking fluid or sticky operation), all old brake fluid should be flushed from the system. Also, the dust created by the brake system may contain asbestos, which is harmful to your health. Never blow it out with compressed air and don't inhale any of it. An approved filtering mask should be worn when working on the brakes. Do not, under any circumstances, use petroleum-based solvents to clean brake parts. Use clean brake fluid, brake cleaner or denatured alcohol only!*

Note: *If you are removing the caliper only to renew or inspect the brake pads, don't disconnect the hose from the caliper.*

Removal

1 Place the bike on its centerstand. **Note:** *If you're planning to overhaul the caliper and don't have a source of compressed air to blow out the pistons, use the bike's hydraulic system instead. To do this, remove the pads (see Section 2) and squeeze the brake lever to force the pistons out of the caliper. Note that on EX500D and E models, and all ER models, the front brake caliper pistons are different sizes – mark the piston heads to aid reassembly.*

2 Remove the brake hose banjo fitting bolt and separate the hose from the caliper **(see illustration)**. Discard the sealing washers. Plug the end of the hose or wrap a plastic bag

2.10 Ensure outer pad fits against tab (arrowed)

3.2 Remove the caliper hose banjo fitting bolt - there's a sealing washer on each side of the fitting

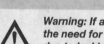

3.5 Remove the insert from each piston

3.9 The dust seal and fluid seal should be carefully removed

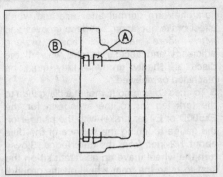

3.13 Seal orientation in the caliper bore

A Piston fluid seal   B Piston dust seal

tightly around it to prevent excessive fluid loss and contamination.

3 Remove the caliper (see Section 2).

Overhaul

4 Remove the brake pads and anti-rattle spring from the caliper (see Section 2).

5 Remove the caliper piston inserts **(see illustration)**. Note that inserts are not fitted on ER500C models.

6 Clean the exterior of the caliper with denatured alcohol or brake system cleaner.

7 Remove the caliper bracket and the slider pin boots from the caliper **(see illustration 2.9a or 2.9b)**.

8 If you didn't blow out the pistons with the bike's hydraulic system in Step 1, place a few rags between the piston and the caliper frame to act as a cushion, then use compressed air, directed into the fluid inlet, to remove the piston(s). Use only enough air pressure to ease the pistons out of the bore. If a piston is blown out, even with the cushion in place, it may be damaged.

 Warning: Never place your fingers in front of the piston in an attempt to catch or protect it when applying compressed air, as serious injury could occur.

9 Using a wood or plastic tool, remove the dust seal(s) **(see illustration)**. Metal tools may cause bore damage.

10 Using a wood or plastic tool, remove the piston seal from the groove in each caliper bore.

11 Clean the pistons and the bores with

denatured alcohol, clean brake fluid or brake system cleaner and blow dry them with filtered, unlubricated compressed air. Inspect the surfaces of the pistons for nicks and burrs and loss of plating. Check the caliper bores, too. If surface defects are present, the caliper must be renewed. If the caliper is in bad shape, the master cylinder should also be checked.

12 Temporarily reinstall the caliper bracket. Make sure it slides smoothly in-and-out of the caliper. If it doesn't, check the slider pins for burrs or excessive wear. Also check the slider pin bores in the caliper for wear and scoring. Renew the caliper bracket, the caliper, or both if necessary. The rubber boots should prevent the escape of lubricant and prevent the ingress of water and road dirt which would lead to sticking caliper operation – renew the boots if they are split or perished.

13 Lubricate the piston seal(s) with clean brake fluid and install the correct way around in the inner groove of the caliper bore **(see illustration)**. Make sure they seat completely and are not twisted. Note that if the front brake caliper pistons are different sizes, the seals will be different sizes also.

14 Lubricate the dust seals with clean brake fluid and install them in their grooves, making sure they seat correctly.

15 Lubricate the pistons with clean brake fluid and install them, closed end first, in the caliper bores. Using your thumbs, push the piston(s) all the way in, making sure it doesn't get cocked in the bore.

16 Install the slider pin boots **(see illustration)**.

17 Apply a thin coat of PBC (poly butyl cuprysil) grease, or silicone grease designed for high-temperature brake applications, to the slider pins on the caliper bracket **(see illustration)**. Install the caliper bracket to the caliper and seat the boots over the lips on the bracket.

Installation

18 If fitted, install the piston insert(s) **(see illustration)**.

19 Install the anti-rattle spring and the brake pads (see Section 2).

20 Install the caliper, tightening the mounting bolts to the torque listed in this Chapter's Specifications.

21 Connect the brake hose to the caliper, using new sealing washers on each side of the fitting. Tighten the banjo fitting bolt to the torque listed in this Chapter's Specifications.

22 Fill the master cylinder with fresh DOT 4 brake fluid and bleed the system (see Section 8). Check for leaks.

23 Check the operation of the brakes carefully before riding the motorcycle.

4 Brake disc – inspection, removal and installation

Inspection

1 Set the bike on its centerstand.

2 Visually inspect the surface of the disc for score marks and other damage. Light

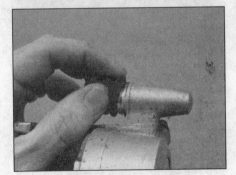

3.16 Install the slider pin boots

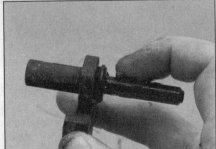

3.17 Apply a thin coat of the specified grease to the slider pins on the caliper bracket

3.18 Install the piston inserts (arrowed) so they seat in the pistons

scratches are normal after use and won't affect brake operation, but deep grooves and heavy score marks will reduce braking efficiency and accelerate pad wear. If the discs are badly grooved they must be machined or renewed.

3 To check disc runout, mount a dial gauge to the fork leg (or to the swingarm for the EX500D or E rear brake) with the plunger on the gauge touching the surface of the disc about 1/2-inch from the outer edge. Slowly turn the wheel (have an assistant sit on the seat to raise the front wheel off the ground) and watch the gauge needle, comparing your reading with the limit listed in this Chapter's Specification. If the runout is greater than allowed, check the wheel bearings for play (see Chapter 1). If the bearings are worn, renew them and repeat this check. If the disc runout is still excessive, it will have to be renewed. On the EX500E model, where a twin front disc brake is fitted, renew both discs at the same time. Always fit new pads when fitting new discs.

4 The disc must not be machined or allowed to wear down to a thickness less than the minimum allowable thickness listed in this Chapter's Specifications. The thickness of the disc can be checked with a micrometer. If the thickness of the disc is less than the minimum allowable, it must be renewed. The minimum thickness is also stamped into the disc **(see illustration)**.

Removal

5 Remove the wheel (see Section 12 front, or Section 13 rear).
Caution: Don't lay the wheel down and allow it to rest on the disc – the disc could become warped. Set the wheel on wood blocks so the disc doesn't support the weight of the wheel.

6 Mark the relationship of the disc to the wheel, so it can be installed in the same position. Remove the Allen bolts that retain the disc to the wheel **(see illustration)**. Loosen the bolts a little at a time, in a criss-cross pattern, to avoid distorting the disc.

7 Take note of any paper shims that may be present where the disc mates to the wheel. If

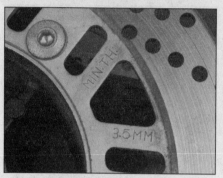

4.4 The minimum allowable thickness is stamped into the disc

there are any, mark their position and be sure to include them when installing the disc.

Installation

8 Position the disc on the wheel, aligning the previously applied matchmarks (if you're reinstalling the original disc). Make sure the arrow (stamped on the disc) marking the direction of rotation is pointing in the proper direction.

9 Apply a non-hardening thread locking compound to the threads of the bolts. Install the bolts, tightening them a little at a time, in a criss-cross pattern, until the torque listed in this Chapter's Specifications is reached. Clean off all grease from the brake disc using acetone or brake system cleaner.

10 Install the wheel.

11 Operate the brake lever (front) or pedal (rear) several times to bring the pads into contact with the disc. Check the operation of the brake carefully before riding the motorcycle.

---

5 Front brake master cylinder – removal, overhaul and installation

Caution: Disassembly, overhaul and reassembly of the brake master cylinder must be done in a spotlessly clean work area to avoid contamination and possible failure of the brake hydraulic system components.

4.6 Loosen the disc retaining bolts a little at a time to prevent distortion

1 If the master cylinder is leaking fluid, or if the lever does not produce a firm feel when the brake is applied, and bleeding the brakes does not help, master cylinder overhaul is recommended.

2 Before disassembling the master cylinder, read through the entire procedure and make sure that you have the necessary rebuild parts (ie a new piston/seal assembly and new sealing washers for the hose banjo union). Also, you will need some new, clean DOT 4 brake fluid, some clean rags and internal circlip pliers. **Note:** *To prevent damage to the paint from spilled brake fluid, always cover the fuel tank when working on the master cylinder.*

Removal

3 Loosen, but do not remove, the screws holding the reservoir cover in place.

4 Pull back the rubber boot, loosen the banjo fitting bolt **(see illustration)** and separate the brake hose from the master cylinder. Wrap the end of the hose in a clean rag and suspend the hose in an upright position or bend it down carefully and place the open end in a clean container. The objective is to prevent excess loss of brake fluid, fluid spills and system contamination.

5 Remove the locknut from the underside of the lever pivot bolt, then unscrew the bolt and withdraw the lever **(see illustration)**.

6 Remove the master cylinder mounting bolts **(see illustration)** and separate the master cylinder from the handlebar.

5.4 Pull back the cover and remove the master cylinder banjo fitting bolt - use a six-point box wrench, and expect some leakage

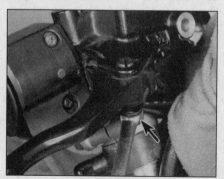

5.5 Remove the locknut, then unscrew the brake lever pivot bolt

5.6 Remove the master cylinder mounting bolts, unplug the electrical connectors and remove the master cylinder

5.9 Remove the rubber boot from the end of the master cylinder piston . . .

5.10a . . . then depress the piston and remove the circlip with a pair of circlip pliers

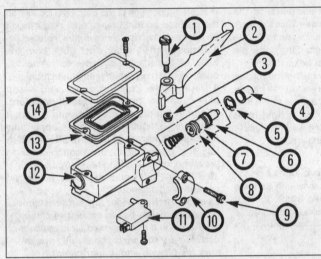

1 Pivot bolt
2 Brake lever
3 Locknut
4 Dust boot
5 Circlip
6 Secondary cup
7 Piston
8 Primary cup
9 Bolt
10 Clamp
11 Brake light switch
12 Master cylinder body
13 Diaphragm
14 Cover

5.10b Exploded view of the master cylinder

Caution: Do not tip the master cylinder upside down or brake fluid will run out.

7 Disconnect the electrical connectors from the brake light switch.

Overhaul

8 Detach the top cover and the rubber diaphragm, then drain the brake fluid into a suitable container. Wipe any remaining fluid out of the reservoir with a clean rag.

9 Carefully remove the rubber dust boot from the end of the piston **(see illustration)**.

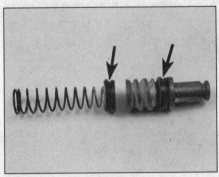

5.12 Make sure the lips of the piston cups (arrowed) are facing away from the lever end of the piston

10 Using circlip pliers, remove the circlip **(see illustrations)** and slide out the piston complete with its seals and the spring. Lay the parts out in the proper order to prevent confusion during reassembly.

11 Clean all of the parts with brake system cleaner (available at auto parts stores), denatured alcohol or clean brake fluid.

Caution: Do not, under any circumstances, use a petroleum-based solvent to clean brake parts. If compressed air is available, use it to dry the parts thoroughly (make

5.15 Master cylinder clamp UP marking

sure it's filtered and unlubricated). Check the master cylinder bore for corrosion, scratches, nicks and score marks. If damage is evident, the master cylinder must be renewed. If the master cylinder is in poor condition, then the caliper should be checked as well.

12 The new piston and seal assembly should come supplied with a new spring **(see illustration)**.

13 Before reassembling the master cylinder, soak the piston assembly in clean brake fluid for ten to fifteen minutes. Lubricate the master cylinder bore with clean brake fluid, then carefully insert the piston and related parts in the reverse order of disassembly. Make sure the lips on the cup seals do not turn inside out when they are slipped into the bore.

14 Depress the piston, then install the circlip (make sure the circlip is properly seated in the groove with the sharp edge facing out). Install the rubber dust boot (make sure the lip is seated properly in the piston groove).

Installation

15 Attach the master cylinder to the handlebar with the arrow and the word 'UP' on the master cylinder clamp pointing up **(see illustration)**. Tighten the bolts to the torque listed in this Chapter's Specifications. **Note:** *Tighten the upper bolt first, then the lower bolt. There will be a gap at the bottom between the clamp and master cylinder body.*

16 Install the brake lever and tighten the pivot bolt locknut to the specified torque.

17 Connect the brake hose to the master cylinder, using a new sealing washer on each side of the hose union. Tighten the banjo fitting bolt to the torque listed in this Chapter's Specifications. Refer to Section 8 and bleed the air from the system.

6 Rear brake master cylinder – removal, overhaul and installation (EX500D/E models)

Caution: Disassembly, overhaul and reassembly of the brake master cylinder must be done in a spotlessly clean work area to avoid contamination and possible failure of the brake hydraulic system components.

1 If the master cylinder is leaking fluid, or if the lever does not produce a firm feel when the brake is applied, and bleeding the brakes does not help, master cylinder overhaul is recommended.

2 Before disassembling the master cylinder, read through the entire procedure and make sure that you have the necessary rebuild parts (ie a new piston/seal assembly and new sealing washers for the hose banjo union). Also, you will need some new, clean DOT 4 brake fluid, some clean rags and internal circlip pliers. **Note:** *To prevent damage to the paint from spilled brake fluid, always cover the surrounding components when working on the master cylinder.*

6.4 Brake caliper hose banjo bolt (arrowed)

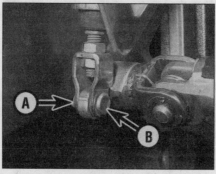

6.5 Remove the cotter pin (A) and clevis pin (B)

6.6 Master cylinder mounting bolts (arrowed)

Removal

3 Release the clamp securing the reservoir hose to the union on the master cylinder, then detach the hose and drain the fluid from the reservoir into a suitable container.

4 Unscrew the brake hose banjo bolt and separate the brake hose from the master cylinder, noting its alignment (see illustration). Discard the two sealing washers as they must be renewed. Wrap the end of the hose in a clean rag and suspend the hose in an upright position or bend it down carefully and place the open end in a clean container. The objective is to prevent excessive loss of brake fluid, fluid spills and system contamination.

5 Remove the cotter pin (split pin) from the clevis pin securing the brake pedal to the master cylinder pushrod (see illustration). Withdraw the clevis pin and separate the pedal from the pushrod. Discard the cotter pin (split pin) as a new one must be used.

6 Unscrew the two bolts securing the master cylinder to the bracket and remove the master cylinder (see illustration). If access to the fluid reservoir is required, remove the right-hand side cover (see Chapter 8); the fluid reservoir is retained to the frame by a single bolt.

Overhaul

7 If required, slacken the clevis locknut on the pushrod, then thread the clevis with its base nut off the pushrod, followed by the locknut (see illustrations). If this is done, it is advisable to mark the position of the top of the locknut on the pushrod so that brake pedal height won't be affected when the clevis is later installed.

8 Dislodge the rubber dust boot from the base of the master cylinder to reveal the pushrod retaining circlip (see illustration).

9 Depress the pushrod and, using circlip pliers, remove the circlip (see illustration). Slide out the piston assembly and spring. If they are difficult to remove, apply low pressure compressed air to the fluid outlet. Lay the parts out in the proper order to prevent confusion during reassembly.

10 Clean all of the parts with clean brake fluid or denatured alcohol.

Caution: Do not, under any circumstances, use a petroleum-based solvent to clean brake parts. If compressed air is available, use it to dry the parts thoroughly (make sure it's filtered and unlubricated).

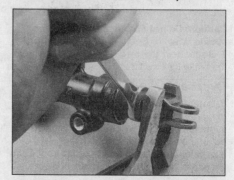

6.7b Hold the clevis and slacken the locknut

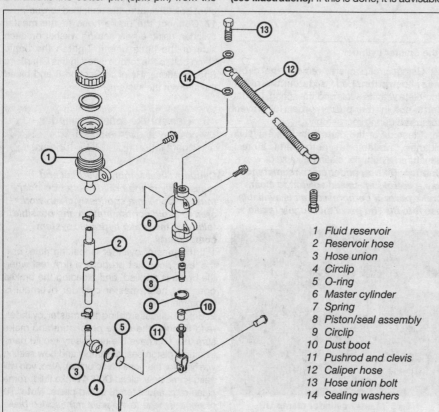

1 Fluid reservoir
2 Reservoir hose
3 Hose union
4 Circlip
5 O-ring
6 Master cylinder
7 Spring
8 Piston/seal assembly
9 Circlip
10 Dust boot
11 Pushrod and clevis
12 Caliper hose
13 Hose union bolt
14 Sealing washers

6.7a Rear brake master cylinder components

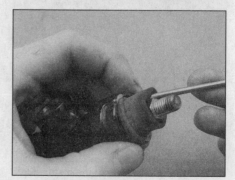

6.8 Remove the dust boot from the pushrod

6.9 Depress the piston and remove the circlip from the cylinder

6.12 Remove the circlip which secures the hose union

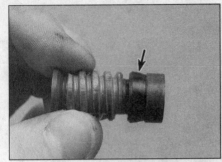

6.13 Make sure the lips of the seals (arrowed) face away from the pushrod end of the piston

11 Check the master cylinder bore for corrosion, scratches, nicks and score marks. If damage or wear is evident, the master cylinder must be renewed. If the master cylinder is in poor condition, then the caliper should be checked as well.

12 If required, remove the circlip securing the reservoir hose union and detach the union from the master cylinder **(see illustration)**. Discard the O-ring as a new one must be used. Inspect the reservoir hose for cracks or splits and renew it if necessary.

13 The new piston will be supplied fitted with new seals and a new spring; use all of the new parts, regardless of the apparent condition of the old ones. If the seal and cup are not already on the piston, fit them according to the layout of the old piston assembly **(see illustration)**.

14 Install the spring in the master cylinder so that its tapered end faces the piston.

15 Before reassembling the master cylinder, soak the piston assembly in clean brake fluid for ten to fifteen minutes. Lubricate the master cylinder bore with clean brake fluid, then carefully insert the piston and related parts in the reverse order of disassembly. Make sure the lips on the cup seals do not turn inside out when they are slipped into the bore.

16 Install and depress the pushrod, then fit a new circlip, making sure it is properly seated in the groove.

17 Install the rubber dust boot, making sure the lip is seated properly in the groove.

18 If removed, fit a new O-ring to the fluid

reservoir hose union **(see illustration)**, then install the union onto the master cylinder and secure it with its circlip.

Installation

19 If removed, install the clevis locknut, the clevis and its base nut onto the master cylinder pushrod end. Position the clevis as noted on removal, then tighten the clevis locknut securely. Note that the clevis position on the pushrod affects the brake pedal height in relation to the rider's footrest. Kawasaki specify a standard position of 80 mm, measured from the centre of the lower mounting point on the master cylinder to the centre of the clevis pin hole in the clevis **(see illustration)**; this should give a brake pedal height of 50 mm (1.97 in) (below the top of the rider's footrest).

20 Install the master cylinder onto the footrest bracket and tighten its mounting bolts to the torque setting specified at the beginning of the Chapter.

21 Align the brake pedal with the master cylinder pushrod clevis, then slide in the clevis pin and secure it using a new cotter pin (split pin). Bend the ends of the cotter pin (split pin) securely.

22 Connect the brake hose to the master cylinder, using a new sealing washer on each side of the banjo union. Ensure that the hose is positioned so that it butts against the lug and tighten the banjo bolt to the specified torque setting.

23 Connect the reservoir hose to the union

on the master cylinder and secure it with the clamp. Check that the hose is secure and clamped at the reservoir end as well. If the clamps have weakened, use new ones.

24 If the fluid reservoir was removed, retain it with its single mounting bolt. Fill the fluid reservoir with new DOT 4 brake fluid (see *Daily (pre-ride) checks*) and bleed the system following the procedure in Section 8. Install the right-hand side cover (see Chapter 8).

25 Check the operation of the rear brake carefully before riding the motorcycle.

7 Brake hoses – inspection and renewal

Inspection

1 Brake hose condition should be checked regularly and the hoses replaced at the specified interval (see Chapter 1).

2 Twist and flex the rubber hose **(see illustration)** while looking for cracks, bulges and seeping fluid. Check extra carefully around the areas where the hose connects to the banjo fittings, as these are common areas for hose failure.

Replacement

3 The brake hose has banjo fittings on each end. Cover the surrounding area with plenty of rags and unscrew the banjo bolts on either

6.18 Use a new O-ring at the reservoir hose union

6.19 Distance from centre of lower mounting to centre of clevis pin must measure 80 mm

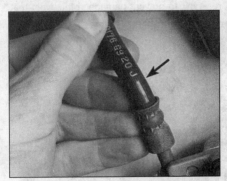

7.2 Flex the brake hoses and check for cracks, bulges and leaking fluid

7.4 Always use a new sealing washer on each side of the banjo union

8.5a Bleeding equipment attached to the front caliper bleed valve

8.5b Rear caliper bleed valve with bleeding equipment attached

end of the hose. Detach the hose from the clips and remove the hose.

4 Position the new hose, making sure it isn't twisted or otherwise strained, between the two components. Install the banjo bolts, using new sealing washers on both sides of the fittings, and tighten them to the torque listed in this Chapter's Specifications **(see illustration)**.

5 Flush the old brake fluid from the system, refill the system with new DOT 4 brake fluid and bleed the air from the system (see Section 8). Check the operation of the brakes carefully before riding the motorcycle.

8 Brake system – bleeding

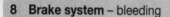

1 Bleeding the brake is simply the process of removing all the air bubbles from the brake fluid reservoir, the lines and the brake caliper. Bleeding is necessary whenever a brake system hydraulic connection is loosened, when a component or hose is renewed, or when the master cylinder or caliper is overhauled. Leaks in the system may also allow air to enter, but leaking brake fluid will reveal their presence and warn you of the need for repair.

2 To bleed the brake, you will need some new DOT 4 brake fluid, a length of clear vinyl or plastic tubing, a small container partially filled with clean brake fluid, some rags and a wrench to fit the brake caliper bleed valve.

3 Cover the area around the brake fluid reservoir to prevent damage in the event that

brake fluid is spilled. Remove the right-hand side cover to access the rear brake fluid reservoir (see Chapter 8).

4 Remove the reservoir cap or cover and slowly pump the brake lever a few times, until no air bubbles can be seen floating up from the holes at the bottom of the reservoir. Doing this bleeds the air from the master cylinder end of the line. Reinstall the reservoir cap or cover.

5 Attach one end of the clear vinyl or plastic tubing to the brake caliper bleed valve and submerge the other end in the brake fluid in the container **(see illustrations)**.

6 Remove the reservoir cap or cover and check the fluid level. Do not allow the fluid level to drop below the lower mark during the bleeding process.

7 Carefully pump the brake lever (front) or pedal (rear) three or four times and hold it while opening the caliper bleed valve. When the valve is opened, brake fluid will flow out of the caliper into the clear tubing and the lever will move toward the handlebar (front) or pedal will move down (rear).

8 Retighten the bleed valve, then release the brake lever/pedal gradually. Repeat the process until no air bubbles are visible in the brake fluid leaving the caliper and the lever/pedal is firm when applied. Remember to add fluid to the reservoir as the level drops. Use only new DOT 4 brake fluid. Never reuse the fluid lost during bleeding; it absorbs moisture from the air, which can lead to brake failure.

9 Replace the reservoir cover, wipe up any spilled brake fluid and check the entire system for leaks.

HAYNES HINT *If bleeding is difficult, it may be necessary to let the brake fluid in the system stabilise for a few hours (it may be aerated). Repeat the bleeding procedure when the tiny bubbles in the system have settled out.*

9 Rear drum brake – removal, inspection and installation (EX500A and ER models)

Removal

1 Before you start, inspect the rear brake wear indicator (see Chapter 1, Section 11).

2 Remove the rear wheel (see Section 13).

3 Lift the brake panel out of the wheel **(see illustration)**.

4 Fold the shoes toward each other to release the spring tension **(see illustration)**. Remove the shoes and springs from the brake panel.

Inspection

5 Check the linings for wear, damage, and signs of contamination from road dirt or water. If the linings are visibly defective, renew them.

6 Measure the thickness of the lining material (just the lining material, not the metal backing) and compare with the value listed in this Chapter's Specifications **(see illustration)**. Renew the shoes if the material is worn to less than the minimum at any point.

7 Check the ends of the shoes where they

9.3 The brake shoes are mounted on a panel that fits into the rear wheel

9.4 Fold the shoes off the panel to remove them

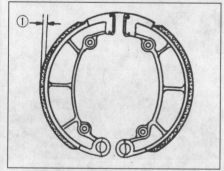

9.6 Measure the shoe linings (1)

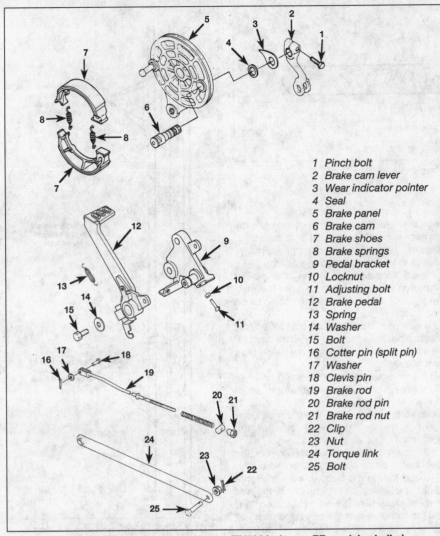

1 Pinch bolt
2 Brake cam lever
3 Wear indicator pointer
4 Seal
5 Brake panel
6 Brake cam
7 Brake shoes
8 Brake springs
9 Pedal bracket
10 Locknut
11 Adjusting bolt
12 Brake pedal
13 Spring
14 Washer
15 Bolt
16 Cotter pin (split pin)
17 Washer
18 Clevis pin
19 Brake rod
20 Brake rod pin
21 Brake rod nut
22 Clip
23 Nut
24 Torque link
25 Bolt

9.8 Exploded view of the rear brake (EX500A shown, ER models similar)

contact the brake cam and pivot post. Renew the shoes if there's visible wear.

8 Check the brake cam and pivot post for wear and damage. If necessary, make match marks across the cam end and cam lever, then remove the pinch bolt, lever, wear indicator pointer, seal and cam **(see illustration)**.

9 Check the brake drum (inside the wheel) for wear or damage. Measure the diameter at several points with a vernier caliper (or have this done by a Kawasaki dealer). If the measurements are uneven (indicating that the drum is out-of-round) or if there are scratches deep enough to snag a fingernail, have the drum turned (skimmed) to correct the surface. If the drum has to be turned (skimmed) beyond the wear limit to remove the defects the wheel must be renewed.

10 Check the brake cam for looseness in the brake panel hole. If it feels loose, measure the diameter of the cam and hole and compare them with those listed in this Chapter's Specifications. Renew worn parts.

Installation

11 Remove all traces of old grease from the surface of the cam and its hole in the brake panel. Apply a smear of high melting-point grease to the two bearing surfaces of the cam

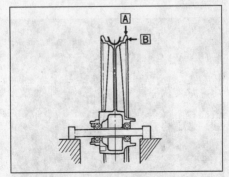

10.2 Check the wheel for radial (out-of-round) runout (A) and axial (side-to-side) runout (B)

and the operating flat on its end. Also apply a smear of high melting-point grease to the brake shoe pivot on the brake panel and the spring hooks where they engage the holes in the brake shoes.

12 Hook the springs to the shoes. Position the shoes in a V on the brake panel, then fold them down into position **(see illustration 9.4)**. Make sure the ends of the shoes fit correctly in the cam and on the anchor pin.

13 The remainder of installation is the reverse of the removal steps.

14 Check the position of the brake pedal and pedal freeplay (see Chapter 1, Section 12) and adjust it if necessary. Check the operation of the rear brake carefully before riding the motorcycle.

10 Wheels – inspection and repair

1 Place the motorcycle on the centerstand, then clean the wheels thoroughly to remove mud and dirt that may interfere with the inspection procedure or mask defects. Make a general check of the wheels and tyres as described in Chapter 1 (wheels) and *Daily (pre-ride) checks* (tyres).

2 With the motorcycle on the centerstand and the wheel being checked off the ground, attach a dial gauge to the fork leg or the swingarm and position the pointer against the side of the rim. Spin the wheel slowly and check the side-to-side (axial) runout of the rim, then compare your readings with the value listed in this Chapter's Specifications **(see illustration)**. In order to accurately check radial runout with the dial gauge, the wheel would have to be removed from the machine and the tyre removed from the wheel. With the axle clamped in a vice, the wheel can be rotated to check the runout.

3 An easier, though slightly less accurate, method is to attach a stiff wire pointer to the fork leg or the swingarm and position the end a fraction of an inch from the wheel (where the wheel and tyre join). If the wheel is true, the distance from the pointer to the rim will be constant as the wheel is rotated. Repeat the procedure to check the runout of the rear wheel. **Note**: *If wheel runout is excessive, refer to the appropriate Section in this Chapter and check the wheel bearings before resorting to wheel renewal.*

4 The wheels should also be visually inspected for cracks, flat spots on the rim and other damage. Since tubeless tyres are involved, look very closely for dents in the area where the tyre bead contacts the rim. Dents in this area may prevent complete sealing of the tyre against the rim, which leads to deflation of the tyre over a period of time.

5 If damage is evident, or if runout in either direction is excessive, the wheel will have to be renewed. Never attempt to repair a damaged cast aluminium wheel.

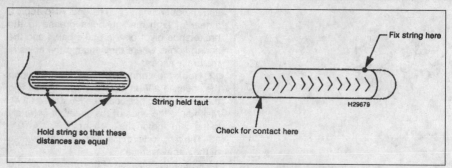

11.5 Wheel alignment check using string

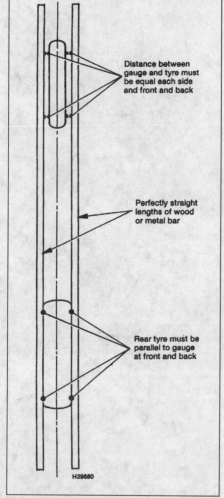

11.7 Wheel alignment check using a straight-edge

11 Wheels – alignment check

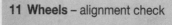

1 Misalignment of the wheels, which may be due to a cocked rear wheel or a bent frame or fork triple clamps, can cause strange and possibly serious handling problems. If the frame or triple clamps are at fault, repair by a frame specialist or replacement with new parts are the only alternatives.

2 To check the alignment you will need an assistant, a length of string or a perfectly straight piece of wood and a ruler. A plumb bob or other suitable weight will also be required.

3 In order to make a proper check of the wheels it is necessary to support the bike in an upright position, using an auxiliary stand. Measure the width of both tyres at their widest points. Subtract the smaller measurement from the larger measurement, then divide the difference by two. The result is the amount of offset that should exist between the front and rear tyres on both sides.

4 If a string is used, have your assistant hold one end of it about halfway between the floor and the rear axle, touching the rear sidewall of the tyre.

5 Run the other end of the string forward and pull it tight so that it is roughly parallel to the floor. Slowly bring the string into contact with the front sidewall of the rear tyre, then turn the front wheel until it is parallel with the string. Measure the distance from the front tyre sidewall to the string (see illustration).

6 Repeat the procedure on the other side of the motorcycle. The distance from the front tyre sidewall to the string should be equal on both sides.

7 As was previously pointed out, a perfectly straight length of wood may be substituted for the string. The procedure is the same (see illustration).

8 If the distance between the string and tyre is greater on one side, or if the rear wheel appears to be cocked, refer to Chapter 1, Section 2 and check that the chain adjuster markings coincide on each side of the swingarm.

9 If the front-to-back alignment is correct, the wheels still may be out of alignment vertically.

10 Using the plumb bob, or other suitable weight, and a length of string, check the rear wheel to make sure it is vertical. To do this, hold the string against the tyre upper sidewall and allow the weight to settle just off the floor. When the string touches both the upper and lower tyre sidewalls and is perfectly straight, the wheel is vertical. If it is not, place thin spacers under one leg of the stand.

11 Once the rear wheel is vertical, check the front wheel in the same manner. If both wheels are not perfectly vertical, the frame and/or major suspension components are bent.

12 Front wheel – removal and installation

Removal

1 Remove the lower fairing on EX models (see Chapter 8). Place the motorcycle on the centerstand, then raise the front wheel off the ground by placing a floor jack, with a wood block on the jack head, under the engine.

2 Disconnect the speedometer cable from the drive unit (see illustration).

3 On EX500A and all ER models, remove the axle nut on the left-hand side, then loosen the right-hand side axle clamp bolt (see illustration).

4 On EX500D and E models, first loosen the axle clamp bolt in the left-hand fork leg then unscrew axle nut set in the left-hand fork leg using an Allen key or Allen socket. Now loosen the axle clamp bolt in the right-hand fork leg.

5 Support the wheel, then pull out the axle

12.2 Unscrew the speedometer cable nut (arrowed)

12.3 Remove the nut from the end of the axle

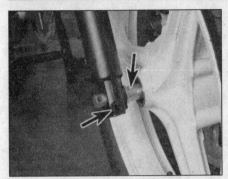

12.5 The axle clamp bolt (left arrow) goes in this hole; remove the collar (right arrow) as the axle is pulled out

13.2 Remove the cotter pin (split pin) from the axle nut

13.3 Loosen the locknut on each chain adjuster (arrowed), then loosen the adjuster bolts all the way

and collar **(see illustration)** and carefully lower the wheel until the brake disc clears the caliper. It will probably be necessary to tilt the wheel to one side to allow removal. Don't lose the collar that fits into the right-hand side of the hub. On EX500D and E models, if necessary tap the axle through the hub with a hammer and drift.

Caution: Don't lay the wheel down and allow it to rest on the disc – the disc could become warped. Set the wheel on wood blocks so the disc doesn't support the weight of the wheel. If the axle is corroded, remove the corrosion with fine emery cloth.
Note: Do not operate the front brake lever with the wheel removed. To prevent accidental operation of the brake, slip a piece of wood between the brake pads.

6 Check the condition of the wheel bearings (see Section 14).

Installation

7 Installation is the reverse of removal. Apply a thin coat of grease to the seal lip, then slide the collar into the right-hand side of the hub. Position the speedometer drive unit in place in the left-hand side of the hub (if it was removed), then slide the wheel into place. Make sure the notches in the speedometer drive housing line up with the lugs in the wheel. If the disc will not slide between the brake pads, remove the wheel and carefully pry them apart with a piece of wood.

8 Slip the axle into place, then tighten the axle nut to the torque listed in this Chapter's Specifications. Tighten the axle clamp bolt(s) to the torque listed in this Chapter's Specifications.
9 Apply the front brake, pump the forks up and down several times and check for binding and proper brake operation.

13 Rear wheel –
removal and installation

EX500A models

Removal

1 Set the bike on its centerstand.
2 Remove the cotter pin (split pin) from the axle nut and loosen the nut **(see illustration)**.
3 Loosen the chain adjusting bolt locknuts and fully loosen both adjusting bolts **(see illustration)**.
4 Unscrew and remove the brake pedal adjusting nut from the rod **(see illustration)**. Slide out the pin and disconnect the brake rod from the cam lever. Remove the R-pin from the torque link bolt, then remove the nut and disconnect the torque link from the brake panel.
5 Push the rear wheel as far forward as possible. Lift the top of the chain up off the

rear sprocket and pull it to the left while rotating the wheel backwards. This will disengage the chain from the sprocket.

⚠ *Warning: Don't let your fingers slip between the chain and the sprocket.*

6 Remove the axle nut and the washer **(see illustrations)**. Note the location of the spacer on each side of the wheel.
7 Support the wheel and slide the axle out. Lower the wheel and remove it from the swingarm, being careful not to lose the spacers on each side of the hub **(see illustration)**.

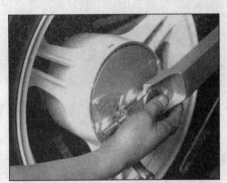

13.4 Remove the nut from the brake rod, then slip the rod out of the pin

13.6a Note the location of the spacer (left arrow) on each side of the wheel, then remove the axle nut . . .

13.6b . . . and the washer

13.7 Slide the wheel rearward, set the chain adjuster down and pull the wheel the rest of the way out

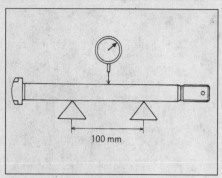

13.8 Check the axle for runout using a dial gauge and V-blocks

13.19a Remove the cotter pin from the axle nut, then unscrew the nut . . .

Inspection

Caution: Don't lay the wheel down and allow it to rest on the sprocket – it could become warped. Set the wheel on wood blocks so the sprocket doesn't support the weight of the wheel.

8 Before installing the wheel, check the axle for straightness. If the axle is corroded, first remove the corrosion with fine emery cloth. Set the axle on V-blocks and check it for runout using a dial gauge **(see illustration)**. If the axle exceeds the maximum allowable runout limit listed in this Chapter's Specifications, it must be renewed.

9 Check the condition of the wheel bearings (see Section 14).

Installation

10 Apply a thin coat of grease to the seal lips, then slide the spacers into their proper positions on the sides of the hub.

11 Place the axle, washer and chain adjuster in the left-hand side of the swingarm so they're ready to go when the wheel is in position **(see illustration)**.

12 Slide the wheel and spacers into place.

13 Pull the chain up over the sprocket, raise the wheel and install the axle and axle nut. Don't tighten the axle nut at this time.

14 Adjust the chain slack (see Chapter 1) and tighten the adjuster locknuts.

15 Tighten the axle nut to the torque listed in this Chapter's Specifications. Install a new cotter pin (split pin), tightening the axle nut an

13.11 Position the left chain adjuster, washer and axle so the axle can be pushed in as soon as the wheel is in position

13.19b . . . and withdraw the axle

additional amount, if necessary, to align the hole in the axle with the castellations on the nut.

16 Tighten the torque link nut to the torque listed in this Chapter's Specifications and install the R-pin.

17 Check the operation of the rear brake before riding the motorcycle.

EX500D and E models

Removal

18 Set the bike on its centerstand.

19 Straighten the cotter pin (split pin) in the rear axle nut and remove it **(see illustration)**. Unscrew the rear axle nut and withdraw the axle and chain adjuster plate from the left-hand side **(see illustration)**. Allow the rear wheel to drop down, then lift the drive chain

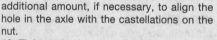

13.23a Insert the right-hand spacer in the hub

off to the left. Roll the wheel backwards out of the swingarm, not forgetting to retrieve the spacers.

Inspection

20 Refer to Steps 8 and 9 of this section.

Installation

21 Apply a thin coat of grease to the seal lips, then slide the left-hand spacer into the hub **(see illustration)**.

22 Position the wheel between the swingarm ends and install the drive chain over the sprocket **(see illustration)**. Check that the wheel spacers are still in position and that the chain adjusters are in place in each end of the swingarm **(see illustration)**.

23 Insert the spacer into the right-hand side of the wheel **(see illustration)**. Locate the

13.22a Engage the chain over the sprocket

13.22b Install the chain adjusters in the swingarm ends

13.21 Insert the left-hand spacer in the hub

13.23b The brake caliper support bracket must locate over the lug on the swingarm

13.25 Make sure that the axle nut is secured correctly

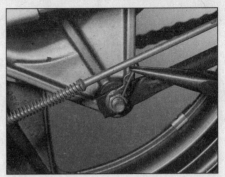

13.28a Remove the R-pin from the torque link bolt

caliper support bracket between the spacer and swingarm so that its slot fits over the lug on the inside of the swingarm **(see illustration)**.

24 Install the axle into the left-hand side and slide it through the wheel, making sure that it passes through the wheel spacers, chain adjusters, chain adjuster plates and brake caliper support bracket. Install the washer and nut on the end of the axle. Tighten the axle nut only lightly at this stage. Check the chain adjustment and adjust it if necessary (see Chapter 1).

25 Tighten the axle nut to the specified torque. Secure the nut using a new cotter pin (split pin) and bend its ends correctly **(see illustration)**.

26 Check that the rear brake works correctly before riding the motorcycle.

ER models

Removal

27 Set the bike on its centerstand.
28 Remove the R-pin from the torque link bolt **(see illustration)**. Unscrew the nut and remove the bolt to separate the torque link from the brake panel **(see illustration)**.
29 Fully unscrew the brake freeplay adjuster nut from the end of the brake rod **(see illustration)**. Press on the rear brake pedal to

draw the rod out of the brake cam **(see illustration)**. Refit the spring and nut back on the brake rod for safekeeping.
30 Straighten the cotter pin (split pin) in the rear axle nut and remove it **(see illustration 13.19a)**. Unscrew the rear axle nut and withdraw the axle from the right-hand side **(see illustration 13.19b)**. Allow the rear wheel to drop down, then lift the drive chain off to the left. Roll the wheel backwards out of the swingarm, not forgetting to retrieve the spacers.

Inspection

31 Refer to Steps 8 and 9 of this section.

Installation

32 Apply a thin coat of grease to the seal lips, then slip the left-hand spacer into the grease seal **(see illustration)**.
33 Position the wheel between the swingarm ends and install the drive chain over the sprocket **(see illustration 13.23a)**. Check that the chain adjusters are in place in each end of the swingarm **(see illustration)**.
34 Install the axle into the right-hand side, complete with the chain adjuster plate and slide it through the wheel, making sure that you insert the right-hand spacer between the brake panel and the swingarm **(see**

13.28b Remove its nut and withdraw the torque link bolt

13.29a Unscrew the adjuster nut from the end of the brake rod

13.29b Disconnect the rod from the brake cam. Note the spring

13.32 Install the left-hand spacer into the grease seal

13.33 Make sure the chain adjusters are in place in the swingarm ends

13.34 Insert the axle from the right-hand side, not forgetting the spacer (arrowed)

illustration). Install the chain adjuster plate, washer and nut on the end of the axle. Tighten the axle nut only lightly at this stage. Check the chain adjustment and adjust it if necessary (see Chapter 1).

35 Insert the torque link bolt through the brake panel and torque link **(see illustration 13.28b)**. Install the nut and tighten it to the specified torque, then slip the R-pin in the hole provided in the bolt **(see illustration 13.28a)**. Place the spring over the brake rod, insert the brake rod through the trunnion in the brake cam **(see illustration 13.29b)** and thread the nut onto the end of the brake rod **(see illustration 13.29a)**. Adjust the brake pedal freeplay as described in Chapter 1.

36 Spin the rear wheel, then apply the rear brake and to centralise the brake shoes in the drum and tighten the axle nut to the specified torque. Secure the nut using a new cotter pin (split pin) and bend its ends correctly **(see illustration 13.25)**.

37 Recheck the rear brake freeplay and rear brake light switch setting (see Chapter 1).

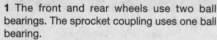

14 Wheel bearings –
inspection and maintenance

1 The front and rear wheels use two ball bearings. The sprocket coupling uses one ball bearing.

2 Set the bike on its centerstand and remove the wheel (see Section 12 or 13).

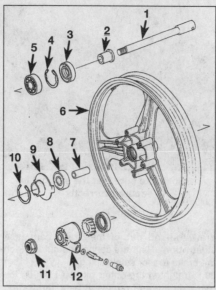

14.4 Front wheel bearing and hub details

1 Axle	8 Bearing
2 Collar	9 Speedometer
3 Seal	drive
4 Circlip	10 Circlip
5 Bearing	11 Nut
6 Wheel	12 Speedometer
7 Spacer	gear and housing

3 Support the wheel rim on blocks so not to allow the weight of the wheel to rest on the brake disc or sprocket.

Front wheel bearings

4 If not already done, remove the speedometer gear housing from the left-hand side of the hub. Pry out the grease seal, then remove the circlip and speedometer drive **(see illustration)**.

5 Turn the wheel over and pry out the grease seal. Remove the circlip.

6 Insert a brass drift from the right-hand side of the hub and tap evenly around the inner race of the opposite bearing to remove it **(see illustration)**. Remove the bearing spacer, then remove the remaining bearing in the same way.

7 Thoroughly clean the inside of the hub with high-flash point solvent and blow it out with compressed air, if available.

8 Drive in the new bearings with a bearing

14.6 Once the circlips have been removed, drive the bearings from the hub with a metal rod and hammer

14.12a Remove the coupling sleeve . . .

driver or a socket the same diameter as the bearing outer race. Don't forget to install the spacer after you've installed the first bearing.

9 Install a new circlip on the right-hand side and make sure it seats securely in its groove.

10 Tap in a new grease seal evenly, using a bearing driver or a socket the same diameter as the seal, until it stops at the circlip.

11 The remainder of installation is the reverse of the removal steps.

Sprocket coupling bearing

12 Lift out the wheel spacer, rear wheel coupling and the shouldered coupling collar **(see illustrations)**.

13 Pry the grease seal out of the coupling **(see illustration)**.

14 Remove the circlip on EX500A models **(see illustration)**.

15 Tap against the back side of the bearing

14.12b . . . and coupling collar

14.13 Pry the grease seal out of the sprocket coupling

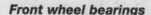

14.14 Remove the circlip

14.15 Drive the bearing out from this side

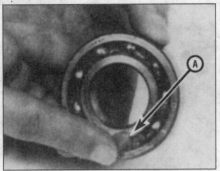

14.17 Pack grease (A) into the bearing until it's full

14.19 Tap a new grease seal in evenly

14.21a Remove the circlip

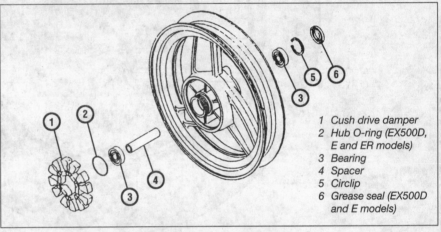

1 Cush drive damper
2 Hub O-ring (EX500D, E and ER models)
3 Bearing
4 Spacer
5 Circlip
6 Grease seal (EX500D and E models)

14.21b Rear wheel bearing details

with a bearing driver or a socket to drive it out of the coupling **(see illustration)**.
16 Thoroughly clean the bearing with solvent. Blow it dry with compressed air, if available, but don't spin the bearing with compressed air while it's dry. Hold the inner race with fingers and spin the outer race. If the bearing feels rough, loose, or makes noise (more than a slight whirring), renew it.
17 Pack the bearing with grease **(see illustration)**.
18 Drive the bearing into the coupling with a bearing driver or a socket the same diameter as the outer race. On EX500A models install the circlip, making sure that it seats fully in the groove.
19 Tap in a new grease seal with a brass or plastic mallet **(see illustration)**. Tap evenly so

14.22 Insert a drift into the hub and tap evenly around the opposite bearing to drive it out

the seal doesn't tilt. If necessary, lay a block of wood across the seal so the hammer's force will be spread evenly.

Rear wheel bearings

20 If you haven't already done so, lift the sprocket coupling out of the hub.
21 On EX500D and E models, pry the grease seal out of the right-hand side of the hub. On all models, remove the circlip from the right-hand bearing **(see illustrations)**.
22 Insert a brass drift into the hub and place it against the opposite bearing **(see illustration)**. Tap evenly around the inner race to drive the bearing from the hub. The bearing spacer will also come out.
23 Lay the wheel on its other side and remove the remaining bearing using the same technique.
24 Refer to Step 16 and inspect the bearings.
25 If the bearings check out okay and will be reused, wash them in solvent once again and dry them, then pack the bearings from the open side with high-quality bearing grease **(see illustration 13.17)**.
26 Thoroughly clean the hub area of the wheel. Install the right-hand bearing into the recess in the hub, with the marked or shielded side facing out. Using a bearing driver or a socket large enough to contact the outer race of the bearing, drive it in until the circlip groove is visible. Install

the circlip. On EX500D and E models, press a new grease into the hub right-hand side.
27 Turn the wheel over and install the bearing spacer and bearing, driving the bearing into place as described in Step 26.
28 Press a little grease into the bearing in the rear wheel coupling (if you haven't just repacked it). On EX500D, E and ER models check the condition of the O-ring around the hub boss on the left-hand side of the wheel; renew the O-ring if it is damaged or deteriorated.
29 Install the coupling to the wheel, making sure the coupling collar is located in the inside of the inner race (between the wheel and the coupling).
30 The remainder of installation is the reverse of the removal steps.

15 Tyres – general information and fitting

General information

1 The wheels fitted to all models are designed to take tubeless tyres only. Tyre sizes are given in the Specifications at the beginning of this chapter.

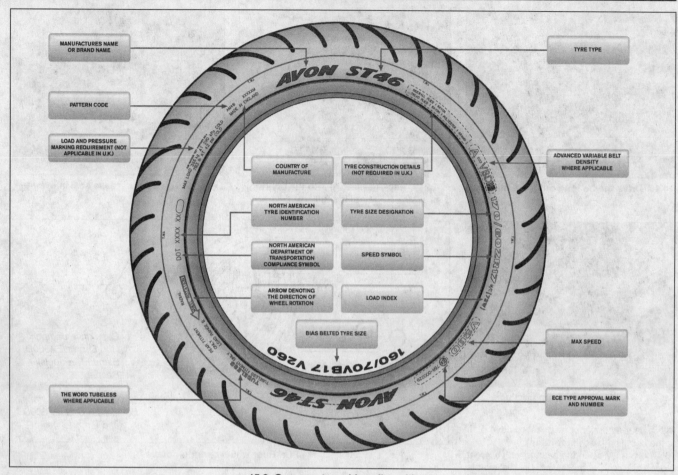

MANUFACTURES NAME OR BRAND NAME

PATTERN CODE

LOAD AND PRESSURE MARKING REQUIREMENT (NOT APPLICABLE IN U.K.)

TYRE TYPE

COUNTRY OF MANUFACTURE

TYRE CONSTRUCTION DETAILS (NOT REQUIRED IN U.K.)

NORTH AMERICAN TYRE IDENTIFICATION NUMBER

TYRE SIZE DESIGNATION

NORTH AMERICAN DEPARTMENT OF TRANSPORTATION COMPLIANCE SYMBOL

SPEED SYMBOL

ARROW DENOTING THE DIRECTION OF WHEEL ROTATION

LOAD INDEX

BIAS BELTED TYRE SIZE

ADVANCED VARIABLE BELT DENSITY WHERE APPLICABLE

MAX SPEED

THE WORD TUBELESS WHERE APPLICABLE

ECE TYPE APPROVAL MARK AND NUMBER

15.3 Common tyre sidewall markings

2 Refer to the *Daily (pre-ride) checks* listed at the beginning of this manual for tyre maintenance.

Fitting new tyres

3 When selecting new tyres, refer to the tyre information label on the swingarm and the tyre options listed in the owners handbook. Ensure that front and rear tyre types are compatible, the correct size and correct speed rating; if necessary seek advice from a Kawasaki dealer or tyre fitting specialist **(see illustration)**.

4 It is recommended that tyres are fitted by a motorcycle tyre specialist rather than attempted in the home workshop. This is particularly relevant in the case of tubeless tyres because the force required to break the seal between the wheel rim and tyre bead is substantial, and is usually beyond the capabilities of an individual working with normal tyre levers. Additionally, the specialist will be able to balance the wheels after tyre fitting.

5 Note that punctured tubeless tyres can in some cases be repaired. Kawasaki recommend that such repairs are carried out only by an authorised dealer. If repairs are made, they should be made internally (on the inside of the tyre) rather than externally. Kawasaki recommend that a repaired tyre should not be used at speeds above 60 mph (100 kmh) for the first 24 hours after the repair, and thereafter not above 110 mph (180 kmh).

Chapter 8
Fairing and bodywork

Contents

Degrees of difficulty

Easy, suitable for novice with little experience	**Fairly easy,** suitable for beginner with some experience	**Fairly difficult,** suitable for competent DIY mechanic	**Difficult,** suitable for experienced DIY mechanic	**Very difficult,** suitable for expert DIY or professional

1 General information

This Chapter covers the procedures necessary to remove and install the fairing and other body parts. Since many service and repair operations on these motorcycles require removal of the fairing and/or other body parts, the procedures are grouped here and referred to from other Chapters.

In the case of damage to the body parts, it is usually necessary to remove the broken component and renew it (or replace it with a used one from a breaker). Note that there are however some companies that specialise in 'plastic welding' and there are a number of bodywork repair kits now available for motorcycles.

2 Lower fairing (belly pan) – removal and installation (EX models)

1 Set the bike on its centerstand.
2 Support the lower fairing and remove the mounting screws, taking note of any washer positions **(see illustrations).**
3 Carefully manoeuvre the fairing out from under the bike.
4 Installation is the reverse of removal.

3 Upper fairing – removal and installation (EX models)

EX500A models

1 Set the bike on its centerstand.
2 Remove the seat. Remove the fuel tank (see Chapter 4).
3 Remove the inner fairing panel from each side of the bike **(see illustration).**
4 Remove the rear view mirrors (see Section 5).
5 Disconnect the front turn signal wiring connectors.

2.2a **Lower fairing is secured by two bolts with washers at the front . . .**

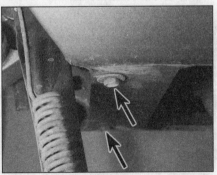

2.2b **. . . and two bolts on the underside at the rear**

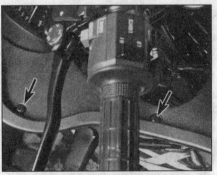

3.3 **Remove the screws (arrowed) and detach the inner fairing on each side of the motorcycle**

3.6 Remove the screw from under the fairing on each side (arrowed)

3.7a Spread the fairing slightly and carefully work it forward to clear the fairing stay

3.7b If you only need access to other components, you can prop the fairing away from the sides of the bike with blocks of wood

6 Remove the screws from the underside of the fairing (see illustration).

7 Spread the fairing slightly and pull it forward to clear the fairing stays, then pull it off (see illustration). Note: *If you're removing the fairing partially for access to other components, prop the rear ends away from the bike with blocks of wood* (see illustration).

8 Installation is the reverse of removal.

EX500D and E models

9 Set the bike on its centerstand.

10 Remove the two mounting bolts from the front underside of the fairing noting their collars and washers (see illustration).

11 Remove the two screws with washers from each side of the fairing (see illustration).

12 Remove the rear view mirrors (see Section 5).

13 Have an assistant support the fairing as you reach inside and disconnect the wiring to the headlight, sidelight (UK models) and front turn signals. Spread the fairing ends slightly and pull it forward to clear the fairing stays as it is removed.

14 Installation is the reverse of removal. Ensure that the fairing fits over the mirror mounting lugs.

4 Windshield – removal and installation (EX models)

1 Remove the screws securing the windshield

to the fairing (see illustration). On EX500D and E models, note that the screws thread into rubber inserts which expand to hold the screen in place (see illustration); it is advisable to remove the instrument cluster trim panel before removing the screen.

2 Carefully separate the windshield from the fairing. If it sticks, don't attempt to pry it off – just keep applying steady pressure with your fingers.

3 Installation is the reverse of the removal procedure. Be sure each screw has a plastic washer under its head. Tighten the screws securely, but be careful not to overtighten them, as the windshield might crack.

5 Rear view mirrors – removal and installation

EX500A models

1 Pull back the rubber cover from the mirror mounting. Remove the two screws and carefully withdraw the mirror with its outer rubber damper (see illustration).

2 When installing the mirror check that the inner rubber damper which locates between the inside of the fairing and the stay is still in place. If necessary remove the inner fairing panel (see Section 3) and relocate it. Install the mirror with its outer rubber damper and

3.10 Fairing mounting bolts at the front . . .

3.11 . . . and on each side

4.1a Windshield mounting screws – EX500A

4.1b Windshield mounting inserts – EX500D and E

5.1 Pull back the rubber cover and remove the mirror mounting screws

5.3 Mirror is retained by two nuts on the inside of the fairing

7.3 Engage tab under tank bracket

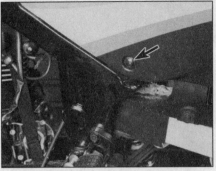

8.2 Remove the side cover mounting screw on each side (arrowed)

tighten the screws securely. Slip the rubber cover back into place. Adjust the mirror angle to suit.

EX500D and E models

3 Remove the two nuts from inside the fairing to release the mirror **(see illustration)**.
4 Refit in a reverse of the removal procedure. Adjust the mirror angle to suit.

ER models

5 Slacken the lower nut on the mirror stalk and unscrew the body of the mirror from the handlebar bracket.
6 On installation, thread the mirror well into its bracket, then position the stalk at the correct angle and tighten down the locknut.

6 Fairing stay – removal and installation (EX models)

1 Remove the fairing (see Section 3).
2 Remove the headlight assembly (EX500A) and instrument cluster from the stay (see Chapter 9).
3 Carefully note how the wiring harness is routed in the area of the fairing stay.
4 Remove the bolts and nut and take the fairing stay off the bike.
5 Installation is the reverse of the removal steps.
6 Check the headlight aim on EX500A models (see Chapter 9).

7 Seat – removal and installation

Removal

1 On EX models, insert the ignition key into the seat lock via the hole in the left-hand tail piece (EX500A) or side cover (EX500D/E) and turn it clockwise to unlatch the seat. Pull the seat up at the rear to remove it.
2 On ER models, insert the ignition key into the seat lock and turn it clockwise to unlatch the seat. Lift the seat at the rear to remove it.

Installation

3 On installation, engage the prong at the front of the seat under the fuel tank mounting bracket and push down on the rear of the seat to lock it **(see illustration)**.

8 Side covers – removal and installation

Side covers – EX500A models

1 Remove the seat (see Section 7).
2 Remove the side cover mounting screw **(see illustration)**.
3 Carefully pull the securing lugs out of the grommets **(see illustration)** and lift the cover off.

8.3 Pull the lugs out of the grommets; if they won't come with a light pull, make sure all fasteners have been removed

4 Installation is the reverse of the removal procedure.

Tail piece – EX500A models

5 Remove both side covers.
6 Unbolt the grab rail and take it off **(see illustration)**.
7 Remove the tail piece bolt on each side **(see illustration)**.
8 Disconnect the electrical connector for the tail lights. Slide the tail piece to the rear until the projections on the tail piece separate from the grommets in the frame, then remove it.
9 Installation is the reverse of removal.

Side covers – EX500D and E models

10 Remove the seat (see Section 7).
11 Remove the grab rail; it is retained by two bolts **(see illustration)**.

8.6 Remove the grab rail mounting bolts

8.7 Remove the bolt on each side of the tailpiece (arrowed) and slide it rearward

8.11 Remove the grab rail bolts (arrowed)

8.12a Side cover retaining screw
(arrowed) at the front . . .

8.12b . . . and at the rear (arrowed)

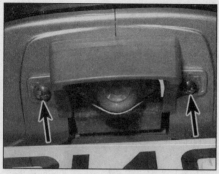

8.12c Licence plate light cover screws
(arrowed)

8.13a Engage the side cover rear peg with
the frame grommet (arrowed) . . .

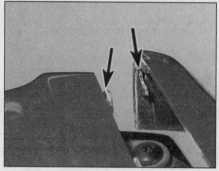

8.13b . . . and engage the fillet projection
in the slot (arrowed) . . .

8.13c . . . then engage the front peg in the
grommet

8.16a Side cover retaining screw . . .

12 Remove the two side cover retaining screws, one at the front lower edge and the other at the top rear edge (see illustrations). Remove the two screws which retain the licence plate light cover below the tail light and remove the cover (see illustration). Pull the side cover out of its grommet at the front upper edge and ease the cover rearwards to disengage its rear peg from the grommet in the frame.

13 On installation be careful to engage the pegs in the side cover with the grommets in the frame (see illustrations). Note also that the projection on the joining fillet must fit into the slot in the side cover (see illustration).

14 Fit the side cover and licence plate cover retaining screws making sure that their washers are in place.

Side covers – ER models

15 Remove the seat (see Section 7).
16 Remove the single screw which retains the side cover to the frame and pull the cover away to release its three pegs from the mounting grommets in the tail piece (see illustrations).

Tail piece – ER models

17 Remove the seat and both side covers (see above).
18 Remove the two bolts and withdraw the grab rail (see illustration).

8.16b . . . and pegs

8.18 Grab rail retaining bolts (arrowed)

8.19a On ER500A models, the tail piece is
retained by a screw at each forward end
(arrowed) . . .

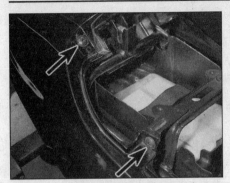

8.19b . . . and by two screws on each side at the rear (arrowed)

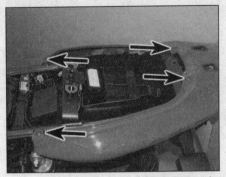

8.19c On ER500C models, the tail piece is retained by four screws (arrowed)

8.19d Take care not to damage the tail piece where it locates on the tabs

19 On ER500A models, remove the six retaining screws **(see illustrations)**. On ER500C models, remove the four retaining screws **(see illustration)**. Very carefully splay the front ends of the tail piece outwards as it is withdrawn as a complete unit towards the rear. On ER500C models, note how the lower edge of the tail piece is located on tabs on the rear subframe **(see illustration)**.

20 If desired the tail piece halves can be separated from the joining fillet my removing the two screws.

21 Installation is a reversal of the removal procedure. Hook the slots on the lower edge over the two hooks on the frame.

> **HAYNES HiNT** *Note that a small amount of lubricant (liquid soap or similar) applied to mounting rubber grommets will assist pegs to engage without the need for undue pressure.*

9 Front mudguard/fender – removal and installation

EX500A models

1 Set the bike on its centerstand.

9.3 The mudguard mounting bolts are accessible from inside the mudguard – EX500A

2 Disconnect the speedometer cable from the speedometer drive.
3 Remove the four bolts from inside the mudguard **(see illustration)**.
4 Installation is the reverse of removal.

EX500D and E models

5 Set the bike on its centerstand.
6 Remove the front wheel (see Chapter 7).
7 Either disconnect the speedometer cable from its drive at the wheel and slip it out of the guide on the mudguard, or carefully ease the guide out of its hole in the mudguard. Very carefully ease the brake hose guide of its hole on the other side of the mudguard.
8 Remove the four bolts and withdraw the mudguard.
9 Installation is a reverse of removal.

ER models

10 Set the bike on its centerstand.
11 Remove the front wheel (see Chapter 7).
12 Either disconnect the speedometer cable from its drive at the wheel and slip it out of the guide on the mudguard, or carefully ease the guide out of its hole in the mudguard.
13 Remove the four bolts from inside the mudguard.
14 Installation is a reverse of removal.

10 Rear mudguard/fender – removal and installation

EX models

Rear section

1 Set the bike on its centerstand.
2 Remove the seat. Remove the tail piece on EX500A models or both side covers on EX500D models (see Section 8).
3 Unplug the electrical connectors for the turn signal lights.
4 Remove the mounting bolts and remove the rear section of the rear mudguard.

5 Installation is the reverse of the removal procedure.

Front section

6 Remove the rear section (see above).
7 Lift the front section out toward the rear.
8 Installation is the reverse of removal. Be sure to route the brake fluid reservoir hose and brake light switch wiring correctly. Ensure that the mudguard flaps locate in the frame slots.

ER models

9 Set the bike on its centerstand and tie it down so that there is no danger of it toppling backwards. As an additional safety measure, position a jack or suitable support underneath the frame at the rear of the engine.
10 Remove the seat and the front and rear side covers (see Sections 7 and 8).
11 Referring the relevant sections of Chapters 5 and 9, remove the battery, regulator/rectifier, fusebox, IC igniter, turn signal relay, starter relay and starter circuit relay.
12 Remove both rear shock absorbers (see Chapter 6) and gently lower the rear wheel and swingarm assembly to rest on the ground.
13 Remove the two bolts which retain the front of the mudguard, and the two bolts with nuts at the rear. It is now possible to withdraw the mudguard from below the rear frame section.
14 Installation is a reverse of the removal procedure, noting the following points:
 a) *Don't forget to install the tail piece mounting hooks on the mudguard rear mounting bolts.*
 b) *Tighten the rear shock absorber bolts/nuts to the specified torque (see Chapter 6).*
 c) *Be careful to reconnect the electrical components correctly.*
 d) *Connect the negative lead last when installing the battery.*

Notes

Chapter 9
Electrical system

Contents

Degrees of difficulty

Easy, suitable for novice with little experience	**Fairly easy,** suitable for beginner with some experience	**Fairly difficult,** suitable for competent DIY mechanic

Difficult, suitable for experienced DIY mechanic	**Very difficult,** suitable for expert DIY or professional

Specifications

Battery

Type
  EX models .... 12 volt, 14 Ah (amp hours)
  ER models .... 12 volt, 10 Ah (amp hours), maintenance free
Electrolyte specific gravity (EX models) .... 1.280 at 20°C (68°F)
Terminal voltage (ER models) .... 12.6 volts or more

Charging system

Charging system regulated output .... 14 to 15 volts DC at 4000 rpm
Alternator unregulated output
  EX500A models .... 60 volts AC @ 4000 rpm
  EX500D and E models .... 56 volts AC @ 4000 rpm
  ER500A models .... 46 to 64 volts @ 4000 rpm
  ER500C models .... 60 volts @ 4000 rpm
Stator coil resistance
  EX500A models .... 0.3 to 0.6 ohms
  EX500D and E models .... 0.37 to 0.55 ohms
  ER500A models .... 0.35 to 0.51 ohms
  ER500C models .... 0.3 to 0.6 ohms

Starter motor

Brush length
  Standard .... 12 to 12.5 mm (0.47 to 0.49 in)
  Minimum – EX models .... 6 mm (0.24 in)
  Minimum – ER models .... 8.5 mm (0.33 in)
Commutator diameter
  Standard .... 28 mm (1.102 in)
  Minimum .... 27 mm (1.063 in)

Fuse ratings

Main fuse	30A
Tail light	10A
Headlight	10A
Cooling fan	10A
Ignition (EX500D, E and ER models)	10A
Horn (EX500D, E and ER models)	10A
Turn signals (EX500D, E and ER models)	10A
Accessory (US/Canada EX models)	10A

Bulb wattages – EX models

Headlight	12V, 60/55W
Sidelight	
EX500A models	12V, 4W
EX500D and E models	12V, 5W
Tail/brake light	
US models	12V, 8/27W x 2
UK models	12V, 5/21W x 2
Licence plate light	
US models	12V, 8W
UK models	12V, 5W
Turn signals – UK models	12V, 21W x 4
Turn signals – US models	
Front (running lights)	12V, 23/8W x 2
Rear	12V, 23W x 2
Instrument cluster lights – EX500A models	12V, 3.4W
Instrument cluster lights – EX500D and E models	
Neutral, oil pressure, high beam, turn signal warning lights	12V, 3W
Meter lights	12V, 1.7W

Bulb wattages – ER models

Headlight	12V, 60/55W
Sidelight	12V, 4W
Tail/brake light	12V, 5/21W
Turn signals	12V, 21W x 4
Instrument cluster lights	
Neutral, high beam, turn signal warning lights	12V, 3W
Oil pressure warning and meter lights	12V, 1.7W

Torque specifications

Alternator rotor bolt	69 Nm (51 ft-lbs)
Alternator stator screws	12 Nm (104 in-lbs)
Alternator cover bolts	
EX500A models	Not specified
EX500D, E and ER models	11 Nm (95 in-lbs)
Oil pressure switch	15 Nm (11 ft-lbs)
Starter motor mounting bolts	11 Nm (95 in-lbs)
Starter clutch bolts	34 Nm (25 ft-lbs)

1 General information

The machines covered by this manual are equipped with a 12-volt electrical system. The components include a crankshaft mounted permanent magnet alternator and a regulator/rectifier unit.

The regulator maintains the charging system output within the specified range to prevent overcharging. The rectifier converts the AC (alternating current) output of the alternator to DC (direct current) to power the lights and other components and to charge the battery.

The alternator consists of a multi-coil stator (bolted to the right-hand engine case) and a permanent magnet rotor.

An electric starter mounted to the engine case behind the cylinders is standard equipment. The starting system includes the motor, the battery, the starter relay, the starter circuit relay (part of the junction box on EX models) and the various wires and switches. If the engine stop switch and the main key switch are both in the On position, the circuit relay allows the starter motor to operate only if the transmission is in Neutral (Neutral switch on) or the clutch lever is pulled to the handlebar (clutch switch on) and the sidestand is up (sidestand switch on).

2 Electrical system – fault finding

 Warning: To prevent the risk of short circuits, the ignition (main) switch must always be OFF and the battery negative (-ve) terminal should be disconnected before any of the bike's other electrical components are disturbed. Don't forget to reconnect the terminal securely once work is finished or if battery power is needed for circuit testing.

1 A typical electrical circuit consists of an electrical component, the switches, relays,

etc. related to that component and the wiring and connectors that hook the component to both the battery and the frame. To aid in locating a problem in any electrical circuit, refer to the wiring diagrams at the end of this Chapter.

2 Before tackling any troublesome electrical circuit, first study the wiring diagram (see end of Chapter) thoroughly to get a complete picture of what makes up that individual circuit. Trouble spots, for instance, can often be narrowed down by noting if other components related to that circuit are operating properly or not. If several components or circuits fail at one time, chances are the fault lies in the fuse or earth (ground) connection, as several circuits often are routed through the same fuse and earth (ground) connections.

3 Electrical problems often stem from simple causes, such as loose or corroded connections or a blown fuse. Prior to any electrical fault finding, always visually check the condition of the fuse, wires and connections in the problem circuit. Intermittent failures can be especially frustrating, since you can't always duplicate the failure when it's convenient to test. In such situations, a good practice is to clean all connections in the affected circuit, whether or not they appear to be good. All of the connections and wires should also be wiggled to check for looseness which can cause intermittent failure.

4 If testing instruments are going to be utilised, use the wiring diagram to plan where you will make the necessary connections in order to accurately pinpoint the trouble spot.

5 The basic tools needed for electrical fault finding include a battery and bulb test circuit, a continuity tester, a test light, and a jumper wire. A multimeter capable of reading volts, ohms and amps is also very useful as an alternative to the above, and is necessary for performing more extensive tests and checks.

HAYNES HiNT *Refer to Fault Finding Equipment in the Reference section for details of how to use electrical test equipment.*

---

3 Battery – inspection and maintenance

Conventional battery – with cell caps (EX models)

1 Most battery damage is caused by heat, vibration, and/or low electrolyte levels, so keep the battery securely mounted, check the electrolyte level frequently (see Chapter 1). If the battery overheats and requires frequent topping up, check the charging system output as described later in this Chapter.

2 The state of charge of the battery can be determined by carrying out a specific gravity check (see Chapter 1). Battery open-circuit (not connected to motorcycle) terminal voltage can be checked by referring to *Fault Finding Equipment* in the Reference section.

3 Check around the base inside of the battery for sediment, which is the result of sulphation caused by low electrolyte levels. These deposits will cause internal short circuits, which can quickly discharge the battery. Look for cracks in the case and renew the battery if either of these conditions is found.

4 Check the battery terminals and cable ends for tightness and corrosion. If corrosion is evident, remove the cables from the battery and clean the terminals and cable ends with a wire brush or knife and emery paper. Reconnect the cables and apply a thin coat of petroleum jelly to the connections to slow further corrosion. When disconnecting the battery, always disconnect the negative (–ve) cable first and reconnect it last when installing the battery (refer to Chapter 1 for details).

5 The battery case should be kept clean to prevent current leakage, which can discharge the battery over a period of time (especially when it sits unused). Wash the outside of the case with a solution of baking soda and water. Do not get any baking soda solution in the battery cells. Rinse the battery thoroughly, then dry it.

6 If acid has been spilled on the frame or battery box, neutralise it with the baking soda and water solution, dry it thoroughly, then touch up any damaged paint. Make sure the

---

battery vent tube is directed away from the frame and is not kinked or pinched.

7 If the motorcycle sits unused for long periods of time, disconnect the cables from the battery terminals. Refer to Section 4 and charge the battery approximately once every month.

Maintenance-free battery (ER models)

8 Maintenance-free batteries do not require topping up of their electrolyte. No attempt should be made to remove the sealing cap on their top surface.

9 The battery is located under the seat. Remove the seat (see Chapter 8), then remove the three screws which retain the battery cover and remove it **(see illustration)**.

10 Periodically check the battery terminals and cables for tightness and corrosion. If corrosion is evident, unscrew the terminal bolts and disconnect the cables from the battery **(see illustration)**, disconnecting the negative (-ve) terminal first, and clean the terminals and cable ends with a wire brush or knife and emery paper. Reconnect the cables, connecting the negative (-ve) terminal last, and apply a thin coat of petroleum jelly to the connections to slow further corrosion.

11 The battery case should be kept clean to prevent current leakage, which can discharge the battery over a period of time (especially when it sits unused). Wash the outside of the case with a solution of baking soda and water. Rinse the battery thoroughly, then dry it.

12 If the motorcycle sits unused for long periods of time, disconnect the cables from the battery terminals (see Step 10) and charge the battery once every month to six weeks.

13 The state of charge of the battery can be assessed by measuring the voltage present at its terminals with the battery removed (open-circuit). Remove the battery from the motorcycle. Connect the voltmeter (set to the 0 – 20 dc volts range) positive (+ve) probe to the battery positive (+ve) terminal, and the negative (-ve) probe to the battery negative (-ve) terminal **(see illustration)**. When fully charged there should be the voltage specified at the beginning of the Chapter. If the voltage falls below this the battery must be recharged as described below in Section 4.

3.9 Three screws (arrowed) retain the battery cover

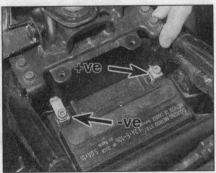
3.10 Battery negative (–ve) cable and positive (+ve) cable

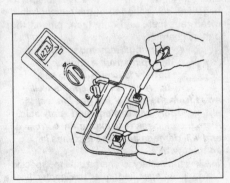
3.13 Measuring battery open-circuit voltage

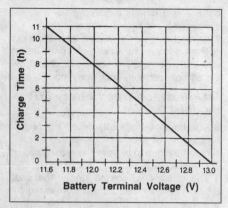

4.10 Battery charging time at 1.2A charge rate

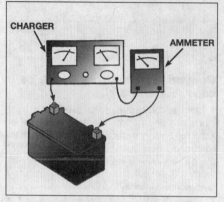

4.11 Battery charger with ammeter connected in series

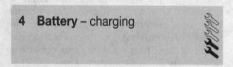

4 Battery – charging

Conventional battery – with cell caps (EX models)

1 If the machine sits idle for extended periods or if the charging system malfunctions, the battery can be charged from an external source.

2 To properly charge the battery, you will need a charger of the correct rating, an hydrometer, a clean rag and a syringe for adding distilled water to the battery cells.

3 The maximum charging rate for any battery is 1/10 of the rated amp/hour capacity. As an example, the maximum charging rate for a 14 amp/hour battery would be 1.4 amps. If the battery is charged at a higher rate, it could be damaged.

4 Do not allow the battery to be subjected to a so-called quick charge (high rate of charge over a short period of time) unless you are prepared to buy a new battery.

5 When charging the battery, always remove it from the machine and be sure to check the electrolyte level before hooking up the charger. Add distilled water to any cells that are low.

6 Loosen the cell caps, hook up the battery charger leads (red to positive, black to negative), cover the top of the battery with a clean rag, then, and only then, plug in the battery charger.

⚠ **Warning: Remember, the gas escaping from a charging battery is explosive, so keep open flames and sparks well away from the area. If the gas ignites, the entire battery can explode and spray acid. Also, the electrolyte is extremely corrosive and will damage anything it comes in contact with.**

7 Allow the battery to charge until the specific gravity is as specified (refer to Chapter 1 for specific gravity checking procedures). The charger must be unplugged and disconnected

from the battery when making specific gravity checks. If the battery overheats or gases excessively, the charging rate is too high. Either disconnect the charger or lower the charging rate to prevent damage to the battery.

8 If one or more of the cells do not show an increase in specific gravity after a long slow charge, or if the battery as a whole does not seem to want to take a charge, it is time for a new battery.

9 When the battery is fully charged, unplug the charger first, then disconnect the leads from the battery. Install the cell caps and wipe any electrolyte off the outside of the battery case.

Maintenance-free battery (ER models)

10 Remove the battery and carry out an open-circuit voltage check as described in Section 3. Determine the battery charge rate and time from the terminal voltage:

12.6 volts or more	no charge is required
11.5 to 12.6 volts	1.2A x 5 to 10 hrs (see illustration) or a quick charge of 5.0A x 1 hr
Below 11.5 volts	1.2A x 20 hrs

11 Use a current controlled battery charger with an in-built ammeter; if the charger

doesn't have an ammeter connect one into the circuit in series (see illustration) – do not use an unregulated charger or the battery could be ruined. Alternatively use one of the new specialised battery condition/chargers such as the Optimate Battery Optimiser.

12 The battery must be removed from the motorcycle before charging. Connect the charger to the battery, making sure that the positive (+ve) lead on the charger is connected to the positive (+ve) terminal on the battery, and the negative (-ve) lead is connected to the negative (-ve) terminal. Where applicable, set the charge rate according to the terminal voltage measured. *Caution: If the battery becomes hot during charging stop. Further charging will cause damage.*

13 If the recharged battery discharges rapidly if left disconnected it is likely that an internal short caused by physical damage or sulphation has occurred and a new battery will be required. After charging, let the battery stand for 30 minutes then measure its terminal voltage. If it measures 12.6 volts or more it is in good condition and fully charged. If it measures between 12 to 12.6 volts charging is insufficient and it should be recharged. If however, the battery measures less than 12 volts after the specified charge period it should be renewed. Note that it is difficult to recover deeply discharged maintenance-free batteries.

5 Fuses – check and renewal

1 All of the fuses except the main fuse are located under the seat (see illustrations). The main fuse is located on the starter relay (see illustrations). The circuit fuses are protected by a plastic cover, which snaps into place. It contains fuses (and spares) which protect individual circuits and their components from damage caused by short circuits.

2 If you have a test light, the fuses can be checked without removing them. Turn the ignition to the ON position, connect one end of the test light to a good earth (ground), then

5.1a On EX models the fusebox is located on the junction box . . .

5.1b . . . and on ER500A models the fusebox is located on the rear mudguard

5.1c Location of the fusebox on ER500C models

5.1d The main fuse is located on the starter relay (arrowed) – EX models

5.1e Main fuse location on starter relay (arrowed) – ER models

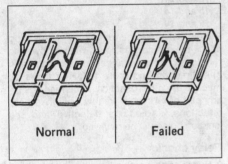

5.3 A blown fuse can be identified by a broken element – be sure to replace a blown fuse with one of the same amperage rating

probe each terminal on top of the fuse. If the fuse is good, there will be voltage available at both terminals. If the fuse is blown, there will only be voltage present at one of the terminals.

3 The fuses can be removed and checked visually. If you can't pull the fuse out with your fingertips, use a pair of needle-nose pliers. A blown fuse is easily identified by a break in the element **(see illustration)**.

4 If a fuse blows, be sure to check the wiring harnesses very carefully for evidence of a short circuit. Look for bare wires and chafed, melted or burned insulation. If a fuse is renewed before the cause is located, the new fuse will blow immediately.

5 Never, under any circumstances, use a higher rated fuse or bridge the fuse block terminals, as damage to the electrical system – including melted wires, ruined components, and fire – could result.

6 Occasionally a fuse will blow or cause an open circuit for no obvious reason. Corrosion of the fuse ends and fuse block terminals may occur and cause poor fuse contact. If this happens, remove the corrosion with a wire brush or emery paper, then spray the fuse end and terminals with electrical contact cleaner.

6 Junction box and diodes – check

Junction box checks – EX models

1 Aside from serving as a mounting for the fusebox, the junction box also houses relays – the fan relay (EX500A1 and A2 only), the starter circuit relay and the headlight relay (US and Canada only). None of these relays are available individually. If one of them fails, the junction box must be renewed.

2 In addition to the relay checks, the fuse circuits and diode circuits should be checked also, to rule out the possibility of an open circuit condition or blown diode within the junction box as the cause of an electrical problem. The terminal pairs given in the following test procedures relate to specific pins on the junction box wiring connectors **(see illustrations)**. Remove the seat and disconnect the battery negative (–ve) cable (see Section 3).

Fuse circuit check

3 Remove the junction box by sliding it out of its holder. Unplug the electrical connectors from the box.

4 If the terminals are dirty or bent, clean and straighten them. Using the accompanying table as a guide, check the continuity across the indicated terminals with an ohmmeter – some should have no resistance and others

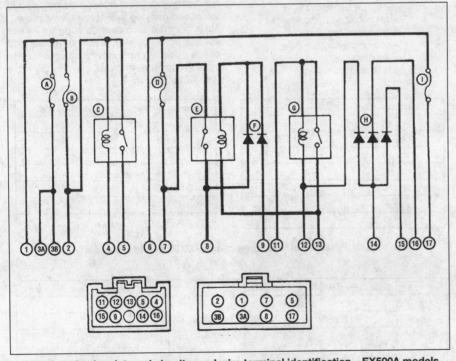

6.2a Junction box internal circuitry and wire terminal identification – EX500A models

A   Accessory fuse*
B   Fan fuse – A3-on models
C   Fan relay – A1 and A2 models
D   Headlight fuse
E   Headlight relay*

F   Headlight relay diodes
G   Starter circuit relay
H   Interlock diodes
I   Tail light fuse
*US and Canada models only

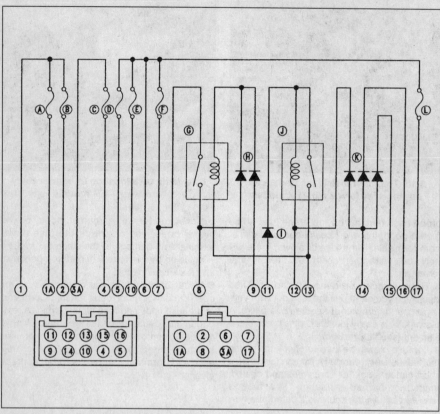

should have infinite resistance **(see illustrations)**.

5 If the resistance values are not as specified, renew the junction box.

Diodes check

6 Remove the junction box by sliding it out of its holder. Unplug the electrical connectors from the box.

7 Using an ohmmeter, check the resistance across the following pairs of terminals, then write down the readings.

Here are the terminal pairs to be checked:
13 and 8 (US and Canada models only)
13 and 9 (US and Canada models only)
12 and 11 (EX500D and E only)
12 and 14
15 and 14
16 and 14

8 Now, reverse the ohmmeter leads and check the resistances again, writing down the readings. The resistances should be low in one direction and more than ten times as much in the other direction. If the readings for any pair of terminals are low or high in both directions, a diode is defective and the junction box must be renewed.

Relay checks

9 Remove the junction box by sliding it out of its holder. Unplug the electrical connectors from the box.

10 Using an ohmmeter, check the conductivity across the terminals indicated in the accompanying table **(see illustrations)**. Then, energise each relay by applying battery voltage across the indicated terminals and check the conductivity across the corresponding terminals shown on the table **(see illustrations)**.

6.2b Junction box internal circuitry and wire terminal identification – EX500D and E models

A	Accessory fuse*	H	Headlight relay diodes*
B	Fan fuse	I	Starter circuit relay diode
C	Turn signal fuse	J	Starter circuit relay
D	Horn fuse	K	Interlock diodes
E	Ignition fuse	L	Tail light fuse
F	Headlight fuse		*US and Canada models only
G	Headlight relay*		

Meter Connection	Meter Reading (Ω)
1 — 2	0
1 — 3	0
6 — 7	0
6 — 17	0
1 — 7	∞
3A — 8	∞
8 — 17	∞

6.4a Fuse circuit test connections – EX500A models

Tester Connection	Tester Reading (Ω)
1 – 1A	0
1 – 2	0
3A – 4	0
6 – 5	0
6 – 10	0
6 – 7	0
6 – 17	0

Tester Connection	Tester Reading (Ω)
1A – 8	∞
2 – 8	∞
3A – 8	∞
6 – 2	∞
6 – 3A	∞
17 – 3A	∞

6.4b Fuse circuit test connections – EX500D and E models

	Meter Connection	Meter Reading (Ω)
Fan Relay[1]	2 – 5	∞
	4 – 5	∞
Headlight Relay[2]	7 – 8	∞
	7 – 13	∞
Starter Relay	11 – 13	∞
	12 – 13	∞

6.10a Relay checks without battery connected – EX500A models

1 Only applies to A1 and A2 models
2 US and Canada models only
∞ = infinite resistance (no continuity)

	Tester Connection	Tester Reading (Ω)		Tester Connection	Tester Reading (Ω)
Headlight Relay	*7 – 8	∞	Starter Circuit Relay	9 – 11	∞
	*7 – 13	∞		12 – 13	∞
	(+) (–) *13 – 9	Other than ∞		(+) (–) 13 – 11	∞
				(+) (–) 12 – 11	Other than ∞

6.10b Relay checks without battery connected – EX500D and E models

* US and Canada models only   ∞ = infinite resistance (no continuity)

	Meter Connection	Battery Connection + −	Meter Reading (Ω)
Fan[1]	2 − 5	2 − 4	0
Headlight[2]	7 − 8	9 − 13	0
Starter	11 − 13	11 − 12	0

6.10c Relay checks with 12V battery connected to indicated junction box terminals – EX500A models

1 Only applies to A1 and A2 models
2 US and Canada models only

	Battery Connection (+) (−)	Tester Connection	Tester Reading (Ω)
Headlight Relay	*9 − 13	*7 − 8	0
Starter Circuit Relay	11 − 12	(+) (−) 13 − 11	Other than ∞

6.10d Relay checks with 12V battery connected to indicated junction box terminals – EX500D and E models

∞ = infinite resistance (no continuity)

6.12 Starter circuit relay (A) and turn signal relay (B) locations – ER models

11 If the junction box fails any of these tests, it must be renewed.

Starter circuit relay and diode – ER models

12 The starter circuit relay is located under the right-hand side cover **(see illustration)**. Disconnect the wiring plug from the relay and slip the relay out of its rubber holder.

13 To test the relay you will need an ohmmeter and a 12V battery, the bike's battery will do. Connect the ohmmeter to the relay terminals shown **(see illustration)**; no continuity (infinite resistance) should be shown on the meter. Now connect the battery

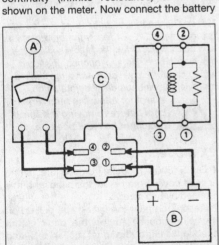

6.13 Starter circuit relay test – ER models

A Ohmmeter
B 12V battery
C Relay connector

as shown; continuity should be indicated on the meter.

14 If the relay does not produce the correct results it should be renewed.

15 There is a single diode set in the wiring between the engine stop switch and the starter circuit relay (see the wiring diagram at the end of this Chapter). Locate the diode **(see illustration)** and unplug it from the wire harness. Connect the probes of an ohmmeter to the diode's two terminals; continuity should be shown in one direction (as indicated by the symbol on the top of the diode) and no continuity (infinite resistance) when the meter probes are reversed.

16 If the diode shows continuity or no continuity in both directions it is faulty and must be renewed.

Interlock diodes – ER models

17 The interlock diode block is located under the seat **(see illustration 6.15)**. Three diodes are contained in the block. Refer to the diode block circuitry shown in the wiring diagram at the end of this Chapter and check each diode by connecting the probes of an ohmmeter to each diode's two terminals; continuity should be shown in one direction and no continuity (infinite resistance) when the meter probes are reversed. If any diode shows continuity or no continuity in both directions it is faulty and the diode block must be renewed.

Coolant temperature warning light diode – ER models

18 The diode is located inside the headlight shell **(see illustration)**. Remove the headlight

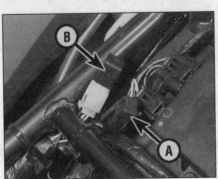

6.15 Starter circuit relay diode (A) and interlock diodes (B)

for access (see Section 8). Unplug the diode from the wire harness. Connect the probes of an ohmmeter to the diode's two terminals; continuity should be shown in one direction (as indicated by the symbol on the top of the diode) and no continuity (infinite resistance) when the meter probes are reversed. If the diode shows continuity or no continuity in both directions it is faulty and must be renewed.

7 Lighting system – check

1 The battery provides power for operation of the headlight, tail light, brake light, licence plate light and instrument cluster lights. If none of the lights operate, always check battery terminal voltage before proceeding (see Section 3). Refer to Chapter 1 for battery checks and Sections 28 through 32 for charging system tests. Also, check the condition of the fuses and renew any blown fuses.

Headlight

2 If the headlight is out when the engine is running and, where necessary, the lighting switch is ON, first check the fuse (see Section 5). Next, unplug the electrical connector for the headlight and use jumper wires to connect the bulb directly to the battery terminals. If the light comes on, the problem lies in the wiring or one of the switches in the circuit. Refer to Sections 19 and 20 for the switch testing procedures, and also the wiring diagrams at the end of this Chapter.

6.18 Coolant temperature warning light diode (arrowed)

7.3 The reserve lighting device is mounted behind the shock absorber

7.4a Location of the headlight relay (arrowed)

7.4b Disconnect the relay wiring connector

7.4c Location of the headlight diode block

3 US and Canada EX500A models use an additonal relay in the system, called the reserve lighting device. On these models, the headlight doesn't come on when the ignition switch is first turned on, but comes on when the starter button is pressed and stays on until the ignition is turned off. The headlight will go out whenever the starter is operated after the engine has stalled (this prevents excessive strain on the battery). The reserve lighting device is located behind the shock absorber **(see illustration)**. US and Canada EX500D models have a headlight relay and diode in the junction box – refer to Section 6 for test procedures.

4 ER500C3, C4 and C5 models have a separate headlight relay and headlight double diode. To access the relay, first remove the battery (see Section 3). Detach the relay from its holder and disconnect the wiring connector **(see illustrations)**. Follow the procedure in Section 6, Step 13 to test the relay. To access the diode block, remove the seat; the diode block is located on the right-hand side of the IC igniter **(see illustration)**. Two diodes are contained in the block. Unplug the block from the wire harness, then refer to the wiring diagram at the end of this Chapter and connect the probes of an ohmmeter to each diode's two terminals; continuity should be shown in one direction and no continuity (infinite resistance) when the meter probes are reversed. If any diode shows continuity or no continuity in both

directions it is faulty and the diode block must be renewed.

Tail light/licence plate light

5 If the tail light fails to work, check the bulbs and the bulb terminals first, then check for battery voltage at the red wire in the tail light with the ignition ON. If voltage is present, check the earth (ground) circuit for an open or poor connection.

6 If no voltage is indicated, check the wiring between the tail light and the ignition (main) switch, then check the switch.

Brake light

7 See Section 14 for the brake light circuit checking procedure.

Neutral indicator light

8 If the neutral light fails to operate when the transmission is in Neutral, check the fuses and the bulb (see Section 17 for bulb removal procedures). If the bulb and fuses are in good condition, check for battery voltage at the light green wire attached to the neutral switch on the left-hand side of the engine. If battery voltage is present, refer to Section 22 for the neutral switch check and replacement procedures.

9 If no voltage is indicated, check the junction box diodes (EX models) or interlock diodes (ER models) as described in Section 6. Refer to the wiring diagrams at the end of this Chapter and check the neutral switch circuit wiring for open circuits and poor connections.

Oil pressure warning light

10 See Section 18 for the oil pressure warning light circuit check.

---

8   Headlight bulb and sidelight bulb – renewal

Note: *The headlight bulb is of the quartz-halogen type. Do not touch the bulb glass as skin acids will shorten the bulb's service life. If the bulb is accidentally touched, it should be wiped carefully when cold with a rag soaked in methylated spirit and dried before fitting.*

⚠️ *Warning: Allow the bulb time to cool before removing it if the headlight has just been on.*

EX models

1 On EX500A models, remove the fairing access cover from below the headlight; it is retained by two screws.

2 Reach up under the fairing and pull up off the wiring connector on the back of the headlight. Grab the dust cover tab and pull the cover off the headlight **(see illustration)**.

3 Lift up the retaining clip and swing it out of the way **(see illustration)**.

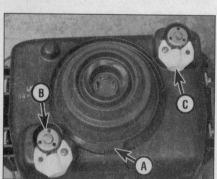

8.2 Pull up on the tab to lift the dust cover away from the headlight

A   Tab   C   Vertical adjuster
B   Horizontal adjuster

8.3 The bulb is held in place by this retaining clip

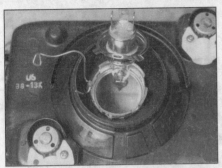

8.4 Lift the bulb out of the headlight

8.7 Remove the screw and its collar from each side of the headlight

8.8a Pull the wiring plug off the headlight . . .

8.8b . . . and pull the sidelight bulbholder out of the headlight

8.9a Disengage the retaining clip . . .

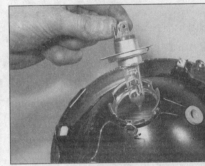

8.9b . . . and lift the bulb out of the headlight

4 Remove the bulb (see illustration).
5 When installing the new bulb, reverse the removal procedure. Be sure not to touch the bulb glass with your fingers – see above **Note.** Fit the dust cover so that its TOP marking is uppermost and the tab is at the bottom; ensure that the dust cover outer edge locates fully in the back of the headlight.
6 The sidelight fitted to UK models is a push fit in the base of the headlight. Ease the bulbholder (and dust cover on EX500A models) out of the headlight. On EX500A models the bulb is of the bayonet fitting and is pushed in and turned anticlockwise to remove, whilst on EX500D and E models the bulb is of the capless type and is simply pulled out of its holder.

ER models

7 Remove the two screws on the lower edge of the headlight shell (see illustration).
8 Ease the headlight unit out of the shell and pull the wiring connector plug off the back of the headlight (see illustration). Pull the sidelight bulbholder out of the base of the headlight (see illustration).
9 Peel the dust cover off the back of the headlight. Lift up the retaining clip and swing it out of the way, then lift out the bulb (see illustrations).
10 The sidelight bulb is a bayonet fit in its holder. Press the bulb in and twist it anticlockwise to remove.
11 When installing the new bulbs, reverse the removal procedure. Be sure not to touch the headlight bulb glass with your fingers – see above **Note.** When fitting the headlight

back into its shell, engage the tab at the top of the rim with the lug in the shell (see illustration).

9 Headlight assembly –
removal and installation

EX500A models

1 Remove the upper fairing (see Chapter 8).
2 Disconnect the wiring connector from the back of the headlight and on UK models disconnect the sidelight wiring connectors. Remove the screws holding the headlight assembly to the fairing (see illustration). Separate the headlight assembly from the fairing stay.
3 Installation is the reverse of removal. Be sure to check the headlight aim (see Section 10).

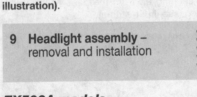

9.2 The headlight assembly is secured by two screws on either side (arrowed)

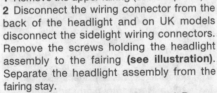
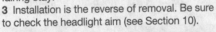

8.11 Engage the tab with the shell lug (arrowed)

EX500D and E models

4 Remove the upper fairing (see Chapter 8).
5 The headlight assembly is secured to the inside of the fairing by four bolts which thread into captive nuts in the fairing (see illustration).

9.5 Headlight retaining bolts (arrowed)

9.7a Remove the throughbolt and nut from each side of the headlight . . .

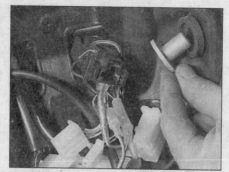

9.7b . . . noting the spacer

9.7c Remove the two bolts at the bottom (arrowed)

6 Installation is the reverse of removal. Be sure to check the headlight aim (see Section 10).

ER models

7 Refer to Section 8 and remove the headlight unit from the shell. The shell is retained to the mounting bracket by two bolts, which pass through rubber dampers and a collar and are secured on the inside of the shell by nuts (see illustrations). A further two bolts retain the shell to the horn bracket at the bottom (see illustration); do not disturb the vertical beam adjuster screw. As the shell is withdrawn, ease the wiring out through the holes in the back of the shell, disconnecting the wiring where necessary.

8 Installation is a reverse of the removal procedure. Be sure to check the headlight aim (see Section 10).

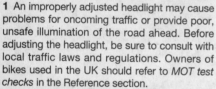

10 Headlight aim –
check and adjustment

1 An improperly adjusted headlight may cause problems for oncoming traffic or provide poor, unsafe illumination of the road ahead. Before adjusting the headlight, be sure to consult with local traffic laws and regulations. Owners of bikes used in the UK should refer to *MOT test checks* in the Reference section.
2 The headlight beam can be adjusted both vertically and horizontally. Before performing the adjustment, make sure the fuel tank has at

least a half tank of fuel, and have an assistant sit on the seat.

EX500A models

3 Remove the fairing access cover from below the headlight; it is retained by two screws. Insert a Phillips screwdriver into the horizontal adjuster guide (see illustration 8.2), then turn the adjuster as necessary to centre the beam.
4 To adjust the vertical position of the beam, insert the screwdriver into the vertical adjuster guide and turn the adjuster as necessary to raise or lower the beam.

EX500D and E models

5 The beam adjusters can be turned by hand by reaching up from the base of the upper fairing (see illustrations).

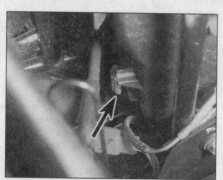

10.5a Horizontal beam adjuster

ER models

6 The horizontal beam adjuster screw is set in the headlight rim and the vertical adjuster screw is set in the bracket at the base of the headlight shell (see illustrations).

11 Turn signal, tail/brake and licence plate bulbs – renewal

Turn signal bulbs

1 Bulb renewal for the turn signals is the same for the front and rear.
2 On US EX500A1, A2 and A3 models and UK ER models, remove the screw that holds the lens/reflector assembly to the turn signal

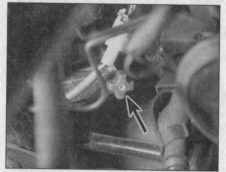

10.5b Vertical beam adjuster

10.6a Horizontal beam adjuster screw

10.6b Vertical beam adjuster screw

11.2a Remove the screw securing the turn signal lens-reflector assembly to the turn signal housing

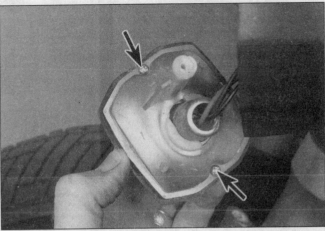

11.2b Remove the screws (arrowed) to detach the lens from the reflector

housing **(see illustration)**. Pull out the lens/reflector assembly. Remove the screws securing the lens to the reflector **(see illustration)**.

3 On UK EX500A models and all market EX500D and E models, remove the single screw from the lens and withdraw the lens and its sealing ring to access the bulb **(see illustrations)**.

4 Push the bulb in and turn it counterclockwise (anticlockwise) to remove it. Check the socket terminals for corrosion and clean them if necessary.

5 Line up the pins on the new bulb with the slots in the socket, push in and turn the bulb clockwise until it locks in place. **Note:** *The pins on the bulb are offset so it can only be installed one way. It is a good idea to use a paper towel or dry cloth when handling the new bulb to prevent injury if the bulb should break and to increase bulb life.*

6 Assemble the turn signal assembly in a reverse of the dismantling order. Check that the turn signals work correctly before riding the motorcycle.

11.3a Remove the lens screw . . .

Tail/brake light bulbs – EX models

7 Remove the seat (see Chapter 8).

8 Turn the bulbholders counterclockwise (anticlockwise) **(see illustration)** until they stop, then pull straight out to remove them from the housing **(see illustration)**. The bulbs can be removed from their holders by turning

11.3b . . . withdraw the lens noting the locating tab

them counterclockwise (anticlockwise) and pulling straight out.

9 Check the socket terminals for corrosion and clean them if necessary. Line up the pins on the new bulb with the slots in the socket, push in and turn the bulb clockwise until it locks in place. **Note:** *The pins on the bulb are offset so it can only be installed one way. It is a good idea to use a paper towel or dry cloth*

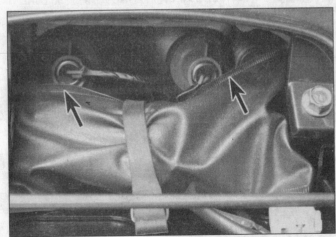

11.8a Unhook the rubber strap and remove the tool bag to gain access to the bulb holders . . .

11.8b . . . then rotate the holders and pull them out of their sockets

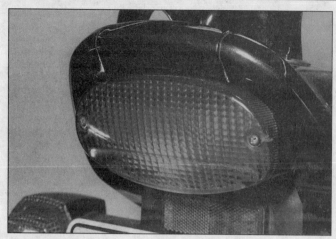

11.12 The lens is retained by two screws

11.16 Licence plate light cover/lens is retained by two screws

when handling the new bulb to prevent injury if the bulb should break and to increase bulb life.

10 Make sure the rubber gaskets are in place and in good condition, then line up the tabs on the holder with the slots in the housing and push the holder into the mounting hole. Turn it clockwise until it stops to lock it in place. **Note:** *The tabs and slots are two different sizes so the holders can only be installed one way.*

11 Reinstall the seat. Wipe any road dirt off the lens surface.

Tail/brake light bulb – ER models

12 Remove the two screws to free the tail light lens **(see illustration).** Carefully withdraw the lens without damaging its sealing ring.

13 Press the bulb in and turn it counterclockwise (anticlockwise) to release it.

14 Check the socket terminals for corrosion and clean them if necessary. Line up the pins on the new bulb with the slots in the socket, push in and turn the bulb clockwise until it locks in place. **Note:** *The pins on the bulb are offset so it can only be installed one way. It is a good idea to use a paper towel or dry cloth when handling the new bulb to prevent injury if the bulb should break and to increase bulb life.*

15 Make sure that is sealing ring is in place and install the lens. Do not overtighten the lens screws. Wipe any road dirt off the lens surface.

Licence plate bulb – EX models

16 Remove the two screws which retain the licence plate light cover/lens **(see illustration).** Withdraw the cover/lens, noting the sealing ring.

17 Push the bulb in and turn it counterclockwise (anticlockwise) to remove it. Check the socket terminals for corrosion and clean them if necessary. Line up the pins on the new bulb with the slots in the socket, push

in and turn the bulb clockwise until it locks in place.

18 Check that the sealing ring is in place and refit the cover/lens; do not overtighten its screws. Wipe any road dirt off the lens surface.

---

12 Turn signal assemblies – removal and installation

1 The turn signal assemblies can be removed individually in the event of damage or failure.

2 To remove a turn signal assembly, first follow the wiring harness from the turn signal to its electrical connectors. Mark the wires with pieces of numbered tape then unplug the electrical connectors.

3 Unscrew the nut that secures the turn signal to the fairing (EX models), headlight bracket (ER models) or rear fender **(see illustration).**

4 Detach the turn signal from the fairing or fender. If you're installing a new turn signal, separate the stalk trim from the old stalk and transfer it to the new one.

5 Installation is the reverse of the removal procedure.

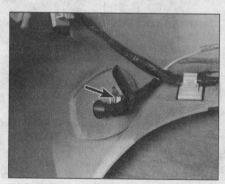

12.3 The turn signals are secured by a nut (arrowed) inside the fender or fairing

---

13 Turn signal circuit – check

1 The battery provides power for operation of the signal lights, so if they do not operate, always check the battery voltage and first and recharge it if necessary (see Sections 3 and 4). Check the main fuse, and on EX500D and E and ER models, also the turn signal circuit fuse (see Section 5).

2 Most turn signal problems are the result of a burned out bulb or corroded socket. This is especially true when the turn signals function properly in one direction, but fail to flash in the other direction. Check the bulbs and the sockets (see Section 11).

3 If the bulbs and sockets check out okay, refer to the wiring diagrams at the end of this Chapter and check for power at the turn signal relay brown wire (UK EX500A models) or orange/green wire (all other models) with the ignition ON **(see accompanying illustrations for EX models and illustration 6.12 for ER models)**. If there's no power at the relay, trace back through the power supply to the ignition switch using the wiring diagrams at the end of this Chapter.

4 If there is power at the relay check the

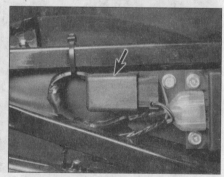

13.3a Turn signal relay (arrowed) on EX500A models

13.3b Turn signal relay (arrowed) on EX500D and E models

orange wire from the relay to the turn signal switch for continuity with the ignition OFF. The turn signal switch can be checked for continuity in each of its positions as described in Section 20.

5 If the wiring and switch checks out okay, renew the turn signal relay.

14 Brake light switches – check and replacement

Circuit check

1 Before checking the electrical circuit, check the main fuse, and on EX500D, E and ER models also check the tail light fuse (see Section 5).

2 On EX500A models, check for voltage at the brown wire terminal in the electrical connector at the brake light switch. If there's no voltage present, check the brown wire between the switch and the ignition switch (see the wiring diagrams at the end of this Chapter). On EX500D, E and ER models, check for voltage at the red/white (UK models) or red/blue (US models) wire terminal in the electrical connector at the brake switch. If there's no voltage present, check the red/white (UK models) or red/blue (US models) wire between the switch and the fuse.

3 If voltage is available, touch the probe of the test light to the other terminal of the switch, then pull the brake lever or depress the brake pedal – if the test light doesn't light up, renew the switch.

4 If the test light does light, check the wiring between the switch and the brake light (see the wiring diagrams at the end of this Chapter).

Switch replacement

Brake lever switch

5 Unplug the electrical connectors from the switch.

6 Remove the mounting screw **(see illustration)** and detach the switch from the brake lever bracket/front master cylinder.

7 Installation is the reverse of the removal procedure. The brake lever switch isn't adjustable.

Brake pedal switch

8 Remove the side cover (see Chapter 8) and unplug the electrical connectors in the switch harness **(see illustration)**.

9 Cut the tie wrap that secures the brake light switch harness to the frame **(see illustration)**.

10 Unhook the spring from the switch plunger. Loosen the adjuster nut **(see illustration)** and unscrew the switch.

14.6 The brake light switch mounted on the brake lever is retained by a screw

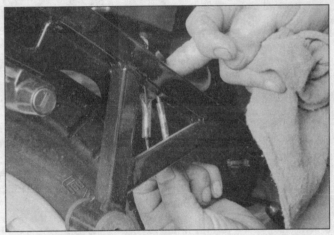

14.8 Unplug the rear brake light switch wire connectors

14.9 Free the wiring from any cable ties (arrowed)

14.10 Loosen the adjuster nut (arrowed) and unscrew the switch

15.1 Location of the cluster electrical connectors

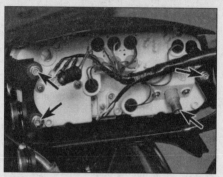

15.2a Disconnect the speedometer cable and remove the cluster mounting nuts (arrowed) – EX500A

15.2b On the EX500D/E, remove the three screws (arrowed) and withdraw the trim panel . . .

11 Install the switch by reversing the removal procedure (use a new tie wrap to secure the harness to the frame).
12 Adjust the switch by following the procedure described in Chapter 1.

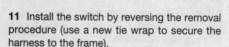

15 Instrument cluster – removal and installation

Caution: Keep the cluster in an upright position while it's off the motorcycle or the gauges will be ruined.

EX models

1 Remove the upper fairing (see Chapter 8) and disconnect the electrical connectors from the cluster harness **(see illustration)**.
2 Disconnect the speedometer cable. On EX500D/E models remove the trim cover **(see illustration),** then on all models remove the three instrument cluster mounting nuts **(see illustrations)**, and detach the cluster from the fairing stay.
3 Installation is the reverse of the removal procedure.

ER models

4 Remove the headlight and its shell (see Section 9).
5 Disconnect the speedometer cable and remove the two instrument cluster mounting nuts **(see illustration)**. Remove the instruments from the mounting bracket.
6 Installation is the reverse of the removal procedure.

16 Meters and gauges – check and replacement

Caution: Always store the cluster with the gauges facing up or the gauges will be ruined.

Check

Temperature gauge (EX models)

1 Refer to Chapter 3 for the temperature gauge checking procedure.

Fuel gauge (ER500A2, A3 and all C models)

2 To check the operation of the fuel gauge, unplug the electrical connector from the fuel level sender.

3 Turn the ignition switch ON. The gauge should read Empty. Connect a jumper wire between the two pins in the gauge side of the connector (not the wires that lead back to the fuel tank). If the fuel level gauge is working properly it should read Full. With the wire disconnected, the needle should fall to the empty mark. Turn the ignition switch OFF and reconnect the sender unit connector.
Caution: Don't leave the wire earthed (grounded) longer than necessary to perform this check. If you do, the gauge could be damaged.
4 If the gauge doesn't respond as described, either the wiring is defective or the gauge itself is malfunctioning. If the gauge does pass the above test, the fuel level sensor is defective. Check the wiring between the sender and gauge unit for continuity. There are no test details for the sender unit, if the gauge and wiring are good, renew the sender unit (see Chapter 4).

Tachometer and speedometer

5 Special instruments are required to properly check the operation of these meters. Take the instrument cluster to a Kawasaki dealer service department or other qualified repair shop for diagnosis.

15.2c . . . then remove the three nuts (arrowed)

15.5 Remove the two nuts (arrowed) and the speedometer cable

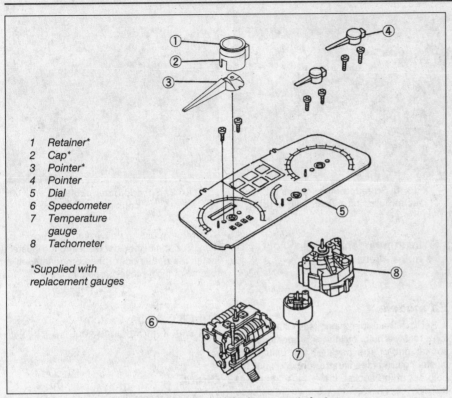

1 Retainer*
2 Cap*
3 Pointer*
4 Pointer
5 Dial
6 Speedometer
7 Temperature gauge
8 Tachometer

*Supplied with replacement gauges

16.6 Exploded view of the instrument cluster

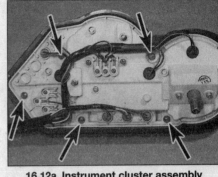

16.12a Instrument cluster assembly screws (arrowed)

16.12b Don't forget to unscrew the tripmeter reset knob

Gauge replacement

EX500A models

6 Remove the screws that secure the instrument cluster cover (see illustration). Detach the cover.
7 Pull the indicator pointer off the gauge to be renewed.
8 Mark the positions of the wires and remove the small screws that secure the gauge to the cluster housing.
9 Detach the gauge from the housing, being careful not to disturb the other components.
10 Inspect the rubber dampers at the cluster screw attaching points. Renew them if they're cracked or brittle.
11 Installation is the reverse of the removal

procedure, noting that new gauges come with a cap and retainer that holds the pointer on.

EX500D and E models

12 Remove the five screws from the base of the instrument cluster and detach the top cover (see illustration). Note that the tripmeter reset knob will have to be unscrewed from its spindle beforehand (see illustration).
13 The gauges can be lifted out of the instrument cluster after removing their retaining screws, although disconnect the gauge wiring from the coolant temperature gauge and tachometer first (see illustration). If the wires aren't marked for identification, label them to aid correct reconnection.

14 Installation is a reverse of the removal procedure. Make sure that the sealing ring is correctly located before fitting the top cover to the instrument cluster.

ER models

15 Remove the three screws from the base of the cluster to detach the bottom cover (see illustration 17.6).
16 Remove the three nuts with washers to free the mounting bracket from the base of the cluster (see illustration).
17 Remove the screw from the centre of the tripmeter reset knob and pull off the knob (see illustration). Remove the six screws from the base of the cluster and withdraw the

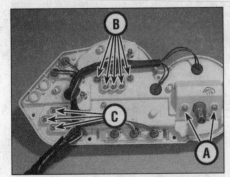

16.13 Speedometer screws (A), tachometer screws (B), temperature gauge screws (C)

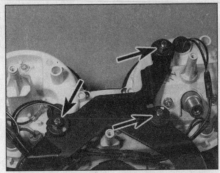

16.16 Mounting bracket retaining nuts (arrrowed)

16.17a Remove the tripmeter reset knob . . .

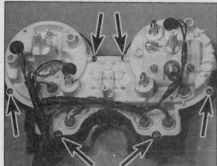

16.17b . . . and the top cover screws (arrowed)

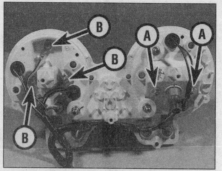
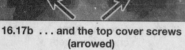

16.18 Speedometer screws (A), tachometer screws and wires (B)

16.21 Speedometer cable lower connection

top cover (with the chrome rings) and the warning light cover **(see illustration)**.

18 Remove the screws to free the speedometer, tachometer and fuel gauge (where fitted) from the instrument cluster **(see illustration)**; label the tachometer and fuel gauge wires beforehand.

19 Installation is a reverse of the removal procedure.

Speedometer cable renewal

20 Disconnect the speedometer cable from the cluster **(see illustration 15.2c or 15.5)**.

21 Disconnect the lower end of the speedometer cable from the drive **(see illustration)**. Note carefully how the cable is routed, then remove it.

22 Installation is the reverse of the removal steps.

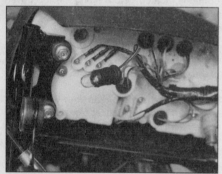

17.2 Pull the bulb socket out of the cluster, then pull the bulb out of the socket

---

17 Instrument and warning light bulbs – renewal

EX models

1 Remove the upper fairing (see Chapter 8).

2 To renew a bulb, pull the appropriate rubber socket out of the back of the instrument cluster housing **(see illustration)**, then pull the bulb out of the socket. If the socket contacts are dirty or corroded, they should be scraped clean and sprayed with electrical contact cleaner before new bulbs are installed.

3 Carefully push the new bulb into position, then push the socket into the cluster housing.

4 Install the fairing.

ER models

5 Remove the headlight and its shell (see Section 9).

6 Disconnect the speedometer cable. Remove the three screws from the base of the cluster to detach the bottom cover **(see illustration)**.

7 The bulbholders are now accessible and can be simply pulled out of the instrument cluster **(see illustration)**.

8 To renew a bulb, pull the bulb out of the socket. If the socket contacts are dirty or corroded, they should be scraped clean and sprayed with electrical contact cleaner before new bulbs are installed.

---

9 Carefully push the new bulb into position, then push the bulbholder back into the cluster. Install the remainder of the components in a reverse of the removal procedure.

18 Oil pressure switch – check and replacement

Check

1 The oil pressure warning light should come on when the ignition is turned on, then extinguish when the engine is running. If the oil pressure warning light fails to extinguish, or comes on while riding the motorcycle, stop the engine and check the oil level (see *Daily (pre-ride) checks*). If the warning light still stays on, carry out an oil pressure check as described in Chapter 2, Section 17.

2 If the oil level and pressure are correct, the fault could lie in the electrical circuit. Disconnect the wire from the oil pressure switch, which is located on the bottom of the engine **(see illustration)**. Turn the main switch ON and ground/earth the end of the wire. If the light comes on, the oil pressure switch is defective and must be renewed (only after draining the engine oil).

3 If the light does not come on, check the oil pressure warning light bulb, the wiring between the oil pressure switch and the light, and the brown power supply wire from the

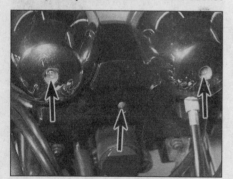

17.6 Bottom cover screws (arrowed)

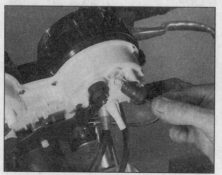

17.7 Pull the bulbholder out of the cluster

18.2 Location of the oil pressure switch

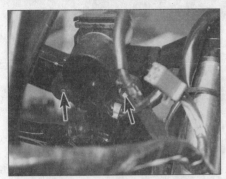

19.7 The ignition switch is retained by shear-head bolts (arrowed)

warning light (see the wiring diagrams at the end of this Chapter).

Renewal

4 To renew the switch, drain the engine oil (see Chapter 1) and unscrew the switch from the case. Coat the threads of the new switch with a non-permanent thread locking agent (not sealant), then screw the switch into its hole, tightening it to the torque listed in this Chapter's Specifications. Reconnect the switch wire

5 Fill the crankcase with the recommended type and amount of oil (see Chapter 1) and check the level (see *Daily (pre-ride) checks*). Check that there are no leaks from the switch.

19 Ignition main (key) switch – check and replacement

> ⚠ **Warning: It is essential that the battery is disconnected (negative lead first) before checking or disturbing the ignition switch.**

Check

1 Remove the upper fairing on EX models (see Chapter 8). This isn't absolutely necessary, but it makes access to the switch electrical connector easier. On ER models, remove the headlight from its shell for access to the wiring connectors (see Section 8).

2 Trace the wiring from the switch to the block connector. Separate the connector and make the checks on the switch side of the connector. Refer to the switch box in the appropriate wiring diagram at the end of this Chapter and check the continuity of the terminal pairs. Continuity should exist between the terminals connected by a solid line when the key is turned to the indicated position.

3 If the switch fails any of the tests, renew it.

Replacement

4 Remove the upper fairing on EX models, if you haven't already done so (see Chapter 8). On ER models, remove the headlight shell (see Section 9).

5 Remove the instrument cluster (see Section 15).

6 Unplug the switch electrical connector.

7 The switch is held to the upper triple clamp with two shear-head bolts **(see illustration)**. Using a hammer and a sharp punch, knock the shear-head bolts in a counterclockwise (anticlockwise) direction to unscrew them. If they're too tight and won't turn, carefully drill holes through the centres of the bolts and unscrew them using a screw extractor (E-Z Out). Detach the switch from the upper clamp.

8 Hold the new switch in position and install the new shear-head bolts. Tighten the bolts until their heads break off.

9 The remainder of installation is the reverse of the removal steps.

20 Handlebar switches – check

> ⚠ **Warning: It is essential that the battery is disconnected (negative lead first) before checking or disturbing the handlebar switches.**

1 Generally speaking, the switches are reliable and trouble-free. Most troubles, when they do occur, are caused by dirty or corroded contacts, but wear and breakage of internal parts is a possibility that should not be overlooked. If breakage does occur, the entire switch and related wiring harness will have to be renewed, since individual parts are not usually available.

2 The switches can be checked for continuity with an ohmmeter or a continuity test light. Remove the fuel tank (see Chapter 4) for access to the switch wire connectors and disconnect them.

3 Using the ohmmeter or test light, check for continuity between the terminals of the switch harness with the switch in the various positions (see the wiring diagrams at the end of this Chapter for the switch position boxes). Continuity should exist between the terminals connected by a solid line when the switch is in the indicated position.

4 If the continuity check indicates a problem exists, refer to Section 21, disassemble the switch and spray the switch contacts with electrical contact cleaner. If they are accessible, the contacts can be scraped clean with a knife or polished with crocus cloth. If switch components are damaged or broken, it will be obvious when the switch is disassembled.

21 Handlebar switches – removal and installation

1 The handlebar switches are composed of two halves that clamp around the bars. They are easily removed for cleaning or inspection

by taking out the clamp screws and pulling the switch halves away from the handlebars.

2 To completely remove the switches, the electrical connectors in the wiring harness should be unplugged; remove the fuel tank for access to the switch wire connectors (see Chapter 4). The right-hand side switch must be separated from the throttle cables (see Chapter 4, Section 9). The left-hand side switch must be separated from the choke cable (see Chapter 4, Section 10).

3 When installing the switches, make sure the wiring harnesses are properly routed to avoid pinching or stretching the wires.

22 Neutral switch – check and replacement

Check

1 Remove the engine sprocket cover (see Chapter 6, Section 15).

2 Disconnect the wire from the neutral switch **(see illustration)**. Connect one lead of an ohmmeter to a good earth (ground) and the other lead to the post on the switch.

3 When the transmission is in neutral, the ohmmeter should read 0 ohms – in any other gear, the meter should read infinite resistance.

4 If the switch doesn't check out as described, renew it. **Note:** *If the neutral light works intermittently, try removing the switch and reinstalling it temporarily without its sealing washer. If the light now works consistently, the switch plunger is worn and the switch should be renewed (don't just leave the old switch in position without the washer).*

Renewal

5 Unscrew the neutral switch from the case and remove the sealing washer.

6 Install the switch with a new sealing washer and tighten it securely.

23 Sidestand switch – check and replacement

Check

1 Place the bike on the centerstand.

22.2 Location of the neutral switch

23.6 The sidestand switch is located between the sidestand and the frame on EX models

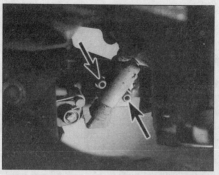

23.7 The sidestand switch is retained by two screws on ER models

24.1 The horn is accessible from the front of the motorcycle

2 Follow the wiring harness from the switch to the connector, then disconnect the connector.

3 Connect the leads of an ohmmeter to the two wire terminals in the switch side of the connector.

4 With the sidestand in the up position, there should be continuity through the switch (0 ohms). With the sidestand down, there should be no continuity (infinite resistance).

5 If the switch fails the test, renew it, although check first that the fault is not caused by the ingress of road dirt and water into the switch plunger.

Replacement

6 On EX models, remove the sidestand (see Chapter 6) then remove the sidestand bracket from the frame. The switch is retained to the inside of the bracket by a single screw (see illustration). Trace the switch wiring up the connector and disconnect it.

7 On ER models, place the machine on its centrestand and retract the sidestand. Remove the two screws and detach the switch from the frame (see illustration). Trace the switch wiring up the connector and disconnect it.

8 Installation is the reverse of the removal procedure.

24 Horn – check, replacement and adjustment
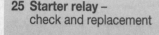

Check

1 Unplug the electrical connectors from the horn (see illustration). Using two jumper wires, apply battery voltage directly to the terminals on the horn. If the horn sounds, check the switch (see Section 20) and the wiring between the switch and the horn (see the wiring diagrams at the end of this Chapter). Check the main fuse, and on EX500D, E and ER models also check the horn fuse (see Section 5).

2 If the horn doesn't sound, renew it. If it makes noise, but sounds 'sick', try adjusting the tone as described below.

Replacement

3 Detach the electrical connectors and unbolt the horn bracket from the frame.

4 Unbolt the horn from the bracket and transfer the bracket to the new horn.

5 Installation is the reverse of removal.

Adjustment

6 Loosen the locknut on the adjustment screw. Have an assistant operate the horn. Turn the adjustment screw in or out until the tone is satisfactory. Tighten the locknut.

25 Starter relay – check and replacement

Check

1 Remove the starter relay as described below.

2 With the starter relay on the bench connect an ohmmeter to its two main terminals. Connect a 12V battery (remove the battery from the bike and use this) to the yellow/red and black/yellow wire terminals on the relay (see illustration).

3 The relay should be heard to click and the ohmmeter should indicate 0 ohms.

4 If the meter doesn't read 0 ohms or the relay doesn't click, renew the relay.

Replacement

5 Remove the seat and disconnect the cable from the negative terminal of the battery.

6 Remove the left-hand side cover on EX models and the right-hand side cover on ER models (see Chapter 8).

7 Detach the large diameter battery positive cable and starter cable, then unplug the wire connector from the relay (see illustrations).

8 Pull the relay out of its mounting.

9 Installation is the reverse of removal. Reconnect the negative battery cable after all the other electrical connections are made.

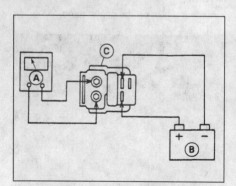

25.2 Starter relay test set-up

A Ohmmeter   B 12V Battery   C Relay

25.7a Starter relay location – EX models

25.7b Starter relay location – ER models

26.3 Pull back the covers and disconnect the starter wires (arrowed)

26.4a Remove the alternator cover bolts (arrowed) . . .

26 Starter motor – removal and installation

Removal

1 Remove the lower fairing on EX models (see Chapter 8). Remove the fuel tank and carburettors (see Chapter 4).

2 Disconnect the cable from the negative terminal of the battery.

3 Remove the nuts retaining the starter cables to the starter (see illustration).

4 Remove the engine sprocket cover. Remove the alternator cover bolts and pull off the cover (see illustrations). Note: *The alternator magnets will hold the cover on. Pull firmly to remove it, but don't pry it off. If it won't come off with a firm two-hand pull, make sure you've removed all of the cover bolts.*

5 Remove the starter chain cover (see illustration).

6 Remove the starter mounting bolts (see illustration).

7 Lift the starter up a little bit and disengage

26.4b . . . and pull off the cover (pull firmly to overcome the pull of the rotor magnets, but don't force it)

the starter sprocket from the chain (see illustration).

8 Check the condition of the O-ring on the end of the starter and renew it if necessary.

Installation

9 Apply a little engine oil to the O-ring and install the starter by reversing the removal procedure.

26.5 Remove the starter chain cover bolts (arrowed)

27 Starter motor – disassembly, inspection and reassembly

1 Remove the starter motor (see Section 26).

Disassembly

2 Mark the position of the housing to each end cover. Remove the two long

26.6 Remove the starter mounting bolts (arrowed)

26.7 Lift the starter and disengage it from the chain

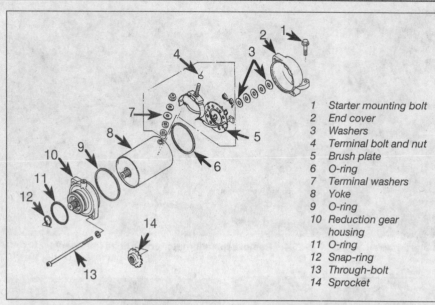

27.4 Remove the brush plate from the housing

1 Starter mounting bolt
2 End cover
3 Washers
4 Terminal bolt and nut
5 Brush plate
6 O-ring
7 Terminal washers
8 Yoke
9 O-ring
10 Reduction gear housing
11 O-ring
12 Snap-ring
13 Through-bolt
14 Sprocket

27.2 Exploded view of the starter motor

27.5 Push the terminal bolt through the housing and remove the plastic brush holder

screws and detach both end covers **(see illustration)**.

3 Pull the armature out of the housing (toward the pinion gear side).

4 Remove the brush plate from the housing **(see illustration)**.

5 Remove the nut and push the terminal bolt

through the housing. Remove the two brushes with the plastic holder from the housing **(see illustration)**.

Inspection

6 The parts of the starter motor that most likely will require attention are the brushes. Measure the length of the brushes and compare the results to the brush length listed in this Chapter's Specifications **(see illustration)**. If any of the brushes are worn beyond the specified limits, renew the brush holder assembly. If the brushes are not worn excessively, cracked, chipped, or otherwise damaged, they may be reused.

7 Inspect the commutator **(see illustration)** for scoring, scratches and discolouration. The commutator can be cleaned and polished with crocus cloth, but do not use sandpaper or emery paper. After cleaning, wipe away any residue with a cloth soaked in an electrical system cleaner or denatured alcohol. Measure

the commutator diameter and compare it to the diameter listed in this Chapter's Specifications. If it is less than the service limit, the motor must be renewed.

8 Using an ohmmeter or a continuity test light, check for continuity between the commutator bars **(see illustration)**. Continuity should exist between each bar and all of the others. Also, check for continuity between the commutator bars and the armature shaft **(see illustration)**. There should be no continuity between the commutator and the shaft. If the checks indicate otherwise, the armature is defective.

9 Check for continuity between the brush

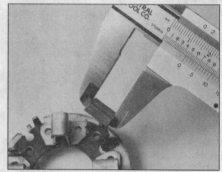

27.6 Measure the length of the brushes

27.7 Check the commutator for cracks and discolouring, then measure the diameter and compare it with the minimum diameter listed in this Chapter's Specifications

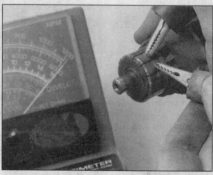

27.8a Continuity should exist between the commutator bars

27.8b There should be no continuity between the commutator bars and the armature shaft

27.9 There should be almost no resistance (0 ohms) between the brushes and the brush plate

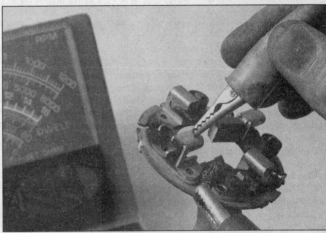

27.10 There should be no continuity between the brush plate and the brush holders (the resistance should be infinite)

27.12 Install the washers on the starter terminal as shown

27.13 When installing the brush plate, make sure the brush leads fit into the notches in the plate (arrowed) – also, make sure the tongue on the plate fits into the notch in the housing (arrowed)

plate and the brushes **(see illustration)**. The meter should read close to 0 ohms. If it doesn't, the brush plate has an open and must be renewed.

10 Using the highest range on the ohmmeter, measure the resistance between the brush holders and the brush plate **(see illustration)**. The reading should be infinite. If there is any reading at all, renew the brush plate.

11 Check the starter reduction gears for worn, cracked, chipped and broken teeth. If the gears are damaged or worn, renew the starter motor.

Reassembly

12 Install the plastic brush holder into the housing. Make sure the terminal bolt and washers are assembled correctly **(see illustration)**. Tighten the terminal nut securely.
13 Detach the brush springs from the brush plate (this will make armature installation much easier). Install the brush plate into the housing, routing the brush leads into the

notches in the plate **(see illustration)**. Make sure the tongue on the brush plate fits into the notch in the housing.
14 Install the brushes into their holders and slide the armature into place. Install the brush springs **(see illustrations)**.

27.14a Install each brush spring on the post in this position . . .

15 Install any washers that were present on the end of the armature shaft. Install the end covers, aligning the protrusions with the notches. Install the two long screws and tighten them securely.

27.14b . . . then pull the end of the spring 1/2 turn clockwise and seat the end of it in the groove in the end of the brush

28 Charging system testing – general information and precautions

1 If the performance of the charging system is suspect, the system as a whole should be checked first, followed by testing of the individual components (the alternator and the voltage regulator/rectifier). **Note:** *Before beginning the checks, make sure the battery is fully charged and that all system connections are clean and tight.*

2 Checking the output of the charging system and the performance of the various components within the charging system requires the use of special electrical test equipment. A voltmeter or a multimeter is the absolute minimum equipment required. In addition, an ohmmeter is generally required for checking the remainder of the system.

3 When making the checks, follow the procedures carefully to prevent incorrect connections or short circuits, as irreparable damage to electrical system components may result if short circuits occur. Because of the special tools and expertise required, it is recommended that the job of checking the charging system be left to a Kawasaki dealer or an electrical specialist.

29 Charging system – regulated output test

Caution: Never disconnect the battery cables from the battery while the engine is running. If the battery is disconnected, the alternator and regulator/rectifier will be damaged.

1 To check the charging system output, you will need a voltmeter or a multimeter with a voltmeter function.

2 The battery must be fully charged (charge it from an external source if necessary) and the engine must be at normal operating temperature to obtain an accurate reading.

3 Remove the left-hand side cover (EX models) or right-hand side cover (ER models) and locate the regulator/rectifier connector **(see illustrations).**

4 Attach the positive (red) voltmeter lead to the white wire terminal and the negative lead to the black/yellow wire terminal; don't disconnect the connector halves.
Caution: The white wire is connected directly to the battery at all times, so don't allow the voltmeter to short this terminal to earth/ground (don't let the voltmeter negative lead touch metal). The voltmeter selector switch (if so equipped) must be in a DC volt range greater than 15 volts.

5 Start the engine. Run it at varying speeds up to 4,000 rpm, with the headlight off (if no ON/OFF switch is fitted on your model, disconnect the headlight wiring connector – see Section 8).

6 The charging system regulated output should be within the range listed in the Chapter's Specifications. It should be at the low end of the range at low engine speeds and at the high end of the range at higher engine speeds.

7 If the output is as specified, the alternator is functioning properly. If the charging system as a whole is not performing as it should, refer to Section 32 and check the regulator/rectifier.

8 Low voltage output may be the result of damaged windings in the alternator stator coils, loss of magnetism in the alternator rotor or wiring problems. Make sure all electrical connections are clean and tight, then refer to Sections 30 and 31 for specific alternator tests.

30 Alternator – unregulated output test

1 Follow the wiring harness from the alternator housing up to the three-pin connector containing the three yellow wires, then disconnect the connector. Make this test on the alternator side of the connector.

2 Connect a voltmeter with a 250-volt AC scale to two of the yellow wire terminals in the alternator connector (at this point, you're measuring the alternator output before it has been rectified from alternating current to

direct current, so the voltmeter must be able to measure AC).

3 Start the engine, run it at 4,000 rpm and note the unregulated vaultage reading. Stop the engine and then connect the meter between another pair of yellow wires so that you take three readings in total.

4 In all cases, the voltage should be as listed in this Chapter's Specifications.
  a) If the voltage reading is correct, the rectifier/regulator is probably defective. Refer to Section 32 for test procedures.
  b) If the voltage reading is low, the alternator may be defective. Test the stator coils as described in Section 31.

31 Alternator stator coils – continuity test

1 If charging system output is low or non-existent, the alternator stator coil windings and leads should be checked for proper continuity. The test can be made with the stator in place on the machine. Follow the wiring harness from the alternator housing up to the three-pin connector containing the three yellow wires, then disconnect the connector. Make this test on the alternator side of the connector.

2 Using an ohmmeter, check for continuity between each pair of the yellow wires coming from the alternator stator, so that you take three readings in total. Continuity should exist between any one wire and each of the others (see the Specifications for the specific resistance figure specified by Kawasaki).

3 Check for continuity between each of the wires and the engine (earth/ground). No continuity should exist between any of the wires and the earth/ground.

4 If there is no continuity between any two of the wires, or if there is continuity between the wires and an engine ground/earth, an open circuit or a short exists within the stator coils. Since repair of the stator is not feasible, it must be renewed, although check first that the fault is not caused by a damaged or broken yellow wire between the connector and the stator.

29.3a The regulator/rectifier and its connector (arrowed) are located behind the left-hand side cover on EX models

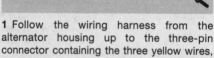

29.3b The regulator/rectifier (arrowed) is located behind the engine unit on ER models . . .

29.3c . . . and the connector (arrowed) is behind the right-hand side cover

Rectifier Circuit Inspection

Range x 100 Ω	Meter (+) Lead Connection					
Terminal	BK	BR	W/R	Y	Y	Y
BK		1 kΩ ~ 5 kΩ	400 Ω ~ 2 kΩ	200 Ω ~ 600 Ω	200 Ω ~ 600 Ω	200 Ω ~ 600 Ω
BR	10 kΩ ~ ∞		10 kΩ ~ ∞	10 kΩ ~ ∞	10 kΩ ~ ∞	100 kΩ ~ ∞
W/R	∞	∞		∞	∞	∞
Y	∞	∞	200 Ω ~ 600 Ω		∞	∞
Y	∞	∞	200 Ω ~ 600 Ω	∞		∞
Y	∞	∞	200 Ω ~ 600 Ω	∞	∞	

(Meter (−) Lead Connection labels the rows)

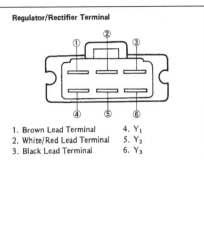

Regulator/Rectifier Terminal

1. Brown Lead Terminal
2. White/Red Lead Terminal
3. Black Lead Terminal
4. Y₁
5. Y₂
6. Y₃

32.3a Rectifier diode test table – EX500A models

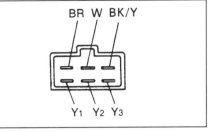

BR W BK/Y

Y₁ Y₂ Y₃

32.3b Rectifier diode test connections – EX500D, E models and ER models

Connect the test meter between the following terminals, then reverse the meter probes (eg W to Y1, then Y1 to W) so that 12 readings are taken in total

W to Y1	BK/Y to Y1
W to Y2	BK/Y to Y2
W to Y3	BK/Y to Y3

32 Regulator/rectifier – check and replacement

1 Remove the left-hand side cover (EX models) or right-hand side cover (ER models) to locate the regulator/rectifier **(see illustrations 29.3a or 29.3b and 29.3c)**.
2 Remove the two bolts securing the regulator/rectifier, then detach the electrical connector. Move the regulator/rectifier to the bench for testing.
3 Using an ohmmeter, check the rectifier diodes across the indicated wire terminals **(see illustrations)**. If the meter readings are not as specified, renew the rectifier/regulator. Note that the actual meter reading may vary depending on the meter used and although specific resistance values are given in the EX500A table, care should be taken to check that in each case continuity is shown in one direction and no continuity (infinite resistance ∞) is shown when the meter probes are reversed.
4 This check, combined with the tests outlined in Sections 29 through 31, should diagnose most charging system problems. If

the voltage regulator/rectifier passes the test described in Step 3, and the stator coil passes the test in Section 31, take the regulator/rectifier to a Kawasaki dealer for further checks, or substitute a known good unit and recheck the charging system output.

33 Alternator – removal and installation

1 Disconnect the cable from the negative terminal of the battery.
2 Remove the starter motor (see Section 26).
3 Prevent the alternator rotor from turning by holding it with Kawasaki tool no. 57001-1313, a strap wrench or a pin spanner wrench, although be very careful not to damage the ignition triggers on the rotor periphery. Remove the rotor bolt **(see illustration)**. **Note:** *The bolt has left-hand threads (loosens in a clockwise direction).*
4 Hold the rotor from turning again, and using tool no. 57001-1216, remove the rotor from the crankshaft taper **(see illustration)**. Remove the Woodruff key from the crankshaft slot if it is loose.

5 If you're going to renew the rotor, remove the starter clutch (see Section 35).
6 Clean all dirt from the crankshaft and the inside of the rotor with high flash-point solvent. If the Woodruff key was removed, install it in the crankshaft slot.
7 Position the rotor on the crankshaft taper, aligning its slot with the Woodruff key. Install the bolt, prevent the engine from turning then tighten the bolt to the torque listed in this Chapter's Specifications.
8 The remainder of installation is the reverse of the removal steps. Before you install the housing, make sure the magnets haven't picked up any pieces of metal that could damage the alternator.

34 Alternator – stator coil replacement

1 Remove the alternator cover (see Section 26).
2 Remove the stator screws **(see illustration)**, remove the wiring harness retainer and lift the stator coils out of the alternator housing.
3 Installation is the reverse of the removal steps. Tighten the stator screws to the torque listed in this Chapter's Specifications.

33.3 The alternator rotor bolt has left-hand threads (turn it clockwise to loosen it)

33.4 This special tool is used to remove the alternator rotor

34.2 The stator coils are secured in the housing by three Allen screws (arrowed)

35.3 Remove the washer and sprocket from the end of the crankshaft

35.4a Compress the springs with a small screwdriver and remove the rollers

35.4b Starter clutch details

35 Starter clutch – removal and installation

1 The starter clutch is mounted on the back of the alternator rotor.

Removal

2 Remove the alternator rotor (see Section 33). At this point check the operation of the starter clutch by installing it and its sprocket back on the crankshaft, but without the chain connected. Try turning the body of the starter clutch in each direction. It should turn freely in a counterclockwise (anticlockwise) direction and lock up with turned in a clockwise direction. If it doesn't function as described, it should be dismantled for inspection.
3 Slide the alternator rotor/starter clutch, washer and starter sprocket off the crankshaft (see illustration).
4 Pull the rollers out of the starter clutch, then remove the spring caps and springs (see illustrations).

Inspection

5 Check all parts for wear and damage. Renew any worn or damaged parts.
6 If you're going to renew the starter clutch housing or rotor, remove the three Allen bolts and separate the starter clutch from the rotor.
7 The starter chain shouldn't suffer from a great deal of wear, but can be checked by pulling the chain taught and measuring a 20 link (21 pin) section (see illustration). Check in a number of places around the chain. If any 20 link measurement exceeds 159 mm (6.26 in), the chain should be renewed.
8 Check the starter chain guide rubber surfaces and renew the guide necessary.

Installation

9 If you removed the starter clutch from the rotor, bolt it back on. Use a non-permanent thread locking agent on the threads of the Allen bolts and tighten them to the torque listed in this Chapter's Specifications.
10 Place the spring caps on the springs. Place the springs in their holes, compress them with a screwdriver and install the rollers (see illustrations).
11 Install the alternator rotor on the engine.

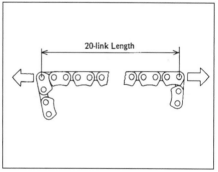

35.7 Starter chain wear measurement

20-link Length

35.10a Press the springs and caps into the holes . . .

35.10b . . . then install the rollers and release the springs

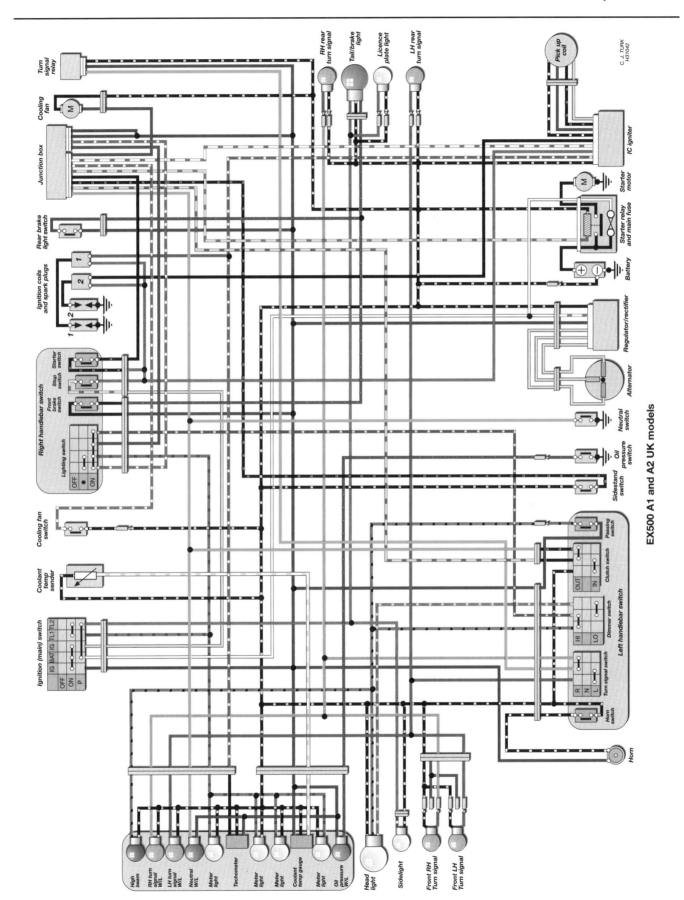

EX500 A1 and A2 UK models

EX500 A3, A4, A5 and A6 UK models

C.J. TURK
H31043

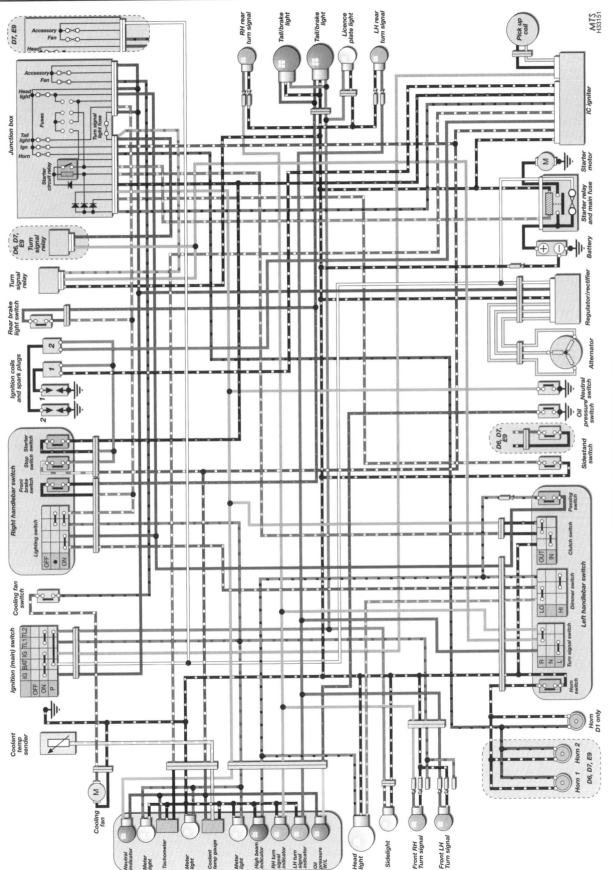

EX500D1 to D7 and E9 UK models

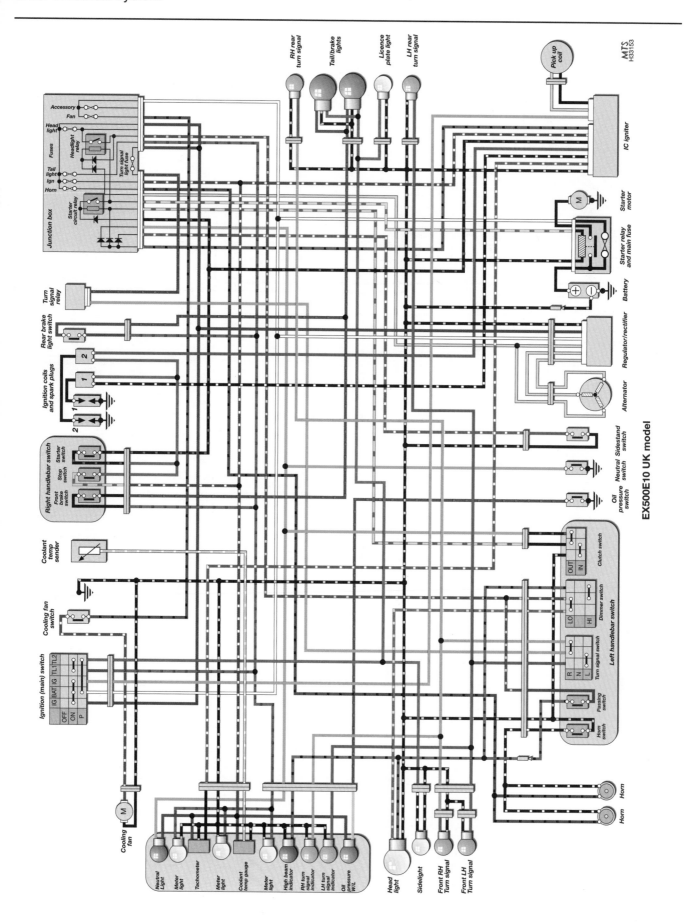

EX500E10 UK model

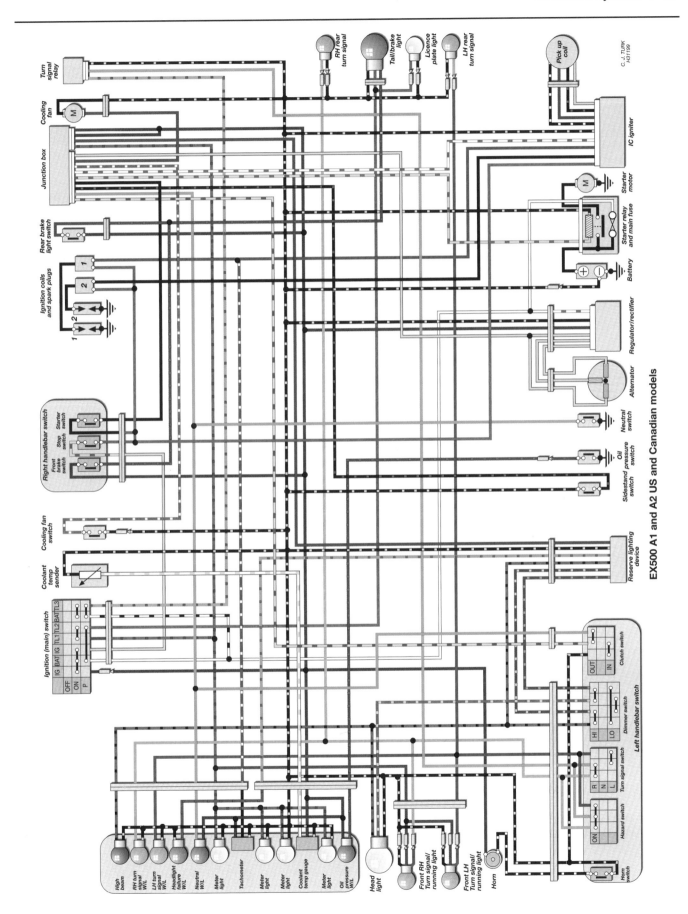

EX500 A1 and A2 US and Canadian models

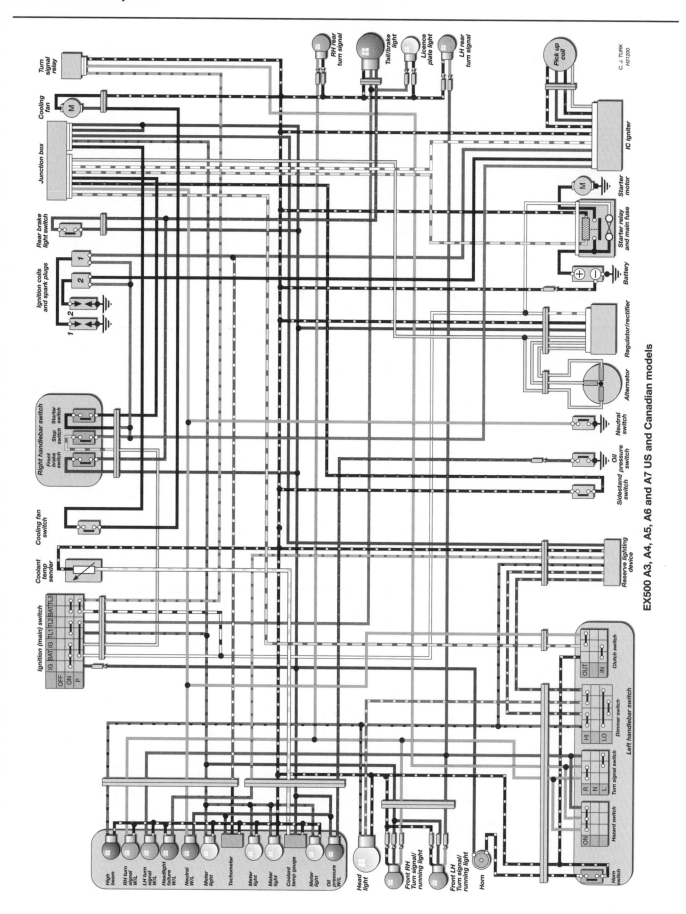

EX500 A3, A4, A5, A6 and A7 US and Canadian models

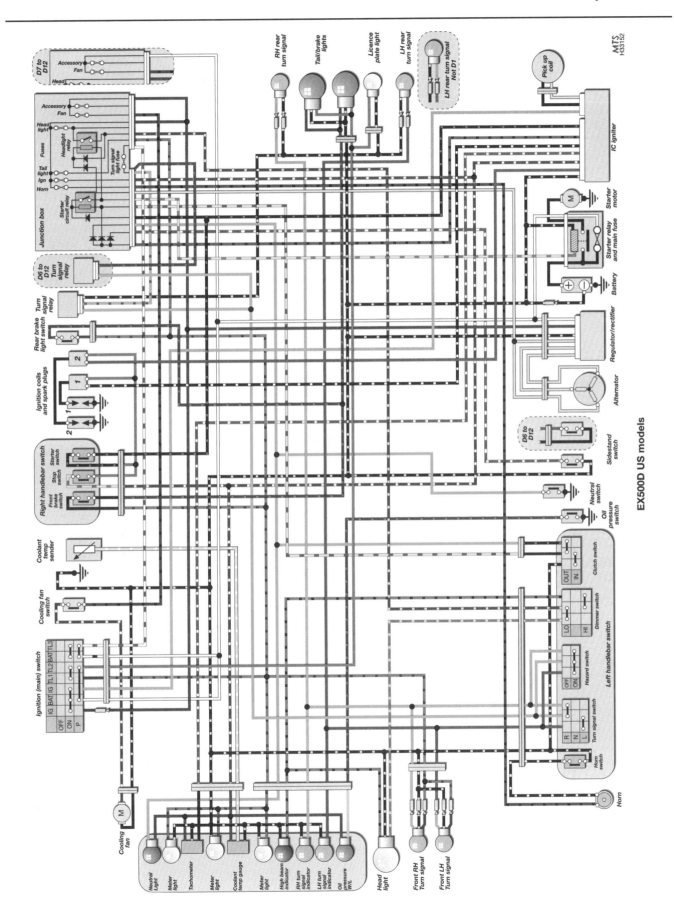

MTS
H33152

EX500D US models

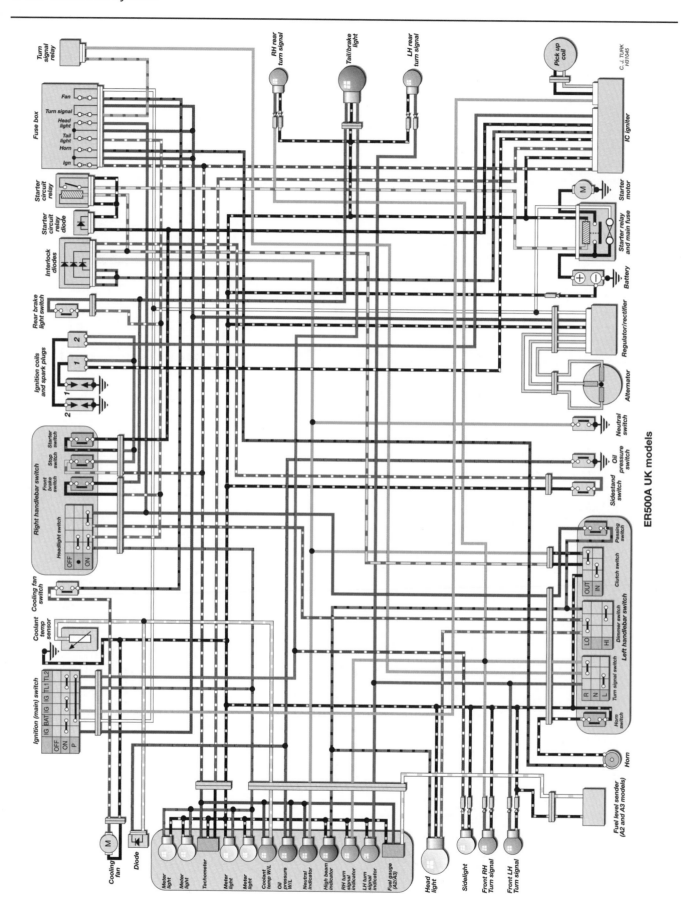

C. J. TURK
H31045

ER500A UK models

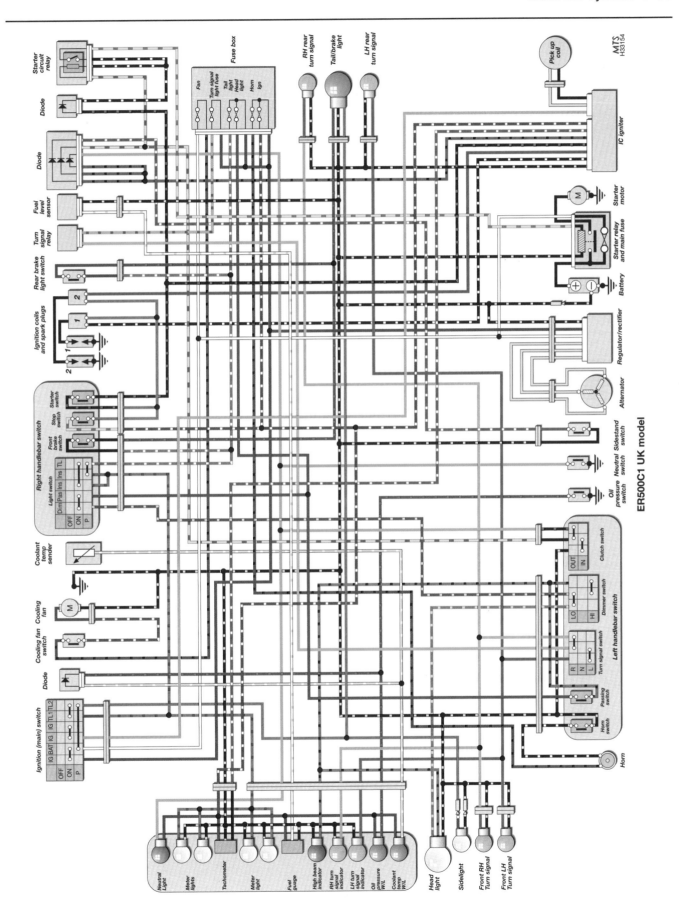

ER500C1 UK model

MTS
H33154

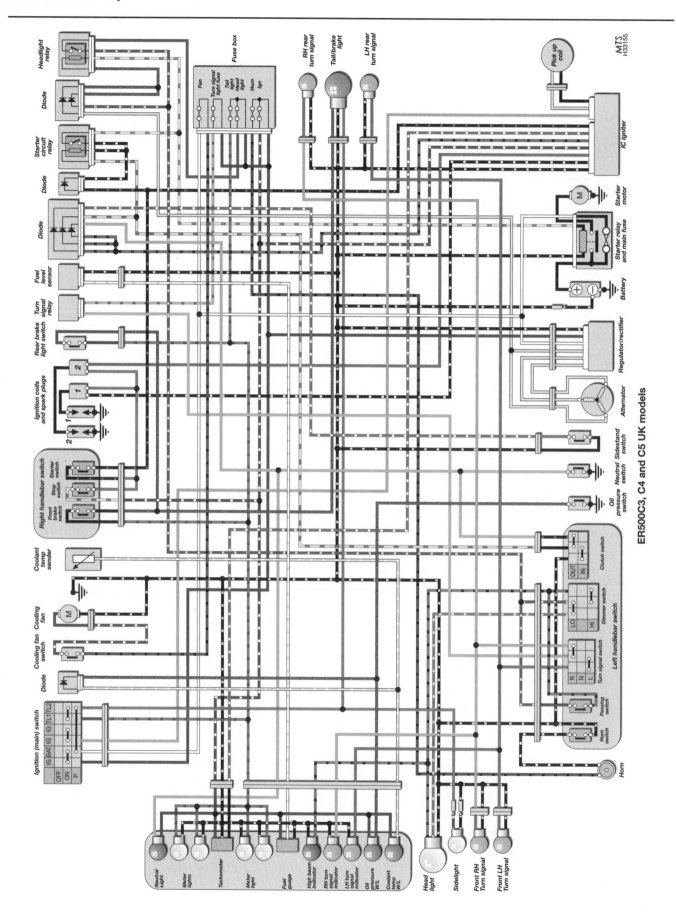

ER500C3, C4 and C5 UK models

Reference

$$34 \, Nm \times 0.738 = 25 \, lbf\, ft$$

Buying tools

A toolkit is a fundamental requirement for servicing and repairing a motorcycle. Although there will be an initial expense in building up enough tools for servicing, this will soon be offset by the savings made by doing the job yourself. As experience and confidence grow, additional tools can be added to enable the repair and overhaul of the motorcycle. Many of the specialist tools are expensive and not often used so it may be preferable to hire them, or for a group of friends or motorcycle club to join in the purchase.

As a rule, it is better to buy more expensive, good quality tools. Cheaper tools are likely to wear out faster and need to be renewed more often, nullifying the original saving.

> ⚠️ **Warning: To avoid the risk of a poor quality tool breaking in use, causing injury or damage to the component being worked on, always aim to purchase tools which meet the relevant national safety standards.**

The following lists of tools do not represent the manufacturer's service tools, but serve as a guide to help the owner decide which tools are needed for this level of work. In addition, items such as an electric drill, hacksaw, files, soldering iron and a workbench equipped with a vice, may be needed. Although not classed as tools, a selection of bolts, screws, nuts, washers and pieces of tubing always come in useful.

For more information about tools, refer to the Haynes *Motorcycle Workshop Practice TechBook* (Bk. No. 3470).

Manufacturer's service tools

Inevitably certain tasks require the use of a service tool. Where possible an alternative tool or method of approach is recommended, but sometimes there is no option if personal injury or damage to the component is to be avoided. Where required, service tools are referred to in the relevant procedure.

Service tools can usually only be purchased from a motorcycle dealer and are identified by a part number. Some of the commonly-used tools, such as rotor pullers, are available in aftermarket form from mail-order motorcycle tool and accessory suppliers.

Maintenance and minor repair tools

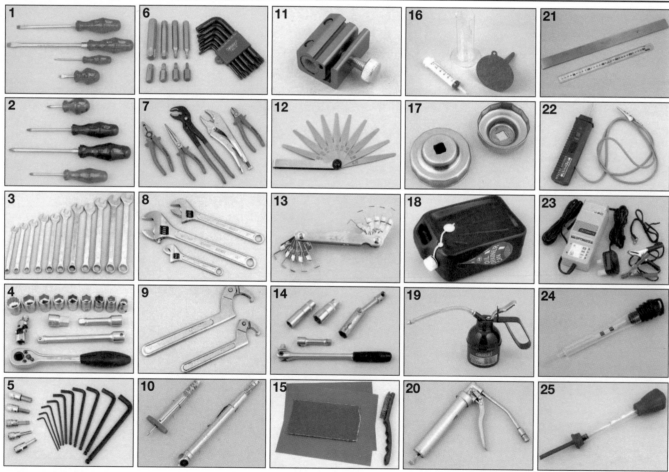

1 Set of flat-bladed screwdrivers
2 Set of Phillips head screwdrivers
3 Combination open-end and ring spanners
4 Socket set (3/8 inch or 1/2 inch drive)
5 Set of Allen keys or bits

6 Set of Torx keys or bits
7 Pliers, cutters and self-locking grips (Mole grips)
8 Adjustable spanners
9 C-spanners
10 Tread depth gauge and tyre pressure gauge

11 Cable oiler clamp
12 Feeler gauges
13 Spark plug gap measuring tool
14 Spark plug spanner or deep plug sockets
15 Wire brush and emery paper

16 Calibrated syringe, measuring vessel and funnel
17 Oil filter adapters
18 Oil drainer can or tray
19 Pump type oil can
20 Grease gun

21 Straight-edge and steel rule
22 Continuity tester
23 Battery charger
24 Hydrometer (for battery specific gravity check)
25 Anti-freeze tester (for liquid-cooled engines)

Repair and overhaul tools

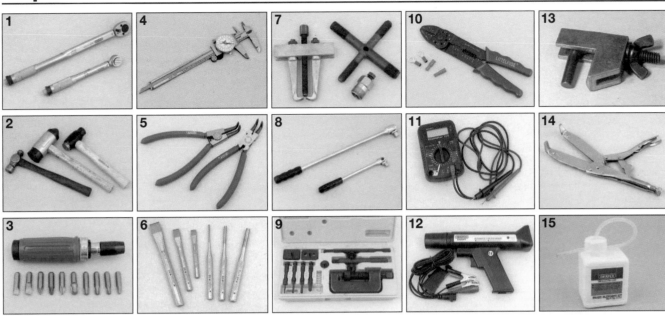

1 Torque wrench
   (small and mid-ranges)
2 Conventional, plastic or
   soft-faced hammers
3 Impact driver set

4 Vernier gauge
5 Circlip pliers (internal and
   external, or combination)
6 Set of cold chisels
   and punches

7 Selection of pullers
8 Breaker bars
9 Chain breaking/
   riveting tool set

10 Wire stripper and
   crimper tool
11 Multimeter (measures
   amps, volts and ohms)
12 Stroboscope (for
   dynamic timing checks)

13 Hose clamp
   (wingnut type shown)
14 Clutch holding tool
15 One-man brake/clutch
   bleeder kit

Specialist tools

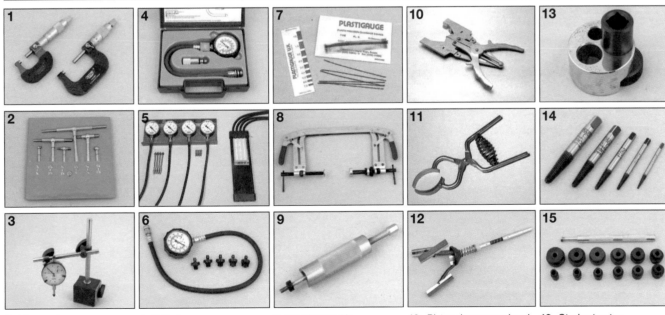

1 Micrometers
   (external type)
2 Telescoping gauges
3 Dial gauge

4 Cylinder
   compression gauge
5 Vacuum gauges (left) or
   manometer (right)
6 Oil pressure gauge

7 Plastigauge kit
8 Valve spring compressor
   (4-stroke engines)
9 Piston pin drawbolt tool

10 Piston ring removal and
   installation tool
11 Piston ring clamp
12 Cylinder bore hone
   (stone type shown)

13 Stud extractor
14 Screw extractor set
15 Bearing driver set

1 Workshop equipment and facilities

The workbench

● Work is made much easier by raising the bike up on a ramp - components are much more accessible if raised to waist level. The hydraulic or pneumatic types seen in the dealer's workshop are a sound investment if you undertake a lot of repairs or overhauls **(see illustration 1.1)**.

1.1 Hydraulic motorcycle ramp

● If raised off ground level, the bike must be supported on the ramp to avoid it falling. Most ramps incorporate a front wheel locating clamp which can be adjusted to suit different diameter wheels. When tightening the clamp, take care not to mark the wheel rim or damage the tyre - use wood blocks on each side to prevent this.
● Secure the bike to the ramp using tie-downs **(see illustration 1.2)**. If the bike has only a sidestand, and hence leans at a dangerous angle when raised, support the bike on an auxiliary stand.

1.2 Tie-downs are used around the passenger footrests to secure the bike

● Auxiliary (paddock) stands are widely available from mail order companies or motorcycle dealers and attach either to the wheel axle or swingarm pivot **(see illustration 1.3)**. If the motorcycle has a centrestand, you can support it under the crankcase to prevent it toppling whilst either wheel is removed **(see illustration 1.4)**.

1.3 This auxiliary stand attaches to the swingarm pivot

1.4 Always use a block of wood between the engine and jack head when supporting the engine in this way

Fumes and fire

● Refer to the Safety first! page at the beginning of the manual for full details. Make sure your workshop is equipped with a fire extinguisher suitable for fuel-related fires (Class B fire - flammable liquids) - it is not sufficient to have a water-filled extinguisher.
● Always ensure adequate ventilation is available. Unless an exhaust gas extraction system is available for use, ensure that the engine is run outside of the workshop.
● If working on the fuel system, make sure the workshop is ventilated to avoid a build-up of fumes. This applies equally to fume build-up when charging a battery. Do not smoke or allow anyone else to smoke in the workshop.

Fluids

● If you need to drain fuel from the tank, store it in an approved container marked as suitable for the storage of petrol (gasoline) **(see illustration 1.5)**. Do not store fuel in glass jars or bottles.

1.5 Use an approved can only for storing petrol (gasoline)

● Use proprietary engine degreasers or solvents which have a high flash-point, such as paraffin (kerosene), for cleaning off oil, grease and dirt - never use petrol (gasoline) for cleaning. Wear rubber gloves when handling solvent and engine degreaser. The fumes from certain solvents can be dangerous - always work in a well-ventilated area.

Dust, eye and hand protection

● Protect your lungs from inhalation of dust particles by wearing a filtering mask over the nose and mouth. Many frictional materials still contain asbestos which is dangerous to your health. Protect your eyes from spouts of liquid and sprung components by wearing a pair of protective goggles **(see illustration 1.6)**.

1.6 A fire extinguisher, goggles, mask and protective gloves should be at hand in the workshop

● Protect your hands from contact with solvents, fuel and oils by wearing rubber gloves. Alternatively apply a barrier cream to your hands before starting work. If handling hot components or fluids, wear suitable gloves to protect your hands from scalding and burns.

What to do with old fluids

● Old cleaning solvent, fuel, coolant and oils should not be poured down domestic drains or onto the ground. Package the fluid up in old oil containers, label it accordingly, and take it to a garage or disposal facility. Contact your local authority for location of such sites or ring the oil care hotline.

OIL CARE
FOLLOW THE CODE
OIL BANK LINE
0800 66 33 66

Note: It is antisocial and illegal to dump oil down the drain. To find the location of your local oil recycling bank, call this number free.

In the USA, note that any oil supplier must accept used oil for recycling.

2 Fasteners -
screws, bolts and nuts

Fastener types and applications

Bolts and screws

● Fastener head types are either of hexagonal, Torx or splined design, with internal and external versions of each type **(see illustrations 2.1 and 2.2);** splined head fasteners are not in common use on motorcycles. The conventional slotted or Phillips head design is used for certain screws. Bolt or screw length is always measured from the underside of the head to the end of the item **(see illustration 2.11).**

2.1 **Internal hexagon/Allen (A), Torx (B) and splined (C) fasteners, with corresponding bits**

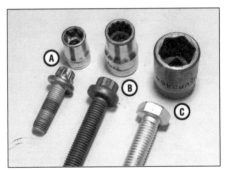

2.2 **External Torx (A), splined (B) and hexagon (C) fasteners, with corresponding sockets**

● Certain fasteners on the motorcycle have a tensile marking on their heads, the higher the marking the stronger the fastener. High tensile fasteners generally carry a 10 or higher marking. Never replace a high tensile fastener with one of a lower tensile strength.

Washers (see illustration 2.3)

● Plain washers are used between a fastener head and a component to prevent damage to the component or to spread the load when torque is applied. Plain washers can also be used as spacers or shims in certain assemblies. Copper or aluminium plain washers are often used as sealing washers on drain plugs.

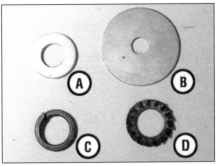

2.3 **Plain washer (A), penny washer (B), spring washer (C) and serrated washer (D)**

● The split-ring spring washer works by applying axial tension between the fastener head and component. If flattened, it is fatigued and must be renewed. If a plain (flat) washer is used on the fastener, position the spring washer between the fastener and the plain washer.

● Serrated star type washers dig into the fastener and component faces, preventing loosening. They are often used on electrical earth (ground) connections to the frame.

● Cone type washers (sometimes called Belleville) are conical and when tightened apply axial tension between the fastener head and component. They must be installed with the dished side against the component and often carry an OUTSIDE marking on their outer face. If flattened, they are fatigued and must be renewed.

● Tab washers are used to lock plain nuts or bolts on a shaft. A portion of the tab washer is bent up hard against one flat of the nut or bolt to prevent it loosening. Due to the tab washer being deformed in use, a new tab washer should be used every time it is disturbed.

● Wave washers are used to take up endfloat on a shaft. They provide light springing and prevent excessive side-to-side play of a component. Can be found on rocker arm shafts.

Nuts and split pins

● Conventional plain nuts are usually six-sided **(see illustration 2.4).** They are sized by thread diameter and pitch. High tensile nuts carry a number on one end to denote their tensile strength.

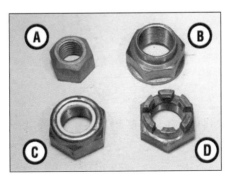

2.4 **Plain nut (A), shouldered locknut (B), nylon insert nut (C) and castellated nut (D)**

● Self-locking nuts either have a nylon insert, or two spring metal tabs, or a shoulder which is staked into a groove in the shaft - their advantage over conventional plain nuts is a resistance to loosening due to vibration. The nylon insert type can be used a number of times, but must be renewed when the friction of the nylon insert is reduced, ie when the nut spins freely on the shaft. The spring tab type can be reused unless the tabs are damaged. The shouldered type must be renewed every time it is disturbed.

● Split pins (cotter pins) are used to lock a castellated nut to a shaft or to prevent slackening of a plain nut. Common applications are wheel axles and brake torque arms. Because the split pin arms are deformed to lock around the nut a new split pin must always be used on installation - always fit the correct size split pin which will fit snugly in the shaft hole. Make sure the split pin arms are correctly located around the nut **(see illustrations 2.5 and 2.6).**

2.5 **Bend split pin (cotter pin) arms as shown (arrows) to secure a castellated nut**

2.6 **Bend split pin (cotter pin) arms as shown to secure a plain nut**

Caution: If the castellated nut slots do not align with the shaft hole after tightening to the torque setting, tighten the nut until the next slot aligns with the hole - never slacken the nut to align its slot.

● R-pins (shaped like the letter R), or slip pins as they are sometimes called, are sprung and can be reused if they are otherwise in good condition. Always install R-pins with their closed end facing forwards **(see illustration 2.7).**

**2.7 Correct fitting of R-pin.
Arrow indicates forward direction**

Circlips (see illustration 2.8)

● Circlips (sometimes called snap-rings) are used to retain components on a shaft or in a housing and have corresponding external or internal ears to permit removal. Parallel-sided (machined) circlips can be installed either way round in their groove, whereas stamped circlips (which have a chamfered edge on one face) must be installed with the chamfer facing away from the direction of thrust load **(see illustration 2.9)**.

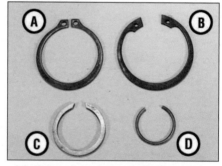

2.8 External stamped circlip (A), internal stamped circlip (B), machined circlip (C) and wire circlip (D)

● Always use circlip pliers to remove and install circlips; expand or compress them just enough to remove them. After installation, rotate the circlip in its groove to ensure it is securely seated. If installing a circlip on a splined shaft, always align its opening with a shaft channel to ensure the circlip ends are well supported and unlikely to catch **(see illustration 2.10)**.

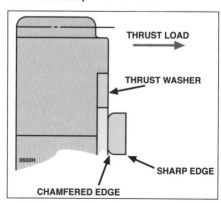

THRUST LOAD

THRUST WASHER

SHARP EDGE

CHAMFERED EDGE

2.9 Correct fitting of a stamped circlip

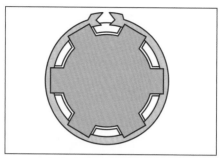

**2.10 Align circlip opening
with shaft channel**

● Circlips can wear due to the thrust of components and become loose in their grooves, with the subsequent danger of becoming dislodged in operation. For this reason, renewal is advised every time a circlip is disturbed.
● Wire circlips are commonly used as piston pin retaining clips. If a removal tang is provided, long-nosed pliers can be used to dislodge them, otherwise careful use of a small flat-bladed screwdriver is necessary. Wire circlips should be renewed every time they are disturbed.

Thread diameter and pitch

● Diameter of a male thread (screw, bolt or stud) is the outside diameter of the threaded portion **(see illustration 2.11)**. Most motorcycle manufacturers use the ISO (International Standards Organisation) metric system expressed in millimetres, eg M6 refers to a 6 mm diameter thread. Sizing is the same for nuts, except that the thread diameter is measured across the valleys of the nut.
● Pitch is the distance between the peaks of the thread **(see illustration 2.11)**. It is expressed in millimetres, thus a common bolt size may be expressed as 6.0 x 1.0 mm (6 mm thread diameter and 1 mm pitch). Generally pitch increases in proportion to thread diameter, although there are always exceptions.
● Thread diameter and pitch are related for conventional fastener applications and the accompanying table can be used as a guide. Additionally, the AF (Across Flats), spanner or socket size dimension of the bolt or nut **(see illustration 2.11)** is linked to thread and pitch specification. Thread pitch can be measured with a thread gauge **(see illustration 2.12)**.

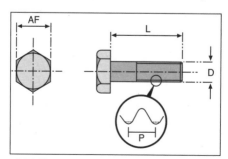

AF

L

D

P

2.11 Fastener length (L), thread diameter (D), thread pitch (P) and head size (AF)

**2.12 Using a thread gauge
to measure pitch**

AF size	Thread diameter x pitch (mm)
8 mm	M5 x 0.8
8 mm	M6 x 1.0
10 mm	M6 x 1.0
12 mm	M8 x 1.25
14 mm	M10 x 1.25
17 mm	M12 x 1.25

● The threads of most fasteners are of the right-hand type, ie they are turned clockwise to tighten and anti-clockwise to loosen. The reverse situation applies to left-hand thread fasteners, which are turned anti-clockwise to tighten and clockwise to loosen. Left-hand threads are used where rotation of a component might loosen a conventional right-hand thread fastener.

Seized fasteners

● Corrosion of external fasteners due to water or reaction between two dissimilar metals can occur over a period of time. It will build up sooner in wet conditions or in countries where salt is used on the roads during the winter. If a fastener is severely corroded it is likely that normal methods of removal will fail and result in its head being ruined. When you attempt removal, the fastener thread should be heard to crack free and unscrew easily - if it doesn't, stop there before damaging something.
● A smart tap on the head of the fastener will often succeed in breaking free corrosion which has occurred in the threads **(see illustration 2.13)**.
● An aerosol penetrating fluid (such as WD-40) applied the night beforehand may work its way down into the thread and ease removal. Depending on the location, you may be able to make up a Plasticine well around the fastener head and fill it with penetrating fluid.

**2.13 A sharp tap on the head of a fastener
will often break free a corroded thread**

● If you are working on an engine internal component, corrosion will most likely not be a problem due to the well lubricated environment. However, components can be very tight and an impact driver is a useful tool in freeing them **(see illustration 2.14)**.

2.14 Using an impact driver to free a fastener

● Where corrosion has occurred between dissimilar metals (eg steel and aluminium alloy), the application of heat to the fastener head will create a disproportionate expansion rate between the two metals and break the seizure caused by the corrosion. Whether heat can be applied depends on the location of the fastener - any surrounding components likely to be damaged must first be removed **(see illustration 2.15)**. Heat can be applied using a paint stripper heat gun or clothes iron, or by immersing the component in boiling water - wear protective gloves to prevent scalding or burns to the hands.

2.15 Using heat to free a seized fastener

● As a last resort, it is possible to use a hammer and cold chisel to work the fastener head unscrewed **(see illustration 2.16)**. This will damage the fastener, but more importantly extreme care must be taken not to damage the surrounding component.

Caution: Remember that the component being secured is generally of more value than the bolt, nut or screw - when the fastener is freed, do not unscrew it with force, instead work the fastener back and forth when resistance is felt to prevent thread damage.

2.16 Using a hammer and chisel to free a seized fastener

Broken fasteners and damaged heads

● If the shank of a broken bolt or screw is accessible you can grip it with self-locking grips. The knurled wheel type stud extractor tool or self-gripping stud puller tool is particularly useful for removing the long studs which screw into the cylinder mouth surface of the crankcase or bolts and screws from which the head has broken off **(see illustration 2.17)**. Studs can also be removed by locking two nuts together on the threaded end of the stud and using a spanner on the lower nut **(see illustration 2.18)**.

2.17 Using a stud extractor tool to remove a broken crankcase stud

2.18 Two nuts can be locked together to unscrew a stud from a component

● A bolt or screw which has broken off below or level with the casing must be extracted using a screw extractor set. Centre punch the fastener to centralise the drill bit, then drill a hole in the fastener **(see illustration 2.19)**. Select a drill bit which is approximately half to three-quarters the

2.19 When using a screw extractor, first drill a hole in the fastener . . .

diameter of the fastener and drill to a depth which will accommodate the extractor. Use the largest size extractor possible, but avoid leaving too small a wall thickness otherwise the extractor will merely force the fastener walls outwards wedging it in the casing thread.

● If a spiral type extractor is used, thread it anti-clockwise into the fastener. As it is screwed in, it will grip the fastener and unscrew it from the casing **(see illustration 2.20)**.

2.20 . . . then thread the extractor anti-clockwise into the fastener

● If a taper type extractor is used, tap it into the fastener so that it is firmly wedged in place. Unscrew the extractor (anti-clockwise) to draw the fastener out.

> ⚠ *Warning: Stud extractors are very hard and may break off in the fastener if care is not taken - ask an engineer about spark erosion if this happens.*

● Alternatively, the broken bolt/screw can be drilled out and the hole retapped for an oversize bolt/screw or a diamond-section thread insert. It is essential that the drilling is carried out squarely and to the correct depth, otherwise the casing may be ruined - if in doubt, entrust the work to an engineer.

● Bolts and nuts with rounded corners cause the correct size spanner or socket to slip when force is applied. Of the types of spanner/socket available always use a six-point type rather than an eight or twelve-point type - better grip

2.21 Comparison of surface drive ring spanner (left) with 12-point type (right)

is obtained. Surface drive spanners grip the middle of the hex flats, rather than the corners, and are thus good in cases of damaged heads **(see illustration 2.21)**.

● Slotted-head or Phillips-head screws are often damaged by the use of the wrong size screwdriver. Allen-head and Torx-head screws are much less likely to sustain damage. If enough of the screw head is exposed you can use a hacksaw to cut a slot in its head and then use a conventional flat-bladed screwdriver to remove it. Alternatively use a hammer and cold chisel to tap the head of the fastener around to slacken it. Always replace damaged fasteners with new ones, preferably Torx or Allen-head type.

A dab of valve grinding compound between the screw head and screw-driver tip will often give a good grip.

Thread repair

● Threads (particularly those in aluminium alloy components) can be damaged by overtightening, being assembled with dirt in the threads, or from a component working loose and vibrating. Eventually the thread will fail completely, and it will be impossible to tighten the fastener.

● If a thread is damaged or clogged with old locking compound it can be renovated with a thread repair tool (thread chaser) **(see illustrations 2.22 and 2.23)**; special thread

2.22 A thread repair tool being used to correct an internal thread

2.23 A thread repair tool being used to correct an external thread

chasers are available for spark plug hole threads. The tool will not cut a new thread, but clean and true the original thread. Make sure that you use the correct diameter and pitch tool. Similarly, external threads can be cleaned up with a die or a thread restorer file **(see illustration 2.24)**.

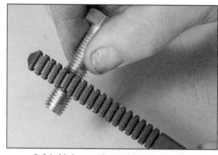

2.24 Using a thread restorer file

● It is possible to drill out the old thread and retap the component to the next thread size. This will work where there is enough surrounding material and a new bolt or screw can be obtained. Sometimes, however, this is not possible - such as where the bolt/screw passes through another component which must also be suitably modified, also in cases where a spark plug or oil drain plug cannot be obtained in a larger diameter thread size.

● The diamond-section thread insert (often known by its popular trade name of Heli-Coil) is a simple and effective method of renewing the thread and retaining the original size. A kit can be purchased which contains the tap, insert and installing tool **(see illustration 2.25)**. Drill out the damaged thread with the size drill specified **(see illustration 2.26)**. Carefully retap the thread **(see illustration 2.27)**. Install the

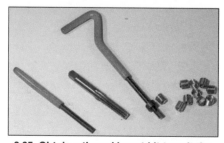

2.25 Obtain a thread insert kit to suit the thread diameter and pitch required

2.26 To install a thread insert, first drill out the original thread . . .

2.27 . . . tap a new thread . . .

2.28 . . . fit insert on the installing tool . . .

2.29 . . . and thread into the component . . .

2.30 . . . break off the tang when complete

insert on the installing tool and thread it slowly into place using a light downward pressure **(see illustrations 2.28 and 2.29)**. When positioned between a 1/4 and 1/2 turn below the surface withdraw the installing tool and use the break-off tool to press down on the tang, breaking it off **(see illustration 2.30)**.

● There are epoxy thread repair kits on the market which can rebuild stripped internal threads, although this repair should not be used on high load-bearing components.

Thread locking and sealing compounds

● Locking compounds are used in locations where the fastener is prone to loosening due to vibration or on important safety-related items which might cause loss of control of the motorcycle if they fail. It is also used where important fasteners cannot be secured by other means such as lockwashers or split pins.

● Before applying locking compound, make sure that the threads (internal and external) are clean and dry with all old compound removed. Select a compound to suit the component being secured - a non-permanent general locking and sealing type is suitable for most applications, but a high strength type is needed for permanent fixing of studs in castings. Apply a drop or two of the compound to the first few threads of the fastener, then thread it into place and tighten to the specified torque. Do not apply excessive thread locking compound otherwise the thread may be damaged on subsequent removal.

● Certain fasteners are impregnated with a dry film type coating of locking compound on their threads. Always renew this type of fastener if disturbed.

● Anti-seize compounds, such as copper-based greases, can be applied to protect threads from seizure due to extreme heat and corrosion. A common instance is spark plug threads and exhaust system fasteners.

3 Measuring tools and gauges

Feeler gauges

● Feeler gauges (or blades) are used for measuring small gaps and clearances (see illustration 3.1). They can also be used to measure endfloat (sideplay) of a component on a shaft where access is not possible with a dial gauge.

● Feeler gauge sets should be treated with care and not bent or damaged. They are etched with their size on one face. Keep them clean and very lightly oiled to prevent corrosion build-up.

3.1 Feeler gauges are used for measuring small gaps and clearances - thickness is marked on one face of gauge

● When measuring a clearance, select a gauge which is a light sliding fit between the two components. You may need to use two gauges together to measure the clearance accurately.

Micrometers

● A micrometer is a precision tool capable of measuring to 0.01 or 0.001 of a millimetre. It should always be stored in its case and not in the general toolbox. It must be kept clean and never dropped, otherwise its frame or measuring anvils could be distorted resulting in inaccurate readings.

● External micrometers are used for measuring outside diameters of components and have many more applications than internal micrometers. Micrometers are available in different size ranges, eg 0 to 25 mm, 25 to 50 mm, and upwards in 25 mm steps; some large micrometers have interchangeable anvils to allow a range of measurements to be taken. Generally the largest precision measurement you are likely to take on a motorcycle is the piston diameter.

● Internal micrometers (or bore micrometers) are used for measuring inside diameters, such as valve guides and cylinder bores. Telescoping gauges and small hole gauges are used in conjunction with an external micrometer, whereas the more expensive internal micrometers have their own measuring device.

External micrometer

Note: *The conventional analogue type instrument is described. Although much easier to read, digital micrometers are considerably more expensive.*

● Always check the calibration of the micrometer before use. With the anvils closed (0 to 25 mm type) or set over a test gauge (for

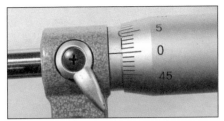

3.2 Check micrometer calibration before use

the larger types) the scale should read zero (see illustration 3.2); make sure that the anvils (and test piece) are clean first. Any discrepancy can be adjusted by referring to the instructions supplied with the tool. Remember that the micrometer is a precision measuring tool - don't force the anvils closed, use the ratchet (4) on the end of the micrometer to close it. In this way, a measured force is always applied.

● To use, first make sure that the item being measured is clean. Place the anvil of the micrometer (1) against the item and use the thimble (2) to bring the spindle (3) lightly into contact with the other side of the item (see illustration 3.3). Don't tighten the thimble down because this will damage the micrometer - instead use the ratchet (4) on the end of the micrometer. The ratchet mechanism applies a measured force preventing damage to the instrument.

● The micrometer is read by referring to the linear scale on the sleeve and the annular scale on the thimble. Read off the sleeve first to obtain the base measurement, then add the fine measurement from the thimble to obtain the overall reading. The linear scale on the sleeve represents the measuring range of the micrometer (eg 0 to 25 mm). The annular scale

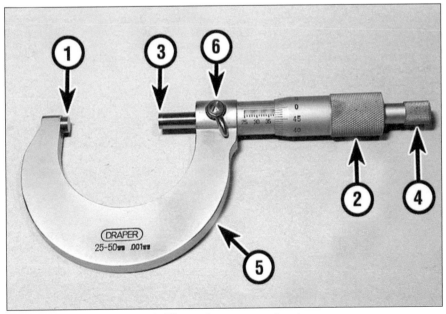

3.3 Micrometer component parts

1 Anvil	3 Spindle	5 Frame
2 Thimble	4 Ratchet	6 Locking lever

on the thimble will be in graduations of 0.01 mm (or as marked on the frame) - one full revolution of the thimble will move 0.5 mm on the linear scale. Take the reading where the datum line on the sleeve intersects the thimble's scale. Always position the eye directly above the scale otherwise an inaccurate reading will result.

In the example shown the item measures 2.95 mm (see illustration 3.4):

Linear scale	2.00 mm
Linear scale	0.50 mm
Annular scale	0.45 mm
Total figure	**2.95 mm**

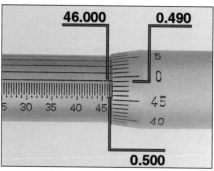

3.5 Micrometer reading of 46.99 mm on linear and annular scales . . .

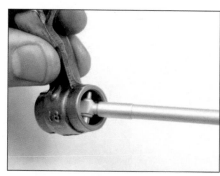

3.7 Expand the telescoping gauge in the bore, lock its position . . .

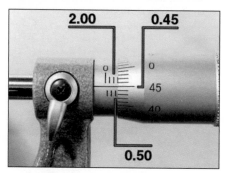

3.4 Micrometer reading of 2.95 mm

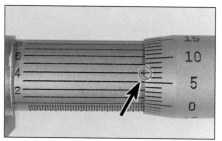

3.6 . . . and 0.004 mm on vernier scale

3.8 . . . then measure the gauge with a micrometer

Most micrometers have a locking lever (6) on the frame to hold the setting in place, allowing the item to be removed from the micrometer.
● Some micrometers have a vernier scale on their sleeve, providing an even finer measurement to be taken, in 0.001 increments of a millimetre. Take the sleeve and thimble measurement as described above, then check which graduation on the vernier scale aligns with that of the annular scale on the thimble **Note:** *The eye must be perpendicular to the scale when taking the vernier reading - if necessary rotate the body of the micrometer to ensure this.* Multiply the vernier scale figure by 0.001 and add it to the base and fine measurement figures.

In the example shown the item measures 46.994 mm (see illustrations 3.5 and 3.6):

Linear scale (base)	46.000 mm
Linear scale (base)	00.500 mm
Annular scale (fine)	00.490 mm
Vernier scale	00.004 mm
Total figure	**46.994 mm**

Internal micrometer

● Internal micrometers are available for measuring bore diameters, but are expensive and unlikely to be available for home use. It is suggested that a set of telescoping gauges and small hole gauges, both of which must be used with an external micrometer, will suffice for taking internal measurements on a motorcycle.
● Telescoping gauges can be used to

measure internal diameters of components. Select a gauge with the correct size range, make sure its ends are clean and insert it into the bore. Expand the gauge, then lock its position and withdraw it from the bore (see illustration 3.7). Measure across the gauge ends with a micrometer (see illustration 3.8).
● Very small diameter bores (such as valve guides) are measured with a small hole gauge. Once adjusted to a slip-fit inside the component, its position is locked and the gauge withdrawn for measurement with a micrometer (see illustrations 3.9 and 3.10).

Vernier caliper

Note: *The conventional linear and dial gauge type instruments are described. Digital types are easier to read, but are far more expensive.*
● The vernier caliper does not provide the precision of a micrometer, but is versatile in being able to measure internal and external diameters. Some types also incorporate a depth gauge. It is ideal for measuring clutch plate friction material and spring free lengths.
● To use the conventional linear scale vernier, slacken off the vernier clamp screws (1) and set its jaws over (2), or inside (3), the item to be measured (see illustration 3.11). Slide the jaw into contact, using the thumb-wheel (4) for fine movement of the sliding scale (5) then tighten the clamp screws (1). Read off the main scale (6) where the zero on the sliding scale (5) intersects it, taking the whole number to the left of the zero; this provides the base measurement. View along the sliding scale and select the division which

3.9 Expand the small hole gauge in the bore, lock its position . . .

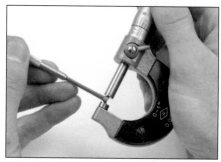

3.10 . . . then measure the gauge with a micrometer

lines up exactly with any of the divisions on the main scale, noting that the divisions usually represents 0.02 of a millimetre. Add this fine measurement to the base measurement to obtain the total reading.

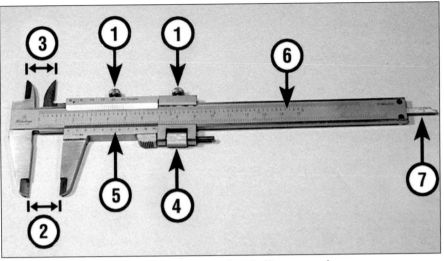

3.11 Vernier component parts (linear gauge)

1 Clamp screws   3 Internal jaws   5 Sliding scale   7 Depth gauge
2 External jaws   4 Thumbwheel   6 Main scale

In the example shown the item measures 55.92 mm **(see illustration 3.12)**:

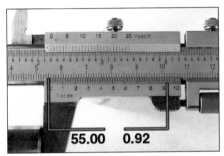

3.12 Vernier gauge reading of 55.92 mm

Base measurement	55.00 mm
Fine measurement	00.92 mm
Total figure	**55.92 mm**

● Some vernier calipers are equipped with a dial gauge for fine measurement. Before use, check that the jaws are clean, then close them fully and check that the dial gauge reads zero. If necessary adjust the gauge ring accordingly. Slacken the vernier clamp screw (1) and set its jaws over (2), or inside (3), the item to be measured **(see illustration 3.13)**. Slide the jaws into contact, using the thumbwheel (4) for fine movement. Read off the main scale (5) where the edge of the sliding scale (6) intersects it, taking the whole number to the left of the zero; this provides the base measurement. Read off the needle position on the dial gauge (7) scale to provide the fine measurement; each division represents 0.05 of a millimetre. Add this fine measurement to the base measurement to obtain the total reading.

In the example shown the item measures 55.95 mm **(see illustration 3.14)**:

Base measurement	55.00 mm
Fine measurement	00.95 mm
Total figure	**55.95 mm**

3.14 Vernier gauge reading of 55.95 mm

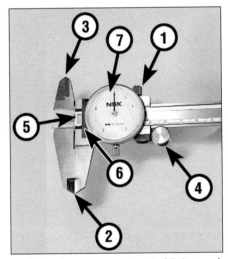

3.13 Vernier component parts (dial gauge)

1 Clamp screw   5 Main scale
2 External jaws   6 Sliding scale
3 Internal jaws   7 Dial gauge
4 Thumbwheel

Plastigauge

● Plastigauge is a plastic material which can be compressed between two surfaces to measure the oil clearance between them. The width of the compressed Plastigauge is measured against a calibrated scale to determine the clearance.

● Common uses of Plastigauge are for measuring the clearance between crankshaft journal and main bearing inserts, between crankshaft journal and big-end bearing inserts, and between camshaft and bearing surfaces. The following example describes big-end oil clearance measurement.

● Handle the Plastigauge material carefully to prevent distortion. Using a sharp knife, cut a length which corresponds with the width of the bearing being measured and place it carefully across the journal so that it is parallel with the shaft **(see illustration 3.15)**. Carefully install both bearing shells and the connecting rod. Without rotating the rod on the journal tighten its bolts or nuts (as applicable) to the specified torque. The connecting rod and bearings are then disassembled and the crushed Plastigauge examined.

3.15 Plastigauge placed across shaft journal

● Using the scale provided in the Plastigauge kit, measure the width of the material to determine the oil clearance **(see illustration 3.16)**. Always remove all traces of Plastigauge after use using your fingernails.

Caution: Arriving at the correct clearance demands that the assembly is torqued correctly, according to the settings and sequence (where applicable) provided by the motorcycle manufacturer.

3.16 Measuring the width of the crushed Plastigauge

Dial gauge or DTI (Dial Test Indicator)

● A dial gauge can be used to accurately measure small amounts of movement. Typical uses are measuring shaft runout or shaft endfloat (sideplay) and setting piston position for ignition timing on two-strokes. A dial gauge set usually comes with a range of different probes and adapters and mounting equipment.

● The gauge needle must point to zero when at rest. Rotate the ring around its periphery to zero the gauge.

● Check that the gauge is capable of reading the extent of movement in the work. Most gauges have a small dial set in the face which records whole millimetres of movement as well as the fine scale around the face periphery which is calibrated in 0.01 mm divisions. Read off the small dial first to obtain the base measurement, then add the measurement from the fine scale to obtain the total reading.

In the example shown the gauge reads 1.48 mm **(see illustration 3.17)**:

Base measurement	1.00 mm
Fine measurement	0.48 mm
Total figure	**1.48 mm**

3.17 Dial gauge reading of 1.48 mm

● If measuring shaft runout, the shaft must be supported in vee-blocks and the gauge mounted on a stand perpendicular to the shaft. Rest the tip of the gauge against the centre of the shaft and rotate the shaft slowly whilst watching the gauge reading **(see illustration 3.18)**. Take several measurements along the length of the shaft and record the

3.18 Using a dial gauge to measure shaft runout

maximum gauge reading as the amount of runout in the shaft. **Note:** *The reading obtained will be total runout at that point - some manufacturers specify that the runout figure is halved to compare with their specified runout limit.*

● Endfloat (sideplay) measurement requires that the gauge is mounted securely to the surrounding component with its probe touching the end of the shaft. Using hand pressure, push and pull on the shaft noting the maximum endfloat recorded on the gauge **(see illustration 3.19)**.

3.19 Using a dial gauge to measure shaft endfloat

● A dial gauge with suitable adapters can be used to determine piston position BTDC on two-stroke engines for the purposes of ignition timing. The gauge, adapter and suitable length probe are installed in the place of the spark plug and the gauge zeroed at TDC. If the piston position is specified as 1.14 mm BTDC, rotate the engine back to 2.00 mm BTDC, then slowly forwards to 1.14 mm BTDC.

Cylinder compression gauges

● A compression gauge is used for measuring cylinder compression. Either the rubber-cone type or the threaded adapter type can be used. The latter is preferred to ensure a perfect seal against the cylinder head. A 0 to 300 psi (0 to 20 Bar) type gauge (for petrol/gasoline engines) will be suitable for motorcycles.

● The spark plug is removed and the gauge either held hard against the cylinder head (cone type) or the gauge adapter screwed into the cylinder head (threaded type) **(see illustration 3.20)**. Cylinder compression is measured with the engine turning over, but not running - carry out the compression test as described in

3.20 Using a rubber-cone type cylinder compression gauge

Fault Finding Equipment. The gauge will hold the reading until manually released.

Oil pressure gauge

● An oil pressure gauge is used for measuring engine oil pressure. Most gauges come with a set of adapters to fit the thread of the take-off point **(see illustration 3.21)**. If the take-off point specified by the motorcycle manufacturer is an external oil pipe union, make sure that the specified replacement union is used to prevent oil starvation.

3.21 Oil pressure gauge and take-off point adapter (arrow)

● Oil pressure is measured with the engine running (at a specific rpm) and often the manufacturer will specify pressure limits for a cold and hot engine.

Straight-edge and surface plate

● If checking the gasket face of a component for warpage, place a steel rule or precision straight-edge across the gasket face and measure any gap between the straight-edge and component with feeler gauges **(see illustration 3.22)**. Check diagonally across the component and between mounting holes **(see illustration 3.23)**.

3.22 Use a straight-edge and feeler gauges to check for warpage

3.23 Check for warpage in these directions

- Checking individual components for warpage, such as clutch plain (metal) plates, requires a perfectly flat plate or piece or plate glass and feeler gauges.

4 Torque and leverage

What is torque?

- Torque describes the twisting force about a shaft. The amount of torque applied is determined by the distance from the centre of the shaft to the end of the lever and the amount of force being applied to the end of the lever; distance multiplied by force equals torque.
- The manufacturer applies a measured torque to a bolt or nut to ensure that it will not slacken in use and to hold two components securely together without movement in the joint. The actual torque setting depends on the thread size, bolt or nut material and the composition of the components being held.
- Too little torque may cause the fastener to loosen due to vibration, whereas too much torque will distort the joint faces of the component or cause the fastener to shear off. Always stick to the specified torque setting.

Using a torque wrench

- Check the calibration of the torque wrench and make sure it has a suitable range for the job. Torque wrenches are available in Nm (Newton-metres), kgf m (kilograms-force metre), lbf ft (pounds-feet), lbf in (inch-pounds). Do not confuse lbf ft with lbf in.
- Adjust the tool to the desired torque on the scale (see illustration 4.1). If your torque wrench is not calibrated in the units specified, carefully convert the figure (see Conversion Factors). A manufacturer sometimes gives a torque setting as a range (8 to 10 Nm) rather than a single figure - in this case set the tool midway between the two settings. The same torque may be expressed as 9 Nm ± 1 Nm. Some torque wrenches have a method of locking the setting so that it isn't inadvertently altered during use.

4.1 Set the torque wrench index mark to the setting required, in this case 12 Nm

- Install the bolts/nuts in their correct location and secure them lightly. Their threads must be clean and free of any old locking compound. Unless specified the threads and flange should be dry - oiled threads are necessary in certain circumstances and the manufacturer will take this into account in the specified torque figure. Similarly, the manufacturer may also specify the application of thread-locking compound.
- Tighten the fasteners in the specified sequence until the torque wrench clicks, indicating that the torque setting has been reached. Apply the torque again to double-check the setting. Where different thread diameter fasteners secure the component, as a rule tighten the larger diameter ones first.
- When the torque wrench has been finished with, release the lock (where applicable) and fully back off its setting to zero - do not leave the torque wrench tensioned. Also, do not use a torque wrench for slackening a fastener.

Angle-tightening

- Manufacturers often specify a figure in degrees for final tightening of a fastener. This usually follows tightening to a specific torque setting.
- A degree disc can be set and attached to the socket (see illustration 4.2) or a protractor can be used to mark the angle of movement on the bolt/nut head and the surrounding casting (see illustration 4.3).

4.2 Angle tightening can be accomplished with a torque-angle gauge . . .

4.3 . . . or by marking the angle on the surrounding component

Loosening sequences

- Where more than one bolt/nut secures a component, loosen each fastener evenly a little at a time. In this way, not all the stress of the joint is held by one fastener and the components are not likely to distort.
- If a tightening sequence is provided, work in the REVERSE of this, but if not, work from the outside in, in a criss-cross sequence (see illustration 4.4).

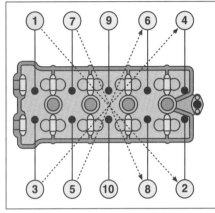

4.4 When slackening, work from the outside inwards

Tightening sequences

- If a component is held by more than one fastener it is important that the retaining bolts/nuts are tightened evenly to prevent uneven stress build-up and distortion of sealing faces. This is especially important on high-compression joints such as the cylinder head.
- A sequence is usually provided by the manufacturer, either in a diagram or actually marked in the casting. If not, always start in the centre and work outwards in a criss-cross pattern (see illustration 4.5). Start off by securing all bolts/nuts finger-tight, then set the torque wrench and tighten each fastener by a small amount in sequence until the final torque is reached. By following this practice,

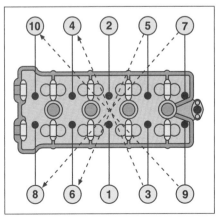

4.5 When tightening, work from the inside outwards

the joint will be held evenly and will not be distorted. Important joints, such as the cylinder head and big-end fasteners often have two- or three-stage torque settings.

Applying leverage

● Use tools at the correct angle. Position a socket wrench or spanner on the bolt/nut so that you pull it towards you when loosening. If this can't be done, push the spanner without curling your fingers around it **(see illustration 4.6)** - the spanner may slip or the fastener loosen suddenly, resulting in your fingers being crushed against a component.

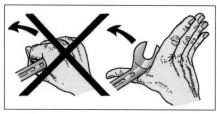

4.6 If you can't pull on the spanner to loosen a fastener, push with your hand open

● Additional leverage is gained by extending the length of the lever. The best way to do this is to use a breaker bar instead of the regular length tool, or to slip a length of tubing over the end of the spanner or socket wrench.
● If additional leverage will not work, the fastener head is either damaged or firmly corroded in place (see *Fasteners*).

5 Bearings

Bearing removal and installation

Drivers and sockets

● Before removing a bearing, always inspect the casing to see which way it must be driven out - some casings will have retaining plates or a cast step. Also check for any identifying markings on the bearing and if installed to a certain depth, measure this at this stage. Some roller bearings are sealed on one side - take note of the original fitted position.
● Bearings can be driven out of a casing using a bearing driver tool (with the correct size head) or a socket of the correct diameter. Select the driver head or socket so that it contacts the outer race of the bearing, not the balls/rollers or inner race. Always support the casing around the bearing housing with wood blocks, otherwise there is a risk of fracture. The bearing is driven out with a few blows on the driver or socket from a heavy mallet. Unless access is severely restricted (as with wheel bearings), a pin-punch is not recommended unless it is moved around the bearing to keep it square in its housing.

● The same equipment can be used to install bearings. Make sure the bearing housing is supported on wood blocks and line up the bearing in its housing. Fit the bearing as noted on removal - generally they are installed with their marked side facing outwards. Tap the bearing squarely into its housing using a driver or socket which bears only on the bearing's outer race - contact with the bearing balls/rollers or inner race will destroy it **(see illustrations 5.1 and 5.2)**.
● Check that the bearing inner race and balls/rollers rotate freely.

5.1 Using a bearing driver against the bearing's outer race

5.2 Using a large socket against the bearing's outer race

Pullers and slide-hammers

● Where a bearing is pressed on a shaft a puller will be required to extract it **(see illustration 5.3)**. Make sure that the puller clamp or legs fit securely behind the bearing and are unlikely to slip out. If pulling a bearing

5.3 This bearing puller clamps behind the bearing and pressure is applied to the shaft end to draw the bearing off

off a gear shaft for example, you may have to locate the puller behind a gear pinion if there is no access to the race and draw the gear pinion off the shaft as well **(see illustration 5.4)**.

> *Caution: Ensure that the puller's centre bolt locates securely against the end of the shaft and will not slip when pressure is applied. Also ensure that puller does not damage the shaft end.*

5.4 Where no access is available to the rear of the bearing, it is sometimes possible to draw off the adjacent component

● Operate the puller so that its centre bolt exerts pressure on the shaft end and draws the bearing off the shaft.
● When installing the bearing on the shaft, tap only on the bearing's inner race - contact with the balls/rollers or outer race with destroy the bearing. Use a socket or length of tubing as a drift which fits over the shaft end **(see illustration 5.5)**.

5.5 When installing a bearing on a shaft use a piece of tubing which bears only on the bearing's inner race

● Where a bearing locates in a blind hole in a casing, it cannot be driven or pulled out as described above. A slide-hammer with knife-edged bearing puller attachment will be required. The puller attachment passes through the bearing and when tightened expands to fit firmly behind the bearing **(see illustration 5.6)**. By operating the slide-hammer part of the tool the bearing is jarred out of its housing **(see illustration 5.7)**.
● It is possible, if the bearing is of reasonable weight, for it to drop out of its housing if the casing is heated as described opposite. If this

5.6 Expand the bearing puller so that it locks behind the bearing . . .

5.7 . . . attach the slide hammer to the bearing puller

method is attempted, first prepare a work surface which will enable the casing to be tapped face down to help dislodge the bearing - a wood surface is ideal since it will not damage the casing's gasket surface. Wearing protective gloves, tap the heated casing several times against the work surface to dislodge the bearing under its own weight **(see illustration 5.8)**.

● Bearings can be installed in blind holes using the driver or socket method described above.

Drawbolts

● Where a bearing or bush is set in the eye of a component, such as a suspension linkage arm or connecting rod small-end, removal by drift may damage the component. Furthermore, a rubber bushing in a shock absorber eye cannot successfully be driven out of position. If access is available to a engineering press, the task is straightforward. If not, a drawbolt can be fabricated to extract the bearing or bush.

5.8 Tapping a casing face down on wood blocks can often dislodge a bearing

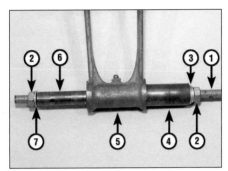

5.9 Drawbolt component parts assembled on a suspension arm

1 *Bolt or length of threaded bar*
2 *Nuts*
3 *Washer (external diameter greater than tubing internal diameter)*
4 *Tubing (internal diameter sufficient to accommodate bearing)*
5 *Suspension arm with bearing*
6 *Tubing (external diameter slightly smaller than bearing)*
7 *Washer (external diameter slightly smaller than bearing)*

5.10 Drawing the bearing out of the suspension arm

● To extract the bearing/bush you will need a long bolt with nut (or piece of threaded bar with two nuts), a piece of tubing which has an internal diameter larger than the bearing/bush, another piece of tubing which has an external diameter slightly smaller than the bearing/bush, and a selection of washers **(see illustrations 5.9 and 5.10)**. Note that the pieces of tubing must be of the same length, or longer, than the bearing/bush.

● The same kit (without the pieces of tubing) can be used to draw the new bearing/bush back into place **(see illustration 5.11)**.

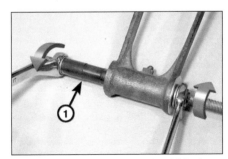

5.11 Installing a new bearing (1) in the suspension arm

Temperature change

● If the bearing's outer race is a tight fit in the casing, the aluminium casing can be heated to release its grip on the bearing. Aluminium will expand at a greater rate than the steel bearing outer race. There are several ways to do this, but avoid any localised extreme heat (such as a blow torch) - aluminium alloy has a low melting point.

● Approved methods of heating a casing are using a domestic oven (heated to 100°C) or immersing the casing in boiling water **(see illustration 5.12)**. Low temperature range localised heat sources such as a paint stripper heat gun or clothes iron can also be used **(see illustration 5.13)**. Alternatively, soak a rag in boiling water, wring it out and wrap it around the bearing housing.

> ⚠️ **Warning: All of these methods require care in use to prevent scalding and burns to the hands. Wear protective gloves when handling hot components.**

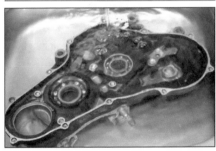

5.12 A casing can be immersed in a sink of boiling water to aid bearing removal

5.13 Using a localised heat source to aid bearing removal

● If heating the whole casing note that plastic components, such as the neutral switch, may suffer - remove them beforehand.

● After heating, remove the bearing as described above. You may find that the expansion is sufficient for the bearing to fall out of the casing under its own weight or with a light tap on the driver or socket.

● If necessary, the casing can be heated to aid bearing installation, and this is sometimes the recommended procedure if the motorcycle manufacturer has designed the housing and bearing fit with this intention.

● Installation of bearings can be eased by placing them in a freezer the night before installation. The steel bearing will contract slightly, allowing easy insertion in its housing. This is often useful when installing steering head outer races in the frame.

Bearing types and markings

● Plain shell bearings, ball bearings, needle roller bearings and tapered roller bearings will all be found on motorcycles (see illustrations 5.14 and 5.15). The ball and roller types are usually caged between an inner and outer race, but uncaged variations may be found.

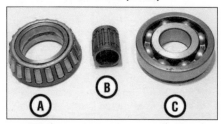

5.14 Shell bearings are either plain or grooved. They are usually identified by colour code (arrow)

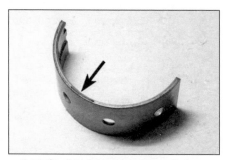

5.15 Tapered roller bearing (A), needle roller bearing (B) and ball journal bearing (C)

● Shell bearings (often called inserts) are usually found at the crankshaft main and connecting rod big-end where they are good at coping with high loads. They are made of a phosphor-bronze material and are impregnated with self-lubricating properties.
● Ball bearings and needle roller bearings consist of a steel inner and outer race with the balls or rollers between the races. They require constant lubrication by oil or grease and are good at coping with axial loads. Taper roller bearings consist of rollers set in a tapered cage set on the inner race; the outer race is separate. They are good at coping with axial loads and prevent movement along the shaft - a typical application is in the steering head.
● Bearing manufacturers produce bearings to ISO size standards and stamp one face of the bearing to indicate its internal and external diameter, load capacity and type (see illustration 5.16).
● Metal bushes are usually of phosphor-bronze material. Rubber bushes are used in suspension mounting eyes. Fibre bushes have also been used in suspension pivots.

5.16 Typical bearing marking

Bearing fault finding

● If a bearing outer race has spun in its housing, the housing material will be damaged. You can use a bearing locking compound to bond the outer race in place if damage is not too severe.
● Shell bearings will fail due to damage of their working surface, as a result of lack of lubrication, corrosion or abrasive particles in the oil (see illustration 5.17). Small particles of dirt in the oil may embed in the bearing material whereas larger particles will score the bearing and shaft journal. If a number of short journeys are made, insufficient heat will be generated to drive off condensation which has built up on the bearings.

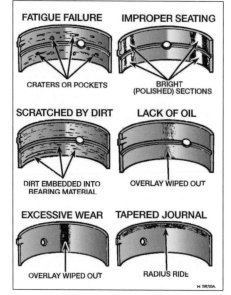

5.17 Typical bearing failures

● Ball and roller bearings will fail due to lack of lubrication or damage to the balls or rollers. Tapered-roller bearings can be damaged by overloading them. Unless the bearing is sealed on both sides, wash it in paraffin (kerosene) to remove all old grease then allow it to dry. Make a visual inspection looking to dented balls or rollers, damaged cages and worn or pitted races (see illustration 5.18).
● A ball bearing can be checked for wear by listening to it when spun. Apply a film of light oil to the bearing and hold it close to the ear - hold the outer race with one hand and spin the inner

5.18 Example of ball journal bearing with damaged balls and cages

5.19 Hold outer race and listen to inner race when spun

race with the other hand (see illustration 5.19). The bearing should be almost silent when spun; if it grates or rattles it is worn.

6 Oil seals

Oil seal removal and installation

● Oil seals should be renewed every time a component is dismantled. This is because the seal lips will become set to the sealing surface and will not necessarily reseal.
● Oil seals can be prised out of position using a large flat-bladed screwdriver (see illustration 6.1). In the case of crankcase seals, check first that the seal is not lipped on the inside, preventing its removal with the crankcases joined.

6.1 Prise out oil seals with a large flat-bladed screwdriver

● New seals are usually installed with their marked face (containing the seal reference code) outwards and the spring side towards the fluid being retained. In certain cases, such as a two-stroke engine crankshaft seal, a double lipped seal may be used due to there being fluid or gas on each side of the joint.

● Use a bearing driver or socket which bears only on the outer hard edge of the seal to install it in the casing - tapping on the inner edge will damage the sealing lip.

Oil seal types and markings

● Oil seals are usually of the single-lipped type. Double-lipped seals are found where a liquid or gas is on both sides of the joint.
● Oil seals can harden and lose their sealing ability if the motorcycle has been in storage for a long period - renewal is the only solution.
● Oil seal manufacturers also conform to the ISO markings for seal size - these are moulded into the outer face of the seal **(see illustration 6.2)**.

6.2 These oil seal markings indicate inside diameter, outside diameter and seal thickness

7 Gaskets and sealants

Types of gasket and sealant

● Gaskets are used to seal the mating surfaces between components and keep lubricants, fluids, vacuum or pressure contained within the assembly. Aluminium gaskets are sometimes found at the cylinder joints, but most gaskets are paper-based. If the mating surfaces of the components being joined are undamaged the gasket can be installed dry, although a dab of sealant or grease will be useful to hold it in place during assembly.
● RTV (Room Temperature Vulcanising) silicone rubber sealants cure when exposed to moisture in the atmosphere. These sealants are good at filling pits or irregular gasket faces, but will tend to be forced out of the joint under very high torque. They can be used to replace a paper gasket, but first make sure that the width of the paper gasket is not essential to the shimming of internal components. RTV sealants should not be used on components containing petrol (gasoline).
● Non-hardening, semi-hardening and hard setting liquid gasket compounds can be used with a gasket or between a metal-to-metal joint. Select the sealant to suit the application: universal non-hardening sealant can be used on virtually all joints; semi-hardening on joint faces which are rough or damaged; hard setting sealant on joints which require a permanent bond and are subjected to high temperature and pressure. **Note:** *Check first if the paper gasket has a bead of sealant*

impregnated in its surface before applying additional sealant.
● When choosing a sealant, make sure it is suitable for the application, particularly if being applied in a high-temperature area or in the vicinity of fuel. Certain manufacturers produce sealants in either clear, silver or black colours to match the finish of the engine. This has a particular application on motorcycles where much of the engine is exposed.
● Do not over-apply sealant. That which is squeezed out on the outside of the joint can be wiped off, whereas an excess of sealant on the inside can break off and clog oilways.

Breaking a sealed joint

● Age, heat, pressure and the use of hard setting sealant can cause two components to stick together so tightly that they are difficult to separate using finger pressure alone. Do not resort to using levers unless there is a pry point provided for this purpose **(see illustration 7.1)** or else the gasket surfaces will be damaged.
● Use a soft-faced hammer **(see illustration 7.2)** or a wood block and conventional hammer to strike the component near the mating surface. Avoid hammering against cast extremities since they may break off. If this method fails, try using a wood wedge between the two components.

Caution: If the joint will not separate, double-check that you have removed all the fasteners.

7.1 If a pry point is provided, apply gently pressure with a flat-bladed screwdriver

7.2 Tap around the joint with a soft-faced mallet if necessary - don't strike cooling fins

Removal of old gasket and sealant

● Paper gaskets will most likely come away complete, leaving only a few traces stuck on

Most components have one or two hollow locating dowels between the two gasket faces. If a dowel cannot be removed, do not resort to gripping it with pliers - it will almost certainly be distorted. Install a close-fitting socket or Phillips screwdriver into the dowel and then grip the outer edge of the dowel to free it.

the sealing faces of the components. It is imperative that all traces are removed to ensure correct sealing of the new gasket.
● Very carefully scrape all traces of gasket away making sure that the sealing surfaces are not gouged or scored by the scraper **(see illustrations 7.3, 7.4 and 7.5)**. Stubborn deposits can be removed by spraying with an aerosol gasket remover. Final preparation of

7.3 Paper gaskets can be scraped off with a gasket scraper tool . . .

7.4 . . . a knife blade . . .

7.5 . . . or a household scraper

7.6 Fine abrasive paper is wrapped around a flat file to clean up the gasket face

7.7 A kitchen scourer can be used on stubborn deposits

the gasket surface can be made with very fine abrasive paper or a plastic kitchen scourer **(see illustrations 7.6 and 7.7)**.

● Old sealant can be scraped or peeled off components, depending on the type originally used. Note that gasket removal compounds are available to avoid scraping the components clean; make sure the gasket remover suits the type of sealant used.

8 Chains

Breaking and joining final drive chains

● Drive chains for all but small bikes are continuous and do not have a clip-type connecting link. The chain must be broken using a chain breaker tool and the new chain securely riveted together using a new soft rivet-type link. Never use a clip-type connecting link instead of a rivet-type link, except in an emergency. Various chain breaking and riveting tools are available, either as separate tools or combined as illustrated in the accompanying photographs - read the instructions supplied with the tool carefully.

> ⚠ **Warning: The need to rivet the new link pins correctly cannot be overstressed - loss of control of the motorcycle is very likely to result if the chain breaks in use.**

● Rotate the chain and look for the soft link. The soft link pins look like they have been

8.1 Tighten the chain breaker to push the pin out of the link . . .

8.2 . . . withdraw the pin, remove the tool . . .

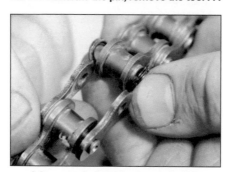

8.3 . . . and separate the chain link

deeply centre-punched instead of peened over like all the other pins **(see illustration 8.9)** and its sideplate may be a different colour. Position the soft link midway between the sprockets and assemble the chain breaker tool over one of the soft link pins **(see illustration 8.1)**. Operate the tool to push the pin out through the chain **(see illustration 8.2)**. On an O-ring chain, remove the O-rings **(see illustration 8.3)**. Carry out the same procedure on the other soft link pin.

> *Caution: Certain soft link pins (particularly on the larger chains) may require their ends to be filed or ground off before they can be pressed out using the tool.*

● Check that you have the correct size and strength (standard or heavy duty) new soft link - do not reuse the old link. Look for the size marking on the chain sideplates **(see illustration 8.10)**.

● Position the chain ends so that they are engaged over the rear sprocket. On an O-ring

8.4 Insert the new soft link, with O-rings, through the chain ends . . .

8.5 . . . install the O-rings over the pin ends . . .

8.6 . . . followed by the sideplate

chain, install a new O-ring over each pin of the link and insert the link through the two chain ends **(see illustration 8.4)**. Install a new O-ring over the end of each pin, followed by the sideplate (with the chain manufacturer's marking facing outwards) **(see illustrations 8.5 and 8.6)**. On an unsealed chain, insert the link through the two chain ends, then install the sideplate with the chain manufacturer's marking facing outwards.

● Note that it may not be possible to install the sideplate using finger pressure alone. If using a joining tool, assemble it so that the plates of the tool clamp the link and press the sideplate over the pins **(see illustration 8.7)**. Otherwise, use two small sockets placed over

8.7 Push the sideplate into position using a clamp

8.8 Assemble the chain riveting tool over one pin at a time and tighten it fully

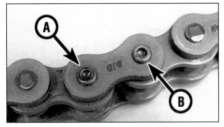

8.9 Pin end correctly riveted (A), pin end unriveted (B)

the rivet ends and two pieces of the wood between a G-clamp. Operate the clamp to press the sideplate over the pins.

● Assemble the joining tool over one pin (following the maker's instructions) and tighten the tool down to spread the pin end securely **(see illustrations 8.8 and 8.9)**. Do the same on the other pin.

 Warning: Check that the pin ends are secure and that there is no danger of the sideplate coming loose. If the pin ends are cracked the soft link must be renewed.

Final drive chain sizing

● Chains are sized using a three digit number, followed by a suffix to denote the chain type **(see illustration 8.10)**. Chain type is either standard or heavy duty (thicker sideplates), and also unsealed or O-ring/X-ring type.

● The first digit of the number relates to the pitch of the chain, ie the distance from the centre of one pin to the centre of the next pin **(see illustration 8.11)**. Pitch is expressed in eighths of an inch, as follows:

8.10 Typical chain size and type marking

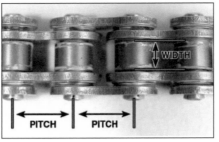

8.11 Chain dimensions

Sizes commencing with a 4 (eg 428) have a pitch of 1/2 inch (12.7 mm)

Sizes commencing with a 5 (eg 520) have a pitch of 5/8 inch (15.9 mm)

Sizes commencing with a 6 (eg 630) have a pitch of 3/4 inch (19.1 mm)

● The second and third digits of the chain size relate to the width of the rollers, again in imperial units, eg the 525 shown has 5/16 inch (7.94 mm) rollers **(see illustration 8.11)**.

9 Hoses

Clamping to prevent flow

● Small-bore flexible hoses can be clamped to prevent fluid flow whilst a component is worked on. Whichever method is used, ensure that the hose material is not permanently distorted or damaged by the clamp.

a) A brake hose clamp available from auto accessory shops **(see illustration 9.1)**.
b) A wingnut type hose clamp **(see illustration 9.2)**.

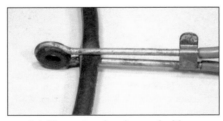

9.1 Hoses can be clamped with an automotive brake hose clamp . . .

9.2 . . . a wingnut type hose clamp . . .

c) Two sockets placed each side of the hose and held with straight-jawed self-locking grips **(see illustration 9.3)**.
d) Thick card each side of the hose held between straight-jawed self-locking grips **(see illustration 9.4)**.

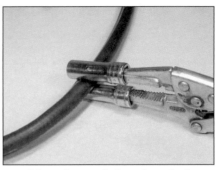

9.3 . . . two sockets and a pair of self-locking grips . . .

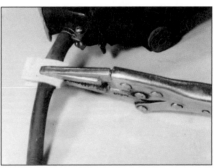

9.4 . . . or thick card and self-locking grips

Freeing and fitting hoses

● Always make sure the hose clamp is moved well clear of the hose end. Grip the hose with your hand and rotate it whilst pulling it off the union. If the hose has hardened due to age and will not move, slit it with a sharp knife and peel its ends off the union **(see illustration 9.5)**.

● Resist the temptation to use grease or soap on the unions to aid installation; although it helps the hose slip over the union it will equally aid the escape of fluid from the joint. It is preferable to soften the hose ends in hot water and wet the inside surface of the hose with water or a fluid which will evaporate.

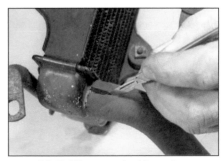

9.5 Cutting a coolant hose free with a sharp knife

Introduction

In less time than it takes to read this introduction, a thief could steal your motorcycle. Returning only to find your bike has gone is one of the worst feelings in the world. Even if the motorcycle is insured against theft, once you've got over the initial shock, you will have the inconvenience of dealing with the police and your insurance company.

The motorcycle is an easy target for the professional thief and the joyrider alike and the official figures on motorcycle theft make for depressing reading; on average a motorcycle is stolen every 16 minutes in the UK!

Motorcycle thefts fall into two categories, those stolen 'to order' and those taken by opportunists. The thief stealing to order will be on the look out for a specific make and model and will go to extraordinary lengths to obtain that motorcycle. The opportunist thief on the other hand will look for easy targets which can be stolen with the minimum of effort and risk.

Whilst it is never going to be possible to make your machine 100% secure, it is estimated that around half of all stolen motorcycles are taken by opportunist thieves. Remember that the opportunist thief is always on the look out for the easy option: if there are two similar motorcycles parked side-by-side, they will target the one with the lowest level of security. By taking a few precautions, you can reduce the chances of your motorcycle being stolen.

Security equipment

There are many specialised motorcycle security devices available and the following text summarises their applications and their good and bad points.

Once you have decided on the type of security equipment which best suits your needs, we recommended that you read one of the many equipment tests regularly carried out by the motorcycle press. These tests compare the products from all the major manufacturers and give impartial ratings on their effectiveness, value-for-money and ease of use.

No one item of security equipment can provide complete protection. It is highly recommended that two or more of the items described below are combined to increase the security of your motorcycle (a lock and chain plus an alarm system is just about ideal). The more security measures fitted to the bike, the less likely it is to be stolen.

Lock and chain

Pros: *Very flexible to use; can be used to secure the motorcycle to almost any immovable object. On some locks and chains, the lock can be used on its own as a disc lock (see below).*

Cons: *Can be very heavy and awkward to carry on the motorcycle, although some types*

will be supplied with a carry bag which can be strapped to the pillion seat.

● Heavy-duty chains and locks are an excellent security measure **(see illustration 1)**. Whenever the motorcycle is parked, use the lock and chain to secure the machine to a solid, immovable object such as a post or railings. This will prevent the machine from being ridden away or being lifted into the back of a van.

● When fitting the chain, always ensure the chain is routed around the motorcycle frame or swingarm **(see illustrations 2 and 3)**. Never merely pass the chain around one of the wheel rims; a thief may unbolt the wheel and lift the rest of the machine into a van, leaving you with just the wheel! Try to avoid having excess chain free, thus making it difficult to use cutting tools, and keep the chain and lock off the ground to prevent thieves attacking it with a cold chisel. Position the lock so that its lock barrel is facing downwards; this will make it harder for the thief to attack the lock mechanism.

Ensure the lock and chain you buy is of good quality and long enough to shackle your bike to a solid object

Figure 2: **Pass the chain through the bike's frame, rather than just through a wheel . . .**

Figure 3: **. . . and loop it around a solid object**

U-locks

Pros: *Highly effective deterrent which can be used to secure the bike to a post or railings. Most U-locks come with a carrier which allows the lock to be easily carried on the bike.*

Cons: *Not as flexible to use as a lock and chain.*

● These are solid locks which are similar in use to a lock and chain. U-locks are lighter than a lock and chain but not so flexible to use. The length and shape of the lock shackle limit the objects to which the bike can be secured **(see illustration 4)**.

U-locks can be used to secure the bike to a solid object – ensure you purchase one which is long enough

Disc locks

Pros: *Small, light and very easy to carry; most can be stored underneath the seat.*

Cons: *Does not prevent the motorcycle being lifted into a van. Can be very embarrassing if you* forget to remove the lock before attempting to ride off!

● Disc locks are designed to be attached to the front brake disc. The lock passes through one of the holes in the disc and prevents the wheel rotating by jamming against the fork/brake caliper **(see illustration 5)**. Some are equipped with an alarm siren which sounds if the disc lock is moved; this not only acts as a theft deterrent but also as a handy reminder if you try to move the bike with the lock still fitted.

● Combining the disc lock with a length of cable which can be looped around a post or railings provides an additional measure of security **(see illustration 6)**.

Alarms and immobilisers

Pros: *Once installed it is completely hassle-free to use. If the system is 'Thatcham' or 'Sold Secure-approved', insurance companies may give you a discount.*

Cons: *Can be expensive to buy and complex to install. No system will prevent the motorcycle from being lifted into a van and taken away.*

● Electronic alarms and immobilisers are available to suit a variety of budgets. There are three different types of system available: pure alarms, pure immobilisers, and the more expensive systems which are combined alarm/immobilisers **(see illustration 7)**.

● An alarm system is designed to emit an audible warning if the motorcycle is being tampered with.

● An immobiliser prevents the motorcycle being started and ridden away by disabling its electrical systems.

● When purchasing an alarm/immobiliser system, check the cost of installing the system unless you are able to do it yourself. If the motorcycle is not used regularly, another consideration is the current drain of the system. All alarm/immobiliser systems are powered by the motorcycle's battery; purchasing a system with a very low current drain could prevent the battery losing its charge whilst the motorcycle is not being used.

A typical disc lock attached through one of the holes in the disc

A disc lock combined with a security cable provides additional protection

A typical alarm/immobiliser system

Indelible markings can be applied to most areas of the bike – always apply the manufacturer's sticker to warn off thieves

Chemically-etched code numbers can be applied to main body panels . . .

. . . again, always ensure that the kit manufacturer's sticker is applied in a prominent position

Security marking kits

Pros: *Very cheap and effective deterrent. Many insurance companies will give you a discount on your insurance premium if a recognised security marking kit is used on your motorcycle.*

Cons: *Does not prevent the motorcycle being stolen by joyriders.*

● There are many different types of security marking kits available. The idea is to mark as many parts of the motorcycle as possible with a unique security number **(see illustrations 8, 9 and 10)**. A form will be included with the kit to register your personal details and those of the motorcycle with the kit manufacturer. This register is made available to the police to help them trace the rightful owner of any motorcycle or components which they recover should all other forms of identification have been removed. Always apply the warning stickers provided with the kit to deter thieves.

Ground anchors, wheel clamps and security posts

Pros: *An excellent form of security which will deter all but the most determined of thieves.*

Cons: *Awkward to install and can be expensive.*

● Whilst the motorcycle is at home, it is a good idea to attach it securely to the floor or a solid wall, even if it is kept in a securely locked garage. Various types of ground anchors, security posts and wheel clamps are available for this purpose **(see illustration 11)**. These security devices are either bolted to a solid concrete or brick structure or can be cemented into the ground.

Permanent ground anchors provide an excellent level of security when the bike is at home

Security at home

A high percentage of motorcycle thefts are from the owner's home. Here are some things to consider whenever your motorcycle is at home:

✔ Where possible, always keep the motorcycle in a securely locked garage. Never rely solely on the standard lock on the garage door, these are usual hopelessly inadequate. Fit an additional locking mechanism to the door and consider having the garage alarmed. A security light, activated by a movement sensor, is also a good investment.

✔ Always secure the motorcycle to the ground or a wall, even if it is inside a securely locked garage.
✔ Do not regularly leave the motorcycle outside your home, try to keep it out of sight wherever possible. If a garage is not available, fit a motorcycle cover over the bike to disguise its true identity.
✔ It is not uncommon for thieves to follow a motorcyclist home to find out where the bike is kept. They will then return at a later date. Be aware of this whenever you are returning

home on your motorcycle. If you suspect you are being followed, do not return home, instead ride to a garage or shop and stop as a precaution.
✔ When selling a motorcycle, do not provide your home address or the location where the bike is normally kept. Arrange to meet the buyer at a location away from your home. Thieves have been known to pose as potential buyers to find out where motorcycles are kept and then return later to steal them.

Security away from the home

As well as fitting security equipment to your motorcycle here are a few general rules to follow whenever you park your motorcycle.
✔ Park in a busy, public place.
✔ Use car parks which incorporate security features, such as CCTV.

✔ At night, park in a well-lit area, preferably directly underneath a street light.
✔ Engage the steering lock.
✔ Secure the motorcycle to a solid, immovable object such as a post or railings with an additional lock. If this is not possible,

secure the bike to a friend's motorcycle. Some public parking places provide security loops for motorcycles.
✔ Never leave your helmet or luggage attached to the motorcycle. Take them with you at all times.

Lubricants and fluids

A wide range of lubricants, fluids and cleaning agents is available for motor-cycles. This is a guide as to what is available, its applications and properties.

Four-stroke engine oil

● Engine oil is without doubt the most important component of any four-stroke engine. Modern motorcycle engines place a lot of demands on their oil and choosing the right type is essential. Using an unsuitable oil will lead to an increased rate of engine wear and could result in serious engine damage. Before purchasing oil, always check the recommended oil specification given by the manufacturer. The manufacturer will state a recommended 'type or classification' and also a specific 'viscosity' range for engine oil.

● The oil 'type or classification' is identified by its API (American Petroleum Institute) rating. The API rating will be in the form of two letters, e.g. SG. The S identifies the oil as being suitable for use in a petrol (gasoline) engine (S stands for spark ignition) and the second letter, ranging from A to J, identifies the oil's performance rating. The later this letter, the higher the specification of the oil; for example API SG oil exceeds the requirements of API SF oil. **Note:** *On some oils there may also be a second rating consisting of another two letters, the first letter being C, e.g. API SF/CD. This rating indicates the oil is also suitable for use in a diesel engines (the C stands for compression ignition) and is thus of no relevance for motorcycle use.*

● The 'viscosity' of the oil is identified by its SAE (Society of Automotive Engineers) rating. All modern engines require multigrade oils and the SAE rating will consist of two numbers, the first followed by a W, e.g. 10W/40. The first number indicates the viscosity rating of the oil at low temperatures (W stands for winter – tested at –20°C) and the second number represents the viscosity of the oil at high temperatures (tested at 100°C). The lower the number, the thinner the oil. For example an oil with an SAE 10W/40 rating will give better cold starting and running than an SAE 15W/40 oil.

● As well as ensuring the 'type' and 'viscosity' of the oil match the recommendations, another consideration to make when buying engine oil is whether to purchase a standard mineral-based oil, a semi-synthetic oil (also known as a synthetic blend or synthetic-based oil) or a fully-synthetic oil. Although all oils will have a similar rating and viscosity, their cost will vary considerably; mineral-based oils are the cheapest, the fully-synthetic oils the most expensive with the semi-synthetic oils falling somewhere in-between. This decision is very much up to the owner, but it should be noted that modern synthetic oils have far better lubricating and cleaning qualities than traditional mineral-based oils and tend to retain these properties for far longer. Bearing in mind the operating conditions inside a modern, high-revving motorcycle engine it is highly recommended that a fully synthetic oil is used. The extra expense at each service could save you money in the long term by preventing premature engine wear.

● As a final note always ensure that the oil is specifically designed for use in motorcycle engines. Engine oils designed primarily for use in car engines sometimes contain additives or friction modifiers which could cause clutch slip on a motorcycle fitted with a wet-clutch.

Two-stroke engine oil

● Modern two-stroke engines, with their high power outputs, place high demands on their oil. If engine seizure is to be avoided it is essential that a high-quality oil is used. Two-stroke oils differ hugely from four-stroke oils. The oil lubricates only the crankshaft and piston(s) (the transmission has its own lubricating oil) and is used on a total-loss basis where it is burnt completely during the combustion process.

● The Japanese have recently introduced a classification system for two-stroke oils, the JASO rating. This rating is in the form of two letters, either FA, FB or FC – FA is the lowest classification and FC the highest. Ensure the oil being used meets or exceeds the recommended rating specified by the manufacturer.

● As well as ensuring the oil rating matches the recommendation, another consideration to make when buying engine oil is whether to purchase a standard mineral-based oil, a semi-synthetic oil (also known as a synthetic blend or synthetic-based oil) or a fully-synthetic oil. The cost of each type of oil varies considerably; mineral-based oils are the cheapest, the fully-synthetic oils the most expensive with the semi-synthetic oils falling somewhere in-between. This decision is very much up to the owner, but it should be noted that modern synthetic oils have far better lubricating properties and burn cleaner than traditional mineral-based oils. It is therefore recommended that a fully synthetic oil is used. The extra expense could save you money in the long term by preventing premature engine wear, engine performance will be improved, carbon deposits and exhaust smoke will be reduced.

Lubricants and fluids

● Always ensure that the oil is specifically designed for use in an injector system. Many high quality two-stroke oils are designed for competition use and need to be pre-mixed with fuel. These oils are of a much higher viscosity and are not designed to flow through the injector pumps used on road-going two-stroke motorcycles.

Transmission (gear) oil

● On a two-stroke engine, the transmission and clutch are lubricated by their own separate oil bath which must be changed in accordance with the Maintenance Schedule.
● Although the engine and transmission units of most four-strokes use a common lubrication supply, there are some exceptions where the engine and gearbox have separate oil reservoirs and a dry clutch is used.
● Motorcycle manufacturers will either recommend a monograde transmission oil or a four-stroke multigrade engine oil to lubricate the transmission.
● Transmission oils, or gear oils as they are often called, are designed specifically for use in transmission systems. The viscosity of these oils is represented by an SAE number, but the scale of measurement applied is different to that used to grade engine oils. As a rough guide a SAE90 gear oil will be of the same viscosity as an SAE50 engine oil.

Shaft drive oil

● On models equipped with shaft final drive, the shaft drive gears are will have their own oil supply. The manufacturer will state a recommended 'type or classification' and also a specific 'viscosity' range in the same manner as for four-stroke engine oil.
● Gear oil classification is given by the number which follows the API GL (GL standing for gear lubricant) rating, the higher the number, the higher the specification of the oil, e.g. API GL5 oil is a higher specification than API GL4 oil. Ensure the oil meets or

exceeds the classification specified and is of the correct viscosity. The viscosity of gear oils is also represented by an SAE number but the scale of measurement used is different to that used to grade engine oils. As a rough guide an SAE90 gear oil will be of the same viscosity as an SAE50 engine oil.
● If the use of an EP (Extreme Pressure) gear oil is specified, ensure the oil purchased is suitable.

Fork oil and suspension fluid

● Conventional telescopic front forks are hydraulic and require fork oil to work. To ensure the forks function correctly, the fork oil must be changed in accordance with the Maintenance Schedule.
● Fork oil is available in a variety of viscosities, identified by their SAE rating; fork oil ratings vary from light (SAE 5) to heavy (SAE 30). When purchasing fork oil, ensure the viscosity rating matches that specified by the manufacturer.
● Some lubricant manufacturers also produce a range of high-quality suspension fluids which are very similar to fork oil but are designed mainly for competition use. These fluids may have a different viscosity rating system which is not to be confused with the SAE rating of normal fork oil. Refer to the manufacturer's instructions if in any doubt.

Brake and clutch fluid

● All disc brake systems and some clutch systems are hydraulically operated. To ensure correct operation, the hydraulic fluid must be changed in accordance with the Maintenance Schedule.
● Brake and clutch fluid is classified by its DOT rating with most motorcycle manufacturers specifying DOT 3 or 4 fluid. Both fluid types are glycol-based and can be mixed together without adverse effect; DOT 4 fluid exceeds the requirements of DOT 3

fluid. Although it is safe to use DOT 4 fluid in a system designed for use with DOT 3 fluid, never use DOT 3 fluid in a system which specifies the use of DOT 4 as this will adversely affect the system's performance. The type required for the system will be marked on the fluid reservoir cap.
● Some manufacturers also produce a DOT 5 hydraulic fluid. DOT 5 hydraulic fluid is silicone-based and is not compatible with the glycol-based DOT 3 and 4 fluids. Never mix DOT 5 fluid with DOT 3 or 4 fluid as this will seriously affect the performance of the hydraulic system.

Coolant/antifreeze

● When purchasing coolant/antifreeze, always ensure it is suitable for use in an aluminium engine and contains corrosion inhibitors to prevent possible blockages of the internal coolant passages of the system. As a general rule, most coolants are designed to be used neat and should not be diluted whereas antifreeze can be mixed with distilled water to provide a coolant solution of the required strength. Refer to the manufacturer's instructions on the bottle.
● Ensure the coolant is changed in accordance with the Maintenance Schedule.

Chain lube

● Chain lube is an aerosol-type spray lubricant specifically designed for use on motorcycle final drive chains. Chain lube has two functions, to minimise friction between the final drive chain and sprockets and to prevent corrosion of the chain. Regular use of a good-quality chain lube will extend the life of the drive chain and sprockets and thus maximise the power being transmitted from the transmission to the rear wheel.
● When using chain lube, always allow some time for the solvents in the lube to evaporate before riding the motorcycle. This will minimise the amount of lube which will

'fling' off from the chain when the motorcycle is used. If the motorcycle is equipped with an 'O-ring' chain, ensure the chain lube is labelled as being suitable for use on 'O-ring' chains.

Degreasers and solvents

● There are many different types of solvents and degreasers available to remove the grime and grease which accumulate around the motorcycle during normal use. Degreasers and solvents are usually available as an aerosol-type spray or as a liquid which you apply with a brush. Always closely follow the manufacturer's instructions and wear eye protection during use. Be aware that many solvents are flammable and may give off noxious fumes; take adequate precautions when using them (see Safety First!).
● For general cleaning, use one of the many solvents or degreasers available from most motorcycle accessory shops. These solvents are usually applied then left for a certain time before being washed off with water.

Brake cleaner is a solvent specifically designed to remove all traces of oil, grease and dust from braking system components. Brake cleaner is designed to evaporate quickly and leaves behind no residue.

Carburettor cleaner is an aerosol-type solvent specifically designed to clear carburettor blockages and break down the hard deposits and gum often found inside carburettors during overhaul.

Contact cleaner is an aerosol-type solvent designed for cleaning electrical components. The cleaner will remove all traces of oil and dirt from components such as switch contacts or fouled spark plugs and then dry, leaving behind no residue.

Gasket remover is an aerosol-type solvent designed for removing stubborn gaskets from engine components during overhaul. Gasket remover will minimise the amount of scraping required to remove the gasket and therefore reduce the risk of damage to the mating surface.

Spray lubricants

● Aerosol-based spray lubricants are widely available and are excellent for lubricating lever pivots and exposed cables and switches. Try to use a lubricant which is of the dry-film type as the fluid evaporates, leaving behind a dry-film of lubricant. Lubricants which leave behind an oily residue will attract dust and dirt which will increase the rate of wear of the cable/lever.

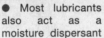

● Most lubricants also act as a moisture dispersant and a penetrating fluid. This means they can also be used to 'dry out' electrical components such as wiring connectors or switches as well as helping to free seized fasteners.

Greases

● Grease is used to lubricate many of the pivot-points. A good-quality multi-purpose grease is suitable for most applications but some manufacturers will specify the use of specialist greases for use on components such as swingarm and suspension linkage bushes. These specialist greases can be purchased from most motorcycle (or car) accessory shops; commonly specified types include molybdenum disulphide grease, lithium-based grease, graphite-based grease, silicone-based grease and high-temperature copper-based grease.

Gasket sealing compounds

● Gasket sealing compounds can be used in conjunction with gaskets, to improve their sealing capabilities, or on their own to seal metal-to-metal joints. Depending on their type, sealing compounds either set hard or stay relatively soft and pliable.

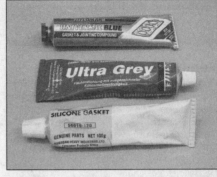

● When purchasing a gasket sealing compound, ensure that it is designed specifically for use on an internal combustion engine. General multi-purpose sealants available from DIY stores may appear visibly similar but they are not designed to withstand the extreme heat or contact with fuel and oil encountered when used on an engine (see 'Tools and Workshop Tips' for further information).

Thread locking compound

● Thread locking compounds are used to secure certain threaded fasteners in position to prevent them from loosening due to vibration. Thread locking compounds can be purchased from most motorcycle (and car) accessory shops. Ensure the threads of the both components are completely clean and dry before sparingly applying the locking compound (see 'Tools and Workshop Tips' for further information).

Fuel additives

● Fuel additives which protect and clean the fuel system components are widely available. These additives are designed to remove all traces of deposits that build up on the carburettors/injectors and prevent wear, helping the fuel system to operate more efficiently. If a fuel additive is being used, check that it is suitable for use with your motorcycle, especially if your motorcycle is equipped with a catalytic converter.

● Octane boosters are also available. These additives are designed to improve the performance of highly-tuned engines being run on normal pump-fuel and are of no real use on standard motorcycles.

Conversion Factors

Length (distance)

Inches (in)	x 25.4	= Millimetres (mm)	x 0.0394	= Inches (in)
Feet (ft)	x 0.305	= Metres (m)	x 3.281	= Feet (ft)
Miles	x 1.609	= Kilometres (km)	x 0.621	= Miles

Volume (capacity)

Cubic inches (cu in; in³)	x 16.387	= Cubic centimetres (cc; cm³)	x 0.061	= Cubic inches (cu in; in³)
Imperial pints (Imp pt)	x 0.568	= Litres (l)	x 1.76	= Imperial pints (Imp pt)
Imperial quarts (Imp qt)	x 1.137	= Litres (l)	x 0.88	= Imperial quarts (Imp qt)
Imperial quarts (Imp qt)	x 1.201	= US quarts (US qt)	x 0.833	= Imperial quarts (Imp qt)
US quarts (US qt)	x 0.946	= Litres (l)	x 1.057	= US quarts (US qt)
Imperial gallons (Imp gal)	x 4.546	= Litres (l)	x 0.22	= Imperial gallons (Imp gal)
Imperial gallons (Imp gal)	x 1.201	= US gallons (US gal)	x 0.833	= Imperial gallons (Imp gal)
US gallons (US gal)	x 3.785	= Litres (l)	x 0.264	= US gallons (US gal)

Mass (weight)

Ounces (oz)	x 28.35	= Grams (g)	x 0.035	= Ounces (oz)
Pounds (lb)	x 0.454	= Kilograms (kg)	x 2.205	= Pounds (lb)

Force

Ounces-force (ozf; oz)	x 0.278	= Newtons (N)	x 3.6	= Ounces-force (ozf; oz)
Pounds-force (lbf; lb)	x 4.448	= Newtons (N)	x 0.225	= Pounds-force (lbf; lb)
Newtons (N)	x 0.1	= Kilograms-force (kgf; kg)	x 9.81	= Newtons (N)

Pressure

Pounds-force per square inch (psi; lbf/in²; lb/in²)	x 0.070	= Kilograms-force per square centimetre (kgf/cm²; kg/cm²)	x 14.223	= Pounds-force per square inch (psi; lbf/in²; lb/in²)
Pounds-force per square inch (psi; lbf/in²; lb/in²)	x 0.068	= Atmospheres (atm)	x 14.696	= Pounds-force per square inch (psi; lbf/in²; lb/in²)
Pounds-force per square inch (psi; lbf/in²; lb/in²)	x 0.069	= Bars	x 14.5	= Pounds-force per square inch (psi; lbf/in²; lb/in²)
Pounds-force per square inch (psi; lbf/in²; lb/in²)	x 6.895	= Kilopascals (kPa)	x 0.145	= Pounds-force per square inch (psi; lbf/in²; lb/in²)
Kilopascals (kPa)	x 0.01	= Kilograms-force per square centimetre (kgf/cm²; kg/cm²)	x 98.1	= Kilopascals (kPa)
Millibar (mbar)	x 100	= Pascals (Pa)	x 0.01	= Millibar (mbar)
Millibar (mbar)	x 0.0145	= Pounds-force per square inch (psi; lbf/in²; lb/in²)	x 68.947	= Millibar (mbar)
Millibar (mbar)	x 0.75	= Millimetres of mercury (mmHg)	x 1.333	= Millibar (mbar)
Millibar (mbar)	x 0.401	= Inches of water (inH₂O)	x 2.491	= Millibar (mbar)
Millimetres of mercury (mmHg)	x 0.535	= Inches of water (inH₂O)	x 1.868	= Millimetres of mercury (mmHg)
Inches of water (inH₂O)	x 0.036	= Pounds-force per square inch (psi; lbf/in²; lb/in²)	x 27.68	= Inches of water (inH₂O)

Torque (moment of force)

Pounds-force inches (lbf in; lb in)	x 1.152	= Kilograms-force centimetre (kgf cm; kg cm)	x 0.868	= Pounds-force inches (lbf in; lb in)
Pounds-force inches (lbf in; lb in)	x 0.113	= Newton metres (Nm)	x 8.85	= Pounds-force inches (lbf in; lb in)
Pounds-force inches (lbf in; lb in)	x 0.083	= Pounds-force feet (lbf ft; lb ft)	x 12	= Pounds-force inches (lbf in; lb in)
Pounds-force feet (lbf ft; lb ft)	x 0.138	= Kilograms-force metres (kgf m; kg m)	x 7.233	= Pounds-force feet (lbf ft; lb ft)
Pounds-force feet (lbf ft; lb ft)	x 1.356	= Newton metres (Nm)	x 0.738	= Pounds-force feet (lbf ft; lb ft)
Newton metres (Nm)	x 0.102	= Kilograms-force metres (kgf m; kg m)	x 9.804	= Newton metres (Nm)

Power

Horsepower (hp)	x 745.7	= Watts (W)	x 0.0013	= Horsepower (hp)

Velocity (speed)

Miles per hour (miles/hr; mph)	x 1.609	= Kilometres per hour (km/hr; kph)	x 0.621	= Miles per hour (miles/hr; mph)

Fuel consumption*

Miles per gallon (mpg)	x 0.354	= Kilometres per litre (km/l)	x 2.825	= Miles per gallon (mpg)

Temperature

Degrees Fahrenheit = (°C x 1.8) + 32   Degrees Celsius (Degrees Centigrade; °C) = (°F - 32) x 0.56

It is common practice to convert from miles per gallon (mpg) to litres/100 kilometres (l/100km), where mpg x l/100 km = 282

About the MOT Test

In the UK, all vehicles more than three years old are subject to an annual test to ensure that they meet minimum safety requirements. A current test certificate must be issued before a machine can be used on public roads, and is required before a road fund licence can be issued. Riding without a current test certificate will also invalidate your insurance.

For most owners, the MOT test is an annual cause for anxiety, and this is largely due to owners not being sure what needs to be checked prior to submitting the motorcycle for testing. The simple answer is that a fully roadworthy motorcycle will have no difficulty in passing the test.

This is a guide to getting your motorcycle through the MOT test. Obviously it will not be possible to examine the motorcycle to the same standard as the professional MOT tester, particularly in view of the equipment required for some of the checks. However, working through the following procedures will enable you to identify any problem areas before submitting the motorcycle for the test.

It has only been possible to summarise the test requirements here, based on the regulations in force at the time of printing. Test standards are becoming increasingly stringent, although there are some exemptions for older vehicles. More information about the MOT test can be obtained from the TSO publications, *How Safe is your Motorcycle* and *The MOT Inspection Manual for Motorcycle Testing*.

Many of the checks require that one of the wheels is raised off the ground. If the motorcycle doesn't have a centre stand, note that an auxiliary stand will be required. Additionally, the help of an assistant may prove useful.

Certain exceptions apply to machines under 50 cc, machines without a lighting system, and Classic bikes - if in doubt about any of the requirements listed below seek confirmation from an MOT tester prior to submitting the motorcycle for the test.

Check that the frame number is clearly visible.

Electrical System

Lights, turn signals, horn and reflector

✔ With the ignition on, check the operation of the following electrical components. **Note:** *The electrical components on certain small-capacity machines are powered by the generator, requiring that the engine is run for this check.*

a) *Headlight and tail light. Check that both illuminate in the low and high beam switch positions.*

b) *Position lights. Check that the front position (or sidelight) and tail light illuminate in this switch position.*

c) *Turn signals. Check that all flash at the correct rate, and that the warning light(s) function correctly. Check that the turn signal switch works correctly.*

d) *Hazard warning system (where fitted). Check that all four turn signals flash in this switch position.*

e) *Brake stop light. Check that the light comes on when the front and rear brakes are independently applied. Models first used on or after 1st April 1986 must have a brake light switch on each brake.*

f) *Horn. Check that the sound is continuous and of reasonable volume.*

✔ Check that there is a red reflector on the rear of the machine, either mounted separately or as part of the tail light lens.

✔ Check the condition of the headlight, tail light and turn signal lenses.

Headlight beam height

✔ The MOT tester will perform a headlight beam height check using specialised beam setting equipment **(see illustration 1)**. This equipment will not be available to the home mechanic, but if you suspect that the headlight is incorrectly set or may have been maladjusted in the past, you can perform a rough test as follows.

✔ Position the bike in a straight line facing a brick wall. The bike must be off its stand, upright and with a rider seated. Measure the height from the ground to the centre of the headlight and mark a horizontal line on the wall at this height. Position the motorcycle 3.8 metres from the wall and draw a vertical

Headlight beam height checking equipment

line up the wall central to the centreline of the motorcycle. Switch to dipped beam and check that the beam pattern falls slightly lower than the horizontal line and to the left of the vertical line **(see illustration 2)**.

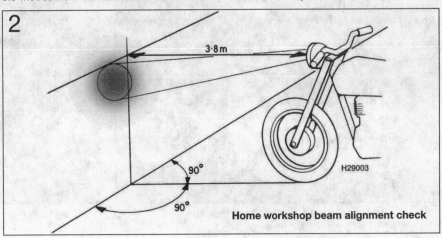

Home workshop beam alignment check

Exhaust System and Final Drive

Exhaust

✔ Check that the exhaust mountings are secure and that the system does not foul any of the rear suspension components.
✔ Start the motorcycle. When the revs are increased, check that the exhaust is neither holed nor leaking from any of its joints. On a linked system, check that the collector box is not leaking due to corrosion.

✔ Note that the exhaust decibel level ("loudness" of the exhaust) is assessed at the discretion of the tester. If the motorcycle was first used on or after 1st January 1985 the silencer must carry the BSAU 193 stamp, or a marking relating to its make and model, or be of OE (original equipment) manufacture. If the silencer is marked NOT FOR ROAD USE, RACING USE ONLY or similar, it will fail the MOT.

Final drive

✔ On chain or belt drive machines, check that the chain/belt is in good condition and does not have excessive slack. Also check that the sprocket is securely mounted on the rear wheel hub. Check that the chain/belt guard is in place.
✔ On shaft drive bikes, check for oil leaking from the drive unit and fouling the rear tyre.

Steering and Suspension

Steering

✔ With the front wheel raised off the ground, rotate the steering from lock to lock. The handlebar or switches must not contact the fuel tank or be close enough to trap the rider's hand. Problems can be caused by damaged lock stops on the lower yoke and frame, or by the fitting of non-standard handlebars.
✔ When performing the lock to lock check, also ensure that the steering moves freely without drag or notchiness. Steering movement can be impaired by poorly routed cables, or by overtight head bearings or worn bearings. The tester will perform a check of the steering head bearing lower race by mounting the front wheel on a surface plate, then performing a lock to

lock check with the weight of the machine on the lower bearing (see illustration 3).
✔ Grasp the fork sliders (lower legs) and attempt to push and pull on the forks (see

Front wheel mounted on a surface plate for steering head bearing lower race check

illustration 4). Any play in the steering head bearings will be felt. Note that in extreme cases, wear of the front fork bushes can be misinterpreted for head bearing play.
✔ Check that the handlebars are securely mounted.
✔ Check that the handlebar grip rubbers are secure. They should by bonded to the bar left end and to the throttle cable pulley on the right end.

Front suspension

✔ With the motorcycle off the stand, hold the front brake on and pump the front forks up and down (see illustration 5). Check that they are adequately damped.

Checking the steering head bearings for freeplay

Hold the front brake on and pump the front forks up and down to check operation

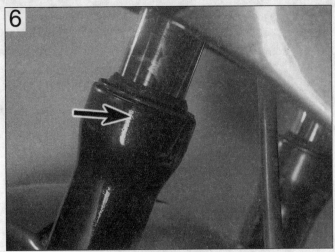

Inspect the area around the fork dust seal for oil leakage (arrow)

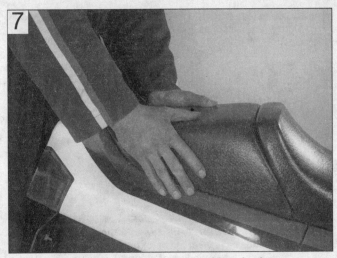

Bounce the rear of the motorcycle to check rear suspension operation

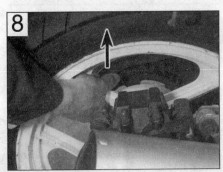

Checking for rear suspension linkage play

✔ Inspect the area above and around the front fork oil seals (see illustration 6). There should be no sign of oil on the fork tube (stanchion) nor leaking down the slider (lower leg). On models so equipped, check that there is no oil leaking from the anti-dive units.

✔ On models with swingarm front suspension, check that there is no freeplay in the linkage when moved from side to side.

Rear suspension

✔ With the motorcycle off the stand and an assistant supporting the motorcycle by its handlebars, bounce the rear suspension (see illustration 7). Check that the suspension components do not foul on any of the cycle parts and check that the shock absorber(s) provide adequate damping.

✔ Visually inspect the shock absorber(s) and check that there is no sign of oil leakage from its damper. This is somewhat restricted on certain single shock models due to the location of the shock absorber.

✔ With the rear wheel raised off the ground, grasp the wheel at the highest point and attempt to pull it up (see illustration 8). Any play in the swingarm pivot or suspension linkage bearings will be felt as movement. **Note:** *Do not confuse play with actual suspension movement.* Failure to lubricate suspension linkage bearings can lead to bearing failure (see illustration 9).

✔ With the rear wheel raised off the ground, grasp the swingarm ends and attempt to move the swingarm from side to side and forwards and backwards - any play indicates wear of the swingarm pivot bearings (see illustration 10).

Worn suspension linkage pivots (arrows) are usually the cause of play in the rear suspension

Grasp the swingarm at the ends to check for play in its pivot bearings

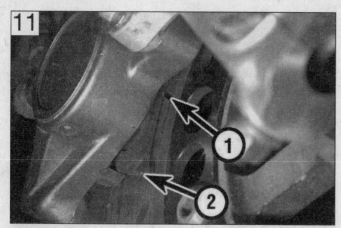

Brake pad wear can usually be viewed without removing the caliper. Most pads have wear indicator grooves (1) and some also have indicator tangs (2)

On drum brakes, check the angle of the operating lever with the brake fully applied. Most drum brakes have a wear indicator pointer and scale.

Brakes, Wheels and Tyres

Brakes

✔ With the wheel raised off the ground, apply the brake then free it off, and check that the wheel is about to revolve freely without brake drag.

✔ On disc brakes, examine the disc itself. Check that it is securely mounted and not cracked.

✔ On disc brakes, view the pad material through the caliper mouth and check that the pads are not worn down beyond the limit **(see illustration 11)**.

✔ On drum brakes, check that when the brake is applied the angle between the operating lever and cable or rod is not too great **(see illustration 12)**. Check also that the operating lever doesn't foul any other components.

✔ On disc brakes, examine the flexible hoses from top to bottom. Have an assistant hold the brake on so that the fluid in the hose is under pressure, and check that there is no sign of fluid leakage, bulges or cracking. If there are any metal brake pipes or unions, check that these are free from corrosion and damage. Where a brake-linked anti-dive system is fitted, check the hoses to the anti-dive in a similar manner.

✔ Check that the rear brake torque arm is secure and that its fasteners are secured by self-locking nuts or castellated nuts with split-pins or R-pins **(see illustration 13)**.

✔ On models with ABS, check that the self-check warning light in the instrument panel works.

✔ The MOT tester will perform a test of the motorcycle's braking efficiency based on a calculation of rider and motorcycle weight. Although this cannot be carried out at home, you can at least ensure that the braking systems are properly maintained. For hydraulic disc brakes, check the fluid level, lever/pedal feel (bleed of air if its spongy) and pad material. For drum brakes, check adjustment, cable or rod operation and shoe lining thickness.

Wheels and tyres

✔ Check the wheel condition. Cast wheels should be free from cracks and if of the built-up design, all fasteners should be secure. Spoked wheels should be checked for broken, corroded, loose or bent spokes.

✔ With the wheel raised off the ground, spin the wheel and visually check that the tyre and wheel run true. Check that the tyre does not foul the suspension or mudguards.

✔ With the wheel raised off the ground, grasp the wheel and attempt to move it about the axle (spindle) **(see illustration 14)**. Any play felt here indicates wheel bearing failure.

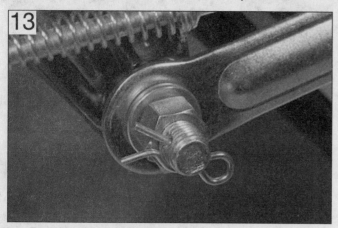

Brake torque arm must be properly secured at both ends

Check for wheel bearing play by trying to move the wheel about the axle (spindle)

Checking the tyre tread depth

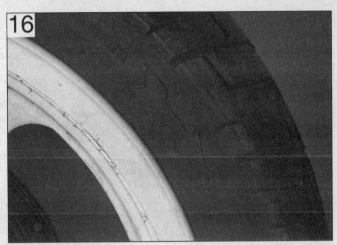

Tyre direction of rotation arrow can be found on tyre sidewall

Castellated type wheel axle (spindle) nut must be secured by a split pin or R-pin

Two straightedges are used to check wheel alignment

✔ Check the tyre tread depth, tread condition and sidewall condition (see illustration 15).
✔ Check the tyre type. Front and rear tyre types must be compatible and be suitable for road use. Tyres marked NOT FOR ROAD USE, COMPETITION USE ONLY or similar, will fail the MOT.

✔ If the tyre sidewall carries a direction of rotation arrow, this must be pointing in the direction of normal wheel rotation (see illustration 16).
✔ Check that the wheel axle (spindle) nuts (where applicable) are properly secured. A self-locking nut or castellated nut with a split-pin or R-pin can be used (see illustration 17).
✔ Wheel alignment is checked with the motorcycle off the stand and a rider seated. With the front wheel pointing straight ahead, two perfectly straight lengths of metal or wood and placed against the sidewalls of both tyres (see illustration 18). The gap each side of the front tyre must be equidistant on both sides. Incorrect wheel alignment may be due to a cocked rear wheel (often as the result of poor chain adjustment) or in extreme cases, a bent frame.

General checks and condition

✔ Check the security of all major fasteners, bodypanels, seat, fairings (where fitted) and mudguards.

✔ Check that the rider and pillion footrests, handlebar levers and brake pedal are securely mounted.

✔ Check for corrosion on the frame or any load-bearing components. If severe, this may affect the structure, particularly under stress.

Sidecars

A motorcycle fitted with a sidecar requires additional checks relating to the stability of the machine and security of attachment and swivel joints, plus specific wheel alignment (toe-in) requirements. Additionally, tyre and lighting requirements differ from conventional motorcycle use. Owners are advised to check MOT test requirements with an official test centre.

Preparing for storage

Before you start

If repairs or an overhaul is needed, see that this is carried out now rather than left until you want to ride the bike again.

Give the bike a good wash and scrub all dirt from its underside. Make sure the bike dries completely before preparing for storage.

Engine

● Remove the spark plug(s) and lubricate the cylinder bores with approximately a teaspoon of motor oil using a spout-type oil can **(see illustration 1)**. Reinstall the spark plug(s). Crank the engine over a couple of times to coat the piston rings and bores with oil. If the bike has a kickstart, use this to turn the engine over. If not, flick the kill switch to the OFF position and crank the engine over on the starter **(see illustration 2)**. If the nature on the ignition system prevents the starter operating with the kill switch in the OFF position,

remove the spark plugs and fit them back in their caps; ensure that the plugs are earthed (grounded) against the cylinder head when the starter is operated **(see illustration 3)**.

⚠ *Warning: It is important that the plugs are earthed (grounded) away from the spark plug holes otherwise there is a risk of atomised fuel from the cylinders igniting.*

> **HAYNES HINT** *On a single cylinder four-stroke engine, you can seal the combustion chamber completely by positioning the piston at TDC on the compression stroke.*

● Drain the carburettor(s) otherwise there is a risk of jets becoming blocked by gum deposits from the fuel **(see illustration 4)**.

● If the bike is going into long-term storage, consider adding a fuel stabiliser to the fuel in the tank. If the tank is drained completely, corrosion of its internal surfaces may occur if left unprotected for a long period. The tank can be treated with a rust preventative especially for this purpose. Alternatively, remove the tank and pour half a litre of motor oil into it, install the filler cap and shake the tank to coat its internals with oil before draining off the excess. The same effect can also be achieved by spraying WD40 or a similar water-dispersant around the inside of the tank via its flexible nozzle.

● Make sure the cooling system contains the correct mix of antifreeze. Antifreeze also contains important corrosion inhibitors.

● The air intakes and exhaust can be sealed off by covering or plugging the openings. Ensure that you do not seal in any condensation; run the engine until it is hot,

Squirt a drop of motor oil into each cylinder

Flick the kill switch to OFF . . .

. . . and ensure that the metal bodies of the plugs (arrows) are earthed against the cylinder head

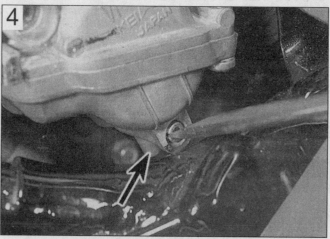

Connect a hose to the carburettor float chamber drain stub (arrow) and unscrew the drain screw

Exhausts can be sealed off with a plastic bag

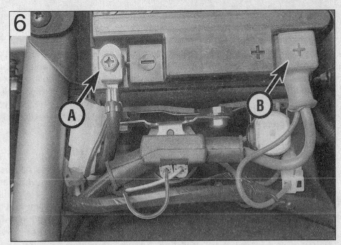

Disconnect the negative lead (A) first, followed by the positive lead (B)

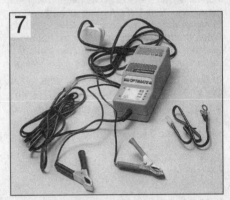

Use a suitable battery charger - this kit also assess battery condition

then switch off and allow to cool. Tape a piece of thick plastic over the silencer end(s) **(see illustration 5)**. Note that some advocate pouring a tablespoon of motor oil into the silencer(s) before sealing them off.

Battery

● Remove it from the bike - in extreme cases of cold the battery may freeze and crack its case **(see illustration 6)**.

● Check the electrolyte level and top up if necessary (conventional refillable batteries). Clean the terminals.
● Store the battery off the motorcycle and away from any sources of fire. Position a wooden block under the battery if it is to sit on the ground.
● Give the battery a trickle charge for a few hours every month **(see illustration 7)**.

Tyres

● Place the bike on its centrestand or an auxiliary stand which will support the motorcycle in an upright position. Position wood blocks under the tyres to keep them off the ground and to provide insulation from damp. If the bike is being put into long-term storage, ideally both tyres should be off the ground; not only will this protect the tyres, but will also ensure that no load is placed on the steering head or wheel bearings.
● Deflate each tyre by 5 to 10 psi, no more or the beads may unseat from the rim, making subsequent inflation difficult on tubeless tyres.

Pivots and controls

● Lubricate all lever, pedal, stand and footrest pivot points. If grease nipples are fitted to the rear suspension components, apply lubricant to the pivots.
● Lubricate all control cables.

Cycle components

● Apply a wax protectant to all painted and plastic components. Wipe off any excess, but don't polish to a shine. Where fitted, clean the screen with soap and water.
● Coat metal parts with Vaseline (petroleum jelly). When applying this to the fork tubes, do not compress the forks otherwise the seals will rot from contact with the Vaseline.
● Apply a vinyl cleaner to the seat.

Storage conditions

● Aim to store the bike in a shed or garage which does not leak and is free from damp.
● Drape an old blanket or bedspread over the bike to protect it from dust and direct contact with sunlight (which will fade paint). This also hides the bike from prying eyes. Beware of tight-fitting plastic covers which may allow condensation to form and settle on the bike.

Getting back on the road

Engine and transmission

● Change the oil and replace the oil filter. If this was done prior to storage, check that the oil hasn't emulsified - a thick whitish substance which occurs through condensation.
● Remove the spark plugs. Using a spout-type oil can, squirt a few drops of oil into the cylinder(s). This will provide initial lubrication as the piston rings and bores comes back into contact. Service the spark plugs, or fit new ones, and install them in the engine.

● Check that the clutch isn't stuck on. The plates can stick together if left standing for some time, preventing clutch operation. Engage a gear and try rocking the bike back and forth with the clutch lever held against the handlebar. If this doesn't work on cable-operated clutches, hold the clutch lever back against the handlebar with a strong elastic band or cable tie for a couple of hours **(see illustration 8)**.
● If the air intakes or silencer end(s) were blocked off, remove the bung or cover used.
● If the fuel tank was coated with a rust

Hold clutch lever back against the handlebar with elastic bands or a cable tie

preventative, oil or a stabiliser added to the fuel, drain and flush the tank and dispose of the fuel sensibly. If no action was taken with the fuel tank prior to storage, it is advised that the old fuel is disposed of since it will go off over a period of time. Refill the fuel tank with fresh fuel.

Frame and running gear

● Oil all pivot points and cables.
● Check the tyre pressures. They will definitely need inflating if pressures were reduced for storage.
● Lubricate the final drive chain (where applicable).
● Remove any protective coating applied to the fork tubes (stanchions) since this may well destroy the fork seals. If the fork tubes weren't protected and have picked up rust spots, remove them with very fine abrasive paper and refinish with metal polish.
● Check that both brakes operate correctly. Apply each brake hard and check that it's not possible to move the motorcycle forwards, then check that the brake frees off again once released. Brake caliper pistons can stick due to corrosion around the piston head, or on the sliding caliper types, due to corrosion of the slider pins. If the brake doesn't free after repeated operation, take the caliper off for examination. Similarly drum brakes can stick

due to a seized operating cam, cable or rod linkage.
● If the motorcycle has been in long-term storage, renew the brake fluid and clutch fluid (where applicable).
● Depending on where the bike has been stored, the wiring, cables and hoses may have been nibbled by rodents. Make a visual check and investigate disturbed wiring loom tape.

Battery

● If the battery has been previously removal and given top up charges it can simply be reconnected. Remember to connect the positive cable first and the negative cable last.
● On conventional refillable batteries, if the battery has not received any attention, remove it from the motorcycle and check its electrolyte level. Top up if necessary then charge the battery. If the battery fails to hold a charge and a visual checks show heavy white sulphation of the plates, the battery is probably defective and must be renewed. This is particularly likely if the battery is old. Confirm battery condition with a specific gravity check.
● On sealed (MF) batteries, if the battery has not received any attention, remove it from the motorcycle and charge it according to the information on the battery case - if the battery fails to hold a charge it must be renewed.

Starting procedure

● If a kickstart is fitted, turn the engine over a couple of times with the ignition OFF to distribute oil around the engine. If no kickstart is fitted, flick the engine kill switch OFF and the ignition ON and crank the engine over a couple of times to work oil around the upper cylinder components. If the nature of the ignition system is such that the starter won't work with the kill switch OFF, remove the spark plugs, fit them back into their caps and earth (ground) their bodies on the cylinder head. Reinstall the spark plugs afterwards.
● Switch the kill switch to RUN, operate the choke and start the engine. If the engine won't start don't continue cranking the engine - not only will this flatten the battery, but the starter motor will overheat. Switch the ignition off and try again later. If the engine refuses to start, go through the fault finding procedures in this manual. **Note:** *If the bike has been in storage for a long time, old fuel or a carburettor blockage may be the problem. Gum deposits in carburettors can block jets - if a carburettor cleaner doesn't prove successful the carburettors must be dismantled for cleaning.*

● Once the engine has started, check that the lights, turn signals and horn work properly.

● Treat the bike gently for the first ride and check all fluid levels on completion. Settle the bike back into the maintenance schedule.

This Section provides an easy reference-guide to the more common faults that are likely to afflict your machine. Obviously, the opportunities are almost limitless for faults to occur as a result of obscure failures, and to try and cover all eventualities would require a book. Indeed, a number have been written on the subject.

Successful troubleshooting is not a mysterious 'black art' but the application of a bit of knowledge combined with a systematic and logical approach to the problem. Approach any troubleshooting by first accurately identifying the symptom and then checking through the list of possible causes, starting with the simplest or most obvious and progressing in stages to the most complex.

Take nothing for granted, but above all apply liberal quantities of common sense.

The main symptom of a fault is given in the text as a major heading below which are listed the various systems or areas which may contain the fault. Details of each possible cause for a fault and the remedial action to be taken are given, in brief, in the paragraphs below each heading. Further information should be sought in the relevant Chapter.

1 Engine doesn't start or is difficult to start

- ☐ Starter motor does not rotate
- ☐ Starter motor rotates but engine does not turn over
- ☐ Starter works but engine won't turn over (seized)
- ☐ No fuel flow
- ☐ Engine flooded
- ☐ No spark or weak spark
- ☐ Compression low
- ☐ Stalls after starting
- ☐ Rough idle

2 Poor running at low speed

- ☐ Spark weak
- ☐ Fuel/air mixture incorrect
- ☐ Compression low
- ☐ Poor acceleration

3 Poor running or no power at high speed

- ☐ Firing incorrect
- ☐ Fuel/air mixture incorrect
- ☐ Compression low
- ☐ Knocking or pinking
- ☐ Miscellaneous causes

4 Overheating

- ☐ Cooling system not operating properly
- ☐ Firing incorrect
- ☐ Fuel/air mixture incorrect
- ☐ Compression too high
- ☐ Engine load excessive
- ☐ Lubrication inadequate
- ☐ Miscellaneous causes

5 Clutch problems

- ☐ Clutch slipping
- ☐ Clutch not disengaging completely

6 Gearchanging problems

- ☐ Doesn't go into gear, or lever doesn't return
- ☐ Jumps out of gear
- ☐ Overselects

7 Abnormal engine noise

- ☐ Knocking or pinking
- ☐ Piston slap or rattling
- ☐ Valve noise
- ☐ Other noise

8 Abnormal driveline noise

- ☐ Clutch noise
- ☐ Transmission noise
- ☐ Chain or final drive noise

9 Abnormal frame and suspension noise

- ☐ Front end noise
- ☐ Shock absorber noise
- ☐ Disc brake noise

10 Oil pressure warning light comes on

- ☐ Engine lubrication system
- ☐ Electrical system

11 Excessive exhaust smoke

- ☐ White smoke
- ☐ Black smoke
- ☐ Brown smoke

12 Poor handling or stability

- ☐ Handlebar hard to turn
- ☐ Handlebar shakes or vibrates excessively
- ☐ Handlebar pulls to one side
- ☐ Poor shock absorbing qualities

13 Braking problems

- ☐ Brakes are spongy, don't hold
- ☐ Brake lever pulsates
- ☐ Brakes drag

14 Electrical problems

- ☐ Battery dead or weak
- ☐ Battery overcharged

1 Engine doesn't start or is difficult to start

Starter motor does not rotate

- [ ] Engine stop switch Off.
- [ ] Fuse blown. Check main fuse (Chapter 9).
- [ ] Battery voltage low. Check and recharge battery (Chapter 9).
- [ ] Starter motor defective. Make sure the wiring to the starter is secure. Make sure the starter relay clicks when the start button is pushed. If the relay clicks, then the fault is in the wiring or motor.
- [ ] Starter relay or starter circuit relay faulty. Check it according to the procedure in Chapter 9.
- [ ] Starter button not contacting. The contacts could be wet, corroded or dirty. Disassemble and clean the switch (Chapter 9).
- [ ] Wiring open or shorted. Check all wiring connections and harnesses to make sure that they are dry, tight and not corroded. Also check for broken or frayed wires that can cause a short to earth (see wiring diagram, Chapter 9).
- [ ] Ignition switch defective. Check the switch according to the procedure in Chapter 9. Renew the switch if it is defective.
- [ ] Engine stop switch defective. Check for wet, dirty or corroded contacts. Clean or renew the switch as necessary (Chapter 9).
- [ ] Faulty clutch switch, neutral switch or sidestand switch. Check the wiring to the switch and the switch itself according to the procedures in Chapter 9.

Starter motor rotates but engine does not turn over

- [ ] Starter motor clutch defective. Inspect and repair or renew (Chapter 2).
- [ ] Damaged idler or starter gears. Inspect and renew the damaged parts (Chapter 2).

Starter works but engine won't turn over (seized)

- [ ] Seized engine caused by one or more internally damaged components. Failure due to wear, abuse or lack of lubrication. Damage can include seized valves, valve lifters, camshaft, pistons, crankshaft, connecting rod bearings, or transmission gears or bearings. Refer to Chapter 2 for engine disassembly.

No fuel flow

- [ ] No fuel in tank.
- [ ] Fuel tap vacuum hose broken or disconnected.
- [ ] Tank cap air vent obstructed. Usually caused by dirt or water. Remove it and clean the cap vent hole.
- [ ] Fuel tap clogged. Remove the tap and clean it and the filter – EX models (Chapter 4). On ER models clean the two fuel filters in the base of the fuel tank.
- [ ] Fuel line clogged. Pull the fuel line loose and carefully blow through it.
- [ ] Inlet needle valves clogged. For both the valves to be clogged, either a very bad batch of fuel with an unusual additive has been used, or some other foreign object has entered the tank. Many times after a machine has been stored for many months without running, the fuel turns to a varnish-like liquid and forms deposits on the inlet needle valves and jets. The carburettors should be removed and overhauled if draining the float bowls does not alleviate the problem.

Engine flooded

- [ ] Float level too high. Check and adjust as described in Chapter 4.
- [ ] Inlet needle valve worn or stuck open. A piece of dirt, rust or other debris can cause the inlet needle to seat improperly, causing excess fuel to be admitted to the float bowl. In this case, the float chamber should be cleaned and the needle and seat inspected. If the needle and seat are worn, then the leaking will persist and the parts should be renewed (Chapter 4).
- [ ] Starting technique incorrect. Under normal circumstances (ie, if all the carburettor functions are sound) the machine should start with little or no throttle. When the engine is cold, the choke should be operated and the engine started without opening the throttle. When the engine is at operating temperature, only a very slight amount of throttle should be necessary. If the engine is flooded, turn the fuel tap off and hold the throttle open while cranking the engine. This will allow additional air to reach the cylinders. Remember to turn the fuel tap back on after the engine starts.

No spark or weak spark

- [ ] Ignition switch Off.
- [ ] Engine stop switch turned to the Off position.
- [ ] Ignition circuit fuse blown. Check fuse (Chapter 9).
- [ ] Battery voltage low. Check and recharge battery as necessary (Chapter 9).
- [ ] Spark plugs dirty, defective or worn out. Locate reason for fouled plug(s) using spark plug condition chart on the inside rear cover and follow the plug maintenance procedures in Chapter 1.
- [ ] Spark plug cap or HT lead faulty. Check condition. Renew either or both components if cracks or deterioration are evident (Chapter 5).
- [ ] Spark plug cap not making good contact. Make sure that the plug cap fits snugly over the plug end.
- [ ] IC igniter defective. Check the unit, referring to Chapter 5 for details.
- [ ] Pick-up coil defective. Check the unit, referring to Chapter 5 for details.
- [ ] Ignition HT coil(s) defective. Check the coils, referring to Chapter 5.
- [ ] Ignition or stop switch shorted. This is usually caused by water, corrosion, damage or excessive wear. The switches can be disassembled and cleaned with electrical contact cleaner. If cleaning does not help, renew the switches (Chapter 9).
- [ ] Wiring shorted or broken between:
  - a) Ignition switch and engine stop switch
  - b) IC igniter and engine stop switch
  - c) IC igniter and ignition coil
  - d) Ignition coil and plug
  - e) IC igniter and pick-up coils
- [ ] Make sure that all wiring connections are clean, dry and tight. Look for chafed and broken wires (Chapters 5 and 8).

Compression low

- [ ] Spark plug loose. Remove the plug and inspect the threads. Reinstall and tighten to the specified torque (Chapter 1).
- [ ] Cylinder head not sufficiently tightened down. If the cylinder head is suspected of being loose, then there's a chance that the gasket or head is damaged if the problem has persisted for any length of time. The head bolts should be tightened to the proper torque in the correct sequence (Chapter 2).
- [ ] Improper valve clearance. This means that the valve is not closing completely and compression pressure is leaking past the valve. Check and adjust the valve clearances (Chapter 1).
- [ ] Cylinder and/or piston worn. Excessive wear will cause compression pressure to leak past the rings. This is usually accompanied by worn rings as well. A top-end overhaul is necessary (Chapter 2).
- [ ] Piston rings worn, weak, broken, or sticking. Broken or sticking piston rings usually indicate a lubrication or carburetion problem that causes excess carbon deposits or seizures to form on the pistons and rings. Top-end overhaul is necessary (Chapter 2).
- [ ] Piston ring-to-groove clearance excessive. This is caused by excessive wear of the piston ring lands. Piston renewal is necessary (Chapter 2).
- [ ] Cylinder head gasket damaged. If the head is allowed to become loose, or if excessive carbon build-up on the piston crown and combustion chamber causes extremely high compression, the head gasket may leak. Retorquing the head is not always sufficient to restore the seal, so gasket renewal is necessary (Chapter 2).

1 Engine doesn't start or is difficult to start (continued)

☐ Cylinder head warped. This is caused by overheating or improperly tightened head bolts. Machine shop resurfacing or head renewal is necessary (Chapter 2).

☐ Valve spring broken or weak. Caused by component failure or wear; the spring(s) must be renewed (Chapter 2).

☐ Valve not seating properly. This is caused by a bent valve (from over-revving or improper valve adjustment), burned valve or seat (improper carburetion) or an accumulation of carbon deposits on the seat (from carburetion, lubrication problems). The valves must be cleaned and/or renewed and the seats serviced if possible (Chapter 2).

Stalls after starting

☐ Improper choke action. Make sure the choke linkage rod is getting a full stroke and staying in the 'out' position. Adjustment of the cable slack is covered in Chapter 1.

☐ Ignition malfunction. See Chapter 5.

☐ Carburettor malfunction. See Chapter 4.

☐ Fuel contaminated. The fuel can be contaminated with either dirt or water, or can change chemically if the machine is allowed to sit for several months or more. Drain the tank and float bowls (Chapter 4).

☐ Inlet air leak. Check for loose carburettor-to-inlet manifold connections, loose or missing vacuum gauge access port cap or hose, or loose carburettor top (Chapter 4).

☐ Idle speed incorrect. Turn throttle stop screw until the engine idles at the specified rpm (Chapters 1 and 4).

Rough idle

☐ Ignition malfunction. See Chapter 5.

☐ Idle speed incorrect. See Chapter 1.

☐ Carburettors not synchronised. Adjust carburettors with vacuum gauge set or manometer as outlined in Chapter 1.

☐ Carburettor malfunction. See Chapter 4.

☐ Fuel contaminated. The fuel can be contaminated with either dirt or water, or can change chemically if the machine is allowed to sit for several months or more. Drain the tank and float bowls. If the problem is severe, a carburettor overhaul may be necessary (Chapters 1 and 4).

☐ Inlet air leak.

☐ Air cleaner clogged. Clean or renew air filter element (Chapter 1).

2 Poor running at low speed

Spark weak

☐ Battery voltage low. Check and recharge battery (Chapter 9).

☐ Spark plugs fouled, defective or worn out. Refer to Chapter 1 for spark plug maintenance.

☐ Spark plug cap or HT lead defective. Refer to Chapters 1 and 5 for details on the ignition system.

☐ Spark plug cap not making contact.

☐ Incorrect spark plug. Wrong type, heat range or cap configuration. Check and install correct plugs listed in Chapter 1. A cold plug or one with a recessed firing electrode will not operate at low speeds without fouling.

☐ IC igniter defective. See Chapter 5.

☐ Pick-up coil defective. See Chapter 5.

☐ Ignition HT coil(s) defective. See Chapter 5.

Fuel/air mixture incorrect

☐ Pilot screw(s) out of adjustment (Chapters 1 and 4).

☐ Pilot jet or air passage clogged. Remove and overhaul the carburettors (Chapter 4).

☐ Air bleed holes clogged. Remove carburettor and blow out all passages (Chapter 4).

☐ Air cleaner clogged, poorly sealed or missing.

☐ Air cleaner-to-carburettor boot poorly sealed. Look for cracks, holes or loose clamps and renew or repair defective parts.

☐ Fuel level too high or too low. Adjust the floats (Chapter 4).

☐ Fuel tank air vent obstructed. Make sure that the air vent passage in the filler cap is open.

☐ Carburettor inlet manifolds loose. Check for cracks, breaks, tears or loose clamps or bolts. Repair or renew the rubber boots.

Compression low

☐ Spark plug loose. Remove the plug and inspect the threads. Reinstall and tighten to the specified torque (Chapter 1).

☐ Cylinder head not sufficiently tightened down. If the cylinder head is suspected of being loose, then there's a chance that the gasket and head are damaged if the problem has persisted for any length of time. The head bolts should be tightened to the proper torque in the correct sequence (Chapter 2).

☐ Improper valve clearance. This means that the valve is not closing completely and compression pressure is leaking past the valve. Check and adjust the valve clearances (Chapter 1).

☐ Cylinder and/or piston worn. Excessive wear will cause compression pressure to leak past the rings. This is usually accompanied by worn rings as well. A top-end overhaul is necessary (Chapter 2).

☐ Piston rings worn, weak, broken, or sticking. Broken or sticking piston rings usually indicate a lubrication or carburetion problem that causes excess carbon deposits or seizures to form on the pistons and rings. Top-end overhaul is necessary (Chapter 2).

☐ Piston ring-to-groove clearance excessive. This is caused by excessive wear of the piston ring lands. Piston renewal is necessary (Chapter 2).

☐ Cylinder head gasket damaged. If the head is allowed to become loose, or if excessive carbon build-up on the piston crown and combustion chamber causes extremely high compression, the head gasket may leak. Retorquing the head is not always sufficient to restore the seal, so gasket renewal is necessary (Chapter 2).

☐ Cylinder head warped. This is caused by overheating or improperly tightened head bolts. Machine shop resurfacing or head renewal is necessary (Chapter 2).

☐ Valve spring broken or weak. Caused by component failure or wear; the spring(s) must be renewed (Chapter 2).

☐ Valve not seating properly. This is caused by a bent valve (from over-revving or improper valve adjustment), burned valve or seat (improper carburetion) or an accumulation of carbon deposits on the seat (from carburetion, lubrication problems). The valves must be cleaned and/or renewed and the seats serviced if possible (Chapter 2).

Poor acceleration

☐ Carburettors leaking or dirty. Overhaul the carburettors (Chapter 4).

☐ Timing not advancing. The pick-up coil unit or the IC igniter may be defective. If so, they must be renewed, as they cannot be repaired.

☐ Carburettors not synchronised. Adjust them with a vacuum gauge set or manometer (Chapter 1).

☐ Engine oil viscosity too high. Using a heavier oil than that recommended in Chapter 1 can damage the oil pump or lubrication system and cause drag on the engine.

☐ Brakes dragging. Usually caused by debris which has entered the brake piston sealing boot or from a warped disc (or from a sticking brake operating cam on drum brakes). Repair as necessary (Chapter 7).

3 Poor running or no power at high speed

Firing incorrect

☐ Air filter restricted. Clean or renew filter (Chapter 1).
☐ Spark plugs fouled, defective or worn out. See Chapter 1 for spark plug maintenance.
☐ Spark plug cap or HT lead defective. See Chapters 1 and 5 for details on the ignition system.
☐ Spark plug cap not in good contact. See Chapter 5.
☐ Incorrect spark plug. Wrong type, heat range or cap configuration. Check and install correct plugs listed in Chapter 1. A cold plug or one with a recessed firing electrode will not operate at low speeds without fouling.
☐ IC igniter defective. See Chapter 5.
☐ Ignition HT coil(s) defective. See Chapter 5.

Fuel/air mixture incorrect

☐ Main jet clogged. Dirt, water and other contaminants can clog the main jets. Clean the fuel tap filter (or tank filters on ER models), the float bowl area, and the jets and carburettor orifices (Chapter 4).
☐ Main jet wrong size. The standard jetting is for sea level atmospheric pressure and oxygen content.
☐ Throttle shaft-to-carburettor body clearance excessive. Refer to Chapter 4 for inspection and part replacement procedures.
☐ Air bleed holes clogged. Remove and overhaul carburettors (Chapter 4).
☐ Air cleaner clogged, poorly sealed or missing.
☐ Air cleaner-to-carburettor boot poorly sealed. Look for cracks, holes or loose clamps, and renew or repair defective parts.
☐ Fuel level too high or too low. Adjust the float(s) (Chapter 4).
☐ Fuel tank air vent obstructed. Make sure the air vent passage in the filler cap is open.
☐ Carburettor inlet manifolds loose. Check for cracks, breaks, tears or loose clamps or bolts. Repair or renew the rubber boots (Chapter 2).
☐ Fuel tap clogged. Remove the tap and clean it and the filter – EX models (Chapter 1). On ER models clean the filters in the base of the fuel tank.
☐ Fuel line clogged. Pull the fuel line loose and carefully blow through it.

Compression low

☐ Spark plug loose. Remove the plug and inspect the threads. Reinstall and tighten to the specified torque (Chapter 1).
☐ Cylinder head not sufficiently tightened down. If the cylinder head is suspected of being loose, then there's a chance that the gasket and head are damaged if the problem has persisted for any length of time. The head bolts should be tightened to the proper torque in the correct sequence (Chapter 2).
☐ Improper valve clearance. This means that the valve is not closing completely and compression pressure is leaking past the valve. Check and adjust the valve clearances (Chapter 1).
☐ Cylinder and/or piston worn. Excessive wear will cause compression pressure to leak past the rings. This is usually accompanied by worn rings as well. A top-end overhaul is necessary (Chapter 2).

☐ Piston rings worn, weak, broken, or sticking. Broken or sticking piston rings usually indicate a lubrication or carburetion problem that causes excess carbon deposits or seizures to form on the pistons and rings. Top-end overhaul is necessary (Chapter 2).
☐ Piston ring-to-groove clearance excessive. This is caused by excessive wear of the piston ring lands. Piston renewal is necessary (Chapter 2).
☐ Cylinder head gasket damaged. If the head is allowed to become loose, or if excessive carbon build-up on the piston crown and combustion chamber causes extremely high compression, the head gasket may leak. Retorquing the head is not always sufficient to restore the seal, so gasket renewal is necessary (Chapter 2).
☐ Cylinder head warped. This is caused by overheating or improperly tightened head bolts. Machine shop resurfacing or head renewal is necessary (Chapter 2).
☐ Valve spring broken or weak. Caused by component failure or wear; the spring(s) must be renewed (Chapter 2).
☐ Valve not seating properly. This is caused by a bent valve (from over-revving or improper valve adjustment), burned valve or seat (improper carburetion) or an accumulation of carbon deposits on the seat (from carburetion, lubrication problems). The valves must be cleaned and/or renewed and the seats serviced if possible (Chapter 2).

Knocking or pinking

☐ Carbon build-up in combustion chamber. Use of a fuel additive that will dissolve the adhesive bonding the carbon particles to the crown and chamber is the easiest way to remove the build-up. Otherwise, the cylinder head will have to be removed and decarbonised (Chapter 2).
☐ Incorrect or poor quality fuel. Old or improper grades of gasoline can cause detonation. This causes the piston to rattle, thus the knocking or pinking sound. Drain old fuel and always use the recommended fuel grade.
☐ Spark plug heat range incorrect. Uncontrolled detonation indicates the plug heat range is too hot. The plug in effect becomes a glow plug, raising cylinder temperatures. Install the proper heat range plug (Chapter 1).
☐ Improper air/fuel mixture. This will cause the cylinder to run hot, which leads to detonation. Clogged jets or an air leak can cause this imbalance. See Chapter 4.

Miscellaneous causes

☐ Throttle valve doesn't open fully. Adjust the cable slack (Chapter 1).
☐ Clutch slipping. Caused by a cable that is improperly adjusted or snagging or damaged, loose or worn clutch components. Refer to Chapters 1 and 2 for adjustment and overhaul procedures.
☐ Timing not advancing.
☐ Engine oil viscosity too high. Using a heavier oil than the one recommended in Chapter 1 can damage the oil pump or lubrication system and cause drag on the engine.
☐ Brakes dragging. Usually caused by debris which has entered the brake piston sealing boot or from a warped disc (disc brakes) or from a sticking operating cam (drum brakes). Repair as necessary.

4 Overheating

Cooling system not operating properly

- ☐ Coolant level low. Check coolant level as described in Chapter 1. If coolant level is low, the engine will overheat.
- ☐ Leak in cooling system. Check cooling system hoses and radiator for leaks and other damage. Repair or renew parts as necessary (Chapter 3).
- ☐ Thermostat sticking open or closed. Check/or renew as described in Chapter 3.
- ☐ Faulty radiator cap. Remove the cap and have it pressure checked by a Kawasaki dealer.
- ☐ Coolant passages clogged. Drain and flush the entire system, then refill with new coolant.
- ☐ Water pump defective. Remove the pump and check the components.
- ☐ Clogged radiator fins. Clean them by blowing compressed air through the fins from the back side.

Firing incorrect

- ☐ Spark plugs fouled, defective or worn out. See Chapter 1 for spark plug maintenance.
- ☐ Incorrect spark plug.
- ☐ Faulty ignition HT coils (Chapter 5).

Fuel/air mixture incorrect

- ☐ Main jet clogged. Dirt, water and other contaminants can clog the main jets. Clean the fuel tap filter (and the fuel tank filters on ER models), the float bowl area and the jets and carburettor orifices (Chapter 4).
- ☐ Main jet wrong size. The standard jetting is for sea level atmospheric pressure and oxygen content.
- ☐ Air cleaner poorly sealed or missing.
- ☐ Air cleaner-to-carburettor boot poorly sealed. Look for cracks, holes or loose clamps and renew or repair.
- ☐ Fuel level too low. Adjust the float(s) (Chapter 4).
- ☐ Fuel tank air vent obstructed. Make sure that the air vent passage in the filler cap is open.
- ☐ Carburettor inlet manifolds loose. Check for cracks, breaks, tears or loose clamps or bolts. Repair or renew the rubber boots (Chapter 2).

Compression too high

- ☐ Carbon build-up in combustion chamber. Use of a fuel additive that will dissolve the adhesive bonding the carbon particles to the piston crown and chamber is the easiest way to remove the build-up. Otherwise, the cylinder head will have to be removed and decarbonised (Chapter 2).
- ☐ Improperly machined head surface or installation of incorrect gasket during engine assembly. Check Specifications (Chapter 2).

Engine load excessive

- ☐ Clutch slipping. Caused by an out of adjustment or snagging cable or damaged, loose or worn clutch components. Refer to Chapters 1 and 2 for adjustment and overhaul procedures.
- ☐ Engine oil level too high. The addition of too much oil will cause pressurisation of the crankcase and inefficient engine operation. Check Specifications and drain to proper level (Chapter 1).
- ☐ Engine oil viscosity too high. Using a heavier oil than the one recommended in Chapter 1 can damage the oil pump or lubrication system as well as cause drag on the engine.
- ☐ Brakes dragging. Usually caused by debris which has entered the brake piston sealing boot or from a warped disc (disc brakes) or by a sticking operating cam (drum brakes). Repair as necessary.

Lubrication inadequate

- ☐ Engine oil level too low. Friction caused by intermittent lack of lubrication or from oil that is 'overworked' can cause overheating. The oil provides a definite cooling function in the engine. Check the oil level (Chapter 1).
- ☐ Poor quality engine oil or incorrect viscosity or type. Oil is rated not only according to viscosity but also according to type. Some oils are not rated high enough for use in this engine. Check the Specifications section and change to the correct oil (Chapter 1).

Miscellaneous causes

- ☐ Modification to exhaust system. Most aftermarket exhaust systems cause the engine to run leaner, which make them run hotter. When installing an accessory exhaust system, always rejet the carburettors.

5 Clutch problems

Clutch slipping

- ☐ No clutch lever play. Adjust clutch lever freeplay according to the procedure in Chapter 1.
- ☐ Friction plates worn or warped. Overhaul the clutch assembly (Chapter 2).
- ☐ Steel plates worn or warped (Chapter 2).
- ☐ Clutch springs broken or weak. Old or heat-damaged (from slipping clutch) springs should be renewed (Chapter 2).
- ☐ Clutch release not adjusted properly. See Chapter 1.
- ☐ Clutch inner cable hanging up. Caused by a frayed cable or kinked outer cable. Renew the cable. Repair of a frayed cable is not advised.
- ☐ Clutch release mechanism defective. Check the shaft, cam, actuating arm and pivot. Renew any defective parts (Chapter 2).
- ☐ Clutch hub or housing unevenly worn. This causes improper engagement of the discs. Renew the damaged or worn parts (Chapter 2).

Clutch not disengaging completely

- ☐ Clutch lever play excessive. Adjust at bars or at engine (Chapter 1).

- ☐ Clutch plates warped or damaged. This will cause clutch drag, which in turn causes the machine to creep. Overhaul the clutch assembly (Chapter 2).
- ☐ Clutch spring tension uneven. Usually caused by a sagged or broken spring. Check and renew the springs (Chapter 2).
- ☐ Engine oil deteriorated. Old, thin, worn out oil will not provide proper lubrication for the discs, causing the clutch to drag. Renew the oil and filter (Chapter 1).
- ☐ Engine oil viscosity too high. Using a heavier oil than recommended in Chapter 1 can cause the plates to stick together, putting a drag on the engine. Change to the correct weight oil (Chapter 1).
- ☐ Clutch housing seized on shaft. Lack of lubrication, severe wear or damage can cause the housing to seize on the shaft. Overhaul of the clutch, and perhaps transmission, may be necessary to repair damage (Chapter 2).
- ☐ Clutch release mechanism defective. Worn or damaged release mechanism parts can stick and fail to apply force to the pressure plate. Overhaul the clutch cover components (Chapter 2).
- ☐ Loose clutch hub nut. Causes housing and hub misalignment putting a drag on the engine. Engagement adjustment continually varies. Overhaul the clutch assembly (Chapter 2).

6 Gearchanging problems

Doesn't go into gear or lever doesn't return

- [ ] Clutch not disengaging. See Section 5.
- [ ] Selector fork(s) bent or seized. Often caused by dropping the machine or from lack of lubrication. Overhaul the transmission (Chapter 2).
- [ ] Gear(s) stuck on shaft. Most often caused by a lack of lubrication or excessive wear in transmission bearings and bushings. Overhaul the transmission (Chapter 2).
- [ ] Selector drum binding. Caused by lubrication failure or excessive wear. Renew the drum and bearings (Chapter 2).
- [ ] Gearchange lever return spring weak or broken (Chapter 2).
- [ ] Gearchange lever broken. Splines stripped out of lever or shaft, caused by allowing the lever to get loose or from dropping the machine. Renew necessary parts (Chapter 2).
- [ ] Gearchange mechanism arm claw ends broken or worn. Full engagement of gears difficult. Renew the shaft assembly (Chapter 2).
- [ ] Gearchange mechanism arm spring broken. Allows arm to 'float', causing sporadic operation. Renew the spring (Chapter 2).

Jumps out of gear

- [ ] Selector fork(s) worn. Overhaul the transmission (Chapter 2).
- [ ] Gear groove(s) worn. Overhaul the transmission (Chapter 2).
- [ ] Gear dogs or dog slots worn or damaged. The gears should be inspected and renewed. No attempt should be made to service the worn parts.

Overselects

- [ ] Selector drum gear positioning lever not functioning or spring broken (Chapter 2).

7 Abnormal engine noise

Knocking or pinking

- [ ] Carbon build-up in combustion chamber. Use of a fuel additive that will dissolve the adhesive bonding the carbon particles to the piston crown and chamber is the easiest way to remove the build-up. Otherwise, the cylinder head will have to be removed and decarbonised (Chapter 2).
- [ ] Incorrect or poor quality fuel. Old or improper fuel can cause detonation. This causes the piston to rattle, thus the knocking or pinking sound. Drain the old fuel and always use the recommended grade fuel (Chapter 4).
- [ ] Spark plug heat range incorrect. Uncontrolled detonation indicates that the plug heat range is too hot. The plug in effect becomes a glow plug, raising cylinder temperatures. Install the proper heat range plug (Chapter 1).
- [ ] Improper air/fuel mixture. This will cause the cylinder to run hot and lead to detonation. Clogged jets or an air leak can cause this imbalance. See Chapter 4.

Piston slap or rattling

- [ ] Cylinder-to-piston clearance excessive. Caused by improper assembly. Inspect and overhaul top-end parts (Chapter 2).
- [ ] Connecting rod bent. Caused by over-revving, trying to start a badly flooded engine or from ingesting a foreign object into the combustion chamber. Renew the damaged parts (Chapter 2).
- [ ] Piston pin or piston pin bore worn or seized from wear or lack of lubrication. Renew damaged parts (Chapter 2).
- [ ] Piston ring(s) worn, broken or sticking. Overhaul the top end (Chapter 2).
- [ ] Piston seizure damage. Usually from lack of lubrication or overheating. Renew the pistons and bore the cylinders, as necessary (Chapter 2).
- [ ] Connecting rod bearing and/or piston pin-end clearance excessive. Caused by excessive wear or lack of lubrication. Renew worn parts.

Valve noise

- [ ] Incorrect valve clearances. Adjust the clearances by referring to Chapter 1.
- [ ] Valve spring broken or weak. Check and renew weak valve springs (Chapter 2).
- [ ] Camshaft or cylinder head worn or damaged. Lack of lubrication at high rpm is usually the cause of damage. Insufficient oil or failure to change the oil at the recommended intervals are the chief causes. Since there are no replaceable bearings in the head, the head itself will have to be renewed if there is excessive wear or damage (Chapter 2).

Other noise

- [ ] Cylinder head gasket leaking. This will cause compression leakage into the cooling system (which may show up as air bubbles in the coolant in the radiator). Also, coolant may get into the oil (which will turn the oil grey). In either case, have the cooling system checked by a dealer service department.
- [ ] Exhaust pipe leaking at cylinder head connection. Caused by improper fit of pipe(s) or loose exhaust flange. All exhaust fasteners should be tightened evenly and carefully. Failure to do this will lead to a leak.
- [ ] Crankshaft runout excessive. Caused by a bent crankshaft (from over-revving) or damage from an upper cylinder component failure. Can also be attributed to dropping the machine on either of the crankshaft ends.
- [ ] Engine mounting bolts loose. Tighten all engine mount bolts to the specified torque (Chapter 2).
- [ ] Crankshaft bearings worn (Chapter 2).
- [ ] Camshaft chain tensioner defective. Renew according to the procedure in Chapter 2.
- [ ] Camshaft chain, sprockets or guides worn (Chapter 2).
- [ ] Loose alternator rotor. Tighten the mounting bolt to the specified torque (Chapter 2).

8 Abnormal driveline noise

Clutch noise

- [ ] Clutch housing/friction plate clearance excessive (Chapter 2).
- [ ] Loose or damaged clutch pressure plate and/or bolts (Chapter 2).

Transmission noise

- [ ] Bearings worn. Also includes the possibility that the shafts are worn. Overhaul the transmission (Chapter 2).
- [ ] Gears worn or chipped (Chapter 2).
- [ ] Metal chips jammed in gear teeth. Probably pieces from a broken clutch, gear or selector mechanism that were picked up by the gears. This will cause early bearing failure (Chapter 2).
- [ ] Engine oil level too low. Causes a howl from transmission. Also affects engine power and clutch operation (Chapter 1).

Driveshaft or final drive noise

- [ ] Chain not adjusted properly (Chapter 1).
- [ ] Sprocket loose. Tighten fasteners (Chapter 6).
- [ ] Sprocket(s) worn. Renew both sprockets and chain as a set (Chapter 6).
- [ ] Rear sprocket warped. Renew (Chapter 6).
- [ ] Wheel coupling worn. Renew coupling rubber damper (Chapter 6).

9 Abnormal frame and suspension noise

Front end noise

- [ ] Low fluid level or improper viscosity oil in forks. This can sound like 'spurting' and is usually accompanied by irregular fork action (Chapter 6).
- [ ] Spring weak or broken. Makes a clicking or scraping sound. Fork oil, when drained, will have a lot of metal particles in it (Chapter 6).
- [ ] Steering head bearings loose or damaged. Clicks when braking. Check and adjust or renew as necessary (Chapter 6).
- [ ] Fork clamps loose. Make sure all fork clamp pinch bolts are tight (Chapter 6).
- [ ] Fork tube bent. Good possibility if machine has been dropped. Renew both tubes (Chapter 6).
- [ ] Front axle or axle clamp bolt loose. Tighten them to the specified torque (Chapter 7).

Shock absorber noise

- [ ] Fluid level incorrect. Indicates a leak caused by defective seal. Shock will be covered with oil. Renew shock (Chapter 6).
- [ ] Defective shock absorber with internal damage. This is in the body of the shock and cannot be remedied. The shock must be renewed (Chapter 6).
- [ ] Bent or damaged shock body. Renew the shock (Chapter 6).

Brake noise (disc brake)

- [ ] Squeal caused by pads not installed or positioned correctly (Chapter 7).
- [ ] Squeal caused by dust on brake pads. Usually found in combination with glazed pads. Clean using brake cleaning solvent (Chapter 7).
- [ ] Contamination of brake pads. Oil, brake fluid or dirt causing brake to chatter or squeal. Clean or renew pads (Chapter 7).
- [ ] Pads glazed. Caused by excessive heat from prolonged use or from contamination. Do not use sandpaper, emery cloth, carborundum cloth or any other abrasive to roughen the pad surfaces as abrasives will stay in the pad material and damage the disc. A very fine flat file can be used, but pad renewal is suggested as a cure (Chapter 7).
- [ ] Disc warped. Can cause a chattering, clicking or intermittent squeal. Usually accompanied by a pulsating lever and uneven braking. Renew the disc (Chapter 7).
- [ ] Loose or worn wheel bearings. Check and renew as needed (Chapter 7).

Brake noise (drum brake)

- [ ] Shoe linings worn or contaminated. Can cause scraping or squealing. Renew the shoes (Chapter 7).
- [ ] Shoe linings warped or worn unevenly. Can cause chattering. Renew the shoes (Chapter 7).
- [ ] Brake drum out of round. Can cause chattering. Renew the wheel or have it skimmed (Chapter 7).
- [ ] Loose or worn wheel bearings. Check and renew as needed (Chapter 7).

10 Oil pressure warning light comes on

Engine lubrication system

- [ ] Engine oil pump defective (Chapter 2).
- [ ] Engine oil level low. Inspect for leak or other problem causing low oil level and add recommended lubricant (Daily (pre-ride) checks).
- [ ] Engine oil viscosity too low. Very old, thin oil or an improper weight of oil used in engine. Change to correct lubricant (Daily (pre-ride) checks).
- [ ] Camshaft or journals worn. Excessive wear causing drop in oil pressure. Renew cam and/or head. Abnormal wear could be caused by oil starvation at high rpm from low oil level or improper oil weight or type (Chapter 1).
- [ ] Crankshaft and/or bearings worn. Same problems as paragraph 4. Check and renew crankshaft and/or bearings (Chapter 2).

Electrical system

- [ ] Oil pressure switch defective. Check the switch according to the procedure in Chapter 9. Renew it if it is defective.
- [ ] Oil pressure warning light circuit defective. Check for pinched, shorted, disconnected or damaged wiring (Chapter 9).

11 Excessive exhaust smoke

White smoke

☐ Piston oil ring worn. The ring may be broken or damaged, causing oil from the crankcase to be pulled past the piston into the combustion chamber. Renew the rings (Chapter 2).

☐ Cylinders worn, cracked, or scored. Caused by overheating or oil starvation. The cylinders will have to be rebored and new pistons installed.

☐ Valve oil seal damaged or worn. Renew the oil seals (Chapter 2).

☐ Valve guide worn. Perform a complete valve job (Chapter 2).

☐ Engine oil level too high, which causes oil to be forced past the rings. Drain oil to the proper level (Daily (pre-ride) checks).

☐ Head gasket broken between oil return and cylinder. Causes oil to be pulled into combustion chamber. Renew the head gasket and check the head for warpage (Chapter 2).

☐ Abnormal crankcase pressurisation, which forces oil past the rings. Clogged breather or hoses usually the cause (Chapter 4).

Black smoke

☐ Air cleaner clogged. Clean or renew the element (Chapter 1).

☐ Main jet too large or loose. Compare the jet size to the Specifications (Chapter 4).

☐ Choke stuck, causing fuel to be pulled through choke circuit (Chapter 4).

☐ Fuel level too high. Check and adjust the float level as necessary (Chapter 4).

☐ Inlet needle held off needle seat. Clean float bowl and fuel line and renew needle and seat if necessary (Chapter 4).

Brown smoke

☐ Main jet too small or clogged. Lean condition caused by wrong size main jet or by a restricted orifice. Clean float bowl and jets and compare jet size to Specifications (Chapter 4).

☐ Fuel flow insufficient. Fuel inlet needle valve stuck closed due to chemical reaction with old fuel. Float level incorrect. Restricted fuel line. Clean line and float bowl and adjust floats if necessary (Chapter 4).

☐ Carburettor inlet manifolds loose (Chapter 4).

☐ Air cleaner poorly sealed or not installed (Chapter 1).

12 Poor handling or stability

Handlebar hard to turn

☐ Steering stem bearing adjuster nut too tight (Chapter 6).

☐ Bearings damaged. Roughness can be felt as the bars are turned from side-to-side. Renew bearings and races (Chapter 6).

☐ Races dented or worn. Denting results from wear in only one position (eg, straight ahead) from impacting an immovable object or hole or from dropping the machine. Renew races and bearings (Chapter 6).

☐ Steering stem lubrication inadequate. Causes are grease getting hard from age or being washed out by high pressure car washes. Disassemble steering head and repack bearings (Chapter 6).

☐ Steering stem bent. Caused by hitting a curb or hole or from dropping the machine. Renew damaged part. Do not try to straighten stem (Chapter 6).

☐ Front tyre air pressure too low (Chapter 1).

Handlebar shakes or vibrates excessively

☐ Tyres worn or out of balance (Chapter 7).

☐ Swingarm bearings worn. Renew worn bearings by referring to Chapter 6.

☐ Rim(s) warped or damaged. Inspect wheels for runout (Chapter 7).

☐ Wheel bearings worn. Worn front or rear wheel bearings can cause poor tracking. Worn front bearings will cause wobble (Chapter 7).

☐ Handlebar clamp bolts loose (Chapter 6).

☐ Steering stem or fork clamps loose. Tighten them to the specified torque (Chapter 6).

☐ Engine mounting bolts loose. Will cause excessive vibration with increased engine rpm (Chapter 2).

Handlebar pulls to one side

☐ Frame bent. Definitely suspect this if the machine has been dropped. May or may not be accompanied by cracking near the bend. Renew the frame (Chapter 6).

☐ Wheel out of alignment. Caused by improper location of axle spacers or from bent steering stem or frame (Chapter 6).

☐ Swingarm bent or twisted. Caused by age (metal fatigue) or impact damage. Renew the arm (Chapter 6).

☐ Steering stem bent. Caused by impact damage or from dropping the motorcycle. Renew the steering stem (Chapter 6).

☐ Fork leg bent. Disassemble the forks and renew the damaged parts (Chapter 6).

☐ Fork oil level uneven.

Poor shock absorbing qualities

☐ Too hard:
   a)   *Fork oil level excessive (Chapter 1).*
   b)   *Fork oil viscosity too high. Use a lighter oil, (see the Specifications in Chapter 1).*
   c)   *Fork tube bent. Causes a harsh, sticking feeling (Chapter 6).*
   d)   *Fork internal damage (Chapter 6).*
   e)   *Shock shaft or body bent or damaged (Chapter 6).*
   f)   *Shock internal damage.*
   g)   *Tyre pressure too high (Chapters 1 and 7).*

☐ Too soft:
   a)   *Fork or shock oil insufficient and/or leaking (Chapter 6).*
   b)   *Fork oil level too low (Chapter 6).*
   c)   *Fork oil viscosity too light (Chapter 6).*
   d)   *Fork springs weak or broken (Chapter 6).*

13 Braking problems

Front brakes are spongy, don't hold (disc brakes)

☐ Air in brake line. Caused by inattention to master cylinder fluid level or by leakage. Locate problem and bleed brakes (Chapter 7).
☐ Pad or disc worn (Chapters 1 and 7).
☐ Brake fluid leak. See paragraph 1.
☐ Contaminated pads. Caused by contamination with oil, grease, brake fluid, etc. Clean or renew pads. Clean disc thoroughly with brake cleaner (Chapter 7).
☐ Brake fluid deteriorated. Fluid is old or contaminated. Drain system, replenish with new fluid and bleed the system (Chapter 7).
☐ Master cylinder internal parts worn or damaged causing fluid to bypass (Chapter 7).
☐ Master cylinder bore scratched. From ingestion of foreign material or broken spring. Repair or renew master cylinder (Chapter 7).
☐ Disc warped. Renew disc (Chapter 7).

Brake lever or pedal pulsates (disc brakes)

☐ Disc warped. Renew disc (Chapter 7).
☐ Axle bent. Renew axle (Chapter 6).
☐ Brake caliper bolts loose (Chapter 7).
☐ Brake caliper shafts damaged or sticking, causing caliper to bind. Lube the shafts and/or renew them if they are corroded or bent (Chapter 7).
☐ Wheel warped or otherwise damaged (Chapter 7).
☐ Wheel bearings damaged or worn (Chapter 7).

Brake lever or pedal pulsates (drum brakes)

☐ Brake drum out of round. Renew wheel or have brake drum skimmed (Chapter 7).
☐ Wheel bearings damaged or worn (Chapter 7).

Brakes drag (disc brakes)

☐ Master cylinder piston seized. Caused by wear or damage to piston or cylinder bore (Chapter 7).
☐ Lever balky or stuck. Check pivot and lubricate (Chapter 7).
☐ Brake caliper binds. Caused by inadequate lubrication or damage to caliper shafts (Chapter 7).
☐ Brake caliper piston seized in bore. Caused by wear or ingestion of dirt past deteriorated seal (Chapter 7).
☐ Brake pad damaged. Pad material separating from backing plate. Usually caused by faulty manufacturing process or from contact with chemicals. Renew pads (Chapter 7).
☐ Pads improperly installed (Chapter 7).

Brakes drag (drum brakes)

☐ Brake pedal freeplay insufficient (Chapter 1).
☐ Brake springs weak or broken. Renew the springs (Chapter 7).
☐ Brake operating cam sticking due to lack of lubrication (Chapter 1).

14 Electrical problems

Battery dead or weak

☐ Battery faulty. Caused by sulphated plates which are shorted through the sedimentation or low electrolyte level. Also, broken battery terminal making only occasional contact (Chapter 9).
☐ Battery cables making poor contact (Chapter 9).
☐ Load excessive. Caused by addition of high wattage lights or other electrical accessories.
☐ Ignition switch defective. Switch either earths internally or fails to shut off system. Renew the switch (Chapter 9).
☐ Regulator/rectifier defective (Chapter 9).

☐ Alternator stator coil open or shorted (Chapter 9).
☐ Wiring faulty. Wiring earthed or connections loose in ignition, charging or lighting circuits (Chapter 9).

Battery overcharged

☐ Regulator/rectifier defective. Overcharging is noticed when battery gets excessively warm or 'boils' over (Chapter 9).
☐ Battery defective. Renew the battery (Chapter 9).
☐ Battery amperage too low, wrong type or size. Install manufacturer's specified amp-hour battery to handle charging load (Chapter 9).

Checking engine compression

● Low compression will result in exhaust smoke, heavy oil consumption, poor starting and poor performance. A compression test will provide useful information about an engine's condition and if performed regularly, can give warning of trouble before any other symptoms become apparent.

● A compression gauge will be required, along with an adapter to suit the spark plug hole thread size. Note that the screw-in type gauge/adapter set up is preferable to the rubber cone type.

● Before carrying out the test, first check the valve clearances as described in Chapter 1.

1 Run the engine until it reaches normal operating temperature, then stop it and remove the spark plug(s), taking care not to scald your hands on the hot components.

2 Install the gauge adapter and compression gauge in No. 1 cylinder spark plug hole (see illustration 1).

Screw the compression gauge adapter into the spark plug hole, then screw the gauge into the adapter

3 On kickstart-equipped motorcycles, make sure the ignition switch is OFF, then open the throttle fully and kick the engine over a couple of times until the gauge reading stabilises.

4 On motorcycles with electric start only, the procedure will differ depending on the nature of the ignition system. Flick the engine kill switch (engine stop switch) to OFF and turn the ignition switch ON; open the throttle fully and crank the engine over on the starter motor for a couple of revolutions until the gauge reading stabilises. If the starter will not operate with the kill switch OFF, turn the ignition switch OFF and refer to the next paragraph.

5 Install the spark plugs back into their suppressor caps and arrange the plug electrodes so that their metal bodies are earthed (grounded) against the cylinder head; this is essential to prevent damage to the ignition system as the engine is spun over (see illustration 2). Position the plugs well

All spark plugs must be earthed (grounded) against the cylinder head

away from the plug holes otherwise there is a risk of atomised fuel escaping from the combustion chambers and igniting. As a safety precaution, cover the top of the valve cover with rag. Now turn the ignition switch ON and kill switch ON, open the throttle fully and crank the engine over on the starter motor for a couple of revolutions until the gauge reading stabilises.

6 After one or two revolutions the pressure should build up to a maximum figure and then stabilise. Take a note of this reading and on multi-cylinder engines repeat the test on the remaining cylinders.

7 The correct pressures are given in Chapter 1 Specifications. If the results fall within the specified range and on multi-cylinder engines all are relatively equal, the engine is in good condition. If there is a marked difference between the readings, or if the readings are lower than specified, inspection of the top-end components will be required.

8 Low compression pressure may be due to worn cylinder bores, pistons or rings, failure of the cylinder head gasket, worn valve seals, or poor valve seating.

9 To distinguish between cylinder/piston wear and valve leakage, pour a small quantity of oil into the bore to temporarily seal the piston rings, then repeat the compression tests (see illustration 3). If the readings show

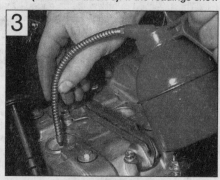

Bores can be temporarily sealed with a squirt of motor oil

a noticeable increase in pressure this confirms that the cylinder bore, piston, or rings are worn. If, however, no change is indicated, the cylinder head gasket or valves should be examined.

10 High compression pressure indicates excessive carbon build-up in the combustion chamber and on the piston crown. If this is the case the cylinder head should be removed and the deposits removed. Note that excessive carbon build-up is less likely with the used on modern fuels.

Checking battery open-circuit voltage

 Warning: The gases produced by the battery are explosive - never smoke or create any sparks in the vicinity of the battery. Never allow the electrolyte to contact your skin or clothing - if it does, wash it off and seek immediate medical attention.

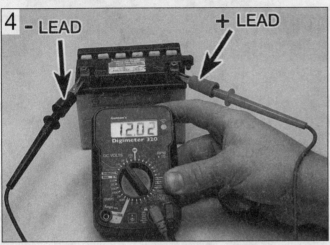

Measuring open-circuit battery voltage

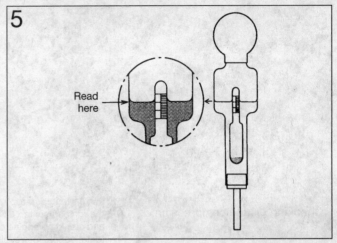

Float-type hydrometer for measuring battery specific gravity

● Before any electrical fault is investigated the battery should be checked.

● You'll need a dc voltmeter or multimeter to check battery voltage. Check that the leads are inserted in the correct terminals on the meter, red lead to positive (+ve), black lead to negative (-ve). Incorrect connections can damage the meter.

● A sound fully-charged 12 volt battery should produce between 12.3 and 12.6 volts across its terminals (12.8 volts for a maintenance-free battery). On machines with a 6 volt battery, voltage should be between 6.1 and 6.3 volts.

1 Set a multimeter to the 0 to 20 volts dc range and connect its probes across the battery terminals. Connect the meter's positive (+ve) probe, usually red, to the battery positive (+ve) terminal, followed by the meter's negative (-ve) probe, usually black, to the battery negative terminal (-ve) **(see illustration 4)**.

2 If battery voltage is low (below 10 volts on a 12 volt battery or below 4 volts on a six volt battery), charge the battery and test the voltage again. If the battery repeatedly goes flat, investigate the motorcycle's charging system.

Checking battery specific gravity (SG)

 Warning: The gases produced by the battery are explosive - never smoke or create any sparks in the vicinity of the battery. Never allow the electrolyte to contact your skin or clothing - if it does, wash it off and seek immediate medical attention.

● The specific gravity check gives an indication of a battery's state of charge.

● A hydrometer is used for measuring specific gravity. Make sure you purchase one which has a small enough hose to insert in the aperture of a motorcycle battery.

● Specific gravity is simply a measure of the electrolyte's density compared with that of water. Water has an SG of 1.000 and fully-charged battery electrolyte is about 26% heavier, at 1.260.

● Specific gravity checks are not possible on maintenance-free batteries. Testing the open-circuit voltage is the only means of determining their state of charge.

1 To measure SG, remove the battery from the motorcycle and remove the first cell cap. Draw

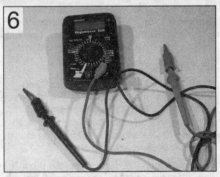

Digital multimeter can be used for all electrical tests

some electrolyte into the hydrometer and note the reading **(see illustration 5)**. Return the electrolyte to the cell and install the cap.

2 The reading should be in the region of 1.260 to 1.280. If SG is below 1.200 the battery needs charging. Note that SG will vary with temperature; it should be measured at 20°C (68°F). Add 0.007 to the reading for every 10°C above 20°C, and subtract 0.007 from the reading for every 10°C below 20°C. Add 0.004 to the reading for every 10°F above 68°F, and subtract 0.004 from the reading for every 10°F below 68°F.

3 When the check is complete, rinse the hydrometer thoroughly with clean water.

Checking for continuity

● The term continuity describes the uninterrupted flow of electricity through an electrical circuit. A continuity check will determine whether an **open-circuit** situation exists.

● Continuity can be checked with an ohmmeter, multimeter, continuity tester or battery and bulb test circuit **(see illustrations 6, 7 and 8)**.

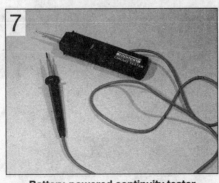

Battery-powered continuity tester

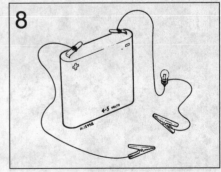

Battery and bulb test circuit

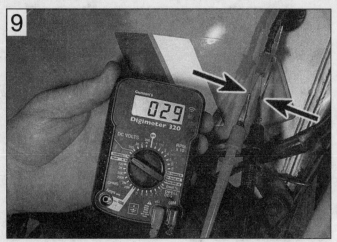

Continuity check of front brake light switch using a meter - note split pins used to access connector terminals

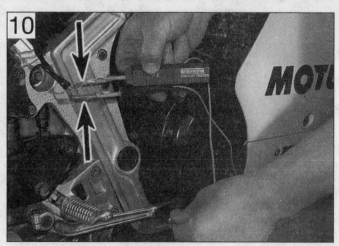

Continuity check of rear brake light switch using a continuity tester

● All of these instruments are self-powered by a battery, therefore the checks are made with the ignition OFF.
● As a safety precaution, always disconnect the battery negative (-ve) lead before making checks, particularly if ignition switch checks are being made.
● If using a meter, select the appropriate ohms scale and check that the meter reads infinity (∞). Touch the meter probes together and check that meter reads zero; where necessary adjust the meter so that it reads zero.
● After using a meter, always switch it OFF to conserve its battery.

Switch checks

1 If a switch is at fault, trace its wiring up to the wiring connectors. Separate the wire connectors and inspect them for security and condition. A build-up of dirt or corrosion here will most likely be the cause of the problem - clean up and apply a water dispersant such as WD40.
2 If using a test meter, set the meter to the ohms x 10 scale and connect its probes across the wires from the switch **(see illustration 9)**. Simple ON/OFF type switches, such as brake light switches, only have two wires whereas combination switches, like the

ignition switch, have many internal links. Study the wiring diagram to ensure that you are connecting across the correct pair of wires. Continuity (low or no measurable resistance - 0 ohms) should be indicated with the switch ON and no continuity (high resistance) with it OFF.
3 Note that the polarity of the test probes doesn't matter for continuity checks, although care should be taken to follow specific test procedures if a diode or solid-state component is being checked.
4 A continuity tester or battery and bulb circuit can be used in the same way. Connect its probes as described above **(see illustration 10)**. The light should come on to indicate continuity in the ON switch position, but should extinguish in the OFF position.

Wiring checks

● Many electrical faults are caused by damaged wiring, often due to incorrect routing or chaffing on frame components.
● Loose, wet or corroded wire connectors can also be the cause of electrical problems, especially in exposed locations.

1 A continuity check can be made on a single length of wire by disconnecting it at each end and connecting a meter or continuity tester

across both ends of the wire **(see illustration 11)**.
2 Continuity (low or no resistance - 0 ohms) should be indicated if the wire is good. If no continuity (high resistance) is shown, suspect a broken wire.

Checking for voltage

● A voltage check can determine whether current is reaching a component.
● Voltage can be checked with a dc voltmeter, multimeter set on the dc volts scale, test light or buzzer **(see illustrations 12 and 13)**. A meter has the advantage of being able to measure actual voltage.
● When using a meter, check that its leads are inserted in the correct terminals on the meter, red to positive (+ve), black to negative (-ve). Incorrect connections can damage the meter.
● A voltmeter (or multimeter set to the dc volts scale) should always be connected in parallel (across the load). Connecting it in series will not harm the meter, but the reading will not be meaningful.
● Voltage checks are made with the ignition ON.

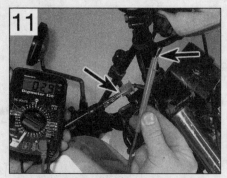

Continuity check of front brake light switch sub-harness

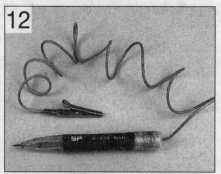

A simple test light can be used for voltage checks

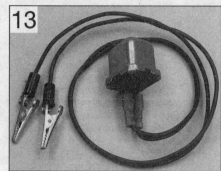

A buzzer is useful for voltage checks

Checking for voltage at the rear brake light power supply wire using a meter . . .

1 First identify the relevant wiring circuit by referring to the wiring diagram at the end of this manual. If other electrical components share the same power supply (ie are fed from the same fuse), take note whether they are working correctly - this is useful information in deciding where to start checking the circuit.

2 If using a meter, check first that the meter leads are plugged into the correct terminals on the meter (see above). Set the meter to the dc volts function, at a range suitable for the battery voltage. Connect the meter red probe (+ve) to the power supply wire and the black probe to a good metal earth (ground) on the motorcycle's frame or directly to the battery negative (-ve) terminal **(see illustration 14)**. Battery voltage should be shown on the meter

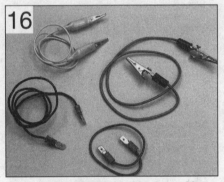

A selection of jumper wires for making earth (ground) checks

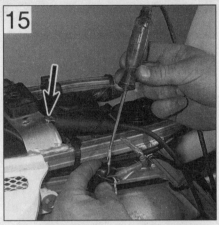

. . . or a test light - note the earth connection to the frame (arrow)

with the ignition switched ON.

3 If using a test light or buzzer, connect its positive (+ve) probe to the power supply terminal and its negative (-ve) probe to a good earth (ground) on the motorcycle's frame or directly to the battery negative (-ve) terminal **(see illustration 15)**. With the ignition ON, the test light should illuminate or the buzzer sound.

4 If no voltage is indicated, work back towards the fuse continuing to check for voltage. When you reach a point where there is voltage, you know the problem lies between that point and your last check point.

Checking the earth (ground)

● Earth connections are made either directly to the engine or frame (such as sensors, neutral switch etc. which only have a positive feed) or by a separate wire into the earth circuit of the wiring harness. Alternatively a short earth wire is sometimes run directly from the component to the motorcycle's frame.

● Corrosion is often the cause of a poor earth connection.

● If total failure is experienced, check the security of the main earth lead from the

negative (-ve) terminal of the battery and also the main earth (ground) point on the wiring harness. If corroded, dismantle the connection and clean all surfaces back to bare metal.

1 To check the earth on a component, use an insulated jumper wire to temporarily bypass its earth connection **(see illustration 16)**. Connect one end of the jumper wire between the earth terminal or metal body of the component and the other end to the motorcycle's frame.

2 If the circuit works with the jumper wire installed, the original earth circuit is faulty. Check the wiring for open-circuits or poor connections. Clean up direct earth connections, removing all traces of corrosion and remake the joint. Apply petroleum jelly to the joint to prevent future corrosion.

Tracing a short-circuit

● A short-circuit occurs where current shorts to earth (ground) bypassing the circuit components. This usually results in a blown fuse.

● A short-circuit is most likely to occur where the insulation has worn through due to wiring chafing on a component, allowing a direct path to earth (ground) on the frame.

1 Remove any bodypanels necessary to access the circuit wiring.

2 Check that all electrical switches in the circuit are OFF, then remove the circuit fuse and connect a test light, buzzer or voltmeter (set to the dc scale) across the fuse terminals. No voltage should be shown.

3 Move the wiring from side to side whilst observing the test light or meter. When the test light comes on, buzzer sounds or meter shows voltage, you have found the cause of the short. It will usually shown up as damaged or burned insulation.

4 Note that the same test can be performed on each component in the circuit, even the switch.

Note: *References throughout this index are in the form "Chapter number" • "Page number". So, for example, 2•15 refers to page 15 of Chapter 2.*

Note: *References throughout this index are in the form* **"Chapter number"** • **"Page number".** *So, for example, 2•15 refers to page 15 of Chapter 2.*

Note: *References throughout this index are in the form* **"Chapter number" • "Page number"**. *So, for example, 2•15 refers to page 15 of Chapter 2.*

Haynes Motorcycle Manuals – The Complete List

The manuals on this page are available through good motorcycle dealers and accessory shops.
In case of difficulty, contact: **Haynes Publishing**
(UK) +44 1963 442030   (USA) +1 805 498 6703
(SV) +46 18 124016
(Australia/New Zealand) +61 2 8713 1400

MCL 07.05.15

Preserving Our Motoring Heritage

WITHDRAWN

< *The Model J Duesenberg Derham Tourster. Only eight of these magnificent cars were ever built – this is the only example to be found outside the United States of America*

Almost every car you've ever loved, loathed or desired is gathered under one roof at the Haynes Motor Museum. Over 300 immaculately presented cars and motorbikes represent every aspect of our motoring heritage, from elegant reminders of bygone days, such as the superb Model J Duesenberg to curiosities like the bug-eyed BMW Isetta. There are also many old friends and flames. Perhaps you remember the 1959 Ford Popular that you did your courting in? The magnificent 'Red Collection' is a spectacle of classic sports cars including AC, Alfa Romeo, Austin Healey, Ferrari, Lamborghini, Maserati, MG, Riley, Porsche and Triumph.

A Perfect Day Out

Each and every vehicle at the Haynes Motor Museum has played its part in the history and culture of Motoring. Today, they make a wonderful spectacle and a great day out for all the family. Bring the kids, bring Mum and Dad, but above all bring your camera to capture those golden memories for ever. You will also find an impressive array of motoring memorabilia, a comfortable 70 seat video cinema and one of the most extensive transport book shops in Britain. The Pit Stop Cafe serves everything from a cup of tea to wholesome, home-made meals or, if you prefer, you can enjoy the large picnic area nestled in the beautiful rural surroundings of Somerset.

> *John Haynes O.B.E., Founder and Chairman of the museum at the wheel of a Haynes Light 12.*

< *The 1936 490cc sohc-engined International Norton – well known for its racing success*

The Museum is situated on the A359 Yeovil to Frome road at Sparkford, just off the A303 in Somerset. It is about 40 miles south of Bristol, and 25 minutes drive from the M5 intersection at Taunton.
Open 9.30am - 5.30pm (10.00am - 4.00pm Winter) 7 days a week, *except Christmas Day, Boxing Day and New Years Day*
Special rates available for schools, coach parties and outings Charitable Trust No. 292048